WINGS ACROSS THE BORDER

A History of Aviation in North Wales and the Northern Marches

Vol III

Derrick Pratt & Mike Grant

bridge
books
Wrexham

Wings Across the Border
First published in Wales by
BRIDGE BOOKS
61 Park Avenue
Wrexham, LL12 7AW

© 2005 Derrick Pratt & Mike Grant
© 2005 Typesetting and design, Bridge Books

A CIP entry for this book is available from the British Library

ISBN 1-84494-010-1

Back cover, lower left: Consolidated PBY-5A Catalina JV928/G-BLSC, in the markings of Nº 210
Squadron, RAF (an aircraft that passed through SARO Beaumaris), as flown by
F/O J. Cruickshank during his VC action. [The Catalina Society]

Printed and bound by
Cromwell Press
Trowbridge, Wiltshire

Contents

Abbreviations

A	'A' series decoys (Army)
A	(plus rank) = Acting
AA	Anti-aircraft
AAPC	AA Practice Camp
AASF	Advanced Air Striking Force
AAS	Air Armament School
AACU	Anti-aircraft Co-operation Unit
ACM	Air Chief Marshal
AEW	Airborne Early Warning
AFDU	Air Fighting Development Unit
AFS	Auxiliary Fire Service
AGS	Air Gunnery School
AI	Air Interception (RADAR)
AMES	Air Ministry Experimental Station
AMRE	Air Ministry Research Establishment
AMWD	Air Ministry Works Directorate
ANBS	Air Navigation & Bombing School
AOG	Aircraft on the ground
AOS	Air Observers School
ARP	Air Raid Precautions
ARV	Armoured Recovery Vehicle
ASE	Admiralty Signals Establishment
ASP	Air Stores Park
ASR	Air/Sea rescue
ASU	Aircraft Storage Unit
ASV	Air to Surface Vessel (RADAR)
ATA	Air Transport Auxilliary
ATC	Air Traffic Control
ATS	Armament Training Station
Aufkl.Gr	*Aufklärung* (Reconnaissance) Unit
AVM	Air Vice Marshal
B&GS	Bombing & Gunnery School
BCBS	Bomber Command Bombing School
BL	Breech loading (guns)
BOAC	British Overseas Airways Corporation
BOP	Battery Observation Post
C	'C' series decoys (civilian)
Calc	Electric calculator
CAPC	Coastal Artillery Practice Camp
CASL	Coastal Artillery Searchlight
CD	Civil Defence
CF	Calibration Flight; Communication Flight
CFS	Central Flying School
CH	Chain Home (RADAR)
CHEL	Chain Home Extra Low
CHL	Chain Home Low
C&M	Care & Maintenance
CN&CS	Central Navigation & Control School
CO	Commanding Officer
CPF	Coastal Patrol Flight
Cpl	Corporal
CWG(C)	Commonwealth War Graves (Commission)
Do	*Dornier*
DTD	Directorate of Technical Development
E/A	Enemy Aircraft
EFTS	Elementary Flying Training School
E&RFTS	Elementary & Reserve Flying Training School
F/O	Flying Officer (RAF)/First Officer (ATA)
FTS	Flying Training School
GCI	Ground Control of Interception
GEC	General Electric Company
GDA	Gun Defended Area
G/Cpt	Group Captain
GL	Gun-laying (RADAR)
HAA	Heavy Anti-aircraft (guns)
HAAPC	HAA Practice Camp
HCU	Heavy Conversion Unit
He	Heinkel
HE	High Explosive
Hs	Henschel
IAZ	Inner Artillery Zone
IB	Incendiary Bomb
JG	*Jagdgeschwader* (fighter unit)
KG	*Kampfgeschwader* (bomber unit)

KSLI	King's Shropshire Light Infantry
LAA	Light Anti-aircraft (guns)
LAC	Leading Aircraftman
LDVF	Local Defence Volunteer Force
LRASV	Long Range ASV
MAEE	Marine Aircraft Experimental Establishment
MAP	Ministry of Aircraft Production
MASB	Motor Anti-submarine Boat
MCU	Mosquito Conversion Unit
Me	Messerschmitt
Mk	Mark (model)
MoHS	Ministry of Home Security
MRU	Mobile Radar Unit
MTB	Motor Torpedo Boat
MU	Maintenance Unit
N	'N' series decoy (Naval)
NFS	National Fire Service
NAVEX	Navigational Exercise
OD	Ordnance Datum (above sea level)
(O)AFU	Observers Advanced Flying Unit
ORs	Other Ranks
ORB	Operational Record Book
OTU	Operational Training Unit
P	'P' series decoy
PE	Permanent echo (RADAR)
PF(F)	Pathfinder (Force)
P/O	Pilot Officer
PPI	Plan Position Indicator (RADAR)
PTS	Parachute Training School
Q	Decoy
Q Code	R/T flying control information codes
QA	Army, military decoy
QF	Quick-firing guns
QD	Drem decoy
QF	Decoy with fires
QL	Decoy with lights
QN	Naval decoy
QP	Petroleum decoy
QT	Decoy with 'T' light system
RAAF	Royal Australian Air Force
RAFVR	Royal Air Force Volunteer Reserve
RATOG	Rocket Assisted Take Off Gear
RAuxAF	Royal Auxilliary Air Force
RCAF	Royal Canadian Air Force
RLG	Relief Landing Ground
RMU	Radion Maintenance Unit
RNAS	Royal Naval Air Station
ROF	Royal Ordnance Factory
RRFU	Radar Research Flying Unit
RSS	Radio Servicing Section
RT	Radio Transmission
Rx	Receiver (RADAR)
SAL	Scottish Aviation Ltd
SEG	Signallers, Engineers, Gunners (course)
SF	Starfish
(S0)PP	(Service) Ferry Pilots Pool
(S)FTS	(Service) Flying Training School
S/L	Squadron Leader
S/Lt	Sub-Lieutenant (RN/FAA)
Sgt	Sergeant
SRDE	Signals Research & Development Establishment
TAF	Tactical Air Force
TFU	Telecommunications Flying Unit
TLC	Tank Landing Craft
TRANSAT	Transatlantic (ferry operations)
TRE	Telecommunications Research Establishment
TSCU	Transport Support Conversion Unit
TTU	Torpedo Training Unit
Tx	Transmitter (RADAR)
UXB	Unexploded Bomb
VCR	Visual Control Room
W/Cmdr	Wing Commander
WO/AG	Wireless Operator/Air Gunner
ZG	*Zerstörer Geschwader* (destroyer unit)

Introduction

By all accounts this present volume has long been anticipated by local historians and aviation buffs alike; the authors hope that you find the wait has been worthwhile. A longer interlude between the appearance of successive volumes was perhaps inevitable as the authors were involved with other books and on-going field work and research. Along with *Wings Across the Border*, Vol. 1 (1998) and Vol. 2 (2002), the greater part of this book was originally written in 1994–5. A third volume was tentatively scheduled to appear in October 2004, but re-writes and revision took longer than expected. Successive deadlines were missed — here tribute must be paid to the forbearance and tolerance of our publisher! But with another sixteen chapters still to revise and with a volume threatening to run out at some 600 pages, it was decided rather late in the day to split the current work into two parts.

Accordingly, *Wings Across the Border*, Vol. 3 is used to sketch the essential background against which the air defence of north Wales and the border country would be fought, ranging from knee-jerk, panic reactions to the first bombs, quaintly comical in today's eyes, to decoys, 'secret fires' and other earth-bound cloak and dagger defensive measures. In this latter category must be included RDF (or Radar) without which the air war would most assuredly have been lost. The authors needed no excuse for shifting the focus of attention slightly from the south and east coasts to Nº 9 Group's fighting area. Ultimately, some fourteen Air Ministry Experimental Stations (AMES) were strung out along the coast of north Wales, not forgetting the inland GCI stations at Hack Green and Comberton. On one of them in particular (RAF Prestatyn) fell much of the ongoing experimental work on radar aerials that Worth Matravers found impossible to carry out in more dangerous locations.

In very much the same sense that the TRE's scientific officers at Prestatyn were 'refugees', so Saro (Saunders-Roe Ltd) sought the relatively calmer waters (bombing and alerts wise) of the Menai Strait to complete its vital flying boat modification contracts. Despite some two dozen Catalinas and other types — Coronado, Mariner, even Spitfire — seen at any one time bobbing at anchor on the Strait between Beaumaris and Bangor Pier over the period January 1941 – July 1945, this particular aspect of the war has received scant attention from local historians. We hope that we have more than compensated for this oversight. RAF Hawarden, built on reclaimed marshland, should never have been built, but having been laid out, official folly was compounded by squeezing a MAP factory, an ASU, a fighter OTU and the largest of the ATA ferry pools on the site — it makes particularly interesting reading!

We find aircraft falling from crowded nursery skies in increasing numbers; somebody had to recover bodies and pick up the pieces. It is behind-the-scenes activity that moved the public at large to empathise more closely with the Junior Service. Chronologically, this history still languishes about 1940–1. Having disposed of fifteen chapters, *Wings Across the Border*, Vol. 4, focussing on RAF Wrexham, Nº 96 Squadron and the art of flying in the dark, will move things on somewhat — to March 1943, Exercise Spartan and Nº 121 Airfield.

This extended local history with its unusual aviation slant, owes much to the generosity of many contributors — 200+ at the last count, some, sadly, passed on since 2002. But, like George Orwell's animals, some contributors are more equal than others. Among this group are the nations' record repositories — RAF Museum Hendon, Peter Elliott (Keeper of Research and Information Service), Nina Banks (Curator), Guy Revell (Assistant Curator), Christine Gregory (Reprographic Services Officer); National Archives, Kew (Air Ministry records); the staff at the RAF Air Historical Branch; the staff of the Commonwealth War Graves Commission, Maidenhead; Science Museum, London; Jane Insley (Curator, Environmental Sciences); staff of the Flintshire Record Office (Hawarden), Denbighshire Record Office (Ruthin), Cheshire Record Office (Chester), Shropshire Record Office (Shrewsbury); Derek Elliott and the staff of the Central Registry of Air Photographs, National Assembly for Wales — with their wonderful machine that can produce seamless aerial mosaics; Medwyn Parry and the staff of the RCAHMW; the National Library of Wales; Ms Annie Woodward and the staff of English Heritage NMR, Swindon; André Berry and colleagues of the former Clwyd Archaeology Service, who, back in 1990, assisted with the research into the Fenn's Moss Bombing Range; Roger J. C. Thomas, RCHME, York; Joy Thomas, A. N. Palmer Centre, Wrexham; Wrexham County Borough Archives; Mrs Hilary Date (Saro, Beaumaris); the Institute of Electrical Engineers (RDF and RADAR); Edward Heap (Cpl RDF/mechanic, RAF Prestatyn); Alan Cleary; David Grocote; Michael Bragg; Ian Brown; Peter Jarvis (ex-RAF Shawbury); Eric Illingworth (ex-Nº 13 Squadron); Mark Chaloner (Airbus); L. D. R. Thomson (McAlpine); George Williams (Minera); Roy Matthews (Haughmond Hill); Mr & Mrs Randle, Keeper's Cottage, Haughmond Hill; Haydn and Mari Jones, Bryn-y-Garth, Penyffordd, re Talacre Firing Range).

To all contributors of fact, photographs, maps and drawings we offer our thanks. Your contribution was welcomed, enabling us to flesh our story lines and plug gaps in our narrative. While your name may not be individually recorded you will recognise where your fragment of information has helped mould the final shape of, not only this particular work, but also *Wings Across the Border*, Vol. 4.

Derrick Pratt, Welsh Frankton, 2005
Mike Grant, Caergwrle, 2005

GB 70 37 b
Nur für den Dienstgebrauch
Bild Nr. 854 b/40 - 740 (Lfl. 3)
Aufnahme vom 18. 9. 40

Shotton
Gußstahlwerk „John Summers & Sons Ltd.
Shotton"
Länge (westl. Greenw.): 3° 02' 00"   Breite: 53° 13' 15"
Mißweisung: — 12° 04' (Mitte 1941)   Zielhöhe über NN 10 m
Maßstab etwa 1 : 11 000

500   0   500m

Genst. 5. Abt.   September 1941
Karte 1 : 100 000
GB/E 12

By September 1940 the Luftwaffe had a dossier on all strategic and military targets in north Wales including this aerial
photograph of the 'cast steel works' of John Summers, Deeside. An early in-line hooded decoy site, top left; anti-glider ditches,
top; broken hedges and trees, airfield camouflage on RAF Sealand, bottom right. [FRO]

1. Panic stations

Wrexham's introduction to the harsh realities of war is generally taken to be the five day period 28 August–1 September 1940, when as part of the first heavy raid on Merseyside, the heather moorlands of Ruabon and Esclusham Mountains were deliberately set alight, and kept burning for several days as a giant decoy successfully attracting hundreds of tons of HE and incendiary bombs otherwise destined for Liverpool and its satellites. This is a twist on the perceived orthodoxy as handed down to successor generation in the Wrexham area. But on going research has revealed that events were perhaps rather more complex than generally suspected. For some eight weeks prior to Wrexham's abrupt precipitation into Liverpool's war, the *Luftwaffe* had been flying isolated data-finding sorties into north-east Wales and border counties as a necessary preliminary to drawing up detailed plans for the imminent invasion of this country. They were armed reconnaissance sorties, with targets of opportunity being seized at every opportunity. Thus on the night of Tuesday, 24/25 June 1940, official records show that for all districts south of a line Hull–Preston (but excluding most of Wales and the south-west) a 'Red Alert' was in force between 2230–0245hrs. During night flying at RAF Shawbury the sirens sounded at 0125hrs. All aircraft were quickly recalled and flare-path lights extinguished. The 'All-clear' was given at 0200hrs. Over on Deeside there was not even a 'Yellow Alert', but at 0045hrs two **SC 50** HE bombs landed in a field at Hope's Place farm, Bretton, barely 1,000 yards from Vickers-Armstrong shadow aircraft factory. Insignificant, unrelated events? Perhaps.

No reports of enemy activity were received locally the following evening. On the night of Wednesday, 26/27 June, although 'Red Alerts' were in force at east coast ports, most of England was under a 'Yellow' warning between 2300–0430hrs. In Flintshire, Areas 7 (Buckley/Hawarden) and 8 (Shotton/Sealand) went on 'Yellow Alert' at 0135hrs, with status 'White' (or 'Cancel') being signalled at 0210hrs. There were no intervening 'Purple' or 'Red' alerts logged and no sirens, which is hardly surprising as all the night's action had occurred without warning ten minutes previously! At 0125hrs a HE bomb landed between the main gate and the Officers' Mess, RAF Sealand, leaving a crater and blowing out windows over a considerable radius as well as bringing down telephone lines. A second **SC 50** bomb landed at Marsh Cottages beyond the West Camp dispersal area and blisters, too close to Chester (otherwise Hawarden Bridge East) Junction on the old Great Central Wrexham–Chester line for comfort. The lone raider droned away at 13,000ft. Aerodrome defences were quickly manned

by the Army, and the civilian workers' LDV (Home Guard) platoon was stood to and issued with guns and ammunition from the armoury. But it was a case of shutting the stable door after the horse had bolted.

Thirty minutes earlier, RAF Shawbury had received the same treatment. Indeed one suspects that the same German bomber may have been responsible for both incidents. The Shropshire airfield was again lit up like a Christmas tree with night flying in full swing. At about 0100hrs a single raider dropped seven **SC 50s**, four inside, and three outside, the perimeter fence. All fell on grass areas and there were no casualties, but there was extensive blast damage to Station HQ, airmen's barrack blocks, the MT section and parked transport. There had been no advance on 'Yellow Alert' status. AA defences were unmanned. Indeed the Royal Engineers were still busy on the construction of gun emplacements — not that much could have been done with Lewis guns against an unseen enemy at 10,000ft! Shawbury would not receive its complement of four 40mm Bofors guns until 9 October (but RAF Tern Hill not until 3 March 1941; although pencilled in, RAF High Ercall appears not to have received its LAA guns). The whole raid took less than ten seconds. Ten minutes later Shrewsbury Police Division went on 'Red Alert'!

On the face of it these were isolated incidents. Flintshire would receive no further attention from the *Luftwaffe* until the night of 28/29 July. Although enemy planes were tracked nightly over the county no further bombs fell on Shropshire until 22/23 July when a questing stick of ten **SC 50s** straddled the A41 at Tern Hill. Local historians still believe, their ideas perhaps shaped by the secrecy, censorship, propaganda and disinformation of the war years, that the apparently random fall of German bombs in rural areas was occasioned purely by their indiscriminate jettisoning from retreating enemy aircraft. But officialdom hints at a possible pattern to be discerned behind these apparently chance hit-or-miss affairs. Twice daily, since he had been appointed Prime Minister on 10 May 1940, a summary and brief strategic appraisal of the previous night's *Luftwaffe* activities fell on Churchill's desk. Such reports were compiled by the Ministry of Home Security, formed in September 1939 from the Air Raid Precautions Department of the Home Office. The effective conduct of civil defence operations was dependent on reliable intelligence channelled into the Home Security War Room from the regions, each of which in turn digested information from their own and RAF and Observer Corps Group and Control centres.

In his appraisal of the events of 24/25 June 1940, Major R. E. MacBryan, War Room Operations Officer, drew attention to the missing of potential targets and suggested that the majority of these raids were either (a) large scale training reconnaissance flights over open, unobstructed wastelands and military and civil aerodromes (including landing strips conveniently listed by the Automobile Association in its Register of Aircraft Landing Grounds), or (b) raids used to produce the exact timings necessary for the co-ordination of any invasion plan. On 2 July Hitler ordered the necessary plans for Operation Sealion to be prepared. In a *Luftwaffe* directive Goering beat him by two days! A feature

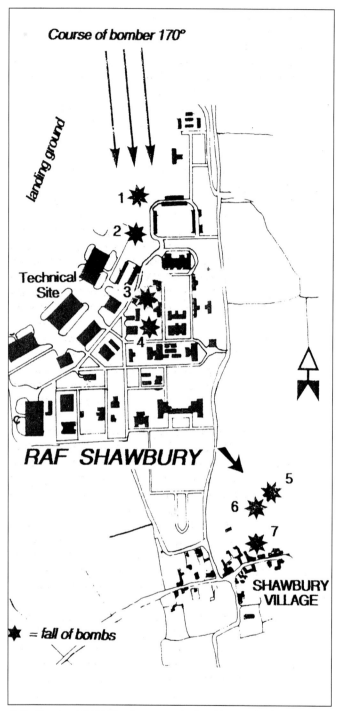

*Fall of bombs at RAF Shawbury — a single raider struck
at 0100 hrs on 27 June 1940.*

of the Danish and Norwegian campaigns had been the accuracy of timings in the assaults. Denmark fell in twelve hours. Norway, apart from the Narvik pocket, took a little longer — eight days. The same meticulous planning saw Holland and Belgium fall in eighteen days. Major MacBryan went on to suggest, that since many of the current series of raids were designed not to cause extensive damage, close attention should be paid by various intelligence departments to the fall of bombs in relation to possible parachute landings at each place with view to capturing landing grounds for use by troop-carrying planes. Against

such an appraisal the apparent sporadic bombing by isolated German aircraft as outlined above, suddenly falls neatly into place, especially if one also considers precautions, *ad hoc* or no, subsequently taken on the ground. Reactions to the Shawbury raids were predictable. The sense of desperate emergency is summed up by former Pte. Eric Evans, KSLI, who in the summer of 1940 was part of a unit detached from Shrewsbury for the ground defence of RAF Shawbury: 'Being Army, we took great delight in seeing these toffee-nosed RAF types running around like chickens with their heads cut off! Jerry had put the fear of God into them. Everything now had to be done yesterday!'

This was a squaddy's succinct summing up of the new preventative measures introduced in great haste, ranging from replacing all lights in living and sleeping quarters with blue bulbs to the sinking of pre-fabricated Stanton type air-raid shelters, 22 on the main technical site, which included N° 11 SFTS, and six for the MU. two each on sites 'A', 'B' and 'C'. Plans for the closure of the roads from Acton Lea and between Moreton Corbet and Shawbury village, drawn up in May 1940, were now suddenly implemented, with double sentries posted at road blocks and passes issued to civilians entitled to use the roads. The Acton Lea–Moreton Corbet road was never re-opened and after the war a permanent diversion was built. Airmen in great numbers, both 'general duties' and 'trades' were siphoned off for guard duties, especially patrolling the five-mile perimeter fence. However, within ten days sixty airmen arrived direct from 'square bashing' at N° 9 Recruit Wing, Blackpool. They would form the nucleus of N° 6 Defence Squadron, formally embodied on 22 July and later strengthened with the arrival of 500 Troop, 142 Battery, of N° 45 LAA Regiment, Royal Artillery, with their Bofors. They would hold the fort until September 1942 when elements of the RAF Regiment took over.

More pertinent to our narrative Pte. Evans found himself part of a squad detached post-haste on 28 June to set up a decoy site on Shawbury's bombing range at Fenn's Moss on the Shropshire/Flintshire border. He recalls being addressed by a 'big RAF type' i.e. the Station Commander, G/Cpt. H. P. Lalo, on the need for secrecy and the dangers of careless talk. Grins were wiped off faces when the CO snarled: 'One word out of place and I'll have you b . . . s shot!' His words must have had some effect for even today there is a marked reluctance to talk about things that went on at Fenn's Moss. However, secrecy had already been compromised to some extent by the appearance of a Fenn's 'Bombing Range' on RAF aeronautical maps, both ¼-inch and 1:500,000 editions, as from editions of June 1939 and so was probably already in the domain of German Intelligence!

Decoys were nothing new even if the tentacles of 'ColonelTurner's Department' were slow to reach out and embrace Shropshire and the Welsh border. The feasibility of setting up decoy dummy airfields had been established as early as September 1939. In the October Colonel John Turner, former Director of of Works and Buildings at the Air Ministry (1936–39), brought out of retirement and charged with putting decoy counter-measures into effect, set up his HQ at Shepperton Film studios. It was an effective 'front'; even the RAF service men who manned the Llandegla

Moors decoy west of Wrexham had only the vaguest inkling that something called the 'The Sound Film Co.' was the mastermind behind their particular strategic complex. The preliminary ground organisation that initially divided the country into four areas, not unnaturally focussed on the east coast and south-east England. It was not until July/August that official 'professional' coverage was extended to the industrial north-west, just in time for the Liverpool and Manchester *Blitz*.

The Shawbury decoy of June 1940, not to be confused with the dual purpose QF-Q/QT site Col Turner was even then trying to set up at Withington on the crest of Haughmond Hill, was a primitive in-house affair, doomed to failure from the start, but more of a morale booster or conscience assuager than anything else. Something was being done. The decoy squad did not enjoy the luxury of a portable generator and electric lights. Each night, after bombing and gunnery had finished for the day, 'money flares' were set out and lit, 'double' or 'single line'. These were drums of paraffin with large wicks that gave off smokey flames 3–4ft high. For the moment little thought was given to realism. The flares were kept burning all night, almost daring German aircraft to drop their bombs. Even when enemy planes were tracked overhead no one thought of dowsing the flares as would happen on a real airfield if attacked. *Luftwaffe* pilots were not fools. The Army ground party was kept busy running up and down topping up drums and relighting wicks — a dangerous pursuit if the enemy had taken it into his head to drop bombs. There was no splinter-proof shelter or blockhouse for the decoy party, only a couple of tents and a sand-bagged observation post re-inforced with blocks of peat.

As they warmed to their new role so the soldiers began to improvise and show touches of ingenuity — occasionally flashing the headlights of their 3-tonner or briefly unmasking Tilley lamps to give the impression of careless movement on the ground. Again this was potentially dangerous, particularly with Army property involved. With some input from RAF personnel they even managed to simulate a landing aircraft, as Pte Evans put it, '... a bizarre method of two lights on a length of wood being towed along the peat cuttings.' Fifty years on he cannot remember who or what did the towing. 'Bizarre' the idea may have seemed to him in 1940, but under prevailing conditions, essentially practical. Bettisfield peat mill and the 'wharves' or yards at Moss Cottages, Whixall, were connected by a 2ft narrow gauge railway. A peat tramway had once run to an exchange siding at Fenn's Moss brickworks. By coincidence its trackbed would be used as a base line to work out the geometry for siting the bombing target and quadrant towers of the later 'Mark IV' bombing range. There were some four miles of track permanently laid on the moss — the 'main line' — and about two miles of temporary track and points that could be taken up and relaid wherever it was needed. Some 300 yards of spare track was commandeered by the Army and a dummy 'aeroplane' fixed onto the chassis of a peat wagon. The system's locomotive was a primitive Simplex, 20h.p., petrol powered, chain driven, bought as new in October 1919. Since it was currently the only one

available on the Moss, it is doubtful if it was imperilled to pull-push the decoy truck. So must one envisage sweating, stumbling, cursing teams of soldiers pulling this contraption by hand up and down the short length of track in the hope that 'someone up there' would drop bombs on them, or worse still, machine-gun them intruder fashion? But not to worry. In the three months this decoy was operational it attracted neither German bomb nor British aircraft attempting an emergency landing, such was its overall ineffectiveness.

As the initial panic subsided and wiser and calmer counsel prevailed, an end was called to the nightly Fenn's Moss charade. Exact date is uncertain, but in August 1940 the KSLI detachment was returned to depôt in Shrewsbury and Nº 10 SFTS, Tern Hill, had almost exclusive use of the bombing range. About this time RAF Shawbury, along with Tern Hill, Cranage, Sealand and Hawarden, got its official Q-site, that on Haughmond Hill (Withington), although the records of Col Turner's Department in the PRO are clearly incomplete and ambivalent in this matter. As will be seen later, the earlier commissioning of Shawbury's Q-site had been frustrated by wrongly siting the control bunker so that it flooded, needing a 24-hour pumping watch, and eventually necessitating a complete rebuild on a drier site.

In September 1941 Fenn's Moss was re-surveyed for the positioning of a 'Strategic Starfish' in between Middle and Top sections of the peat workings. In August 1943 the range was again resurveyed and enlarged to accommodate 'train busting' facilities. Thereafter there was very little alteration to lay-out, through a re-survey of June 1944 and the final disposition of January 1945, for which a diazo or dye-line drawing exists in the English Nature archive, and which has served as a basis for the maps in the following chapters. Fortunately, too, until his death in 1996 the range control and safety officer for the last eighteen months of its existence, lived not far away, in Whixall, and was able to fill in on the day-to-day running of the range, although he was more reticent on the decoys, worried, as he still was, about the 'Official Secrets Act'!

The *ad hoc* deceptions as outlined above must be seen in the context of darkness and night raids. Preventative measures during daylight hours were a different matter altogether, and in 1940–41 relied heavily on attempts to persuade the enemy that a 350+ acre aerodrome did not exist, in other words reliance was paced on airfield camouflage and/or elementary decoys as yet not standardised but left very much to schemes devised by the various AMWD area Clerks of the Works and the initiative of individual station commanders, with success commensurate with the attention and care to detail or indifference, negligence, even inertia shown by these officers. Of Shawbury's efforts at daylight deception we know little, save perhaps in 1940 it was caught up in the general indecision over rival camouflage schemes. Its huge 'C'-type hangars were neatly wrapped up in 'disruptive' green, brown and black paint, even then going out of fashion, but traces of which still survive on brickwalls some sixty years later. In contrast smaller hangars and other buildings on the technical site are painted in single tone

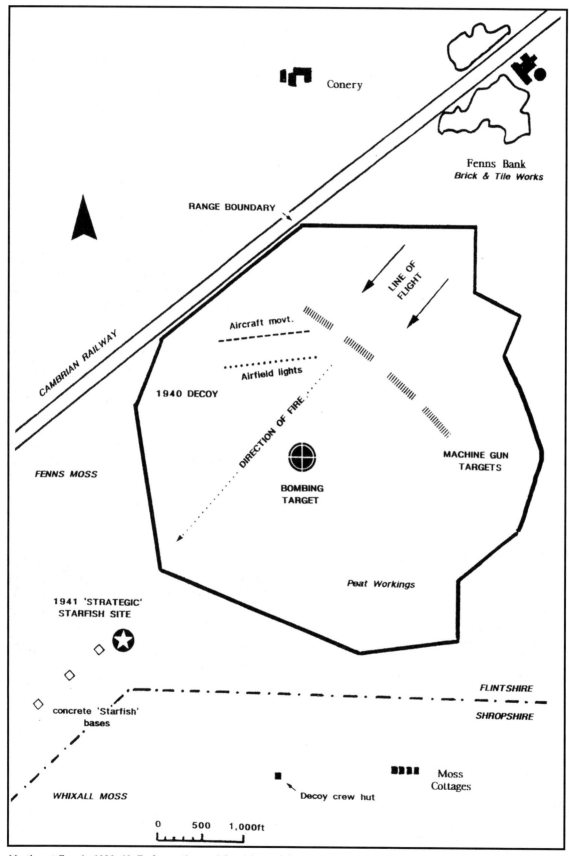

North-east Fenn's, 1939–40. Early wartime aerial activity and decoy.

schemes, varying in density to obtain maximum disruptive effect. This would be the recommended norm after May 1941. The pattern of agriculture on surrounding farms produced a patchworks of colours and textures against which the vast mono-coloured landing-ground would stand out from the air. Hence attempts to artificially reproduce hedge lines and the strip effects of growing crops and managed grasslands that would, hopefully, break up runways, roads, peri-tracks and hardstandings. We have not found a photograph of Shawbury so camouflaged but reproduce the efforts to make Cranage, Wrexham and Tern Hill aerodromes reasonably invisible, the first two taken by RAF PRUs, but the last, however by *Luftwaffe* photo reconnaissance, and a very illuminating example of how NOT to do camouflage!

Tern Hill had first been raided on 23 July 1940, when a stick of HE bombs straddled the A41 outside the main entrance and guard room. The main picture overleaf is a German 'snap shot' of 29 September 1940, the same day as the RLG at Wrexham (Borras Lodge) and Hawarden aerodrome were photographed. But the construction work had not yet started on the former, and the latter was still a large chaotic building site. The camouflage measures at Tern Hill are clearly those put in place twelve months previously, at the end of the 1939 growing season. The characteristic Expansion period 'arc' of the main technical and communal site is easily recognisable — the Officers' Mess stands out, although side annexes are less obvious; the 'C'-type aircraft sheds carry disruptive camouflage of varying hues, but only in the one case has an attempt been made to break the rectangular outline by draping camouflage nets over the

entrances; MT sheds and the AMWD/M&EE depots are mono-toned, owing more to constructional materials than change in camouflage policy; hutted camps have been built without reference to the camouflage potential of the adjacent woodland. The MU/ASU sites on Stoke Heath fare a little better. On 'B' and 'C' sites the turf-covered 'L'-type aircraft sheds blend perfectly into the background. 'A' site, however, is a right mess, the disruptive camouflage of the 'C'-type shed almost succeeding in hiding the saw-tooth roof, leaving the two 'D'-types standing out like sore thumbs, the one obviously newly erected and as yet bereft of any paint at all. A dead give-away are the aeroplanes picketed out around the landing ground, between the perimeter fence and the peri-track, like a string of beads. Indeed, the intervals are so regular as to make one wonder whether these planes were part of some early primitive decoy system. The hedges of open fields adjacent to these sites attempt to shelter dispersed aircraft from the prying eye of the camera but there are no visible means of access which would point to them being 'genuine' aircraft rolled into place.

The wider landing ground as a whole represents a poor effort at deception having been allowed to decay, literally gone to seed, through neglect or downright indolence. There is no excuse for it; if German PR could see through these attempts surely RAF top-brass who overflew the area daily could see what was going amiss and act accordingly? A one-dimensional attempt has been made to simulate hedgerows, fence lines and trees to make it appear as if the vast open landing ground was broken into segments too small to land aircraft; but such hedgelines are too thick and obtrusive compared with the real field boundaries adjacent. It may be

Above, left: Desolate peat cuttings on Fenn's Moss, ideal for air-to-ground gunnery ranges.
Below, left: The 1919 vintage loco which propelled the decoy 'aircraft'.

Top right: The narrow gauge tramway, parts of which were utilised for a makeshift decoy.
Bottom right: Flat-bed peat wagons used to simulate moving aircraft.

RAF Tern Hill, 27 September 1940, showing how difficult it was to maintain camouflage on an all grass aerodrome. Luftwaffe photograph. [American National Archive Photographic Library]

Below: RAF Tern Hill, 1942 with its new concrete runways and a more defined camouflage. [English Heritage N.M.R.]

that the undue thickness is a misconceived attempt to create a three-dimensional 'shadow' effect, but some illusion is immediately lost by hedgelines stopping short at the peri-track without being painted over the latter. Similarly the spring and summer growing season has diluted the effectiveness of the interior camouflage; this is not to mention actual physical attrition caused by the tyres of taxying planes and service vehicles and aircraft landing or taking off, leaving long streaks in the field which have rubbed out the bogus hedgerows. Again, in comparison with the general tatty, dog-eared aspect of the landing ground, the surrounding fields have a decidedly clean and neat look in comparison and aircraft parked here, although perhaps requiring a second glance to locate, are definitely visible. Overall, then, small wonder that Tern Hill received a second visitation from the *Luftwaffe* on 16 October 1940, perhaps not so opportune or fortuitous as is often thought. On this occasion four 250kg HE bombs and several canisters of IB were dropped, hitting the easternmost of the 'C'-type hangars (paradoxically the best camouflaged), destroying two Blenheims and some twenty training aircraft belonging to N° 10 SFTS. Only the side annexes of the hangar remain, to this day known as the 'Sunshine Hangar'.

RAF Cranage, 1940, illustrates the problem of camouflaging an 'Expansion' period all-grass aerodrome.
[English Heritage NMR]

Early camouflage efforts at RAF Wrexham, 1942. Not an aeroplane in sight, N°s 96 and 285 Squadrons having moved south.
[National Assembly for Wales]

Luftwaffe aerial photograph of RAF Tern Hill, September 1940. Decoy work shown incompleted with decoy bombers laid out on the fields.. [US National Archives Aerial Photo Library)

Across the A41 (top of picture) the armoury and ammunition stores and the approach road stand out 'camouflaged' as they are in some sort of 'blotchy', very unsuitable paint scheme, but at least one can see that hedges have been breached to permit dispersal of aircraft in the adjacent field, which is more than can be said for the disposition visible on the next following exposure, which shows the MU 'D'-site (bottom left) and fields running towards Buntingsdale Hall, an imposing building in formal gardens just relinquished as HQ Training Command, but still HQ to Nº 25 (Armament Training) Group and later Nº 29 (Flying Training) Group — so not exactly the best place to plant a decoy site. The whole area is now occupied by former RAF married quarters housing, but here in 1940 German Intelligence saw but a small crescent of six semi-detached houses with some very basic and dodgy decoys too close for comfort. The painted or cut-out silhouettes of largely single engine aircraft - one twin engine outline noted — overlie or stand on bases of darker material — paving or ash. They were of little value in daylight, being flat, not raised off the ground or sitting at an angle and so casting no shadow. They, like the main airfield, appear to have been badly maintained and parts of the shapes have faded away. An alternative explanation is that the *Luftwaffe* has caught Tern Hill's first home-spun decoy in an unfinished state with some silhouettes possibly unpainted, and the paved bases as

yet to be toned down to match their surrounds, as has obviously happened to the aircraft dispersed in adjoining fields! Whether one can consider these decoy aircraft too remote from the airfield to be credible is a moot point. They do indeed lack clear taxi paths to the airfield, but having said that, one must remember that at Tern Hill, in addition to the SFTS there was an even more valuable ASU and one should perhaps consider that some of these decoy aircraft are actually decoying the storage facilities at Nº 24 MU, Stoke Heath.

2. To fool the enemy ...

At the end of August 1940, as the mountains of east Denbighshire burned for over a week smothering Wrexham in a pall of grey smoke and a thick layer of white wood ash, William Joyce alias 'Lord Haw Haw' claimed in one of his nightly broadcasts to the British nation that the *Luftwaffe* had destroyed a large munitions dump and oil storage complex near the town.

There was some initial panic in five counties, for three miles east of Wrexham, in Isycoed parish, Nᵒˢ 34 and 35 Royal Ordnance Factories were even then nearing completion and would be commissioned on 10 December. The two contractors, Holland & Hannen and Cubitts Ltd. and Pauling & Co. Ltd. employed between them some 2,000 men, drawn from all over the north-west as far afield as Merseyside and the Potteries. Management, work-force and relatives were relieved to find that the ROF was unscathed. Fortunately throughout the war the ROF would not be bombed although there were several near misses during the construction phase. Incendiary bombs fell on 31 August 1940, parachute flares on 6 September, ten high explosive bombs on 29 October, and ten more on 14 November. There was another parachute flare on 22 October 1941 but this did not set off an invasion scare as previously! All these fell outside the perimeter fence. In retrospect the munitions factory was perhaps in greater danger from aircraft falling unexpectedly out of the sky than from the nightly forays of the *Luftwaffe*. Masters AZ698 and AZ593 of 17 (P)AFU, Wrexham, on 16 September and 5 October 1943 respectively come immediately to mind. But with the middle Dee valley being a high density 'Low Flying Area' one can cheerfully add training aircraft from all over Shropshire, for example, a High Ercall Mosquito on 13 December 1943 or an Atcham-based Thunderbolt of 495 Fighter Training Group, USAF, on 11 April 1944.

Some seven weeks into the Battle of Britain the bombing of 'military targets' on Ruabon Mountain (which term also covers Minera and Esclusham Mountains) was Wrexham's rude introduction into the harsh realities of an air war, Liverpool's air war. As such, the incident still looms large in the local folk lore and legend of an older generation. An

Right: Just two of the hundreds of IBs (incendiary bombs) that fell on or about the Royal ordnance Factory, Wrexham on 30/31 August 1940 as collected by Ernest Woodfine, a local smallholder, within hours of burning out. The label reads: 'Found August 31st 1940 up the fields in front of the house at 1.30am. Gate House. Friday night.

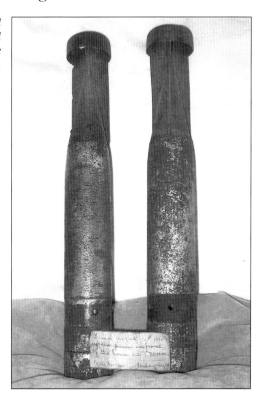

Above: Yellow painted fins of a SC50 High Explosive bomb dropped on Edward Dickens' farm, Hugmore Lane, Llan-y-pwll, close to the ROF, killing livestock.

Below: What look like marl pits in a 1960s agricultural landscape are actually water-filled HE bomb craters dating back to the raid of 31 August 1940. Former ROF top right. Holt–Cock Bank road (B5130) bottom right. [Pilkington Brothers]

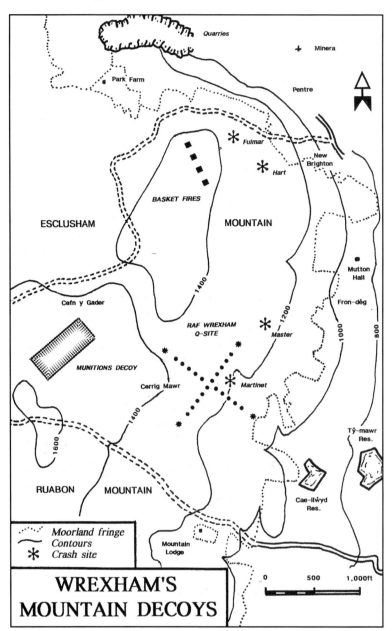

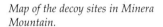

Map of the decoy sites in Minera Mountain.

upland farm in Penycae was obliterated, UXBs caused fatal casualties in Rhos and Gresford, and in the mortuary of the War Memorial Hospital duty orderlies carefully entered the first names in the town's War Casualty Register. As things turned out, these were the only names so entered. An eight-month lull would be broken only by entries relating the crews of the Heinkel He111 that was brought down on the outskirts of Wrexham on 7/8 May 1941 and the Junkers Ju88 that came to a fiery end at Pulford on 1 November 1941.

Although raids would occur right through to January 1942, with 'peak periods' in October 1940 and May 1941, nothing was to compare with the intensity and savagery of the nights of the 28 August–1 September 1940. Not surprisingly, in view of the strict censorship imposed on the local press and the tight security around the mountain itself, it is difficult to get a true picture of events, not in the least an adequate reason for the bombing of the mountain. There are as many different versions of events as there are survivors of the war years!

The biggest uncertainty centres upon whether the fires on the mountain were started accidentally or deliberately. Everyone agreed, however, that they succeeded in diverting hundreds of tons of IBs and HE otherwise destined for Merseyside targets. For our present purpose the bombing of 28/29 August and the next four days is a convenient watershed, enabling the researcher to focus on developments 'before' and 'after'. Much of what follows is derived from fieldwork and the oral evidence of former serving members of both the newly formed LDVF (Home Guard) and holding companies at the Barracks, Wrexham, in particular W. G. Parry-Ralphs, Ruabon, Home Guard messenger/runner and decoy maintenance man, and Len Jones, Hightown, Wrexham, ex-RWF.

On 14 May 1940 the new Secretary of State,

Bomb craters on Esclusham Mountain show the effectiveness of the early decoy system.
[NLW, Geoffrey Charles Collection]

Anthony Eden, announced the formation of the Local Defence Volunteer Force. Two days later over 2,000 men in Denbighshire and 1,800 in Flintshire had registered with the police, with all the attendant problems of accommodation, training and equipping. The Zone 3, Wrexham Group, area ultimately supported two battalions of Home Guard, the 6th (originally 4th) Denbighshire Battalion drawing upon Wrexham and the industrial villages to the north and north-west, and the 7th Den/Flint Battalion covering the area to the south and the detached part of Flintshire. Battalion reorganisation was completed on 17 July 1940. To this date, lacking any other, may tentatively be attributed the complete sealing off of Ruabon Mountain and its zoning for patrol purposes between various Home Guard units backed by detachments of the RWF.

Patrols were made and road-blocks manned round the clock. Thus upon the Penycae, Rhos, and Ponciau platoons of 'C' (later 'E') Company, 7th Den/Flint Batt. Home Guard fell the onus of securing that part of the mountain from Penycae to Esclusham. The Llangollen platoon (later D' Company) and Cefn/Acrefair platoon patrolled the southern approaches. Their HQ at the Drill Hall, Osborne Street, Rhos, was shared by RWF guard, maintenance details, and liaison officers. Upon the regulars fell the burden of the 'day shift'. Each unit manned road blocks in, and patrolled, their own areas. Ignorance of what went on in another company's territory made for enhanced security. The Rhos platoon had special responsibility for the Plas Drain access, with road blocks and check points at Llanerchrugog Hall and Onen-fawr and observation post at Mountain Lodge. North of them responsibility for the 'buffer end' security was taken over by 'D' Company, 6th Den. Batt. Home Guard, co-ordinated from HQ first at Cerrig Farm, Tanyfron, and then North Wales Power offices at Rhostyllen.

Apart from the fact that the Army may have been using large tracts of mountain for live ammunition training — they

were certainly doing this in 1942 — what was on this mountain that necessitated it being closed for the duration? The measure was a blow to the landed shooting fraternity and a serious curtailment of civilian movement. Pre-war Rhos Mountain was a popular week-end rendezvous for miners and their families, with some people suffering from tuberculosis and industrial diseases setting up temporary homes in huts on the 1,000ft contour, and eking out their existence by selling teas etc. to week-end picnickers.

The first clue is afforded by the appearance of a Royal Engineer unit on Wynnstay Park, Ruabon, setting up camp at the School Lodge. As well as beginning to 'upgrade' former mining roads to the long disused Pool Park and South Minera lead mines at 1,200–1,300ft OD, they commenced to skin a large gently sloping site at Cefn y Gader, near enough on the former Wynnstay mine site, for something that for ease of reference is referred to as a 'munitions factory' decoy. This was remote from the seat of the great mountain blaze that would ensue. As yet there is some uncertainty as to whether the decoy was in place before 28 August. It was certainly there after the 'big fire'. The fact that the *Luftwaffe* attempted to bomb it, and William Joyce gloated over its destruction, would seem to suggest that it was up and running and doing an effective deception job in late July or early August. It was one of Mr Parry-Ralphs' daily chores to maintain 'inflatables' on the decoy site with the aid of a lorry-mounted compressor. There were dummy guns, muzzles pointing to the sky, Army tanks, lorries, and searchlights 'that never lit'. Although many of these lifesized models had been built by film company 'prop.' departments, their early efforts were rather pathetic and soon began to warp and disintegrate under the sun and the dry scorching summer winds that swept the mountain top. The ply-wood mock-ups were interspersed with scrap versions of the real thing, salvaged from the breaker's yard, and increasingly by inflatables as manufacturers such as

Officers and men of HQ 'F' Company, 6th (Denbighshire) Bn, Home Guard, outside the Drill Hall, Poyser Street, Wrexham.
[W. Alister Williams Collection]

Colonel John Turner, Director of Decoys. [Royal Engineers Journal]

Vauxhall and Crossley were persuaded to produce 'blow-up' versions of their production models.

In order to create the illusion that the decoy site was being actively used Army lorries ran up the mountain roads at irregular intervals and parked in different positions about the site during the day. Twice a week on rotation sections of the static display were re-arranged. This was a necessary precaution for during this period *Luftwaffe* reconnaissance aircraft were penetrating Wrexham air space with relative impunity. We have noticed elsewhere the recording of 5 SFTS 's relief landing ground at Borras and the partly-built ROF adjacent by a cheeky intruder He111 on Saturday, 28 September 1940. Two days later, 30 September, the same He111 that at *c.*1530hrs dropped two HE bombs at the gates of Llay Main Colliery also buzzed Minera Mountain and shot up a Home Guard foot patrol. It was not an isolated strafing. What else was to be expected when a low-flying reconnaissance aircraft came under concentrated rifle fire? A little retaliation, sport even, was always on the cards. Such one-sided engagements pointed to a military presence and, if nothing else, might have served to emphasise the genuineness of the decoy sites in the eyes of German Intelligence. Essentially a daytime decoy, the Cefn y Gader facility also had a night-time version although it amounted to little more than sheep hurdles covering a Tilley lamp to give an irregular blinking light and the impression of some careless black-out. This complex miraculously survived the moorland fire and would gradually spill over the lip of its shelf into Nant Cwm-mawr in an attempt to give some legitimacy to the RAF's new 'K'-cum-'Q' site.

All this careful deception, although rather primitive compared with what would later be produced, bears the hall-mark of Colonel John Turner's department, with its HQ at Shepperton Film Studios, set up as early as October 1939 to co-ordinate and supervise the new 'cloak and dagger' measures. The department was probably involved more in an advisory capacity although the approximate dates suggested for the Ruabon Mountain decoy also fit in with the expansion of Colonel Turner's ground organisation, from the original four 'K' areas, covering only eastern counties and the south-east, to thirteen areas country-wide by January 1941. Fifty years on the only problem with this 'munitions factory' decoy is that it seems to be self-standing and bears no relation to any known military ordnance site. The ROF east of Wrexham was an explosives factory, an extension of the Royal Gun Powder Factory at Waltham Abbey, producing nitro-glycerine, gun-cotton etc. Apart from the Acid Factory and boiler houses its landscape was largely one of Nitrating Buildings, Purification, Mixing,

Washing and Weighing Houses, Stoves and Paste Stores etc. all hidden in their protective 'hills'. The Royal Artillery Depôt and School at Kinmel, near Abergele, was the nearest military establishment that from the air would remotely resemble the Minera Mountain decoy. While Kinmel was bombed and strafed several times, Minera is too far removed to be considered its decoy, even if, at a time of material shortages, every two-bit regimental depôt warranted its own strategic decoy. Thus in a sense the 'munitions factory' decoy can only be considered as a carrot dangled in front of a *Luftwaffe* donkey, inviting the mountain to be bombed! But there were easier ways of setting a mountain alight. Also in place on Minera Mountain in July 1940 was a set of 'pan fires' of crudest construction. This was on a broad shelf along side the tailings of the Park Lead Mine, completely invisible from immediately below. By all accounts there were other sets of pans further south along the mountain fringe, but their position has not been ascertained although they were seen to ignite on 'the night of the fire'. All 'pan' sites were apparently linked and capable of being ignited simultaneously. The 'pans' were nothing more than the ends of huge fuel drums cut in half and supported on steel scaffolding or pieces of iron girder. With more than one on the mountain their prime function was to show fire at night and attract bombs. They had been built at great speed. There were no concrete bases. The pans were simply set straight on the Upper Grey Limestone which underlies the thin soils and heather at this point. Any spillage of paraffin or other combustibles and a moorland fire was inevitable.

It has been suggested that the Minera pans were a protective decoy for Brymbo Steelworks two miles to the north. Steelworks with blast furnaces were notoriously difficult to black out. Brymbo was of vital importance to the war effort, having been selected to supply quality steels to the Air Ministry. Seven months before the outbreak of war work had commenced on the installation of four electric arc furnaces, three of which, ironically, were of German origin, manufactured by Siemens Schuckert, whose experts oversaw the installation! With the formation of the Ministry of Aircraft Production in May 1940 the works was put under the control of Thomas Firth and John Brown Ltd. But there would be few better documented potential targets on the files of *Luftwaffe* Intelligence! Was it coincidence, or just part of the general mayhem, that the steelworks was bombed on the night of 31 August/1 September 1940? Fortunately damage was confined to the scrap yard so that there was no disruption in steel production.

The evening of Wednesday, 28 August 1940, although industrial targets in the Midlands were the main objective, marked the first of four successive nights of bombing on Merseyside, each increasing in severity. A short 'Purple Alert' (0050–0130hrs) was logged by Flintshire Police. A half-hearted attempt at 0300hrs to bomb the RA Training Depôt at Kinmel Park was probably associated with minelaying activity in Liverpool Bay. But the following night all hell broke loose as Liverpool suffered the heaviest night raid yet on a British city, not only because it was the country's second port but also as a reprisal for the attack on Berlin the previous evening. As an adjunct to these raids Flintshire

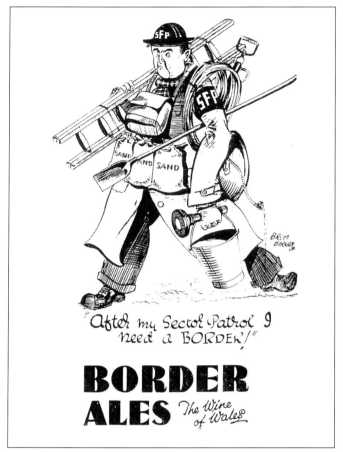

There was no way of knowing that Wrexham's 'Blitz' was to be short-lived. Border Breweries introduced a bit of humour into an otherwise potentially disaterous scenario. [Wrexham Leader/Border Breweries/Marstons Brewery]

Police divisions reported over thirty incidents in the county. Inexplicably Denbighshire Civil Defence logged just the two bombs (one an UXB) at Gresford. No mention is made of the fire on Ruabon Mountain.

For this one turns to Colin Eaborn, FRS, lately Professor of Chemistry at the University of Sussex, but then of Rhosymedre (and earlier of Holt) and a 17-year old sixth-former at Ruabon Boys Grammar School. As a member of the recently formed LDVF he was doing his regular Thursday night stint of guard and patrol duty. He writes:

On a Thursday in August 1940, as a member of the Local Defence Volunteers, I was on guard on the railway viaduct at Newbridge along with a fellow sixth-former and two veterans of the 1914-18 War. One of the latter, a holder of the Military Medal, was the corporal in charge of our group. In the early part of the night we were watching the flashes from the bombs dropping on Liverpool and the lights in the sky from the flames, when suddenly a long line of fire appeared on the moors in the area between Garth and Rhos. I would estimate that it was at least half-a-mile long, and its nature was such that the corporal shouted, "They have hit a pipe line", though we quickly recognised that it was an unlikely place for such a thing! The flames quickly spread as the bracken caught fire.

From then on many of the planes turned away from Liverpool to drop their bombs, mainly harmlessly, onto the burning area, and continued to do so for the duration of the raid. The bombs sounded, and felt, alarmingly close to us, but in fact could not have been less than two miles away! At one point one of the bombers flew very low directly over us, probably no more than 300ft, going south along the main railway line, which in the bright moonlight would have provided an excellent pointer to its way home.

The next day some of us from the LDV, mostly schoolboys, were taken to the moors to help firemen fight the fires which were threatening some farmhouses. We succeeded in protecting the building assigned to us but, not realising that the fires had been started deliberately, I was puzzled by the feebleness of the overall effort being made to put it out. The blaze, which continued to burn for about a week, attracted some bombers every night, though it is my recollection that the proportion going there rather than to Liverpool fell away fairly quickly after the first two nights. There were some deaths from the bombs in the Rhos area, including that of a boy from my school.

What Professor Eaborn saw was the detonation of the southernmost decoy pans. At exactly the same moment a platoon of Cheshire Home Guard, from their vantage point high on the Bickerton Hills, were startled to see the faint after-glow of the western night sky riven by sheets of flame as all the pans along the moorland edge were ignited. Uncomprehendingly, they could only settle back and watch as the blazing heather began to attract its quota of incendiary and high-explosive bombs. Writing in October 1977, former Pte. A. T. Hughes of Brown Knowl, Broxton, reported: 'I had a grandstand view of this occasion. Four of us were on Home Guard duty on Maiden Castle, Bickerton Hill. My son, then aged fifteen, had come with us that night and he and I went for a stroll across the front of the hill. We quickly became aware of the streams of German aircraft coming over and saw the first batch of incendiaries start the fires. I went across to the hut to fetch the other three Home Guards and we lay in a depression on the hill top and viewed the rest of the raid. It was a truly terrible sight. When we came to leave the post at daybreak we could not see anything of the mountain for the smoke. I was told by a person who had been to Wilmslow that day that the smoke could be smelled there. After the first planes had got the fires going successive waves arrived with the high explosives that caused the damage and the casualties.

Duty done, Army personnel had fled the mountain. But they were back in force the next day to control and contain, rather than extinguish, the fires. Thrown up in haste, the improvised pans now lay empty, smoking and holed. No thought had been given to staggered detonation or keeping some in reserve for use on successive nights. This would come with experience. W. G. Parry-Ralphs recalls the Army 'up on top keeping the fire stoked up', with loads of used tyres and 'pine cuttings', in other words pit-props scrounged from Bersham and Hafod collieries, being off-loaded to form the next night's decoy pyres, the aim being 'to make as much smoke and flames as possible'.

If the pounding given to Ruabon Mountain is any yardstick the decoy ploy was a success, admittedly with diminishing returns as the week ended. Inevitably there was a debit side, with farms, hamlets and villages receiving a dose of IBs and a leavening of HE. Each incident on its own gives the impression of indiscriminate bombing, a haphazard jettisoning of a bomb load. Viewed overall one can discern a broad belt of secondary bomb damage flanking three sides of the burning mountain — from Llandegla, round through Glascoed, Cae-llo, Pentresaeson and Brymbo, then south via Summerhill, Coedpoeth, Plas Power, Frondeg and Bronwylfa to Rhos, where an UXB in Osborne Street would kill seven people and injure five, and on to Penycae,

Bombing pattern in the Wrexham area, 30 August–1 September 1940. Wrexham's air war was three days of saturation bombing of decoys, .

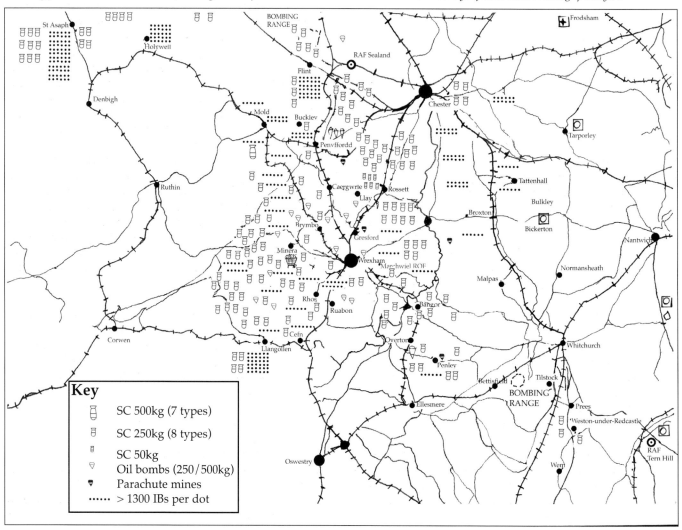

where the Plas Ucha family and farmhouse were wiped out. The trail of destruction petered out on Garth Mountain although Shropshire people would like to move the whole scenario southwards to Bronygarth Mountain!

Colin Eaborn's reference to German aircraft flying along the railway is not far off the mark. Providing they could be seen railways, canals and rivers were flawless navigational aids to friend and foe alike. These early raids on Merseyside were trailblazing 'Adolf's Railway' that ran via Lyme Bay, Bristol Channel, Severn estuary, Welsh border, Dee estuary and thence to Liverpool, with a right turn for Manchester at Shocklach! Additionally, by following railways, one never knew what targets of opportunity might present themselves in the shape of trains, marshalling yards and railway junctions. The seemingly haphazard visitations of Shropshire over the same four nights might best be interpreted as railway orientated.

The fires of August/September 1940 seemed to have established the bona fides of Ruabon Mountain as a suitable site for decoys. As noted earlier, adjacent to the gradually expanding 'munitions factory' decoy was erected an RAF decoy site. From the Appendix to Chapter 6, based on the official list in the PRO, it will be seen that almost every operational and training aerodrome in 9 Group Fighter Command area, commissioned in 1941 or earlier, had its statutory decoy site. They were all abandoned by 30 November 1943, with RAF Cosford's for some reason hanging on until 31 December.

Even as RAF Shawbury, following the opportunist night time raid of 26/27 June 1940, tinkered with a primitive decoy on Fenn's Moss bombing range and even more basic static bonfires on Cherrington Moor, Newport, so an attempt was also made to establish a more 'sophisticated' Q-site on Haughmond Hill, north of Shrewsbury, straddling the favoured southern approach to the aerodrome along 'Adolf's Railway'. In retrospect the search-light and Bofors gun at Hunkington on the Withington road was probably a more effective deterrent! Sophisticated it may have become in later years, but in 1940, by Colonel Turner's standards, it was still a risible affair — one suspects that early efforts on this hill were also station or 'in-house' based.

In peacetime the heathland on Haughmond Hill formed part of Sundorne Castle's game preserve. Pheasant breeding pens had to be moved to accommodate 'a command centre for monitoring enemy air activity', a feeble fiction immediately questioned by the Keeper's Cottage family when a further 20 acres was requisitioned to build 'an aerial runway with a lighting system' on which, incredibly, 'no aircraft was to land'. Initially, the lighting scheme was pecked out with paraffin lamps, converting to T-type pattern and electricity early in 1940, after the control centre had been requisitioned on a drier site further up the small eminence which dominates the area. Against all local advice and knowledge, the AMWD had built — and buried up to the air vents — the first control shelter on a faulted natural hill drain. For the first nine months it had to be continually pumped out by hand, a real chore in the bad winter of 1939–40. Despite offers of rehousing, the keeper's family remained in their cottage and spent the next two or three years waiting to be bombed. In its earliest incarnation the RAF decoy was crewed by two corporals and two AC1s who were billeted at the cottage. As the decoy expanded so did the numbers of crew, most of whom were billeted in Upton Magna.

Eye witnesses refer to 'structures resembling aircraft frames covered with sacking' — were these a short-lived daylight decoy on the lines of the misguided efforts at Tern Hill? What sort of impression were they intended to convey when they had lamps glowing dully in their interiors? Co-located on the hill was an 'A' Series QF decoy for Harlescott, a strategic suburb of Shrewsbury, with its giant Sentinel and Perkins works and a 'Spitfire factory'. The Sentinel works produced and repaired Bren-gun carriers for the Army, which were also trialled on Haughmond Hill. Large squares were 'shaved' or cleared in the bracken. In these, arranged in diverse patterns, stood roughly constructed wooden 'firebaskets', lined with chicken wire and filled with assorted combustibles soaked in creosote, kept dry whilst

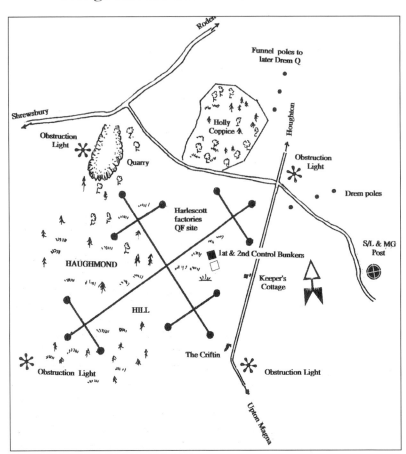

Haughmond Hill A.23 (No 72 dual decoy, north-east of Shrewsbury) built to protect RAF Shawbury and the Harlescott factories.

Two views of the first decoy control building at Haughmond Hill. despite being warned by locals, the Army went ahead and built the decoy over an underground stream which caused it to be flooded. It was abandoned and rebuilt further up the hill..

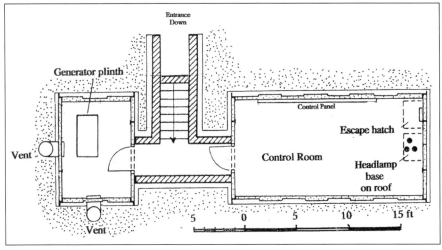

Left: Ground plan of the original control building at Haughmond Hill.

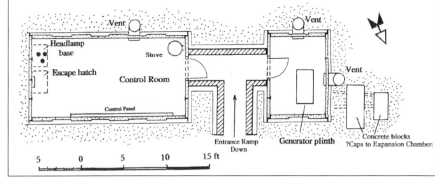

Ground plan of the resited decoy control building at Haughmond Hill, built on a drier site.

dormant by roofing felt, hessian or scrim, and ignited by flare cans and wicks. These early fire baskets did not burn with the same ferocity as those later provided by Colonel Turner's department which had to replicate the 'fire-ribbons' and *Brand-bombfelder* ('fire bomb fields') of incendiary patterns dropped from December 1940 onwards. Primitive contraptions or otherwise, a fire basket had a short life. If it was intended they should burn for a long period, they had to be lit in relays, hence their proliferation on Haughmond Hill. Twice during 1941, the inhabitants of Shrewsbury, accustomed to a diffused light surrounding the hill were treated to a pyrotechnic display 'as the whole combustible side of the decoy site caught fire during an electrical storm' — at least this was the official verdict of a court of inquiry. Such an occurrence would ruin the careful correlation between airfield and decoy. When enemy aircraft trundled overhead, Shawbury's lights would be extinguished; those of the decoy dulled, but not put out completely. Both sets of decoys on the hill would be officially abandoned by 30 November 1943, too early to be associated with the crashes of a Nº 60 OTU DH Mosquito (DZ244) and an as yet unidentified Republic Thunderbolt on the hill, both in 1944. However, one might note the demise of a Nº 57 OTU Miles Master (TA364) at the decoy cross-roads on 5 April 1942. It was on a NAVEX, when its engine failed and the pilot had to make a forced landing.

Keeping track of both RAF Hawarden's and RAF Sealand's Q-sites is a complicated affair. Pre-Colonel Turner there were local initiatives on the Burton Marshes in the Dee estuary. Engineers of Western Command, Chester, were busy off Burton Point, west of the railway embankment, 'with their scaffolding, sacking and lights', easing their way over the mud and tidal gutters 'on little railway buggies', which points to some sort of narrow gauge railway system, perhaps using contractors' prefabricated tracking. The ruse obviously worked; the Army decoy was plastered during the last week of July and throughout August and September 1940, 'hits' falling off as the main thrust of decoying moved east of the railway. There was a downside. Army detachments daily had to trawl the marshes between tides to recover unexploded items and other fragments potentially dangerous to boatmen, anglers and farmers who still had limited access to the marsh. These early initiatives have no place in the regional listing of decoy sites appended to Chapter 6. Land for RAF Sealand's 'Q' site was requisitioned

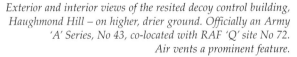

Exterior and interior views of the resited decoy control building, Haughmond Hill – on higher, drier ground. Officially an Army 'A' Series, No 43, co-located with RAF 'Q' site No 72. Air vents a prominent feature.

Sentinel Works, Harlescott

The Sentinel Works, Harlescott, a 'vital point' and the reason for the Haughmond Hill "A' series QF Decoy site, manufactured a wide variety of wartime equipment. [All pictures via R. Pilsbury]

Left: An aeroplane wing riveting machine.

Below: Bow ramp operating gears, as used on naval landing craft.

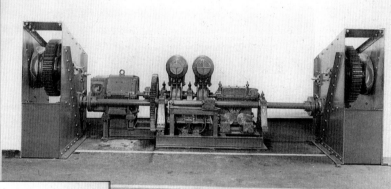

Left: Locust tank being collected from Harlescott by the Royal Armoured Corps .

Above : Portabole Oxygen Generating Plant for the RAF .

Left: Universal (Bren gun) carriers awaiting collection by the Army.

Right: the chassis and engine of a Loyd Carrier 3.

Below left: The 4-ton Loyd carrier 3, capable of carrying eight men.

Above: The front view of a RAM II ARV tank, designed to assist in the recovery of other armoured vehicles on the battlefield.

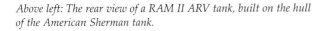

Above left: The rear view of a RAM II ARV tank, built on the hull of the American Sherman tank.

Right: Two Stuart light tanks.

as of Marsh Farm estates on 21 July 1940, in the first instance for a standard 't'-type lighting affair; lights and other equipment were installed by electrical engineers from the AMWD as per Drawing N° 10239/40, but with groundwork in the hands of the station commander so that Colonel Turner had difficulty in keeping tabs on the work progress and when the sites became operational. Work was obviously incomplete by 14 August 1940 on which evening Sealand aerodrome was bombed by a rogue Heinkel He111 causing considerable damage and casualties. Puddington made its first appearance in Turner's records on 1 August 1941. This late date is puzzling, even allowing for official lethargy and red tape and points to this particular PRO file as possibly being incomplete. The Sealand decoy is registered as 'Q' N° 205, but for some reason changed to 'Q' N° 153, an earlier running number, on 15 December 1941, which number it carried forward until closure in 1943. Not surprisingly, in view of its position *vis-a-vis* Merseyside, Puddington was a 'busy' decoy during November–December 1940, May–June 1941 and October 1941–January 1942. Liverpool sirens sounded for the last time on 9 August 1942, so the upgrading of the electrics three days later was, in practice, a waste of time. The same might be said for one of Liverpool's 'Civil' (C.60) and 'Starfish' (SF.11m) decoys which had been near enough co-located by 1 January 1942 on another piece of the salt marsh north of the RAF decoy. To confuse matters, the seaward side of all Puddington 'Q' sites, i.e. west of the Wrexham–Bidston railway line, would transmogrify into yet another bombing range. 'Reactivated' is possibly a more suitable word, for this range was first purchased by the Air Ministry in 1924, for use by N° 5 FTS and is shown as a 'Danger Area' on peacetime air charts until 1940. The re-opening of the range was made more urgent after May 1942 with the formation of N° 60 OTU, High Ercall, Shropshire, whose Mosquitoes were the prime users of the range, in addition to those also used on the Ribble estuary.

One should note that the principle of establishing decoys to airfields, especially those in eastern and southern England, had been approved as early as June 1939, but with a typical lack of urgency on the part of the RAF very little was done until four days before the actual outbreak of hostilities, when operational Commands were advised to put airfield decoy measures in hand — much attenuated, less sophisticated than envisaged, with no guarantee of any of the specially designed 'props' if the airfield lay west of a line Southampton–Birmingham–Perth. In practice, the onus fell directly upon Group commanders and individual station COs to act 'as they saw fit', hence the early unco-ordinated shambles that we have noticed at Shawbury and Tern Hill. But allowing for their training rôle in a 'back area' that some decoy provision actually got off the ground at all, before a certain Colonel John Turner was appointed as 'Dictator of Dummies' i.e. facilitator and overseer of the whole decoy programme, is to be commended. Naturally, there was a time lag in the Welsh borderland and north-west.

By August 1940 Tern Hill had disposed of its in-house day-time deception system. As noted in the previous chapter this comprised home-made dummy aircraft and crude attempts to paint hedgelines on the landing ground. If not ill-conceived, these elements were certainly ill-managed. In their place a night Q-site was set up at Chipnall, five miles to the east on the Shropshire/Staffordshire border, its 'flare path' running along a soggy bottom of the Coal Brook. This was no longer the responsibility of the station commander acting off his own bat; but now came under the aegis of the 'professionals' namely Colonel Turner's department. Chipnall was N° 71 (out of an eventual 231) on the latter's running list of airfields provided with Q-sites, which may hint at the priority being given to vital training aerodromes, particularly those that had already been visited by the *Luftwaffe*. RAF Shawbury was N° 72 in the pecking order. The RAF failed to evict the Shropshire family of Chipnall Mill Farm and they spent the next three years waiting to be bombed, living with an obstruction light just over the hedge and their windows painted with a green anti-glare substance. Electricity cables were slung for nearly two miles between Dales Wood and Old Springs Farm, carried over deep water on larch poles. In 1940 it comprised but a single row of lights, but 'grew very quickly to a magnificent wonderous sight as far as the eye could see in the blackout'. This is a layman's description of expansion from 'In-line Hooded Flarepath' via 'T'-type to full 'Drem'. Three crew maintained the decoy and were billeted at the Lloyd Farm, just down the lane from the control bunker. The latter was only demolished in 2001 as the watermeadows were converted to a wildlife sanctuary.

Late in 1940 the Chipnall decoy was constantly in action as the *Luftwaffe* roamed the Midland skies with relative impunity. Work had been sufficiently forward to attract bombs on 30 August 1940, when HE and IBs were scattered between Park Springs, Keeper's Lodge, Johnson's Wood and Lipley. This was the same night that Manchester, Merseyside and the Wrexham area were *blitzed.* Bombs had also fallen in the Sutton upon Tern area between Woodseaves and Colehurst Manor on the night of 23 July. Whether this was due to the infant 'Q'-site is debatable. However, at 2110 hrs on the evening of Tuesday, 15 October 1940, Chipnall was illuminated by magnesium flares dropped from a solitary German aircraft, obviously on a nocturnal reconnaissance. No other bombs were dropped that night, but early the following morning, 16 October, a single Junkers Ju88 dropped four 250kg HE bombs on RAF Tern Hill, causing considerable damage. This incident is covered in greater detail elsewhere in this book, but suffice it here to note that the same evening William Joyce *aka* 'Lord Haw Haw' informed the British nation in his nightly propaganda broadcast that the German air force 'had destroyed a major RAF base in Shropshire at 'Tern Hill' and that they knew of the decoy for this base, near Market Drayton — 'It had not fooled the *Luftwaffe*'. Not surprisingly, the 'Q'-site had little impact on the next raid on 20 October when Tern Hill airfield was obviously the target but bombs actually straddled the dispersed sites of N° 24 MU between Stoke Heath and Sutton heath. In the 'last big raid' bombs fell north-west of Market Drayton in the Shavington, Spoonley, Norbridge, Adderley and Newstreet Lane areas. Notwithstanding the German claim, the Chipnall site continued to operate for the next three years before being abandoned in November 1943.

The establishment by 1 August 1941 of an 'A' (Army) Series QF/QL decoy for the Royal Ordnance Factory, Marchwiel, in thinly tenanted farmland across the Dee on the border of Shocklach, Oviatt and Cuddington must signify the abandonment of the out-moded, incongruous site 'munitions factory' day-time decoy on Ruabon Mountain, always assuming that this locally improvised 'K'-site did indeed replicate the ROF. Following local usage the latter was known to Colonel Turner's department as 'Marchwiel' although strictly not in Marchwiel parish at all but in Isycoed; likewise, although the decoy site is placed officially at Worthenbury, Flintshire, it was located in its entirety in Cheshire. No 35 ROF came on stream in December 1940 — the same month work started on RAF Wrexham — and it sprawled over some three square miles. It had been photographed by the *Luftwaffe* on 28 September, its existence probably heralded by the 'chattering' rural class in the pub or by that leaky grape vine (purely involuntarily) that was the local War Agricultural Committee. IB and HE bombs fell outside the perimeter fence on 31 August and 14 November 1940; parachute flares lit up the factory on 6 September 1940. A decoy was urgently needed.

When built (A.36 co-located with C.64) it, too, was widely dispersed over an estimated 400 acres over four farms, on roughly the same latitude as the real factory was 3¼ miles further east. Such was the number of agencies that it had to be consulted before land could be released, the researcher would not be surprised to discover that the secrecy surrounding its existence was also compromised. Additionally the decoy was traversed by a network of lanes to which the public had access. It stretched from the Purser, Hitchen's and Soughan's Farms in the north to Flennen's

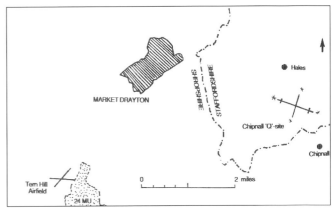

Location of RAF Tern Hill's Q decoy site at Chipnall.

Brook Bridge i.e. the Cheshire/Flintshire border in the south. Responsibility for securing such a large site was put firmly and squarely in the lands of the local Home Guard detachment, namely 'B' (Tilston) Company, 5th Cheshire (Broxton) Battalion, of which most of the farmers involved were members anyway. Basket fires, crib fires, 'boiling oil troughs' and oil drips were located in pasture fields taken out of normal cultivation and banned to close family members, farm workers and, of course, livestock. The site is noted as operational before July 1941. The earliest control bunker was in the Purser Lane, standard 'early Army', brick gables, 13ft x 15ft x 7ft constructed from galvanised iron sheets bent on steel formers, standing on the surface but covered with layers of aggregate, earth and turves, the sole entrance (apart from an escape hatch) protected by three blast walls. By May 1943, the decoy had shrunk to more manageable proportions and a new control bunker built off the drive to Hitchin's Farm, this time completely buried. The decoy would be abandoned by 29 October 1943, and the fields quickly reclaimed for agriculture. The control bunkers were finally cleared in 1976.

If McAlpine's workmen moved into Borras on 16 December 1940 and RAF Wrexham's opening-up party began to trickle in from 5 June 1941 onwards, to what did the RAF decoy that was already on Ruabon Mountain relate? As so often happens with RAF records it is difficult to establish an exact chronology as significant dates tend not to tally. On 6 May 1942 RAF Wrexham's

Above: Looking north over the water meadows at Chipnall, near Market Drayton, at the site of N° 71 Decoy for RAF Tern Hill

Right: Chipnall, looking south from the Control Bunker over the site of N° 71 Decoy for RAF Tern Hill.

The reason for a co-located 'A' and 'C' series decoy at Shocklach, the Royal Ordnance Factory, Marchwiel. An RAF reconnaissance photograph of 2 April 1946, showing part of the giant works. The concrete ROF roads stand out clearly. The river Clywedog can be seen meandering in the lower quarter of the photograph. [National Assembly for Wales]

ORB contains the sole entry 'Q-site became operational.' This is very late for a decoy to be built *ab initio* and conflicts with Colonel Turner's department's own listings which notes the commissioning of RAF Wrexham's decoy as imminent ('details to follow') on 1 November 1941 and as functioning on 15 November 1941. These dates follow closely on the arrival of Nº 96 Squadron at Wrexham on 20–22 October 1941, when the aerodrome became a fully operational night-fighter station.

The decoy was known officially as 'Minera' and its map reference centres it fairly and squarely on the earlier RAF decoy on the mountain. On 12 August 1942 a general circular announced that Wrexham's decoy had been re-classified as a 'Q/D' site, in other words now encapsulating the basic features of a Mk II ('Drem') Airfield Lighting system. Almost

certainly the cryptic station ORB entry relates to the completion of the giant task of rewiring the mountain top to include runway lighting as before but with the addition of lead-in strings, outer, middle and inner 'funnels', 'distance to go' cross-bar lights, warning 'totem. poles', Chance lights or floodlights on 'runway thresholds' (not all that portable owing to the boggy, heather grown terrain), approach 'funnels', and even outer lights. Being somewhat distant from the putative centre of the dummy airfield, outlying poles that carried the outer circle of lights still (1996) stand proud on the moorland above Frondeg albeit in the last stages of decay.

The control bunker, perhaps more familiar to hill walkers as an *ad hoc* mountain refuge, still exists, covered by its protective camouflage of fine aggregate, soil and turf. It comprises three sections. The west end is a narrow 16ft semi-sunk Anderson shelter-type 'hut' with a steel-plated door on an angle-iron frame in the exterior brick end gable. This is fronted by a 14ins thick blast wall and further protected by stepped lateral blast walls. These terminate in a 5ft-square concrete roof platform, once railed, and reached by a wall ladder from the door well. This was the look-out and 'hearing' platform. A hole in the floor took phone, inter/com. and W/T wiring into the shelter below. In the inner end gable a wooden door gives access to a cramped brick-lined central 'vestibule' which has the only other entrance to the facility on the north side, again protected by blast walls. This was the switch room, with mimic board and panel controlling the entire decoy airfield lighting system, incorporating brilliance adjustments and lamp failure indicator, the latter essential for easier maintenance in such difficult terrain. Repair work was best carried out by day. Off the 'vestibule' the bunker's eastern component comprised a

10ft long structure made up of prefabricated concrete sections bolted together. This may have been a relic of the Stanton air-raid shelter that went with the living accommodation of the earliest decoy on site, but now recycled and extended. Here were housed the two Lister generators. Their plinths have vanished, deliberately smashed to provide shelter for animals in the post-war period; but ducting holes and pipes in walls and floor indicate access for cables and wiring and to the exterior expansion chambers whose position is still marked by concrete slabs set in the peat.

The site was staffed on a rota system by a corporal and three airmen, but, compared with many decoy crews elsewhere, they did not stay on the mountain, hence the lack of sleeping accommodation apart from a bed and mattress. The tedious, routine work was done during the day — testing lights and phone lines, cleaning peaty dust from lamps, overhauling the generator etc. — then back to RAF

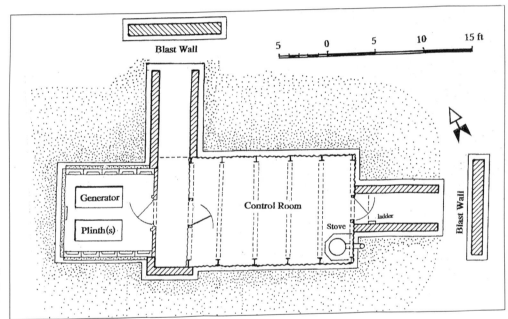

Ground plan of the control room at RAF Wrexham's Drem Q-site on Esclusham Mountain.

Cross-section of the control room at RAF Wrexham's Drem Q-site on Esclusham Mountain.

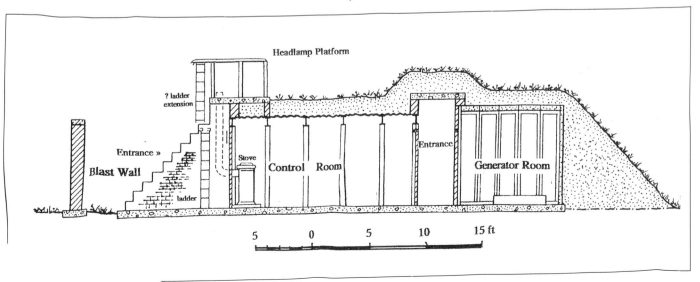

Above: Decoy (Q site) shelter on Esclusham Mountain.

Right: Looking west over the decoy (Q site) shelter on Esclusham Mountain towards the real airfield at RAF Wrexham.
Below: Decoy (Q site) shelter on Esclusham Mountain.

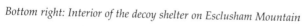

Right: Entrance to the decoy shelter on Esclusham Mountain. Control building Stanton to the left, control to the right.

Bottom left: Inside the decoy shelter on Esclusham Mountain. Note the pipes coming in at floor level.

Bottom right: Interior of the decoy shelter on Esclusham Mountain

Wrexham. At night, when Atcham Sector Control thought that there might be a chance of stray visitors from Midlands raids, there would be a mad rush as the decoy crew were 'scrambled'. They piled into the truck kept at readiness in the MT yard near the guard-room and went hurtling along the blacked-out roads for their tiny bunker on the mountain.

With hindsight the Minera decoy was something of a white elephant, redundant even as it was being commissioned. In June 1941 tactics in the air war changed abruptly as a high proportion of *Luftwaffe* units based in France and the Low Countries were transferred en bloc to meet the enormous demands of new offensives on the Russian Front, in the Mediterranean, Balkans and against the Arctic convoys. This reduced almost overnight the weight of the *Blitz* on Britain. Henceforth a maximum of some 700 aircraft remained in north-west Europe, only 200 of them bombers. At first Home Security found the reduced level of enemy activity, despite improving weather conditions, difficult to explain. It was only after the 22 June 1941 that they cautiously ventured to suggest that 'The enemy's offensive against Russia may reasonably be expected to prolong his present small scale effort against this country'.

This notwithstanding, the new Minera decoy was put to the test on the night of 1/2 November 1941, a week or so before it was fully operational. Enemy activity was on a was on a larger scale than for some time, with some 56 aircraft roaming at large against targets as far afield as the Wirral, north Wales and the Midlands. All four German planes lost that night had been briefed to attack Liverpool. Two were brought down as they crossed the Dorset coast. A third, a Heinkel He111 of 7/KG4O was blown out of the sky by a Beaufighter of 'A'-flight, N° 68 Squadron, on a five-month detachment to Valley from High Ercall. The fourth, a Junkers Ju88 of Epro/KG3O, was shot down by the Kinnerton HAA battery and crashed at Pulford, north of Wrexham, killing all its crew.

The decoy attracted no bombs and this set the pattern for the ensuing months. Nights of mindbending monotony and boredom were broken only by a precautionary alert of 26/27 November. Decoy lights were switched on 'just in case'. Although enemy activity in N° 9 Group area was confined largely to anti-shipping strikes in the Irish Sea, several German aircraft were disorientated or lost owing to effective British 'Meacon' counter-measures or 'beam bending'. It had to be one of these that deposited a parachute mine just over the ridge from the decoy, but whether the intended target was the small Brymbo Water Works reservoir at Pendinas or the actual 'Q'-site will never be known.

It would be another two years before the decoy sites were officially abandoned. A reprieve was afforded in April–July 1942 by an unexpected escalation of the night offensive as *Luftflotte 3*, by scraping the bottom of every available barrel and flying double missions, mustered sufficient aircraft to embark upon the notorious 'Baedeker raids'. After the destruction of the beautiful medieval city of Lübeck on the night of 28/29 March retaliation was sought against British historic cities — Exeter, Bath, York, Norwich, Ipswich, Poole, Canterbury, King's Lynn, Colchester, Swansea — and some not so 'historic', such as Weston-super-Mare, Cowes and Nuneaton. Birmingham was a particular target being raided three times in July. To conserve meagre resources the 'Baedeker' raids were short and sharp, aircraft following devious routes to mislead defences. For example, the Birmingham raids were routed west of Lands End, and along the Irish coast to Arklow Head before turning east across mid-Wales at high speed, using Lake Vyrnwy and Elan Valley reservoirs as check-markers. Raids on Chester and Shrewsbury appeared on the cards but never materialised. The offensive petered out in September 1942.

Nevertheless, despite not seeing much in the way of 'active' service, the Minera 'Q'-site was put to good use. It was regularly lit up during night-exercises for the Beaufighters of N° 96 Squadron at RAF Wrexham. Busy converting in May/June 1942 from Defiants to Beaufighters — significantly the same time as the Minera decoy's electrics were upgraded this unit, too, was also beginning to feel the numbing paralysis brought about by lack of action in No 9 Group area since they had arrived from Cranage in October 1941. Still, this was sufficient to keep the specialist decoy crews out of the clutches of the Station Warrant Officer and for the moment to resist the claims of the Army for a larger slice of mountain for mortar and live ammunition training by Royal Marine Commandos who had moved in to the Hermitage Camp at Wrexham.

The Minera decoy functioned between November 1941 and November 1943. So much is clear from official listings. What is not so clear is the history of the decoy site that preceded it. As remarked upon elsewhere, PRO lists would appear incomplete, the earliest listing dating only from 1 August 1941. From the evidence of the military who were responsible for the security of the mountain the 'dummy airfield' was in situ by mid-October 1940, perhaps earlier. It would appear to have been basically a daytime 'K-site but with facilities for night time deception. This was a standard progression, for in the early months of the *Blitz* the *Luftwaffe* operated largely by daylight. But as the enemy switched increasingly to night bombing, so the maintenance of 'K'-sites would have become superfluous, the emphasis switching to night-time decoys with their lights and/or fires. Sixty years later it seems remarkable that anybody would think that the Germans would be fooled by a passive unauthentic-looking 'K'-site airfield planted in a moorland depression between the 1,200 and 1,400ft contours! However, the effort was made, but at a considerable cost in human and material resources.

There were two camouflaged 'aeroplane sheds' or hangars built out of canvas, hessian and corrugated iron sheets draped about a frame of scaffolding. In front of these were parked three or four dummy aircraft vaguely identified as a 'Wellington' and 'Battles'. These were dismantled daily and re-erected in different positions, presumably to give the site that 'lived in' look! If, as was forthcoming, the decoy crew had been trained in this art at N° 2 Balloon Centre, Hook, Surrey, a link with Colonel Turner's Department is established. Running away SW–NE along the slope was an 'in-line hood flare path', at this time a single line of lights, with a screened bar of red lights across the 'landing threshold' (to warn off friendly aircraft mistaking the decoy for a real aerodrome and attempting to land).

Hard by the old mining track running up from Plas Drain were the 'living sites', first just tents then, in time for the worst winter of the war, two small wooden huts and and an even smaller cookhouse. Nearby was an air-raid shelter, possibly the same Stanton that formed part of RAF Wrexham's later control bunker. On top of this was perched a searchlight, controlled by a long handle, which when lit would hopefully convey he impression that a plane was about to land. There was also a dummy ammunition dump and petrol store. At least two sand-bagged machine-gun emplacements were for real and were manned round the clock. The place was given further touches of authenticity by a liberal sprinkling of typical airfield impedimenta such as oil drums and a scrap van and lorry tarted up to resemble an ambulance and fire tender.

The unit had its own truck which brought in rations and stores daily and took out men for sick parade and 'rest and recuperation' (including weekly baths!). Establishment on site was a sergeant, two corporals and 15–20 airmen. They did not mix locally (language problem?) except for the occasional visit to a film in the Miners' Institute, Rhos. But irritatingly, while so much is known about this 'K'-cum-'Q'-site no one can recall its parent station, presumably the aerodrome for which it was acting as a decoy.

On reflection the only candidate at this time is RAF Hawarden, sharing its airfield with a Vickers-Armstrong shadow aircraft factory and, since June 1940, home to N° 7 OTU, one of only two Spitfire OTUs in the country. The other was at Aston Down (Gloucestershire). In a sense Hawarden, more correctly Broughton, was a dual 'Key Point' installation for which some protection was demanded other than camouflage paint on the roofs or tar-painted hedge lines across the aerodrome surface.

The PRO listings lack data for 1940 and early 1941 but indicate that by 1 August 1941 and obviously earlier — RAF aerodrome and MAP factory at Hawarden were sharing the same decoy on the empty ill-drained farmland on The Lach Eyes south-east of Bretton Hall. By coincidence, east of the GWR railway, is a 'Decoy Farm', which place-name, however, has a pedigree going back to 1633! The airfield decoy is Serial No 207 in the RAF list and the Vickers factory N° C.42 in the 'C' Series. But all entries relating to the airfield are qualified 'transferred to C.42' as if there had been some streamlining of manning and responsibilities. On 22 November 1942 the Q/F decoy complex is redesignated a 'Starfish' decoy, but reverts to a Q/F site in May 1943. For earlier references to Hawarden's decoys the researcher turns to D. J. Smith's *Hawarden. A Welsh Airfield 1939–79*, published in 1979. He writes:

The [Vickers-Armstrongs] works was very well camouflaged and the deception was completed by the erection of a dummy factory made of wood and canvas in open country south of Saltney. It was considered likely that any German bomber flying in daylight would approach from the south and would therefore see the decoy first and hopefully waste its bombs on it. The dummy was quite convincing, from the air at any rate, even to the extent of having derelict cars on a cinder car park. Like other similar sites near factories, the dummy was cunningly devised to look as though an attempt had been made to camouflage it.

This indicates that the Bretton decoy, like that on Minera, started out as a 'K'-site, in which rôle its would quickly become redundant, it forms no part of Colonel Turner's listings for August 1940. Smith also mentions 'another decoy at Buckley for night use', but no trace of this can be found in official lists. The older inhabitants of Buckley recall only one military installation — the unwelcome intrusion onto the cricket square of a searchlight battery associated with the HAA guns at Kinnerton. One should note that a 'Q/L' or 'Q/F' site in Buckley amidst the myriad of badly blacked out brickworks and small potteries would have been superfluous. Again, if daytime decoys needed a convincing night-time version, they were, for economy as well as strategy, usually located on the same site.

The attendant map, reinforced with appropriate images, shows a provisional lay-out for Hawarden's various deception efforts, based on the authors' field work. It is self-explanatory, with the exceptions of the features labelled 'D' and 'E'. Six decades of fairly intensive agriculture have eradicated any minor surface blemishes that may have facilitated meaningful re-interpretation of the sites — an abrasive process hastened by construction works associated with the building of the A55(T) express way in the late 1970s. But there is no doubt that something was going on in these two fields, as witness the heavy duty electric cable that is still being turned up by the plough as drains are laid. The survival (only just) of a command bunker alongside Site 'D' would seem to confirm this. If one is looking for somewhere to position Hawarden's enigmatic 'K'-site, it is tentatively suggested one can do no worse than begin with these two fields.

Smith further states, 'In addition the fighter OTU had a Q-site which is said to have been on what was later to be Borras aerodrome near Wrexham'. The PRO list, inadequate though it is, may indicate the existence of an earlier site for RAF Hawarden. It is given the Serial No 157, and that is all, apart from a note that it has been superseded by decoys N°ˢ 207 and C.42. No location is given and there is no map reference; in other words No 157 is defunct. But the OTU's 'Q'-site could not have been at Borras. As seen elsewhere, between April November 1940 the former civilian flying ground at Borras was being intensively used by 5 SFTS, Sealand, as a relief landing ground. In December the contractors moved in, but in March 1941, even before they had finished, the Spitfires of N° 7 OTU were themselves in temporary residence and would remain so until the December — therefore no room at Borras for a decoy. Additionally the proximity of the Acton and Rhosnesni suburbs of Wrexham and the newly operational ROF below the airfield would have ruled out Borras as a site inviting the enemy to bomb it!

There is no precise date for the establishment of the

Vickers decoy. If N⁰ 7 OTU had a separate decoy before it was merged with that at Bretton it must post-date June 1940 when the unit moved into Hawarden. If not at Borras, Wrexham, then in all probability it was the 'K'-cum'Q'-site on Minera, the tenuous association with Wrexham arising from the fact that RAF Wrexham's 1941 'Q'-site sprang out of the ashes of a pre-existing decoy site.

In the provision of decoys early priority was given to RAF stations and their satellites. There was nothing like a raid or two to hasten matters. N⁰ 27 MU at RAF Shawbury had a visitation at 2222hrs on 5 September 1940. Again, during night-flying on 25 September, the aerodrome and village received eight HE and two dozen IBs. Within the week the Haughmond Hill decoy was operational! Similarly it needed a prod from the *Luftwaffe* on 11 September, when HE and IBs fell around Cleobury Mortimer and Ditton Priors before the Royal Navy ordnance depot at the latter place was duly paired with its 'QP'-site at Neenton.

Some fifteen Airfield 'Q'-sites in No 9 Group area are listed in the appendix attached to Chapter 6. Aerodromes completed in 1942 or later — Tilstock, Sleap, Rednal, Montfort Bridge, Calveley, Condover — do not seem to have warranted a decoy site, at least in the north-west 'back area'. Airfields north of the Mersey seemed also to have been

Vickers aircraft factory QF decoy site on the Lache Eyes, Bretton.

denied a strategic decoy. The Royal Naval Air Station at Stretton, otherwise HMS *Blackcap*, was commissioned as a RNAS on 1 June 1942 to cater primarily for aircraft flying directly to and from carriers moored in the Mersey. It was also an 'Air Yard', housing the naval equivalent of an RAF Maintenance Unit. But, as betrayed by runway layout, standard RAF watch tower, buildings and hangars, and

Map showing the location of the decoy sites for RAF Hawarden and the Vickers factory at Broughton. A – Fire baskets; B – Anti-glider ditches; C – QL site. [1951 base map, 2½-inch sheet SJ36 (33/36) reproduced by kind permission of the Ordnance Survey]

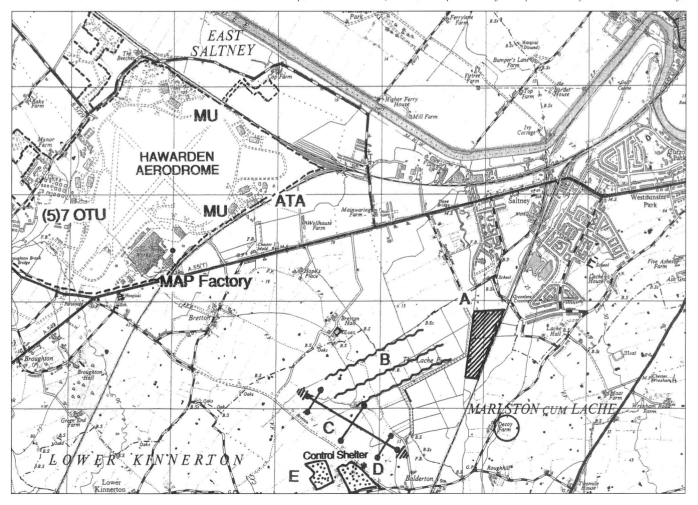

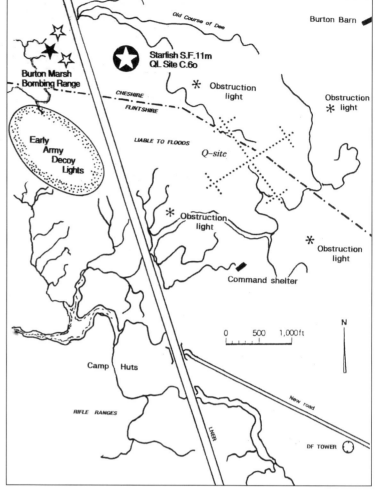

fighter dispersal pens around the perimeter Stretton began life in 1941 as a No 9 Group Fighter Command aerodrome, along with Wrexham and Calveley, hence the provision of a 'Q'-site (N.29) at Budworth., which was taken over and manned by the Navy. It was abandoned on 22 August 1943.

Even if a daytime 'K'-site did not stand up to minute aerial scrutiny — hence their rapid phasing out — when acting as a night-time 'Q'-site it was difficult for enemy bomber crews to pick out the offending decoy and ignore it. Their general effectiveness at night may be gauged by the fate a Beaufighter VIF (X8190) of N° 456 Squadron RAAF, based at Valley, Anglesey. At 2305hrs on 8 October 1942 — late in the effective life of a decoy — the starboard engine of X8190 cut out. Heading for base the pilot mistook the the lights of Valley's decoy on Newborough Warren, lit up for a Bullseye exercise, for the home station and ploughed straight into a 30ft high sand-dune, disintegrating and catching fire, killing the two Australians, Sgts R. Scott, pilot, and C. Wood, observer.

RAF Wrexham's 'Q'-site also collected aircraft. On Wednesday, 3 November 1943, barely three weeks before the decoy was officially abandoned, a Miles Martinet (HP227) of N° 41 OTU, Poulton, crashed smack in the middle of the site, where the two flare paths crossed. The Polish pilot was killed. He was not found until the 'Q'-site crew came up from Borras on the Thursday to make their daily checks. Interestingly the predecessor decoy, whatever its status and deception arrangements, also had an aircraft come to grief on it. On 30 October 1940 a Miles Master (N7445) of N° 5 SFTS Sealand, came down on or in direct line with the decoy's flare path just in front of the warning cross-bar lights. It was burnt out and the two crew seriously injured. But there is nothing in the subsequent inquisition records to suggest that the two decoys had any connection with either crash. HP227 was on target towing duties and entered cloud. N7442 was flying on instruments. Esclusham Mountain just happened to be in the way!

After the fall of France thoughts also turned to providing alternate decoy sites for some strategic civilian centres vital to the war effort. It was a daunting proposition. There were 4,325 designated 'Key Point' installations alone out of a massive 16,000 factories engaged overall on Government contracts. These were divided into:

(a) Royal Ordnance and Government factories and depôts
(b) Commercial factories
(c) Shipbuilding yards
(d) Raw material dumps and stores
(e) Steelworks
(f) Oil installations of all types
(g) Food processing plant and storage depôts
(h) Ports, docks and harbours
(i) Telecommunications (including the BBC)
(j) Public utilities
(k) Railways

As far as north Wales and the north-

Looking out over the Q and QF sites towards Burton Point.

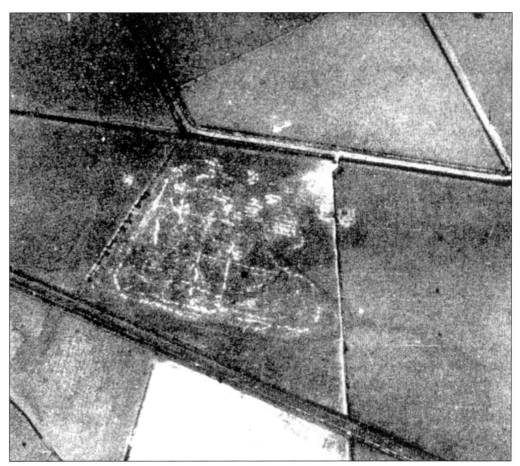

Above: Looking at the Vickers aircraft factory Broughton QF decoy site straddled between the Great Western Railway (bottom left–right) and the Great Drainage ditch (top left–right). [National Assembly for Wales]

Left: The RAF Hawarden Q decoy site now split in two by the A55 Expressway at Broughton South.

Bottom left: Looking north-east down the Lache Eyes towards Chester at the RAF Hawarden decoy site.

Bottom right: Site of the control bunker of the RAF Hawarden Q decoy site.

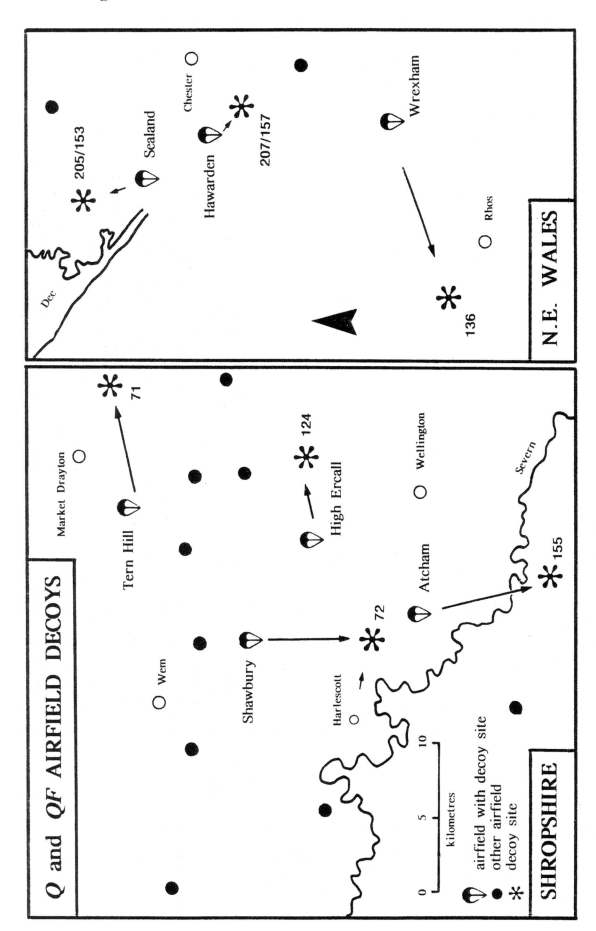

Q and *QF* AIRFIELD DECOYS

N.E. WALES

SHROPSHIRE

☂ airfield with decoy site
● other airfield
✳ decoy site

west are concerned most of these categories are covered in the N, A, P, Miscellaneous and C-Series 'Q'-sites listed in the Appendix to Chapter 6. Logistically only major installations could be protected by decoys. Thus, while the Stanlow oil terminal and refinery at Ellesmere Port rated a 'Q/F'-site on Ince Marshes, the aviation fuel and oil reserves depots at Much Wenlock and Beeston Castle had to fend for themselves. It will also be noted that many of the 'C-Series' decoys about Liverpool, Manchester, Crewe and Northwich also doubled as Starfish' sites. Chronology remains confused, but some of the Liverpool decoys may have started life as 'Starfish' before graduating to the more sophisticated 'Q/L' status. On the other hand, if map references are accurate, the Stanlow 'Q/F' decoy on Grinsome Farm at Ince sprouted a separate 'Starfish' site 100 yards away but doubtless mannned by the same crews and controlled from the same bunker.

The thirty-two 'Starfish' sites in the north-west multiplied after the crushing pounding suffered by Coventry on 14 November 1940. The design and installation of 'Special Fires' as they were originally known — began on 23 November around Sheffield, Derby, Birmingham, Bristol, Coventry and Crewe. By December each city had two or three 'Starfish' up and running, with Middlesborough and Wolverhampton added to the list as a matter of priority. The latter, with Intelligence fearing an imminent Coventry-type attack, was promised a decoy in four, instead of the usual seven, days. On Merseyside existing 'Q/F'-sites were initially considered sufficient although these were later augmented by additional 'Starfish' at Ince, Wallasey, and an outer quadrant of three 'Strategic Starfish' at Fenn's Moss, Llandegla and Llanasa in north-east Wales. In addition to its three 'Q'-sites Manchester added 'Starfish' at Tatton Park, Park Moor, Chunal Moor, Mossley, and Ludworth Moor. Some of these had been abandoned by 1 March 1942. The choice of Tatton Park seems rather ill-conceived. Since July 1940 it had been used both day and night as a Dropping Zone by the Parachute Training School at Ringway with occasional landings in the park by the Whitleys of the PTS. As already noted, while Crewe's second 'Starfish' was officially at Hack Green, the actual combustion site was a mile to the south-east of the future GCI station but nevertheless continued operational even after the latter was opened in May 1941.

'Starfish' sites had only one thing in common — they all came under the control of N° 80 (Signals) Wing, formed on 7 September 1940 at Radlett, near St Albans. Each 'Starfish' and 'Q' site had telephone links to their respective Sector Operations Room, but the latter rarely operated on their own initiative. It was N° 80 Wing who would give the order to ignite. The layouts of typical 'Starfish' sites have been discussed elsewhere in relation to Fenn's Moss and Llandegla. There would appear as many variations on means of combustion as there were sites! On the first occasion when Liverpool's 'Q/L'-cum-'Starfish' on Little Hilbre Island (No C.6(n) or SF.11(l)) at the mouth of the Dee estuary was lit it appeared to have discharged its paraffin directly onto the sea where it was spectacularly ignited — to such an effect that the incident has found an indelible place in *Luftwaffe* official histories.

In April 1944 a certain *Hauptmann* Otto Bechtle prepared a 'Staff Study' entitled *Der Einsatz der Luftwaffe gegen England, ihre Taktik und die Lehren 1940–43* ('The *Luftwaffe's* Offensive against England, Tactics and Lessons 1940–43') preserved at the *Bundesarchiv* in Freiburg-im-Breisgau. He summed up the current situation in the air as follows:

As compared with today [1944] the enemy defences were poor … But now and then the enemy had considerable success in diverting crews from their destined targets by cleverly designed decoy installations … Special mention must be made of the raid on Liverpool on the night of 29/30 [*recte 28/29*] November [1940]. Major fires had been faked by the pouring of oil onto the Dee estuary west of Birkenhead, with the majority of crews mistaking these for fires in Liverpool.

It is not certain whether or not Little Hilbre was in its 'Starfish' mode. Officially the first 'Starfish' were fired on 2 December 1940, at Bristol, when some 121 aircraft of *Luftflotte* 3 raided the city. Be that as it may, the conflagration was reported by N° 7 Group (Royal) Observer Corps posts at Hoylake (7/H.1) and Mostyn (7/H.3). Early decoys had been fired only after the commencement of an attack, but on this particular night Little Hilbre seems to have been functioning as a direct decoy — unless the whole thing was an accident! On the night of Thursday, 28/29 November over 300 aircraft of *Luftflotten* 2 and 3 attacked Merseyside, with the six miles of docks on the east bank of the Mersey and the dry docks, floats, mills, grain silos etc. of Birkenhead as the *Schwerpunkt* or main objective.

A former member of the Little Hilbre decoy, writing in 1956, had this to say about this particular incident: 'Our decoy was lit regularly; in fact it was never out. We used to joke about our site being the beacon by which German aircraft could find north Wales and safety — it was a black as the Ace of Spades over there! During the very heavy raids of 29/30 November 1940 we poured petrol onto the incoming tide and waited for the signal to ignite. As luck had it, the wind was blowing off-shore and the vapour went out into the estuary. We fired the baskets from our command shelter, and the whole area for miles round went up in dense smoke. But, on the negative side, we began to get bombs. We kept our heads down, and did not get to see the light show and fireworks going on outside. Talking later to local people, the rumour was about that Jerry had dropped a new bomb called an 'oil bomb'. According to our sergeant, bombs rained down on the Wirral coast as far as Gayton. Jerry really did think he had hit Liverpool.

Cloud cover was intense and visual bombing rarely possible. Most of the aiming was done by dead reckoning or by the glow of fires on the ground — hence the apparent success of the Little Hilbre fire. On Deeside a 'Yellow' Alert was given at 1901hrs, 'Purple' at 1905hrs, followed by the sirens at 1945hrs. The decoy was ignited shortly afterwards, within minutes of the first Heinkels of II/KG55 from Chartres, pathfinders for the night, dropping their flares. Significantly the decoy fires were on the east side of the Dee estuary. As often happened, some crews may have thought they were actually hitting targets on the east bank of the Mersey. But for all the intensity of aerial activity — the raids lasted until 0335hrs on the Friday morning when the 'All clear' was sounded — and the great weight of bombs dropped on Merseyside — 350 tons of HE and over 30,000 IBs — there is little of the usual overspill into Flintshire and Denbighshire. Apart from ten HE bombs falling harmlessly in Kinnerton fields, Flintshire incidents were confined to HE and UXBs in Iscoed, Bronington and Willington parishes in the detached portion of Maelor. These essentially rural parishes straddled 'Adolf's Railway' along the Welsh border and one wonders if one of the early marks of Fenn's Moss decoy was ignited that night.

Not all results from decoy deployment were as satisfying as the Little Hilbre fire. German aircrews were not fools. For example, the Boulton Paul decoy at Coven (No M.2 in the Appendix) was attacked on 14 August 1940, permitting the real factory at Upper Pendeford alongside Wolverhampton Airport to continue its production of Defiant aircraft. But this was one off! *Luftwaffe* vertical aerial photographs taken later that month showed both real and decoy factories. Cover was blown! At 1845hrs on Sunday 29 September 1940 a lone Junkers Ju88 dived out of cloud above Codsall, swept over the Boulton Paul factory and then swung round, passing over the decoy at Brewood/Coven and back on to the real thing, ignoring the threat from mock-up AA guns on the nearby hill. It dropped five HE bombs which fortunately missed the aircraft factory and exploded harmlessly in the filter tanks at Barnhurst Farm sewage works causing not a little environmental unpleasantness! The Bofor gunners on the roof of the factory were taken completely by surprise and did not open fire until after the bombs had dropped. However, they claimed hits on the Ju88 and local tradition has it that the raider was that which crashed the same evening in the Nuneaton area. The researcher is immediately put at a disadvantage by this, as according to the *Luftwaffe's* own statistics the three Ju88s lost on operations that evening all crash-landed on the French side of the Channel after suffering engine failure and/or combat damage! However, two weeks earlier, on Monday, 16 September, a Ju88 of 1/KG54 on a raid to Banbury did get lost and collided with balloon cables near Coventry. Its two engines caught fire and it exploded and crashed over Hopsford Old Hall Farm, Withybrook, south-east of Nuneaton. Thus, possibly, the threads of oral history have become slightly twisted with the passage of time.

By their very nature decoys were ephemeral, covering large areas of open, sparsely populated or waste land. Very little tends to survive, perhaps the concrete base of a fire basket or a firebreak trench. If on good agricultural land they have long been removed or filled in as obstacles to post-war farming. On the Wrexham ROF decoy site near Shocklach, the control bunker was removed by the farmer only in 1976. Its blast walls, used as 'back scratchers' by his cattle had become unstable and therefore dangerous. It is on the mountain moorlands of north-east Wales that such bunkers yet survive. In addition the bunker on RAF Wrexham's Minera decoy, a control centre also exists on Ffrith Mountain, a lobe of Moel Famau, south of Cilcain village.

This latter was a 'C'-Series decoy, Nº C.62 in the Appendix. Its parent station or the site it protected is referred to rather ambiguously as Mold. More exactly it was the 'ROF, Rhydymwyn', a low profile euphemism for a potentially controversial chemical warfare establishment. During the Second World War the labyrinth of old mine workings in the Rhydymwyn area was used to store thousands of tons of TNT. Additionally, between September 1939 and November 1940 special deep tunnels and chambers were excavated for the storage of toxic chemicals and the stockpiling of charged chemical weapons. The whole complex was managed by the General Chemicals Division of ICI.

This top-secret ROF was given its own decoy two miles away on the slopes of Moel Famau. The control bunker yet stands, smack on the 1,000ft contour, partially hidden behind a fifty-year old screen of alder trees, and lost to official records until rediscovered during the course of the current upland archaeological survey of the Clwydian Range. It resembles a small Nissen hut or Anderson shelter, some 13ft long by 15ft across, let into the hillside, its eighteen sheets of corrugated steel, now dangerously corroded and holed, giving seven foot of headroom in the centre. The access end is closed by an $8^1/2$ft wall, 14ins thick with doorway placed centrally. The latter is fronted by a blast wall, partially demolished to allow cattle ingress, and further protected by two more blast walls offset obliquely. Above the doorway a GPO telephone-pole bracket, minus insulator, indicates that the bunker had its own dedicated phone line out. Remains of the ignition wire that ran uphill to the combustion site still cling to the exterior brickwork. On the opposite end wall the metal treads of a vertical ladder lead up to what must have been an escape hatch in the roof and/or an observation/hearing platform. The whole of this structure had originally been covered with a thick layer of aggregate topped by soil and turf, both to give protection from bomb blast and to camouflage the installation. With the passage of time much of this covering has been eroded, sliding off on the down-slope side or falling through the gaping holes in the roof to add body to the composted 'bedding' on the floor.

Although starting life as an Army decoy, the bunker was latterly manned by RAF personnel based in and about Cilcain village, using the 'Red Lion' inn as their HQ. The combustion site(s) were 700 yards along the path to Moel Famau summit and 300ft higher in altitude. Here the slope levels to give a broad step which would have made the decoy fires invisible from below and from across the Alun and Gain valleys. There is now nothing to be seen here, the combustion units probably being self-standing on the underlying limestone. The Ffrith Mountain site was still operational on 1 May 1943, but on 18 May it was finally abandoned. Fifty years on it has at least become a card and number in the Sites and Monument Record. Sadly, it is unlikely to be granted 'Listed Building' status!

The C.62 Decoy Site above Cilcain

Left: The corrugated steel roof about to collapse on the control bunker

Below: The entrance to the unusual control bumker

Left: The control bunker viewed from above..

Below: Interior view of the control bunker at Cilcain. The escape ladder on the far wall went out through the roof.

Above and right: The C.62 decoy site above Cilcain. The Jubilee Tower on Moel Fannau can be seen in the background of the lower photograph.

The reason for the QF decoy (C.62) above Cilcain — the top secret ICI chemical weapons plant at Rhydymwyn, Mold. [National Assembly for Wales]

3. Gunnery/bombing ranges

On their northern extremities both Flintshire and Denbighshire possessed substantial stretches of coastline fringed by sand-dunes, saltings and partially reclaimed estuarine marshes, home to sheep, Army rifle ranges, and the odd golf club. Apart from a sprinkling of wooden shacks, converted bus bodies and railway coaches half hidden in the sand-hills they were as yet innocent of today's highly organised camping sites and holiday camps. Inland, compared with the spinous Clwydian Range, the rounded massif of Ruabon and Esclusham Mountains afforded by far the greater extent of desolate moorland. Further east, on the Flintshire/Shropshire border, a diverse lowland glacial landscape — retreat moraines, drumlins, eskers, meres and mosses — carried extensive heathlands and raised mires. Of the latter, the melancholy wilderness of Fenn's and Whixall Moss, at over 2,500 acres, reflected a long history of peat cutting on a domestic scale. Commercial over-exploitation and a conservation back-lash would be reserved for the post-war years.

Large tracts of such marginal lands were quickly lost to airfield construction — Sealand, Hawarden, Tilstock, Sleap, Tern Hill — not without inherent, and often insuperable, physical problems. It was almost pre-ordained that the more intractable peripheral areas, isolated, unpopulated and agriculturally unproductive, should be scrutinised for the possible provision of gunnery and bombing ranges and decoy sites, as at Talacre, north-east Fenn's Moss, and Burton Marshes. Inevitably, as the pace of training quickened in the run-up to D-Day, the demand for such facilities far out-stripped provision. On occasion, despite local protests, the RAF would trespass further upon good farm land albeit the relatively ill-drained water meadows in broad valley bottoms, remote from road, bridging point, farmhouse or hamlet. Such were the bombing ranges established on Baggy Moor and Cherrington Moor respectively on the Perry and Strine rivers in Shropshire.

The use of the latter was exclusively localised and concentrated over a short period of time. Cherrington Moor was used between May–October 1944 by the Wellington Ills and Xs of N° 83 OTU, No 93 Group Bomber Command, at Peplow, some three miles to the north. The insatiable demand for trained crews to underpin *Operation Overlord* was leading to congestion on the Cannock Chase ranges and so prompted the laying out of their own bombing range in a section of Shropshire's 'empty quarter' north of Wellington, known generically as the Weald Moors ('the wild marsh'). The range was prepared at great speed on a DIY basis, utilising station and unit labour. Warning boards and flags, a wooden hut and a tent, sand-bagged quadrant observation posts, a portable generator for night-time illumination of target, a standing picket by the RAF Regiment — and the range was open for business. Despite adding to the congestion of Shropshire air space, especially with RNAS Hinstock and RAF Chetwynd in such close proximity, the use of the Cherrington range gave trainee pilots and air bombers a valuable introduction to day and night bombing before they embarked upon 'stick bombing' and high altitude bombing on specialist ranges during night navigation and bombing exercises.

The use of Baggy Moor as an improvised range must be seen against the widening rôle of the Supermarine Spitfire as a fighter-bomber in *Rhubarb* and *Circus* operations over Europe. Within No 81 Group Training Command, Nº 61 OTU's Spitfires from Rednal popped daily to the Talacre range for air-to-ground gunnery practice or squeezed in a short residency at RAF Llanbedr for air-to-air firing, but from September 1942 the first steps in dive bombing (with dummy or 8lb practice bombs) was aerodrome based, with a target, reminiscent of the 'bombing circle' of the interwar years, set up in the middle of the airfield. For a busy training establishment this was a dodgy practice to say the least, notwithstanding that the bulk of courses at Rednal were multi-national, with some problems in communication. There were several near misses but it was not until 12 September 1943, when two Spitfires collided over the target, that the makeshift 'range' was actually moved.

Spitfire V, R7127, fell directly onto the airfield killing its pilot Sgt D. G. Keith, aged 22. Spitfire I, X1473, although badly damaged managed a circuit and landed safely with a badly shaken pilot. (For the record, X1473 would crash again at the Talacre range on 19 May 1944, when it stalled over the targets as pulling out of a dive). The accident also meant the

end of dive-bombing practice at Rednal's satellite, Montford Bridge, where the last three weeks of OTU courses were spent honing up on skills. At week-ends the normally lax security was tightened up and, for safety reasons, the three lanes around the perimeter were closed to the public. A portable 'target hut' was erected at the runway junction in the middle of the aerodrome and bombing practice proceeded unhindered.

Rednal's 'home range' did not move very far, just onto Baggy Moor beyond the aerodrome's eastern perimeter and runway 16/34. Rednal airfield, when built, had swallowed up the greater part of Haughton Tory and The Buildings farms, but for obvious reasons excluding the water meadows on the west bank of the River Perry. Now it was the turn of this unwanted area to play a more vital rôle in the war effort other than yielding a hay crop. Being so close to the airfield, range furniture or ground equipment was minimal, the most important innovation being the provision of a separate Range Control Officer, who took some of the responsibility from the shoulders of the harrassed Airfield Control Pilot. But even under the revised arrangements accidents continued to happen.

On 18 March 1945 Spitfire Vc, EE601, suffered engine failure on a bombing run over Baggy Moor and belly-landed on the range. The plane was written off, but the pilot managed to walk away. A week earlier, on 10 March, a North American Mustang III, FZ150 — to which make Nº 61 OTU had been steadily converting since January 1945 — crashed on Rednal Moss near Station Farm after hitting a telegraph pole whilst making a tight turn to starboard after a low-level attack on Baggy Moor. The Polish pilot, Sgt Z. Boleslaw, aged 27, lost control and spun in.

The 'bombing' range on Burton Marsh, on the seaward side of the 'Broken Bank', was the particular preserve of Nº

Cannock Chase Bombing Range

Right: The centre marker of the bombing range photographed in 1994.
[Keith Jones]

Below: The general destruction caused by the practice bombs is still evident sixty years on.
[Keith Jones]

The grave of F/O R. B. Bowran from N° 96 Squadron, RAF Wrexham, in Cannock Chase Military Burial Ground. Bowran was killed on 27 May 1942 (flying Beaufighter AA546) on the edge of the Cannock Range whilst carrying out a mock attack on a machine gun installation.

60 OTU, High Ercall. The latter was established in May 1942 for the specific purpose of training Mosquito night intruder crews. From June 1943, with the rapid expansion of Bomber Command's night offensive and the development of new tactics such as pathfinding, new elements — PF duties and target marking — crept into the training syllabus. But where to drop flares at no risk to property and the environment? A section of Burton Marsh in Air Ministry ownership since 1918 was reactivated. There was already a crew and communications infra-structure in place. Since early 1941 there had been QL and Starfish decoys adjacent, east of the railway. The last alert on Merseyside was (with hindsight) 9 August 1942. After waiting for raids that never materialised, the decoy sites were abandoned the following year, to be put to new use by N° 60 OTU.

By its very different nature accidents over the range were very few. Engine failure could occur anywhere, any time. But on 30 May 1944 as Mosquito VI, HX984, was coming off the range it had to feather its starboard engine, lost height and made a forced landing at Ford Hill, Birkenhead, unfortunately hitting a tree in the process, killing the navigator. More spectacular was the demise of Mosquito VI, LR263, which crashed on the range on 30 August 1944, killing its crew. Control had been lost after it was struck by flares dropped by another No 60 OTU Mosquito. This was not an uncommon occurrence, almost an occupational hazard amongst bomber and fighter-bomber OTUs exercising in strength at night. One immediately recalls the fate of a Wellington X, NC678, attached for all its working life to N° 30 OTU at Hixon, Staffs. On the night of Sunday, 16 July 1944 it was one of several making their run on to the illuminated target at Cannock Chase bombing range. A flash bomb from another Wellington flying at a higher altitude came through the fuselage roof of NC678 and exploded, causing a massive fire which the crew could not extinguish. The pilot ordered them to bale out, reducing airspeed to assist. Then, believing all had complied, he himself took to his parachute, but in the confusion either the order had been misunderstood or was never received. Four crew had stayed with the aircraft and were killed as NC678 crashed at Huntington, near Cannock. Three, all Canadians, lie buried in the Imperial War Graves Commission Cemetery at Blacon, near Chester — F/Sgt John Harrison Jones (WO/AG), Sgt Patrick Charles Mullins (bomb-aimer), and F/O Stanley Dickenson Mann (navigator). The pilot was injured on landing. Sgt J. D. Wall (air-gunner) is buried in Aberdeen.

When Burton Marsh ceased to be a target marking practice range is uncertain, but it must have been before March 1945 when N° 60 OTU dissolved into N° 13 OTU on moving to Finmere (Oxfordshire) and Hampstead Norris (Berkshire). Here, although nominally under the control of No 2 Group, 2nd TAF, training focussed on producing crews for Far East squadrons.

The great lowland raised mire or sphagnum moss peat bog that is Fenn's Moss is the southernmost and third largest of its type in the country. It is bisected by the Flintshire/Shropshire border and today is a National Nature Reserve, protected by English Nature and the Countryside Council for Wales. In addition to those factors that in the 1980s made the moss a SSSI — a remote, unpopulated wasteland with a unique fauna and flora — the fact that it lay within five minutes flying time of three Flying Training Schools and two fighter

Looking out over the Dee estuary from Denhall with the red flag flying at the bombing range on Burton Point Marsh.

and bomber OTUs and their satellites made it almost inevitable that a Second World War gunnery and bombing range and sundry decoy sites should be located here. However, as regards military use a precedent had perhaps been set in the First World War with the building of large military camps in the immediate vicinity of the moss.

It is difficult to unearth precise information, but there were apparently two sets of Army ranges on Fenn's Moss that on the north-east Fenn's pre-dates the OS 1909 re-survey of the area. The second, smaller, range is on the western edge of the moss in an area known locally as *The Batters* (presumably from 'battery' in the sense of 'gun emplacements'), and was used just for the period 1915–19. More specifically *The Batters* refers to the butts area, a high wall of railway sleepers against which peat, rather than the usual sand, was piled to absorb spent bullets. This was fronted by a similarly constructed rampart to protect the butt party. This was a 300-yard range with access only from the tow-path of the Shropshire Union Canal (Liangollen Branch) via a cinder track, the only 'enriched' path on the whole moss.

The Batters range was used by soldiers stationed at Bettisfield Park, and some credence must be given to the strong oral tradition of troops arriving at the range by canal barge. This makes better sense than picturing a large body of men lumbered with ammunition boxes (if not carried by a mule!), negotiating a narrow, overgrown and occasionally deficient, canal towpath for nearly 1¹/₂ miles. Barges were already being used for the movement of peat from the moss to the wharf at Bettisfield for horse bedding at the artillery lines. In an era of horses, before the development of a market for horticultural compost, stables were the major non-domestic users of ground peat from the Fenn's. With changing industrial practice peat was also used for packing crockery etc. in transport, in the manufacture of cardboard, and as a filtration or purification element in gas production. In the 1914–18 War dozens of women descended upon Fenn's Moss to pick the green moss for field dressings and the extraction of iodine.

Some time before 1899, in catering for markets further afield, a narrow gauge tramway was laid connecting peat workings in The Canal section [SJ492368] with the Peat Litter Moss Works at Moss Cottages, Whixall [SJ502367], and on to an exchange siding at Fenn's Moss Brick & Tile Works [SJ508389]. This was a horse-drawn tramway. In 1915, as distinct from local provision and to meet the ever burgeoning demands of the Army, the War Office established, or contracted out, its own Peat Moss Works [SJ178367] at the Bettisfield end of the Moss, with its own siding from the Cambrian Railway main line. From here another horsedrawn tramway ran off into the Railway and Middle peat workings [SJ4736, 4836, 4937]. The whole complex was dismantled in 1919.

If the 1,100-yard range on the Top N.E. Fenn's was in existence before 1909 it has its roots either in the South

African war years or the expansion of local militia/territorial units. It was a standard ten-target 600-yard range with provision for a four-target 800, and single target 900, 1,000 and 1,100-yard firing points. Up to 800 yards the firing points were made up of peat blocks held in place by timber revetments. Like *The Batters* the target gallery had ramparts made up of timber with peat to front and rear, and a range hut behind. The whole was kept relatively dry by two lateral drainage ditches 2,300ft and 2,500ft long, still discernible in places. However, come the Great War a single range proved woefully inadequate for the Army units stationed in the neighbourhood. It was therefore abandoned and three new 600-yard ranges and one 300-yard range were laid out over and adjacent to it, spilling into Fenn's Wood which was then just scrub land through which firing lines were easily cleared. In that two of the ranges and several firing points straddled the line of the 1890s peat tramway, 1915 might mark the latter's abandonment prior to the focussing, post-War, of peat-cutting activity upon the Bettisfield Mill. This move was concident with the introduction of 'loco-power' onto the tramway system in October 1919.

In 1995 a very fragile, possibly incomplete, blueprint for the Proposed Rifle Range at Fenn's Moss came to light amongst a former Whixall freeholder's funeral effects. Each

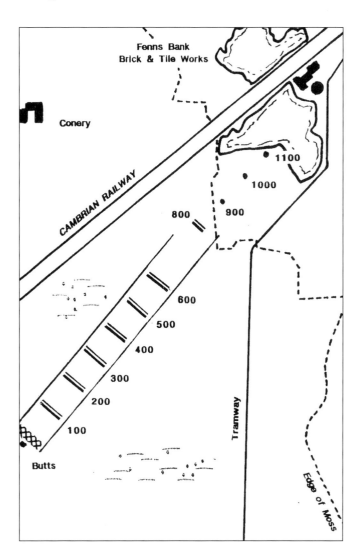

Pre-1909 Volunteers rifle range, north-east Fenn's.

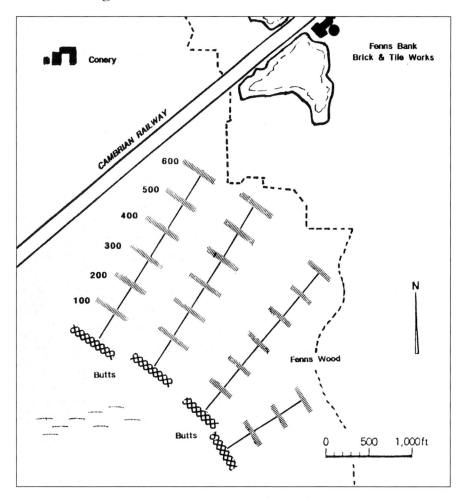

1914–19 rifle ranges on north-east Fenn's.

railway sleepers at 4ft intervals, tied in by iron rods anchored to pickets set in the base of the rampart. Strangely, according to these plans, there was no provision for a rampart or stop-butt to the rear of the targets as is the norm with present-day rifle ranges. This has all sorts of implications for security and safety precautions. One can only assume that large scale peat cutting had not yet spread to the N.E. Fenn's!

Main use of the ranges was made by troops from the large First World War camp on Prees Heath, near Whitchurch, and occasionally by soldiers from Park Hall, Oswestry. They would arrive by train, an extra long siding being provided off the passing loop at nearby Ferns Bank Station to accommodate them. With the closure and demolition of these camps after the war the ranges became redundant. Such fittings as were not salvaged by the Army were quickly stripped and 'recycled' by local smallholders. Galleries and butts fell into decay, dissolving quietly into the surrounding peat, to disappear under a mat of heather, purple moor grass, birch scrub and the odd Scots pine, or vanishing completely as peat cutters moved in to skin the area. Post-1963 tree planting in the Fenn's Wood area has further helped to obliterate traces of the firing points.

target gallery, separated by a target storage shed behind a protective wall of peat sods, now held thirty-two 6-ft square targets delicately balanced in pairs on a double pivot so that they could either be 'at rest' i.e. not showing to marksmen above the 8-ft front rampart, or with one target elevated for firing and its counterpart 'grounded' for pasting-up and other repairs by the range party. This gave sixteen firing positions to a range, each marked by a 4-ft square number board at the foot of the protective rampart.

The latter was 8ft high, the 2/3 slope stabilised on the firing side by $1^{1}/_{2}$-inch boards held down by 'pickets' (pointed wooden stakes or pegs). The flat crest of the rampart was further protected by $^{3}/_{4}$-inch steel plate. On the target side, the gallery floor, some 14ft wide, comprised compacted ash on top of peat and had a slight fall to a rear drainage channel. The almost vertical inner face of the rampart was consolidated by tightly packed peat blocks fronted by six inches of broken stone or hard slag held in place by old boarding, and the whole buttressed by

Paradoxically information on Second World War activities on Fenn's Moss is even more difficult to obtain. Neither range nor decoy sites were independent units, but are rarely mentioned in parent station ORBs, possibly, in the case of the latter on grounds of stringent secrecy. Almost every spade of peat contains the fragmentary remains of the thousands of practice bombs that were dropped over a five-

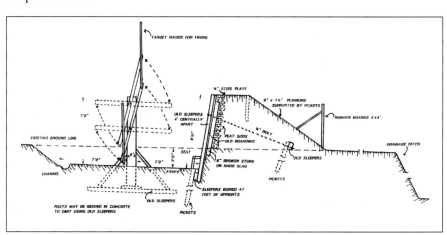

Cross section of the target gallery, Fenn's Moss.

A   Peat tramway

B   First World War rifle ranges
    converted to Second World
    War use.

C   Air-to-ground machine-gun
    range

D   Second World War bombing
    target circle.

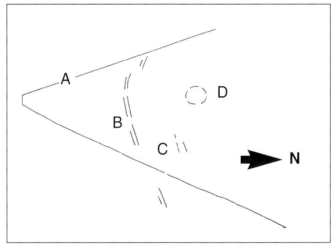

Fenn's Moss Bombing Range. Traces of the military use of this area were still visible in 1994.
[RCAHMW & André Berry]

year period, and every Whixall schoolboy carefully picked over the range for spent .303 and .50 ammunition to augment his pocket money. Yet there are few physical remains apart from a brick battery hut, concrete plinths that once carried control buildings, quadrant towers and Starfish bowls, and sundry baulks of peat from which still protrude iron rods that supported machine-gun targets. Air Ministry Works Directorate (AMWD) drawings for the period February 1940–January 1945 that would show the evolution and expansion of range facilities no longer survive, at least in official repositories. However, 'crop marks' and other

detail on a series of vertical and oblique aerial photographs covering the period 1946–94 enable some tentative reconstructions to be made.

From February 1940 the parent unit was Nᵒ 11 SFTS, Shawbury. They shared the range with Nᵒ 10 SFTS, Tern Hill, which latter would have a monopoly of use from August-November 1940. From 7 November 1940–8 February 1942 the range was used by Nᵒˢ 306, 605, 403 and 131 Squadrons, operational units posted into Tern Hill for the defence of Merseyside and the West Midlands, and between April–October 1941 also by 'D' Flight, Nᵒ 57 OTU, refugees

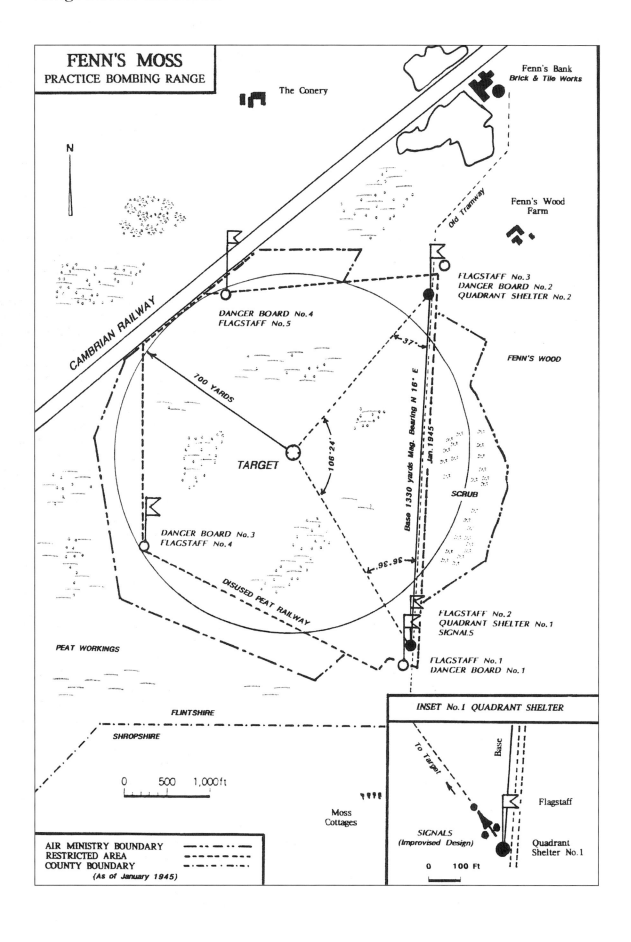

from RAF Hawarden where runway construction was under way. Rarer visitors were the 5-gun Masters which N° 5 SFTS had taken with them to Tern Hill. In October 1941 even the Wellingtons of N° 27 OTU, Lichfield, crowded off the Cannock ranges, pinched the odd day — and night — at Fenn's Moss for bombing and flare dropping practice.

From April–August 1942 Fenn's Moss was used by the Spitfires of N° 61 OTU at Rednal. The first aircraft had flown in from their temporary base at Heston (near Heathrow) on 13 April 1942. The first training accident was logged on 4 May when P/O Pensa and Sgt P. R. Wright were killed in Miles Master W9003. But the first accident involving a Spitfire occurred over the Fenn's Moss range on 14 June 1942. According to eye-witnesses Spitfire II P7622, piloted by Sgt G. G. Mager, was seen coming off the target area, flying very low. Over Cadney Bank it started a low, steep banking turn to port but then slowly flipped onto its back and dived into Cadney Moss, the other side of the Llangollen Canal from the range area. Sgt Mager was killed instantly. Like most of the Spitfires in N° 61 OTU P7622 was a rather war weary machine having entered service with N° 616 ('South Yorkshire') Sqadron at Kirton-in-Lindsey in February 1941 and passing through the hands of seven other operational squadrons before being put out to grass in the Shropshire countryside. It had come to N° 61 OTU in March 1942 from N° 154 Squadron at Coltishall, Norfolk, as the latter converted to Spitfires VA and VB. However, the resultant inquiry blamed inexperience and pilot error rather than poor maintenance.

In September 1942 Ferns Moss was taken over solely as a bombing range by N° 81 OTU, N° 92 Group, Bomber Command, at Tilstock and (after April 1943) Sleap. N° 61 OTU had perforce to look further afield for its air-to-ground gunnery, namely the Talacre range. In January 1944 RAF Tilstock came under the control of N° 38 Group (Airborne Forces) and home to the Stirlings of N° 1665 HCU and a Whitley/Horsa combination glider training establishment. But it still retained the day-to-day running of the Fenn's Moss range now increasingly used by Wellingtons from OTUs at Peplow (until squeezed out), Pershore, Honeybourne and elsewhere on their cross-country navigational exercises, as well as the Spitfires and Mustangs from N°s 41 and 58 OTUs at Hawarden and Poulton.

It was the demise of a Broughton-built Wellington III, BK430, whilst using the Fenn's Moss range that brought the horrors of war home to the tiny hamlet of Little Green, Bronington, on the northern edge of the range. The late Mrs Marie Mottershead, then newly married with a young family, recalled her father coming into the house early morning his clothes blackened and singed by the heat, smelling of smoke and carrying the unmistakable stench of burning flesh, a stink that neither would experience again until the great foot-and-mouth epidemic of 1967–8. He issued the grim warning that women and children should best keep away from the crash site where police, Home Guard, range crew and farm-workers stood helplessly by, unable to approach the wreckage because of the heat and fear of exploding ammunition. The fire crews and crash tenders from Whitchurch and RAF Tilstock arrived within twenty minutes. All they could do was to dampen down.

N° 23 OTU, based at Pershore (Worcestershire), had the responsibility of training Canadian crews for the new Commonwealth squadrons. BK430 had taken off at 2200hrs on Friday, 6 August 1943 on a night NAVEX which included dropping practise bombs on the Fenn's Moss range. As it cleared Dawley and Wellington the crew reported engine trouble, but pressed on and actually communicated with the Fenn's Moss safety and control officer and took their place in the circuit over Whixall. But, as the post-crash investigation revealed, the supply of oil to the bigend bearing of the master con-rod of the port engine had failed. With the pilot unable to feather the engine the Wellington went into a steep dive from which it was just pulling out when it ploughed into the ground on the edge of the moss and immediately burst into flames, trapping and killing all five crew members despite valiant efforts of the range crew and civilians living nearby.

But as the sun rose next morning only the occasional wisp of smoke and a strange pungent odour mingling with the mists that hung over the moss suggested that something untoward had recently happened in this remote part of Flintshire. At the crash site the Bronington police constable and two Home Guard sentries with fixed bayonets, their reliefs long overdue, prowled restlessly around the blackened geodetic skeleton of a Wellington that had survived bombing and minelaying missions with N° 196 Squadron (Leconfield) and N° 429 Squadron RCAF (East Moor, Yorks.) only to meet an inglorious end thus.

The Canadian crew of BK430 comprised F/Sgt J. P. R. Labbe (26, pilot); W/O F. C. J. Therien (25, WO/AG); F/Sgt J. P. G .M. de Bellefeuille (19, pupil bomb-aimer); F/O N. Solomka (23, navigator), and F/Sgt W. McKenzie Arril (25, air bomber). They all lie buried in the CWG Cemetery, Blacon, Chester.

Whether the Wellington was loaded with 10lb. Mk III or 11^1/$_2$lb. Mk I (flash) practice bombs is uncertain, but the result would be the same. Practice bombs with flash filling (gunpowder and magnesium turnings) for night work would have had the cotter pin securing the striker removed as loaded into the aircraft, leaving just the safety-pin that would springload out upon release. The impact of the crash would have shaken the bombs loose, triggering off an instantaneous conflagration which would have given the dazed and possibly injured crew no chance to escape.

The subsequent inquiry attributed the crash to 'failure to jettison practice bomb load. Pilot left it too late to order crew to bale out, which possibly led to confusion and the loss of control. Duration of flight was one hour'. To confuse the researcher RAF records claim six dead and attribute the site of the crash to a place called 'Badmington, Salop' or 'Bodrington, near Shropshire'! The loss of BK430 was not an isolated incident. Even restricting one's overview to casualties in Welsh border country N° 23 OTU has a melancholy record of crashes, fatalities and near misses, inevitable, perhaps, in training units where new crews were in the process of shaking down. Of course, Pershore did not have a monopoly of such incidents and similar lists could be compiled for N°s 15 OTU (Harwell), 16 OTU (Upper

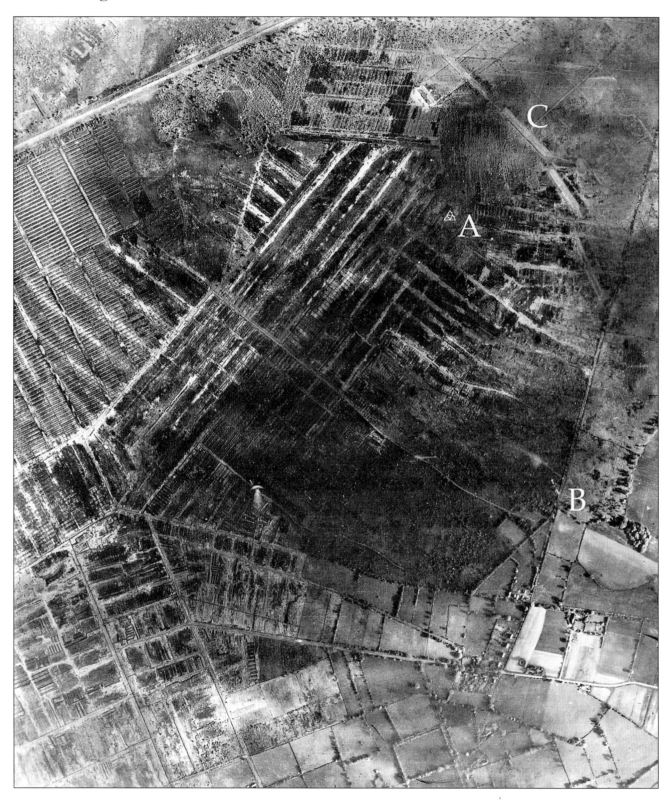

Fenn's Moss Bombing Range, 1946. Traces include:

A — *Bombing target*   B — *Quadrant No 1 & direction arrow*   C — *Former rifle ranges*

[National Assembly for Wales]

Heyford), 17 OTU (Upwood), 18 OTU (Bramcote), 21 OTU (Moreton-in-the-Marsh) and others. Causes of accidents were varied and many.

On 8 April 1942, N° 23 OTU lost Wellington Ic, R1597, struck by lightning during a storm. All five crew perished when it crashed near Llangamarch Wells, Brecon. Welsh weather also claimed Wellington III, X3608, on the last leg of a night NAVEX on 12 February 1943. The pilot, Sgt A. N. E. White, RAFVR, ordered the crew to bale out when the aircraft started to ice up over Betws-y-coed, Snowdonia. He stayed at the controls to allow the crew to clear the aircraft but died in the ensuing crash at Cefn Glaniwrch, south-east of Llanrhaeadr-ym-Mochnant. Sgt White lies buried in Oswestry Cemetery.

Things did not always work out for the best even if there was a 24-hour watch airfield conveniently to hand when in trouble. Whilst on a night exercise from Pershore on 25 January 1943 one of the engines of Wellington III, X3956, ran rough and then failed completely. RAF Shawbury was alerted, runways cleared, and a forced landing made at 2140hrs. It was only partially successful. The undercarriage collapsed as the aircraft landed on its belly after overshooting and running off into the adjoining fields, damaging engines and ripping out the underside of the fuselage. Remarkably this time the crew walked away from the wreckage with only the WO/AG sustaining slight injuries.

When N° 23 OTU was formed in April 1941 night fighter pilots were not as trigger-happy as they were the previous year when they exhibited a disturbing tendency to fire upon anything with two engines. There were still itchy fingers about, but positive identification was now demanded before opening fire. There must be several former crews of Pershore's Wellingtons still blissfully unaware how close they came to be shot down as they trundled across N° 9 Group's congested night skies. An entry in 96 Squadron's ORB from their Wrexham Beaufighter days suffices to illustrate the point: '27.7.42. ... Five operational patrols carried out this evening. A magnificent evening with full moon, and should have brought us some success, but Sector were troubled with something like 100 training aircraft flying around in the Group. P/O J. Birkbeck had two contacts, one a Wellington from Pershore, the other a Hun ....' P/O Birkbeck and his 'Navigator Radio', Sgt D. Nicholas would be killed as 'A' Flight, 96 Squadron, took off from Wrexham on 6 September 1942 on the unit's move to Honiley. After take-off their Beaufighter went up almost vertically, stalled at 300ft and crashed on to the aerodrome, bursting into flames.

Practice interceptions on N° 23 OTU's Wellingtons were common place, ideal for both bomber crews and fighter pilots from training units en route. Nine times out of ten these were incident free but the tenth could be fatal to one or both parties. Thus on Friday, 14 May 1943 F/Sgt A. A. Webb (21, RAAF) was flying Spitfire IIA, P8268, of N° 61 OTU, Rednal, on a fighter affiliation exercise. He was making a mock attack on Wellington III, BK186 (another Broughton-built aircraft), from Pershore, when unfortunately both aircraft collided. The Spitfire crashed at Wittingslow, one

mile south of Little Stretton, at 1120hrs, killing the pilot. (Other records give the crash as occurring at Marshbrook, near Church Stretton). F/Sgt Webb was buried at Oswestry Cemetery five days later. There were no casualties aboard the Wellington. When N° 23 OTU was disbanded in March 1944 BK186 was transferred to N° 22 OTU, Stratford, where on 11 June it suffered a further accident when its undercarriage collapsed on landing.

It is sobering to consider that from July 1941 N° 23 OTU's Wellingtons were regularly dispatched on 'Nickels' or propaganda leaflet raids over northern France and that between July and September 1942 they made up numbers for bombing raids over Dusseldorf, Essen and Bremen, not without loss. Nothing like throwing crews in at the deep end! Then to try and reconcile this with the depressing losses sustained on ordinary cross-country training flights!

Continuing the story of Fenn's Moss range, since 1 April 1937, N° 5 Armament Training Camp (later N° 9 AOS/9 BGS) at Penrhos and Hell's Mouth in the Llŷn had provided the Advanced Training Flights from Tern Hill, Shawbury, Digby, Netheravon and other FTSs with their final aerial gunnery and bombing practices, a month at a time, fitting them in around the summer and week-end practice camps for regular, auxiliary and Royal Naval squadrons. But with the outbreak of war this happy arrangement was not to last.

Until the Miles Master and the North American Harvard came on stream in 1940 both N°s 10 and 11 FTS used the Hawker Hart, Audax and Fury, the Avro Tutor, and the Gloster Gauntlet for single-engine training. Theoretically a FTS took in pilots who had already totted up 50 hours (including 30 hours dual) air experience at an Elementary & Reserve FTS. But courses never reached the optimum nine months and by 1938, as the RAF geared itself for war, were already reduced to 22 weeks, divided into two equal terms. In the first term the aim was to produce pilots competent in the handling of service aircraft in addition to mastering the theory of flight and the rudiments of engines, rigging, elementary meteorology, RAF law and administration etc. During the second term pilots of the Advanced Training Squadron picked up on those skills which were a necessary pre-requisite to joining an operational unit i.e. formation flying, dog-fighting, air-to-air and air-to-ground gunnery, bombing from the air etc. But before proceeding to the Llŷn, to accelerate a pupil's skills in the handling of aircraft at low altitude and high speed and with live weaponry, a practice range was set up on Fenn's Moss. Such a facility was also essential for making up time and experience that might be lost at the Armament Practice Camp due to bad weather.

As seen from the accompanying map, the Fenn's Moss range was initially nothing elaborate, a mere extension of the traditional 'bombing circle', with machine-gun targets set up along the galleries of the old First World War rifle ranges. Target circles could not be painted onto a moss, heather or moor grass surface so they were constructed out of timber and placed in situ. Each section was 3ft wide, painted white, and when assembled formed a hollow circle some 20–25ft in diameter. In the centre was a squat, square 'funnel' made out of galvanised metal sheeting. The latter could represent

Tail unit from a 250lb L.C. bomb found on the range prior to re-opening. In the background is the Heath Robinson structure of the circular bombing target 1949/53 which appears to have taken some punishment. [Peter Jervis]

View taken from Nº 1 Quadrant, showing directional arrow to target. [Peter Jervis]

anything from a military truck to a gun emplacement.

But it was not long before the first accident on the range emerges from No 23 Group (Training Command) records. On 6 May 1940 Acting-P/O D. C. Leary, with 106 flying hours to his credit (49 on the Audax and 47 on other ATS types), was flying at Fenn's Moss in Hawker Audax K2011. This venerable bi-plane was delivered to the RAF in February 1932 and had seen service with Nº 13 Squadron at Netheravon and (1937–8) with Nº 211 Squadron at Grantham. When the latter squadron moved to Egypt K20111 was taken over by Nº 45 E&RFTS and in 1939 by Nº 11 FTS Shawbury.

At 1045hrs on the Monday morning A-P/O Leary had taken off from Shawbury to carry out low bombing and strafing attacks on the Fenn's Moss range. According to witnesses he had successfully dropped his practice bomb and was turning at low altitude on a north-westerly heading over the GWR railway when 'he lost power, it seemed, and slipped sideways in the turn, ever so slowly and then plummeted into the peat workings. From where we were standing we could see people running over to the aircraft which looked just like a crumpled kite. There was no fire, and we learnt later that the pilot had survived his ordeal'. The crash is now part of Moss folklore, with details varying according to the narrator. It is often asserted that the Audax actually clipped a stack of drying peat as it turned, but official records make no mention of this.

As so often happens in isolated rural areas where there was no resident police constable, it was railway workers to the rescue. Station staff from Bettisfield and permanent way workers took control of the situation and carefully freed the pilot from the crumpled wreckage. They were no strangers to aircraft crashes. As noted Volume II of this work, only a few months previously they had dealt effectively with the Miles Magister that crashed the other side of Bettisfield Station on 16 March 1939 whilst on a ferry flight from its Woodley factory to Nº 10 FTS, Tern Hill, and came perilously close to blocking the single line track.

At the subsequent inquiry the pilot claimed that his attention was diverted for a vital second during the turn, with subsequent loss of control. The Chief Instructor put it more bluntly: 'It was just damn bad piloting!' Thirty-five years later such remains of K2011 as had not been cleared at the time came to light during peat digging

Cross-sections of 8¹/2 lb (left, 10lb (centre) and 11¹/2 lb (right) practice bombs, as used on Fenn's Moss bombing range.
[Timothy Morgan via André Berry]

operations. Unfortunately no aviation archaeologist was contacted and the de-rated Rolls-Royce Kestrel X engine, of which so few now remain, promptly found its way to Furber's scrapyard just along the canal!

N° 81 OTU, as we have seen, primary latter day users of the Fenn's Moss range, passed into aviation history in August 1945 with its redesignation as N° 1380 (Transport Support) Conversion Unit with satellite at Sleap. This in turn was disbanded in January 1946. In March 1946 RAF Tilstock was reduced to care and maintenance under Tern Hill, which might explain why the latter station still had titular oversight of the Fenn's Moss range as late as 1949–50. But No 6 FTS, then resident at Tern Hill, with its due establishment of North American Harvards and Percival Prentices, had little need for the luxury of an in-house range. Neither on paper did the Central Navigation and Control School at Shawbury, which station took over the Fenn's Moss range towards the end of 1949, a responsibility which lasted until early 1953 at least.

So much is known from a unique corpus of images that have survived and are reproduced here for the first time. They illustrate, 1949–52, the main access to the range, quadrant posts, mess and 'rest room', members of the range crew, and, more importantly, specimens of obsolete but live ordnance awaiting disposal by controlled explosions, which have been cleared off the range 'prior to re-opening', implying a specific purpose to reactivating a wartime bombing facility. To this end senior NCOs and range crew had been transferred from Tern Hill onto the books of RAF Shawbury. F/Sgt MacCabe was nominally i/c range, with F/Sgt Walker as relief. They filled the role of Range Safety Officer under the eagle eye of W/O C. Turner, station armaments officer, Shawbury. Corporal P. Jervis oversaw the disposal of UXBs on site, along with any unwanted explosives from local military units. Seven airmen completed the range crew, to operate the Hill's Mirror, run the tiny 'cookhouse', drive the unit truck, and staff the two quadrant towers, two men in each, one to mark the strike the second on the telephone.

Apparently, because of the drastic reduction in the strength of Bomber Command after the war there was a desperate shortage of bomb aimers. This deficiency was partly made good by the establishment at Lindholme (Yorkshire) of a series of courses 'SEGs to Bomb Aimers', in other words offering the chance to change speciality role to 'Signallers, Engineers and Gunners' aircrew. The course used Wellington Mk Xs on the books of the N° 5 ANS (NA780, NA845, NB117, NC892, NC958, NC981, NC987) — to list but a few of the hundreds of Mark Xs converted for specialist training purposes in the peacetime RAF. N° 5 ANS had a chequered history as N° 5 AOS and the Air Navigation and Bombing School, Jurby (Isle of Man), before being re-established at Lindholme, where, in November 1952, it would be replaced by Bomber Command Bombing School. Overcrowding at Lindholme meant that the 'SEG to Bomb Aimer' retraining component was farmed out to RAF Shawbury. Here the courses were headed up by one Major Earl G. Hunt (USAF) as Bombing Leader. he was on an exchange posting from the USA. F/Lts Dewey and Morris,

Recovered nose and tail fragments of an 11lb practice bomb from Fenn's Moss bombing range.

RAF, were Assistant Bombing Leaders. A a result of the 'Cold War' developments the RAF were faced with the problem of training crews American fashion for the Boeing B-29 Super Fortresses, even then, under the American military aid programme for Europe, being taken out of 'cocooned' storage and modernised before reaching RAF operational units. Due to financial economies there was no British aircraft currently available to replace the superannuated Avro Lincoln as a long-range strike aircraft. The Boeing B-29 (or 'Washington' as it was known to the RAF) proved a useful temporary stop-gap in this respect. The four-jet V bombers were still some years away — the first production Vickers Valiant taking to the air in December 1953 and appearing in strength at the Farnborough Air Display in 1955. Whether the Valiants appeared over Fenn's Moss is doubtful. However, a frequently chronicled visitor to the range as part of long haul navigational exercises was the Avro 706 Ashton, WB492, one of a series of six experimental aircraft, but this particular one attached to the Radar Research Establishment, Defford, for radar bombing research, hence WB492's large under-wing bomb containers, and an advanced radar bombsight in a ventral dome.

Interestingly, accident records throw up the loss of a Washington (WF502) of N° 90 Squadron* on 8 January 1953 in the hills east of Wrexham. The aircraft had taken off from RAF Marham at 1440hrs, an element in *Exercise Kingpin*, a

Left: Cpl Peter Jervis at the main entrance to the Fenn's Moss Bombing Range. [Peter Jervis]

Below: View of Nº 1 Quadrant. The Hill's Mirror positioning block can be seen in front of the Quadrant. [Peter Jervis]

Above: Group in front of No 1 Quadrant. L–R: Cpl P. Jervis, Flt Sgt MacCabe, W/O C. Turner (Station armament officer, Shawbury). MT driver. [Peter Jervis]

Above: A Hill's Mirror. [Science Museum, London]

Below: Due for demolition: 25lb flash bombs, sea markers, incendiary bombs and a smoke float. [Peter Jervis]

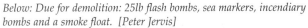

Below: View from Nº 1 Quadrant. 'X' marks Nº 2 Quadrant. [Peter Jervis]

An RAF B-29 Washington bomber similar to the aircraft which crashed near Llanarmon-yn-Iâl in 1953. [MoD PRB4047]

sixteen-hour slog involving several high altitude radar and visual bombing attacks. At about 2110hrs WF503 ploughed through a small pine wood on the 1,000ft contour at Wern Goed, between Chweleiriog and Gelligynan farm, Llanarmon-yn-Iâl, in an inverted position, killing all ten people on board before catching fire. The crew list is interesting —

S/Ldr W. J. Sloane	pilot
P/O C. B. Speller	co-pilot
P/O Lightfowler	navigator
Sgt E. D. Pearton	navigator 2
Sgt A. Martin	flight engineer
Sgt R. Anderson	signaller
F/Sgt K. A. Reakes	gunner
Sgt R. G. Hughson	gunner
Sgt E. F. Wheeler	gunner
Sgt M. J. Clinton	gunner

Preliminary investigation of the B-29 crash site by the Wartime Recovery Group in 1980 at Wern Goed, Llanarmon-yn-Iâl. This daylight photograph gives a good impression of the difficulty of operating in such dense woodland. The white items scattered on the ground are pieces of aluminium from the crashed aircraft.

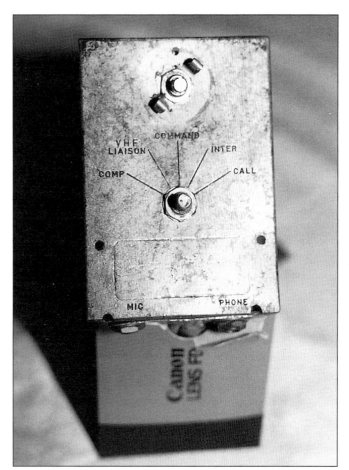 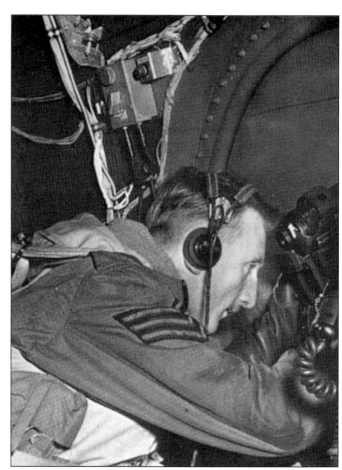

Left: One of the communications selector boxes (minus its knobs) recovered from the B-29 Washington (WF502) which crashed near Llanarmon-yn-Iâl.
Right: A complete box can be seen directly above the airman sitting in the remote control side-blister position
of a B-29 Washington. [MoD PRB1696]

The graves of sixof the crew of the B-29 Washington (WF502) in Hawarden Cemetery, Flintshire. [W. Alister Williams Collection]

Avro Ashton (WB492), a regular visitor over Fenn's Moss. Note the large under-wing bomb containers.

— all the hallmarks of a 'SEG' crew under training. Subsequent investigations and a Court of Inquiry were at a loss to account for why the aircraft should have been flying at such a low altitude and why it should have entered into that fatal dive which put undue stress on the airframe causing structural failure and the partial disintegration of the aircraft, resulting in a scatter of wreckage over a four mile swathe south-west of Llanarmon-yn-Iâl. Whether its 'duty' included a visit to Fenn's Moss range is not known. The Washington was certainly on course for it.

The wreckage was taken to RAF Shawbury for investigation before some of it eventually found its way into local scrapyards.

* Nº 90 Squadron was formed at Shawbury on 8 October 1917, moving to Shotwick (Sealand) on 5 December 1917. In its early days this was a fighter squadron equipped with the F.E.2b, the Avro 504K and the Sopwith Dolphin.

4. Accident blackspot

Point of Ayr, Flintshire, where the Dee estuary opens out into Liverpool Bay, derives its name from the Old Norse *eyrr* = 'a gravel- or sand-bank' or perhaps its Old English cognate *ear* = 'gravel, earth, mud'. Both hint at the spit's complex geological history and a long history of accretion and erosion at this point. The postglacial cliff-line running between Ffynnongroyw and Gwesbyr is fronted by flats of blue estuarine clays upon which rest poorly developed gravel and shingle ridges marking successive stages in the seaward growth of point and spit. Fringing the High Water Mark a magnificent line of dunes reaches over 12m OD except where, post-war, they were robbed for building sand. On their inner side a more sporadic line of dunes and ridges of blown sand branch away following the old beach ridges.

The dunes are fed by blown sand from the extensive inter-tidal beach and move except where stabilised by vegetation. Their renewal about the lighthouse is being encouraged by the building of wood walls and brushwood traps. Much of the original salt-marsh was embanked and drained under the Lianasa Enclosure Act of 1811, leaving the seaward margins with their high and well-formed dunes as a natural wilderness, subject only to pre-war encroachment by the indiscriminate planting of holiday shacks — huts, railway coaches, bus bodies etc. that would render valuable war-time service in sheltering evacuees and harbouring deserters.

But on 19 January 1940 it is doubtful whether Sgt Harry Moorby, piloting an Avro Anson, had time to appreciate such niceties of geology and historical geography. Anson N5050 was one of four that, since November 1939, had been on detachment at Hooton Park from Nº 502 'Ulster' Squadron, a general reconnaissance unit of Coastal Command based at Aldergrove, near Belfast. Between them they maintained a dawn-to-dusk patrol of Liverpool Bay, the sea area between the North Wales coast and the Isle of Man and from the Bar Lightship to some fifteen miles west of the inward convoy routes through the North and St George's Channels.

The weather had not been ideal when N5050 had taken off on the mid-morning shift — dull, overcast, with heavy rain showers. The Tiger Moths of Hooton's inshore Coastal Patrol Flights, 'scarecrow' units in more than job description, had long returned to base, having no radio, just two carrier pigeons for inward communication, and an inflated car inner-tube as a survival kit! Under such circumstances discretion was always better than valour.

The decision to take off in the face of an advancing cold front was a calculated risk. The crew of N5050 were mindful of how close the detachment had come to losing Anson N5234 on 3 January when in almost identical weather conditions it had stalled on take-off from Hooton Park owing to icing on its wings. Nevertheless they pressed on. As they cleared Point of Ayr crew would have been very alert, remembering how three days earlier F/O Chambers of Nº 3 CPF in his Tiger Moth had seen a large oil slick made turbulent by air bubbles just off the Chester Bar, the first bit of excitement for nearly three months. It had warranted the sending of a pigeon back to base and the eventual token dispatch of an Admiralty trawler to investigate. But as N5050 ploughed on over the Irish Sea the weather worsened, rain changing to blinding sleet and snow. Sgt Moorby turned about to make landfall whilst conditions yet permitted. They picked up the Welsh coast at the Great Orme and set course for base. But approaching Abergele they ran into a blizzard and lost control over Rhyl as the Anson iced up. Anson N5050 plummeted to earth on the beach between Gronant and Talacre.

Two of the crew, Sgt Moorby and AC1 Robert Beattie, were killed instantly; Thomas Christopher McClure died from his injuries at Rhyl Hospital later the same day. First on the scene were Civil Defence workers from Prestatyn and Gronant. They retrieved the bodies and injured crewman, but because of the tides it was the following day before a salvage team from RAF Sealand could tackle the recovery of the aircraft's wreckage.

At least the aircraft was then relatively accessible. Six months later there would be immense problems as the wide inter-tidal flats were sown with larch poles to prevent German glider landings. On the High Water Mark a double row of Dannert Concertina wire with intervening minefield was reinforced by hastily planted Norcon pill-boxes carefully hidden in the base of the sand dunes, all aimed to discourage landings from the sea. Strategically placed 'corridors' gave safe access to the beach, ostensibly for range crews, who frequently had to recover straying target drogues, and for the rescue services whose task had immediately become more dangerous and unpleasant.

Pilots contemplating a forced landing now made for the mud flats around Point of Ayr Colliery — tackle was often available to winch aircraft ashore before the tide turned — and the Dee estuary, or even the Hoyle Bank, exposed for a couple of hours at low water. But frequently they had no choice in the matter, with usually fatal and horrible results. Thus, much later in the war, on 19 May 1944 a Spitfire Va, X4173, of Nº 61 OTU Rednal, was on air-to-ground firing practice at Talacre. Its steep diving approach was made from an unusual direction from the south-west over Gronant — which may explain why, after firing, F/Sgt Feliks Wares (Poland) failed to pull out of his dive and hit the first line of larch poles. The Spitfire was literally ripped apart at the wing roots before ricocheting into the Dannert wire and triggering off several of the anti-personnel mines. Pieces of the aircraft were scattered over 300 yards of beach. The unfortunate pilot lies buried in Hawarden Churchyard.

Human error or mechanical or structural failure? The

Above: Avro Ansons of 'A' Flight, Nº 502 Squadron based at RAF Hooton Park, spring, 1940.

Left: Avro Anson K8754 of Nº 206 Squadron. A detachment from this squadron was based at RAF Hooton Park before the arrival of Nº 502 Squadron.

An Avro Anson Mk I of N° 48 Squadron on patrol in the western approaches during the Battle of Britain. The squadron was at Hooton Park from 16 July 1940 to 24 July 1941.

Avro Anson K6155 of N° 48 Squadron, coded 'J'. This aircraft was transferred to N° 2 SAN RAF Cranage on 25 September 1940 and four weeks later, on 18 October, it crashed at Ludlow in Shropshire.

truth behind the crash of X4173 will never be known. The Spitfire was a veteran of the Battle of Britain and nine operational squadrons as well as a lengthy stint with N° 57 OTU at Hawarden in 1941–2. On the other hand, while the Talacre Range fulfilled three basic requirements of site, in the fourth it was somewhat deficient. It experienced relatively good weather, was backed by a large sea area free from shipping (a reflection of the historic decline of the Dee estuary ports) and had convenient airfields to hand. But unobstructed approaches to targets from the landward side it did not possess unless aircraft came off the Dee estuary at an awkward tangent. Generally they approached the Talacre ground targets in a steep dive from over Gwesbyr village and Talacre Abbey, themselves on a 350ft ridge, but with the Clwydian Range rising quickly to 600–900ft behind. Such a feature may even have been considered a plus factor, testing flying skills to the utmost and approximating more closely to operational realities.

However, like so many Second World War ranges, some military precedent underlay the selection of Talacre Warren apart from the absence of objections on planning and amenity grounds. In 1915 three 600-yard Army rifle ranges had been established at Llawndy, remaining in use until *c*.1922. After April 1917, with the establishment of through-running facilities for the Kinmel Park Military Railway, troops would arrive at Talacre via a rail shuttle service, using the Up siding to Point of Ayr Colliery screens as a shunt. Prior to that the unfortunates from Kinmel Park and Bodelwyddan camps had to march to the ranges! The tidal flats off Point of Ayr were also used for air-to-ground gunnery practice by the training squadrons from RAF Shotwick (otherwise Sealand).

At first targets were simply mounted on piles driven 6–8ft into the sand, the limits of the range being marked by other poles surmounted by a basket or lobster pot! Fishing boats from Mostyn and Llinegr were subcontracted to paint and repair these targets and to act as range patrols in case of emergency. But someone omitted to remind officialdom of the fate of that great wonder of Victorian engineering, the third Point of Ayr lighthouse, a skeletal steel structure erected in 1844 on piles on the edge of the Welsh Channel, abandoned as dangerous by 1866 and which finally

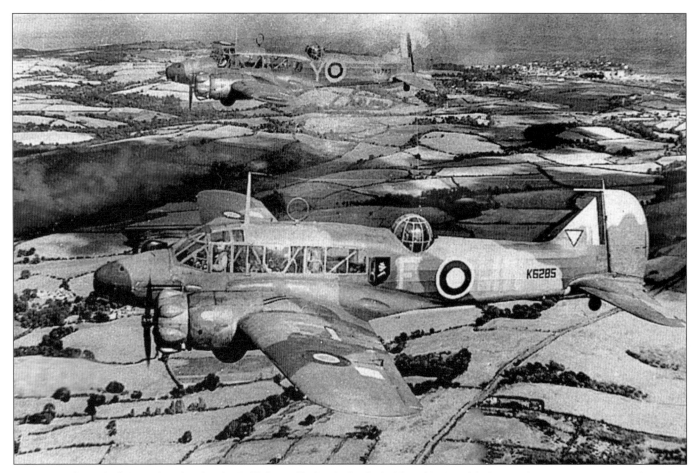

Avro Anson (K6285) of Nº 321 Squadron based at RAF Carew Cheriton in Pembrokeshire. This aircraft had an accident on 9 August 1940 when it hit an invasion obstacle during a forced landing on the beach at Pendine Sands. The squadron flew 'scarecrow' patrols at night trying to intercept enemy aircraft that were mine laying at the approaches to Milford Haven. The squadron also carried out patrols around the Llŷn peninsula and up beyond Holyhead into the Irish Sea. The aircraft in the background is Anson N9742 which experienced engine failure whilst on convoy patrol and ditched into the sea off Holyhead on 29 November 1940.

disappeared without trace during a gale in 1869. The static targets were reputedly swept away and were quickly replaced by cork float targets and marker buoys anchored to the sea bed. Painting, tying down and replacing was again entrusted to local boats. The use of this 'range' was short-lived and ceased abruptly in 1918, leaving Talacre to the Army.

Construction of the Vickers-Armstrong 'shadow' factory at Broughton, near Hawarden, began in 1937. In 1938 the Air Ministry requisitioned land adjacent for an airfield. Nº 48 MU moved in as the lodger unit in March 1940. In June, temporarily under Nº 10 Group, Fighter Command, Nº 7 (later Nº 57) OTU with its Hurricanes and Spitfires, took over the station. In July it would standardise on Spitfires, which explains why in the early years so few Hurricanes are noted as coming to grief on Talacre ranges. One such was Hurricane I, P3829, which on 20 July 1940 stalled off a steep turn after firing but managed a belly-landing on the beach at Gronant. The plane was damaged and the pilot suffered cuts and whip-lash injuries. But at least he had abided by the newly promulgated instruction issued at every briefing, to land on sand banks and mud flats with wheels up. Later, the Spitfires of Nº 61 OTU (Rednal) and the Mosquitos of Nº 60

OTU (High Ercall) would share Talacre range, along with the aircraft of operational units such as the Tomahawks of Nº 403 Squadron, ostensibly on 'rest and recuperation' in Nº 9 Group's 'back area'. Hurricanes would reappear on RAF Talacre's casualty lists in 1942–3 as Nº 41 OTU from Andover replaced Nº 57 OTU at Hawarden.

Most of Talacre Warren lying between Lifeboat Cottage and Ty'nmorfa was taken over for the coastal air-to-ground firing range. Entry was prohibited whilst gunnery was in progress. The usual strategic red flags indicated whether or not the range was 'active'. Before the advent of VHF the range was controlled by Aldis lamp and Very light, green for 'Go', red for 'Overshoot' and 'Don't fire'. The white, wooden framed targets, about 12ft square, angled to the sky, were set in their iron sliding frames on top of the outer rampart or dunes. Over 30ft high they necessitated the posting of additional lookouts equipped with very pistols to cover the dead ground. Safety precautions were frequently compromised by range crews leaving out the red flags day and night. Local school children searching for spent bullets or going to the beach for a paddle became complacent and put themselves at risk. An older and wiser Richard Hughes, retired schoolmaster of Denbigh, recalls: '…you just had to

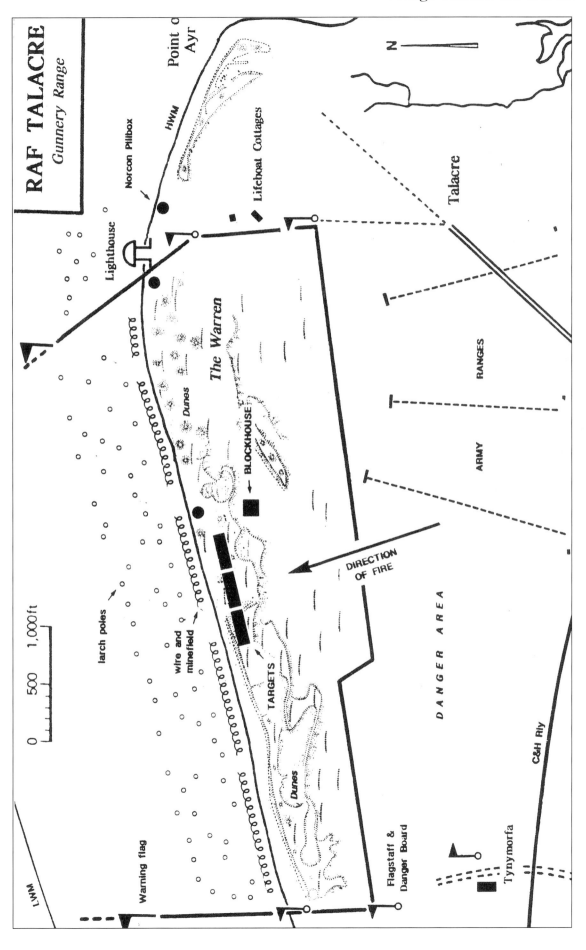

Left: The blockhouse at Talacre Range, used for the protection of the range crew, target making and replacement was carried out here. [Marie & Heddy Jones]

Below: The lighthouse at Talacre. It was here that N° 57 OTU installed a VHF radio station. This beach was the site of many forced landings. Now cleared of mines and barbed wire, a Norcon pill box lies half buried in the foreground.

exercise judgement when crossing the range. I was once crossing it on my bike when a Spitfire hurtled out of the overcast and bore down on the targets. Fear lent me wings and the pilot did not fire until his second pass. Thanks, whoever you are!' Mrs Marie Ann Jones (*née* Dowell), grand-daughter of one of the last Talacre lifeboat men, and brought up in Lifeboat Cottages, daily took her life in her hands to get to school in Gwesbyr. She also remembers: '... a boy by the name of Robert Keegan hiding behind one of the targets with a Spitfire bearing down off the hills. We all thought he was going to get it when the range lookout fired a red Very flare, and the aircraft overshot without firing. Things tightened up after that, but it soon went back to red flags being left out again. being on the range at Lifeboat Cottages we could collect the different ammo in safety as we knew when the range was in use. We collected three types, 0.303. 0.5 and 20mm. Then a rain of spent cases dropped over the old rifle ranges on the seaward side of the railway'. Obviously girls were as much an authority on 'collectables' as the lads. Much of Marie's inside information was derived from the fact that RAF range personnel were billeted at both Lifeboat and Lighthouse Cottages.

The range was alarmingly close to habitation, especially Warren House and the Merseysiders' makeshift holiday shanty town on the southern edge of the warren. If the incidence of non-indigenous vegetation in the warren is any indication of the former extent of encroachments plants such as red hot pokers, rambler roses, euonymus, Russian vine, aspens, and apple and pear trees — some of these homes were less than 100 yards from the concrete blockhouse used for the storage of target equipment and sheltering range crews. This in turn was frequently 'shot up' by errant marksmen. Sad to relate, after surviving the war and vandals for half a century, the blockhouse was summarily demolished in the so-called 'Year of the Fortress' (1995) as part of an alleged 'conservation scheme' to protect natter-jack toads in an adjacent pond!

As its title suggests N° 7 OTU was formed ostensibly to brush up and polish a pilot's operational training before joining a squadron. To this end air-to-ground and air-to-air

gunnery facilities were needed. Bottom line of operational flying, whatever the aircraft, was the ability of a pilot to set his flying and shooting skills against those of the enemy. The ultimate objective of a fighter pilot was air combat and it seems obvious and fundamental that a pilot should be able to fire straight and accurately at a hostile. But strangely, in the period 1936–41, there prevailed the false premise that as a fighter pilot one automatically could shoot. In practice there was little air gunnery and even less talk or theory about it, which confirms how out of date the higher echelons of Fighter Command were and how little they knew of air fighting and the capabilities of the modern aircraft the Command was beginning to receive.

During the latter part of 1940, at the height of the Battle of Britain, N° 7 OTU's courses were so attenuated — a fortnight long and subject to further curtailment by adverse weather — that a pilot's time was spent almost entirely on mastering the Spitfire, with the merest lip-service paid to tactics and the niceties of operational flying, outmoded as they were. In July and August 1940 pilots were leaving the OTU with as little as ten hours flying time on Hurricane or Spitfire and, incredibly, without firing guns, potential cannon fodder to an enemy who had cut their teeth on combat over Spain, Poland and the Low Countries. One such was AVM J. E. ('Johnny') Johnson, who, however, ended the war as the top scoring Allied fighter pilot — 38 air kills — and with the rank of Group Captain! Whilst at Hawarden P/O Johnson came close to being grounded or back-squaded after a writing off his Spitfire in a heavy landing at RAF Sealand! What a loss it would have been to N° 616 Squadron!

As the Battle of Britain progressed gunnery was taken more seriously, particularly after N° 7 OTU's restructuring as a specialist Spitfire OTU and when blooded 'veterans' were seconded from the squadrons to OTUs to give of their hard-earned experience and expertise. A 'Tactics Officer' was appointed and an 'Air Firing Flight' established at Hawarden, initially under the command of F/Lt H. C. Flemmons. It took on strength eight Fairey Battles as in house target-towing aircraft. Obsolescent as bombers even before the outbreak of war and suffering appalling losses during the period May–June 1940, the Battle found itself relegated to training establishments at home and abroad or to target-towing. Hawarden's Battles were all completed as target-towers either on Austin's Longbridge assembly line (L5705, L5716, L5770) or by Fairey Aviation Co. itself at Stockport (R7372–R7376). All these were delivered as new from ASUs, and being new some were soon lost to more urgent priorities elsewhere. In August 1940 Battles R7373 and R7374 were transferred to N° 12 OTU, Bomber Command, at RAF Benson, where Polish aircrew — it is difficult to comprehend why — were being trained for new Battle squadrons. However frustrating it must have been for allies dying to get to grips with the enemy this possibly was a case of marking time until supplies of suitable aircraft caught up with demand! These trainees would form the cadres of N°s 300, 301, 304 and 305 (Polish) Squadrons which would not begin to convert to Wellington ICs until October/November 1940.

Battle R7372 simply moved out to the eastern perimeter of RAF Hawarden to N° 3 FPP's dispersal, where it served as an ATA communications aircraft until final obsolescence in 1944. R7375 and R7376 were transferred to N° 1 FTS at Netheravon, Wilts., which concentrated on producing naval pilots. Both would return to north Wales in March 1942, more specifically to N° 3 AGS at RAF Mona (Anglesey). L5709 went to N° 1 AAS (Air Armament School), Manby Lincolnshire, while L5761 suffered engine failure and crashed at Hawarden in November 1940 and was written off. Such losses were made good by an infusion of Battle tugs from other OTUs — L5773 flew in from N° 55 OTU, Aston Down, and L5631 and L5714 from N° 56 OTU, Sutton Bridge. The rump soldiered on and moved with N° 57 OTU to Eshott in November 1942 where they took on strength Battle L5625 from N° 54 OTU, Charterhall (Berwick) being only struck off charge in July 1943, exactly a year before all remaining RAF Battles in the UK were finally declared irrevocably obsolete.

The lack of, and poverty in, front gun instruction, produced a breed of pilots who basically were bad shots unable to assess range, a fact glossed over by the Spitfire's 'shot-gun spread' as favoured by Dowding, and many squadron commanders faced with taking 'sprogs' on ops. due to recent heavy losses. Even Johnny Johnson had problems with judgement of distance. Inevitably the more successful pilots were those who followed the simple rule: 'The closer you get the greater the chance of success', that is the closing range was alright, even if the opening range was

way out! Additionally most 'aces' preferred point-harmonisation of guns and in their Spitfire IIBs, VBs and VCs fired .303 machine guns and 20mm cannon together always. One was only in a firing position for a fraction of a second and the more one could squirt in the better! In expert hands the devastating Hispano cannon could cut a big fat FW190 and the leaner Me109 to bits! 'That the Battle of Britain was won with just the .303 guns — pea shooters really — had never ceased to amaze me' thus wrote Johnny Johnson half a century later.

Such was the theory of practicalities finding its way back to N° 7 OTU. To implement it was another matter. One can visualise F/Lt Flemmons's frustrations when seen against the pressures by the Ministry of Aircraft Production in August 1940 to evict N° 7 OTU from Hawarden, and the atrocious weather of autumn/winter 1940-41 which made the aerodrome unserviceable and for seven months, until it had dried out, saw N° 7 OTU scattered throughout the land to Speke, Cranage, Sealand (a case of 'out of the frying-pan into the fire'), Tern Hill and Wrexham (the latter still under construction).

For those fortunate few able to take to the air for gunnery practice the first stop was the air-to-ground range at Talacre Warren. Only when considered proficient would they graduate to air-to-air firing on the 'range' out to sea. Here F/Sgt McNaughton was in charge. Having to pick up the day's firing programme from the Flight Office he had the doubtful privilege of not being billeted locally in comfortable digs, but travelled daily to and from the aerodrome in the ambulance that took up an ominous 'ready' position by Lifeboat Cottage, geared to any emergency.

There were many accidents, several of them fatal. The representative list at the end of Chapter 7 only scratches the surface. Point of Ayr was literally a cross-roads for air traffic without the benefit of traffic lights! The Dee estuary was a 'High Activity' low flying area, especially at its eastern end where the circuits of three aerodromes and one SLG overlapped. Out towards Hilbre it became N° 7 OTU's preferred 'combat' area, occasionally spilling up the Vale of Clwyd. Out to sea the flying circles of N° 7 OTU's target-towers were transected by N° 6 AACU's motley collection of Battles, Lysanders, Leopard Moths and Dominies as they trundled up and down the coast calibrating artillery, AA guns, searchlights and, later, radar. Overflying the whole were Hooton's coastal patrols and convoy escorts and a steady stream of aircraft from Ferry Pools and bomber OTUs which used Point of Ayr as a convenient landfall and departure point. Scything through the lot at full throttle would race the Spitfires, Mosquitos and Tomahawks intent on the destruction of Talacre's ground targets. It would be interesting to discover how the CHL radar station at Gwaunysgor, to say nothing of the Royal Observer Corps posts at Hoylake, Halkyn, Mostyn and Rhyl, coped with so much local traffic!

Local inhabitants quickly became immune to the chatter of machine guns and the roar of Merlin, Griffon, Mercury and Pratt & Whitney engines. It was only when a rain of spent cartridge casings fell in unaccustomed places or the distinctive throb of a Jumo or Daimler-Benz engine intruded into the awareness of the mind did one realise that something untoward was amiss and glance upwards. So recalls Glyn Williams of Holywell, who as a youngster of eleven was busy picking mushrooms on his farm on the Dee estuary near Bagillt: 'When we heard the familiar rat-tat-tat of machine guns we did not bother looking up as we were accustomed to fighter planes firing at cone-shaped targets towed by Tiger Moth biplanes. However, when we eventually looked up we noticed to our horror that neither aircraft was towing a target and instead of the familiar RAF roundels one of the planes had the feared and dreaded black cross. We dropped our mushrooms and fled home. I have since regretted that we did not stay and watch the dog fight, but we assumed that our fighter won'. The same incident is also remembered by Richard Hughes save that the scenario has now shifted to over Talacre: 'Once as I walked along Abbey Drive I was startled by the pinging of cartridge cases and clips dropping around me. Overhead a German bomber was being attacked by a Spitfire. It was eventually forced down near Abergele'.

The incident may be pin-pointed exactly from official records. The German bomber was a Dornier Do215 reconnaissance plane, possibly of *4/AufkJärungsgruppe Ob.d.L.* — a more precise identification cannot be made since it crashed into the sea (variously at Rhyl, Abergele or off Anglesey). On Wednesday, 18 September 1940, the main enemy activity was centred on London but with substantial raids made early evening on Liverpool. Since the pounding of 28–31 August 1940 the port was averaging a raid every other night, often short and sharp, some reconnaissance, some mine-laying in Liverpool Bay. The raid of 18 September is noted in folk memory for direct hits scored on Walton Gaol. Twenty-one bodies were recovered. The Governor insisted that there should be 22 prisoners, and one was thought to have escaped. He hadn't. His body was found under the rubble in 1951, eleven years later!

There was no alert on Deeside that evening, but at about 1915hrs information was received from Observer Corps centres at Shrewsbury and Wrexham that a formation of enemy aircraft was making for Liverpool. Three Spitfires of Hawarden's 'Battle Flight', in what turned out to be the last of their spectacular operational sorties, were scrambled to intercept them. With the exception of the Spitfires on detachment at Ringway from 'B' Flight N° 64 Squadron, Leconfield (Yorkshire), the unofficial *ad hoc* flight at N° 7 OTU, armed, fuelled and at stand-by after a day's flying, was the only day defence of Merseyside. They were crewed in rota by the OTU's instructors most of whom had combat experience. The enemy aircraft were caught as they turned for home. S/Ldr J. S. McLean engaged a Do17 reconnaissance plane at 16,000ft, silencing the rear gunner, but then being forced to break off the engagement having exhausted his ammunition. Sgt J. F. Armitage, a veteran of N° 242 Squadron at Biggin Hill and Coltishall, harried a Ju88 until he lost sight of it in the gathering gloom. P/O G. F. Brotchie engaged, pursued and finally shot down the Do215. His rather incoherent Combat Report reads as follows:

I have the honour to report that on the evening of the 18th September, whilst flying Spitfire N° (N)3235, I engaged and destroyed one enemy aircraft, a Dornier 215. I took off with my section on patrol at 1930hrs. Shortly after taking off my N° 2 had to return to the aerodrome with engine trouble. I continued to climb to a height of 10,000ft and spotted some AA fire over Liverpool. I then received a message from control to the effect that bandits were reported over Liverpool at 8,000ft. I climbed towards Liverpool and almost immediately received a message that there was a bandit over base at 8,000ft. I turned again towards base and received a message that there were eight bandits at various heights. It was just after this message that I sighted the enemy aircraft at about 20,000ft, some distance apart. flying south over Hoylake. My N° 3 broke off and chased one and I went after the other.

I chased the enemy aircraft down the coast of Wales, climbing all the time. At about 20,000ft I closed on the aircraft. At 250 yards I was sitting on its tail but, on the point of opening fire, the enemy aircraft spotted me and dived steeply towards the ground. I followed down on its tail, firing about four long bursts. Its rear gunner only replied with one burst. Its dive gradually got steeper and at about 4,000ft it dived through some low cloud almost vertically. I eased out of my dive slightly and followed him down through the cloud just in time to see him dive into the sea off the coast of Anglesey. No flames were seen to come from the machine so I judged it to be either out of control or that the pilot had been killed. Speed at the time he entered cloud was at least 350mph. As it was now dark I climbed back over the clouds and returned to the aerodrome.

Spitfire N3235 would come to a more inglorious end when it made a forced landing at Carmel, near Holywell on 21 October 1940, bursting into flames and killing its pilot, Sgt Stanley Smith.

The latter had taken off from N° 7 OTU Hawarden at i7i5hrs for an hour's dogfighting practice with another Spitfire. Both Osborne Jones, farmer, of Highbrook, Carmel, and ex-Police Inspector W. J. Parry, who was at the Holway Farm at the time, vividly recalled subsequent events. Their evidence was corroborated by Sgt A. L. Hughes of N° 21 MU Sub-Depôt at Grange Quarry, Holywell. Whilst manoeuvring over Gorsedd, N3235 was seen to break away eastwards, with smoke pouring from the starboard side of the engine cowling/fuselage.

The Spitfire described a huge circle to port, gradually losing altitude. As Osborne Jones recalled, 'The engine appeared to be out of action as I saw the propellor going round quite slowly'. The significance of this was not lost upon Sgt Lewis: 'Suddenly it stalled and struck the ground. It ripped along the ground for about 30 yards, crashing through a hedge and then striking a large tree. It immediately burst into flames'.

The three men were already running across the fields to

the aircraft. The first on the scene plunged into the burning wreckage to drag away the body of the pilot slumped limply against the trunk of the tree. Sgt Hughes recalled this act of heroism: 'They had dragged his body about six or seven yards when the petrol tanks exploded. How they ever survived I will never know. I felt the air pressure and almost stopped running as the blast of the explosion hit me. But they were not deterred, and whilst I got my breath back, they carried on dragging him until satisfied he was no longer in danger of being burnt. As it was the pilot had severe head injuries and lower limbs burnt. The area reeked of high octane fuel, the stench mingling with the sweet smell of roasting turnips, ploughed up as the aircraft careered down the field'. Holywell police, doctors and AFS were quickly on the scene. It was adjudged that Sgt Smithson had been killed instantly. The N° 21 MU ambulance conveyed the body to the old Holywell Workhouse mortuary.

The use of the ground targets at Talacre, whether by 'learners' from fighter OTUs or operational fliers from squadrons 'resting' in N° 9 Group 'back area', was not without attendant problems, occasioned largely by the difficult terrain on Talacre's landward approach. Firing was by one or more aircraft who were expected to fly level at 200 yards, closing to 150ft. Such parameters at Talacre meant that there was little leeway for error. Thus on 26 July 1943 the pilot of Spitfire V, P7692, from N° 61 OTU Rednal, stood no chance at all when he screamed down the hill from Gwesbyr and ploughed straight through his target on top of the 35ft dunes, to belly-flop amidst the anti-invasion larch poles and wire on the seaward side of Talacre's minefield. These poles in their own right could catch inexperienced pilots unawares as they crested the dunes. On 5 February 1943 a North American Mustang, AP216, from N° 41 OTU, was virtually ripped to pieces coming off the ground targets and crashed into deep water below the Low Water Mark, killing its pilot. This was the first accident on the range by a N° 41 OTU aircraft since that unit had moved into RAF Hawarden from Andover on 14 November 1942.

If it wasn't the targets it could be the miniature desert storms raised as a procession of aircraft flew over an extensive apron of dunes only lightly anchored by marram grass. Such happened on 4 April 1943 to Spitfire I, X4425, again of N° 61 OTU, which, however, despite filters and intake being clogged with sand, did manage to stagger along the coast to find an unencumbered stretch of beach at Llandulas to make an almost perfect belly-landing. Denbighshire Civil Defence log records 'Fuselage, propeller and radiator badly damaged'. RAF Hawarden handled the recovery.

A greater hazard than sand were birds, not just the thousands of seagulls, but land birds such as skylarks and meadow pipits nesting in the dunes and rough grass, and the terns that favoured the shingle banks. This does not include the hundred plus species of migratory birds that persisted in using this favoured staging post despite Ministry of Defence warning notices and red flags! Particularly nasty was the fate of Mustang AG585 of N° 41 OTU on 28 February 1943. Coming off the range P/O E. W. G. Verley smashed into a rising wall of panic-stricken seagulls. With perspex shattered and flying instruments, including the air-speed indicator, badly damaged, the crippled plane managed to reach RAF Hawarden. But on turning to land the engine stalled and AG585 crashed outside the perimeter fence between the aerodrome and Hawarden village, and caught fire. The pilot, with multiple fractures to limbs, head and chest and badly burnt, was pulled from his blazing aircraft by two young ATC cadets of N° 928 (Hawarden County School) Flight, and a merchant seaman on shore leave. Their heroism was to no avail; P/O Verley died from his injuries the following day. He lies buried in Hawarden Cemetery.

Behind every accident at Talacre there has to be a cause, be it snowstorm, icing up, engine failure, mid-air collision or hitting obstacles on the ground and so on. But even the most superficial perusal of the accident data-base held by the RAF Museum and the AHB, however compromised its overall integrity, throws up many cases that have not been fully explained. Thus between 19 June 1940 (two days after their arrival) and 14 October 1942 (three weeks before their departure) some 22 Spitfires of N°s 7 and 57 OTU Hawarden dived lemming-like into the Irish Sea and Dee estuary or onto sand banks and mud flats exposed at low tide. This seemingly set a precedent which other OTUs and operational squadrons tried hard to emulate!

Away from the ground targets at Talacre the sea area off Point of Ayr was the air-to-air gunnery range. Two main types of aerial target were used — the 'flag', a flat length of canvas towed vertically or horizontally, and the 'drogue', like an overgrown windsock. Both would approximately match the dimensions of an enemy bomber or fighter fuselage. They would be streamed out behind a target tug on about 1,000ft of Bowden cable, adjudged sufficient a safety margin! Tugs flew at varying heights, usually between 1,500–2,000ft, along the coast between Mostyn and Abergele or diffidently described large circles or figures of eight over Liverpool Bay, anything as long as they did not put themselves in direct line of fire and were comfortably clear of the lunatics streaking off the dune targets 1,000ft below them. Firing commenced on a hand signal from the target-tug operator/observer. Again, pilots were aiming ideally to dive onto the drogue at not less than 200 yards and close to 150ft before opening fire. Easier said than done. Results, especially when ciné-camera guns were used, showed that few pilots could bring to bear for the vital split-second that accurate perception of distance, height, angle, speed, attitude of plane etc. which makes for the born marksman.

The more modern target tugs — Lysanders, Martinets and redundant Battles and Defiants could carry up to three targets. Units like N° 61 OTU, Rednal, and N° 60 OTU, High Ercall, had their own tugs which would fly out to Talacre for the morning or afternoon session. The ammunition of each aircraft briefed for firing practice would be smeared with a distinctively coloured mastic type paint prior to loading. Theoretically the paint would show clearly around shot holes in the drogue or 'flag'. When practice was complete the drogue would be dropped at the blockhouse in Talacre's 'Hidden Valley' and the performance of a particular pilot estimated. Pilots would have had something like 200 rounds of ammunition to literally make their mark! Such, then, was the simple theory behind air-to-air firing. But in practice things inevitably went badly wrong — engines failing, guns refusing to work, targets accidentally being shot away, the weather, especially low cloud a sea mist, interfering, and either target tug or 'customer' failing to meet up for one reason or another.

N° 61 OTU, Rednal, seemed to be just as unfortunate with its in-house target tugs at Talacre as with its Spitfires. On 3 April 1943 it lost Martinet HP263 due to engine failure over the range. It did manage to land safely on the Low Water Mark with a badly shaken crew. Slightly further up the beach, amidst the anti-invasion defences, and they would have been in trouble. This was in the middle of quite a flurry of forced landings in the area. As noted above, the following day Spitfire X4425 came to grief. Three days earlier, on 31 March, an Airspeed Oxford of N° 6 AACU, Wrexham, had suffered a broken propellor whilst calibrating guns at Kinmel but made a safe landing on the beach 150 yards north of the erstwhile 'Sunny Vale Holiday Camp'. On 26 March Anson N5382 of N° 3 (O)AFU, Halfpenny Green, ditched with engine failure during a NAVEX, just 'north of Rhyl' according to the local Civil Defence log; a lot further out to sea if AHB records are to be credited.

Four months later, on 15 August 1943 Rednal lost another Martinet at Talacre. JN294 stalled at low altitude whilst trying to drop its drogue at the blockhouse. It belly-landed in almost exactly the same spot as HP263; again the crew managed to wade to safety. More fortunate was the unidentified Martinet tug which took off from Rednal for Talacre on 24 July 1944 to work with a flight of eight Spitfires from N° 61 OTU. Whilst awaiting their turn to fire the Spitfires had been briefed to work individually or in pairs at aerobatics and dogfighting tactics out over the Dee. Eventually P/O A. J. Goldman (RCAF) in a Spitfire V, BM113, a fighter-bomber conversion with wings stiffened to take bomb racks, was called to the range. He broke and dived in approved fashion at the drogue, closing to the stipulated 150ft but then failed to break off at the apposite moment and ploughed straight through the drogue and cable. He lost control and plunged into the deep water of the Welsh channel at the mouth of the Dee. The pilot of the Martinet regained control of his aircraft, aborted the exercise and made it safely back to Rednal. No trace of P/O Goldman was found, despite an intensive air and sea search. He was posted 'Missing, presumed dead'. The subsequent Court of Inquiry ruled 'Pilot error of judgement'.

Was it coincidence that six months later the sea began to yield up its dead? On 9 February 1945 the Denbighshire Civil Defence log briefly recorded: 'Human foot in a long woollen stocking and inside a shoe similar to RAF issue, found on the shore at Kinmel Bay'. Four weeks later, on 2 March 1945, a badly decomposed body of an airman was washed ashore at Abergele. He was buried as 'An Unidentified Airman of the Second World war' in the Imperial War Graves Cemetery at Blacon, Chester. Was it P/O Goldman at long last laid to rest?

N° 60 OTU's Mosquitos from High Ercall added a new dimension to the otherwise monotonous recital of Spitfires,

Mustangs and Martinets lost over Point of Ayr. There were not all that many since, once the rudiments of air-to-air firing had been mastered during daylight hours, would-be night-intruders transferred to the Banks Range in the Ribble estuary or used ranges along the lower Severn and Bristol Channel. Here, as already hinted, the more spectacular accidents would occur. Magnificent flying machine as it was, under certain conditions e.g. with one engine failed, the Mosquito was more than an inexperienced pilot could handle. One only has to recall Mosquito HJ816 which came to grief on Banks Range on 10 September 1944. When pulling out of a steep attacking dive the aircraft started to break up and the starboard wing folded! Both crew were killed.

There was nothing so spectacular over Talacre; 'loss of control' and 'engine failure' were normally held to blame. Mosquito DZ751 was lost on 28 December 1943 whilst trying to make an emergency landing at Newton, near Hoylake, on the Wirral bank of the Dee estuary. Both crew were killed — a 'Black Tuesday', indeed, a 'Black Christmas', as N° 60 OTU lost two further aircraft that same day! On 14 February 1944 Mosquito HX863 broke off its attack, described a huge circle to port losing height all the while and crashed into the sea at Prestatyn, not quite making the Golf Course which for so long had served almost as a relief landing ground to RAF Talacre! The precedent had been set way back on 19 October 1941 when Spitfire X4033, of N° 131 Squadron, Atcham, crash landed there whilst on 'air firing duty'.

When HX967 was lost whilst on the Talacre range on 3 February 1945 an overheated engine which had to be shut down was possibly to blame. Gradually losing height the pilot finally ditched in the sea off Rhos-on-Sea. Official RAF records and Denbighshire Civil Defence log differ in detail as to the actual crash. The former have HX967 as ditching 'off the Caernarvonshire coast' and both crew killed, drowning before rescue boats could reach them, with their dinghy only 50 yards away but being carried ever further by the wind. But it is doubtful if the RAF were familiar with the historical configuration of the county of Caernarfon which gave it two detached portions — the Creuddyn Peninsula and (until 1922) Llysfaen parish in Denbighshire. The Civil Defence log has the ditching 200 yards off the end of Rhos-on-Sea pier, the pilot killed and navigator injured and both recovered by a fishing boat manned by Mr H. Large, Colwyn Bay and the Menai ASR launch.

Within the present corpus of aviation history the dense aerial activity over and around the Point of Ayr and the high incident rate stemming therefrom perhaps throws up no more curious a set of coincidences than the magnetic, yet benevolent, influence exerted by a single field up in the hills behind the Talacre gunnery range — 'benevolent' in that no lives were lost.

On Saturday morning, 5 July 1941, three Spitfire Is of N° 57 OTU's detachment at RAF Speke set off for the Talacre range. RAF Hawarden was still largely unserviceable after a bad winter and wet spring, hence N° 57 OTU dispersed to the four winds. Only two days previously it had lost two Spitfires on Ruabon Mountain — they had been operating out of RAF Wrexham for several months before that station was handed over by the contractors! As the section crossed the Dee estuary at Heswall X4274 developed engine problems. Approaching the hills between Gronant and Llanasa the engine cut out completely and the Spitfire's Polish pilot, F/Sgt Czezowski, had no option other than to attempt an emergency landing. But what made him pick Sheep Pens Field belonging to Kelston Farm? The landing was near enough perfect save that the undercarriage collapsed on the third bounce. F/Sgt Czezowski was able to walk away and raise the alarm. X4274 was recovered and flew again.

It would be the very same field that at about 1200hrs on 9 December 1943 an Airspeed Oxford, ED128, of N° 6 OTU (Coastal Command), Silloth (Cumberland), with a crew of two aboard, chose to make a forced landing. It was on a delivery flight to N° 32 MU, St Athan (Glamorgan), for electronics updating. Several other Oxfords were in transit at the same time. From Solway Firth the Point of Ayr was the final landfall before turning on the last leg for South Wales.

As ED128 crossed the West Hoyle Bank, its starboard engine packed up (officially problems with the inlet valve!). The pilot, F/Sgt H. N. Wash, contemplated trying to reach Hawarden, but he was losing height too quickly. Bryn Glas (= green hill), a 700ft saddle between Gronant and Lianasa, beckoned. Sloping fields look deceptively flat from the air — but the pilot had little choice. Choosing the second largest field — the first had a string of high tension cables running across it — he made a near perfect a belly-landing and skidded to a halt on the exact spot where Spitfire X4274 had landed. F/Sgt Wash was shaken otherwise uninjured, but his Canadian radio operator was badly gashed about the head. The Home Guard were quickly on the scene. After a check-up at the Military Hospital, Prestatyn, F/Sgt Wash proceeded to St Athan by train. ED128 was recovered, patched up and served with N° 1 TTU (Torpedo Training Unit), N° 50 OTU and N° 131 OTU before ending up with N° 540 Squadron, a photographic reconnaissance unit that had transferred from RAF Benson to Coulommiers (A.58), France, in March 1945. On 30 April 1945 Airspeed Oxford ED128 made its final belly-landing near Varreddes, France, again with starboard engine trouble!

These two aircraft, X4274 and ED128, found the same field in daylight. But the first plane to actually use it and establish a precedent was a Whitley IV of N° 51 Squadron, Dishforth (Yorkshire), which touched down on Bryn Glas in low cloud and blanket fog at 0500hrs on the night of 21/22 May 1940. Whitley K9038 had been delivered to the RAF in July 1939. After a short spell at N° 1 AAS (Air Armament School) at Manby, Lincolnshire, it was transferred in November of that year to N° 51 Squadron. On that eventful night in May 1940, with P/O Peter Rutter in the pilot's seat, K9038 had taken off at 2015hrs to raid the marshalling yard at Krefeld, north of Düsseldorf. At 0100hrs, duty done, they turned for home. Crossing the Channel they found the whole of south-east England under a blanket of fog. Radio trouble meant that they could not raise a navigational fix. The Whitley continued to fly a northwesterly course, but things were becoming desperate. They had been airborne for over eight hours and fuel was getting low — a Whitley's range was some 1,500 miles, about nine hours flying time.

Suddenly, some fifteen minutes after nosing round a red navigational beacon (which may have been Shawbury's 'lighthouse') and drawing no response, a slice of hillside loomed through the murk and mist. They slowly closed with it, there being no alternative but to try and make an emergency landing, bad enough in daylight but at night! The crew had refused to bale out. Landing lights picked out the high tension wires; these were leap-frogged with a touch of throttle and the Whitley slowly sank onto Sheep Pens Field and, with brakes hard on, came to rest in one piece but tilted at an acute angle. Time 0500hrs; the crew had been airborne 8hrs 50mins! A cursory examination showed that they had not burst a tyre but were at a cant on a slope — and also that they had landed with a couple of hang ups', in other words there were two 500lb bombs still in the racks!

Within an hour the fog had begun to lift. The slow process of rescue began by following phone wires to Golden Grove, the Elizabethan manor house nearby. A startled household was awoken at 0630hrs. Dishforth was contacted and told that the crew were uninjured and the Whitley undamaged. Help was on the way. At about 0830hrs the Chief Flying Instructor from N° 5 FTS Sealand reconnoitred the site in his yellow Miles Master and vanished. At 1200hrs an RAF van arrived from Dishforth complete with Cpl. Lawrence Elliott of the Whitley's regular ground crew, an armourer and a Rolls-Royce engineer from Armstrong Whitworth's Baginton factory who just happened to be at Dishforth. They set about defusing and removing the bombs and checking the aircraft which was eventually pronounced airworthy. An Army guard was provided by the Royal Corps of Signals based at one of the Prestatyn holiday camps. They also busied themselves filling in a ditch and removing a couple of hedges to give a clear run of some 1,000 yards for an attempted take off the following day.

The next morning the Whitley was lightened by removing guns and ammunition and non-essential equipment. The Rolls-Royce engineer tuned the two engines for maximum boost. Men from the North Wales Power Company stood by to cut off electricty and lower the high-tension cables. Petrol arrived from RAF Sealand in cans, fifty gallons to each engine, which was deemed sufficient to get the aircraft airborne and to Sealand for refuelling. At 1645hrs an apprehensive but loyal crew climbed into the shell of their aircraft. Engines were started. K9038 taxied as far up Sheep Pens Field as possible and turned. Brakes hard on, throttles opened wide, brakes off — and the Whitley leapt forward along the canting slope, a bumpy run of about thirty seconds — and was airborne, clearing the trees by a few feet, and out over Kelston Farm and Talacre Schools. A cheer from the huge crowd of onlookers, a final circuit, and on to Sealand for refuelling. At 1950hrs Whitley K9038 took off again for Dishforth. Mission accomplished, albeit 40 hours behind schedule!

This gentle dalliance on the Clwydian Range was virtually the last operational sally by K9038. By the end of May No 51 Squadron had phased out its Mark IVs and re-equipped with the Whitley Mark V, with its more powerful 1,145hp Rolls-Royce Merlin X engines, a slightly longer fuselage, and re-designed tail fins. K9038 was put out to

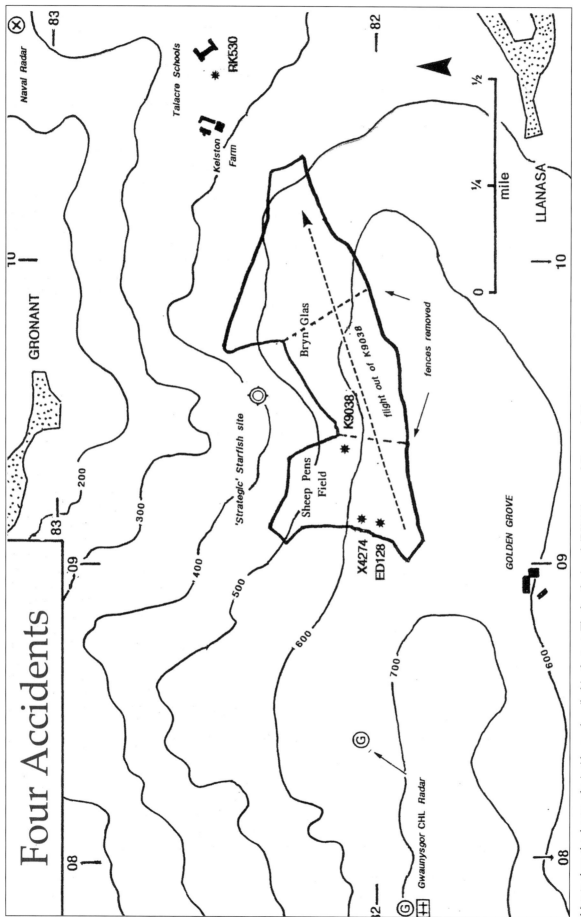

Map to show the chapter of coincidences described in the text. The fourth aircraft (RK530) a naval Barracuda V, came to grief on a ferry flight on 22 November 1945.

grass, first a couple of weeks with Nº 10 OTU at Abingdon (Berkshire), and then with Nº 19 OTU at Kinloss (Morayshire). Here on 5 August 1940 it crashed again, undershooting on approach, drifting off line and collapsing its undercarriage. However, it was repaired and thence survived unscathed until being honourably discharged on 1 December 1943.

As if, three aeroplanes in one field were not concidence enough, the fate of a Whitley V, BD204, came close to making it 'straight flush'. On Monday, 17 May 1943, piloted by Sgt J. W. Clarke, BD204 was on a NAVEX from Nº 24 OTU, Honeybourne (Wiltshire). Approaching the Irish Sea and Point of Ayr, their departure point for the Isle of Man, Sgt Clarke was in something of a dilemma. His port engine was giving high and fluctuating radiator temperature readings. However, a decision was made for him. The engine cut and at 1715hrs BD204 splashed down on the mudflats at Point of Ayr Colliery. Didn't they know about Sheep Pens Field? A concealed gutter made for a hefty impact, Sgt Clarke sustaining a fractured skull. The rest of the crew waded ashore. Because it would become an obstacle to shipping as the tide turned, the Whitley was quickly winched onto dry land by surface workers at the colliery.

Obviously, while Nº 34 MU from Monkmoor had salvaged essentials such as engines, instruments, guns etc. the greater part of the fuselage had been left on the water's edge to be 'picked over' by local entrepreneurs. In March 1990, amidst renewed media publicity surrounding the quasi-50th anniversary of the crash of ED128 and the meeting up of surviving air- and ground-crews, the spotlight happened to focus on an ancient, improvised goat shed on a farm at Ffynnongroyw. It still boasted a faded RAF roundel and the 'Y' of Nº 24 OTU's 'TY' code letters — which is how part of the fuselage of Whitley V BD204 today rests on deposit at the Midland Air Museum, Baginton (otherwise Coventry Airport).

The disbanding of Nº 58 OTU, Hawarden, in July 1945, the departure of Nº 24 EFTS from Sealand in March 1945, and the closure of the Talacre ranges, moves precipitated by the cessation of hostilities, put an end almost overnight to the great aerial circus that for six years had performed daily over the Point of Ayr. But where ever peacetime RAF units continued to use Dee estuary air space for training it was perhaps inevitable that its mudbanks and the gently sloping beaches at Gronant and Talacre should still attract the odd involuntary caller.

One of the last so recorded was a Spitfire P.22 of the redesigned type — with rear view bubble-hood and cut-down rear fuselage — that between 1946–51 was the major aircraft in service with the Royal Auxiliary Air Force (RAuxAF). PK385 had been taken on strength by Nº 610 (County of Chester) Squadron, Hooton Park, in September 1949. On Sunday, 21 May 1950, with 25-year old P/O Kenneth John Evans, Wallasey, at the controls, it had taken off on aerobatics duty off the Point of Ayr. Between Rhyl and Prestatyn, according to eye-witnesses, its engine began to falter. At about 50ft above the deck the Spitfire screamed between sand-dunes and the sea towards Gronant, began to climb, but suddenly turned on to its back, performed a

double-somersault and plunged nose-first into the wet sand near the Low Water Mark. P/O Evans was killed instantly. He had made no attempt to crash-land, possibly because of a number of children playing on the sand but more probably because of the larch poles, planted ten years previously as an anti-invasion measure, still standing proud. Time, approximately 11.10hrs. Twenty minutes later, after his tiny office had been inundated by emergency telephone calls, P.C. Tom Hughes arrived on the scene with ropes and tools borrowed from the Mitford Garage, Ty'nymorfa, to find a crowd of onlookers standing gawping at the crumpled wreckage now half submerged by the rapidly advancing tide. The dead pilot had just been cut free from the cockpit by Richard Nichols, a Dee & Clwyd Rivers Board worker, who had waded out to the wreckage with a couple of week-enders. They carried the broken body over the dunes to the long abandoned blockhouse on the former firing range, whence it was conveyed to the mortuary in Prestatyn and later to RAF Sealand where the inquest preliminaries were held the next day.

5. Bay watch

Decoy sites as described in Chapter 2 were passive elements in the air defence of this country, but, as seen, were shrouded by an impenetrable cloak of secrecy. Playing a more active role, but equally cloak and dagger, was Radio Direction Finding (RDF), a 'cover' name given to British pioneer efforts in the the electronic scanning of air space from 1935 but since 14 July 1943, officially recognised as RADAR an acronym for *RA*dio aid for *D*etection *A*nd *R*anging, a term in use in the USA since 1940. Radar stations rarely figure in regional aviation histories, or excite the attention of local historians and/or local history societies generally. This is due (a) to the aura of secrecy that theoretically cloaked such establishments during the Second World War when parenting aerodrome ORBs were not permitted to mention the existence of their dependent AMES, and (b) the paucity of official records pertaining to individual sites although with the creation of Nº 60 (Signals) Group ORBs were started for the units under their control. With the cessation of hostilities most radar station ORBs were destroyed either on security grounds or simply to lessen the pressure on shelf space at the PRO. Representative documents, contents usually leaving much to be desired, were retained, but on a seemingly haphazard basis, with signficant dates and events contributing to the preservation lottery. It goes without saying that record repositories in Wales itself have turned out to be completely barren on the subject. This, if no other reason, has prompted the writing of this particular chapter.

A useful starting point are the 'period' maps found in most official publications dealing with wartime radar. They have been redrawn here for the area ultimately the responsibility of N⁰ 9 Group Fighter Command — the North-west, Irish Sea approaches to Liverpool and Belfast, and north and mid-Wales. The first shows radar stations added to the original twenty of the East Coast CH Chain. in the period September 1939–July 1940, the run up to the Battle of Britain. Three CHLs only in our area — Glenarm, Cregneash, and Prestatyn, the latter name chosen because officialdom could not get its tongue around 'Gwaunysgor'. The second map overleaf shows the Home Chain at ostensibly 'maximum' development in March 1945. Nationally this is to ignore many stations which had closed by this arbitrary date. The radar chain would actually have been at its greatest extent in late 1942. Nevertheless within N⁰ 9 Group's fighting area three stations have increased to sixteen, but, as just hinted, this does not give a true picture as some stations shown were already non-operational and on 'Care & Maintenance' e.g. Rhuddlan and Prestatyn. Not one is mapped as part of the Radar Research and Development scene 1946–50, although three former GCI stations — Hack Green, Trewen Sands (both 'Readiness') and St Annes ('Ops') — will be resuscitated as part of the ROTOR control and reporting plan in 1954–8 in the wake of the Korean War while Prestatyn would re-emerge as a CHEL ('Ops') in early 1958. Additionally there were many radar stations that were short lived, usually because of insuperable technical problems or in a enforced gradual 'wind down' to meet the demand for technicians and operators to man new radar units abroad, particualrly in the run-up to, and after, D-Day. An attempt has been made therefore to show on a third map (page 71), as far as present state of knowledge allows, all known radar stations that operated within our area, including Army and Navy establishments.

This map does not include the inter-Service experimental radio/radar stations, often short lived, very secret and extremely mobile, so rarely leaving physical traces of their presence. These experimental stations, with their locations and path lines plotted cartographically (see map, right), were refugees from the south coast where war-time operational conditions did not lend themselves to relatively long term experimental projects, in this particular case the development of very short wave and centimetric radar, and the impact made by reflection from sea and land, physical obstacles and varying atmospheric conditions. It was the striking increases in the range of CH and CHL stations on the Welsh coast and elsewhere observed in the summers of 1940 and 1941 which prompted a renewed attack on the problem of long-rage radio waves/radar, basically signals beyond the optical horizon on wavelengths of about 9, 6 and 3cm.

Full time operation of the first of the 9cm measuring circuits (Fishguard–Aberdaron) started in July, 1943, following earlier ASE/SRDE/GEC-supervised preliminary trials in May and June. One also notes 11–16 May, 1942, 'Sea III', shore to ship experiments, over a path of ¹/2–40 miles, centred upon Douglas where the Admiralty had *inter alia* the naval Radar Training School. 'Sea IV' was a longer leg of some 103–114 miles between Snowdon (3,480ft) and the Mourne Mountains (980ft), Co. Down. There was a second station lower down the slopes of Snowdon at 1,175ft, but its exact location has not yet been ascertained. The first 'short period trial' took place 1–12 June 1942, testing effects of atmospheric absorption and fading signals and weather dependence for longer optical paths. Experiments along the other Irish Sea paths as mapped lasted into 1946. That from Fishguard across Cardigan Bay was 57 miles in length. 'Fishguard' is an omnibus term covering high and low transmitters at Garn-Fawr (540ft OD) and Strumble Head (901ft OD) 'Aberdaron' covers receivers at Rhiw (825ft OD) and Aberdaron (951ft OD). Portpatrick's receiver was at 93ft OD, but also included one at Knockharnahan at 375ft. The path between here and Fishguard was 200 miles. Four foot parabolic dishes were used for all transmissions and receivers; for secrecy these were mounted within their respective 'stations' behind large hessian covered 'windows'.

Rhiw radar station still exists, courting controversy in November 1995 and making headlines in the Welsh press — 'Villagers' radar rage' — when, after a six year planning wrangle, permission was finally granted for a £1 million upgrade of the 50-year old facility. Rhiw was essential to successful tracking operations on the integrated MoD missile range at Llanbedr, near Harlech, and at Aberporth, south of Aberystwyth. But, despite being a diversionary aerodrome to RAF Valley and its very long runway being much used by the Hawks of N⁰ 4 FTS for 'touch and goes', RAF Llanbedr has since closed (28 October 2004), the last Jindvik

CHL Station

GLENARM

CREGNEISH

PRESTATYN

Scale

50   0   50   100 Miles

CHL radar stations 1939–40 (Battle of Britain period).

Experimental centrometric radio/radar stations about the Irish Sea, 1942, some of which may have been co-located with conventional CH/CHL stations e.g. Kilkeel, Strumble Head and Llandudno.

flights taking place on 26 October 2004. Aberporth, too, has seen some changes. Part of the MoD aerodrome is currently being developed as a civil 'West Wales Airport', and the remainder as a 'cutting edge technology park', Parc Aberporth, with a focus on UAV and associated technologies. There might still be a role for Rhiw radar station. Only time will tell.

The former radar station on the summit of Snowdon still stands, having for some sixty years provided refreshments to climbers and train buffs. But there are moves to demolish it as an unfitting ornament to a National Park. But even in its present structural state, one suspects that it was a considerable advance, comfort-wise, on the horse-box trailer which at lower levels housed the experimental equipment in the preliminary trials! Owing to the problem of securing dedicated land lines, communication between stations was by radio-telephone, Army-led experimental circuits first being used across Cardigan Bay. All four possible links across Cardigan Bay became operational in November 1943, although transmission from the Fishguard high site (Gam-Fawr) had been running since July. On the 200 miles sea path Portpatrick's 9cm receiver started work at the end of August 1943, but apart from a short period in September, for some technical reasons no signals were received at all until March 1944, shortly before the installation of a higher station. On 3 cm all stations mapped were operational by July 1944 (June on the 200 miles sea path). The surveillance arc centred on Llandudno represents both a naval ship/U-boat watching and experimental presence at the RAF CHL station on Great Orme's Head, and a naval/TRE 3-cm MRU on the Morfa below, tackling another problem given to boffins — the adequate detection of dielectric coated signal-absorbing, snorkels (*Schnorchel*) of enemy submarines. This particular line of investigation, literally hunting for needles in a haystack, was never successfully concluded before the end of hostilities in Europe.

Reverting to 'main stream' radar, earliest developments in Flintshire must be seen against the background of events nationally. Radar is a technique for detecting and determining the position of aircraft by means of reflected radio waves. A practical demonstration of the potential of RDF as an 'early warning' instrument was given at Daventry on 26 February 1935 before, *inter alia*, one A. P. Rowe a young scientific officer, personal assistant to the Director of Scientific Research, Air Marshal Sir Hugh Dowding (later, July 1936–November 1940, C-in-C, Fighter Command). In October 1935, following the success of these experiments, the Air Staff approved the establishment of a chain of RDF stations along the east coast, every twenty miles or so between the Tyne and Southampton, twenty stations in all.

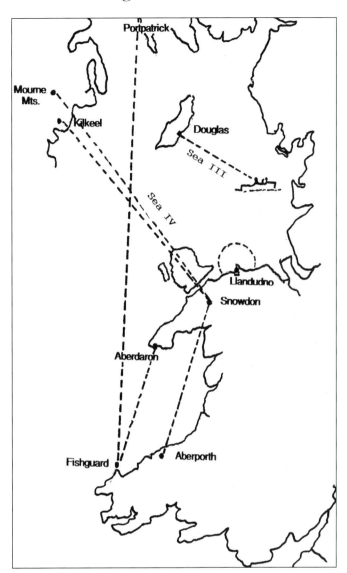

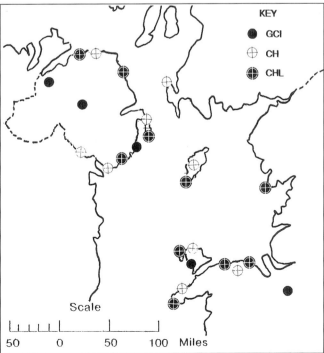

N° 9 Group Fighting Area – radar stations as of 1944–5.

This is the beginning of the 'Chain Home' (CH) with which every schoolboy is familiar. Improvements were quickly made to simple prototypes so that bearings and heights could be estimated at every station, avoiding cumbersome triangulation procedures

At the outset the CH reporting system, providing early warning and tracking of enemy aircraft was maintained and operated by technical personnel of Nº 60 (Signals) Group, Fighter Command, specially established 23 March 1940 (instead of a RDF Command) to control the Air Ministry Experimental Stations (AMES), otherwise radar stations. It immediately found itself overwhelmed. On top of some 21 existing CHs and 16 CHLs a huge backlog of new stations would soon accumulate. A string of CHLs between Liverpool and the Clyde had been mooted at an RDF policy meeting of 27 February 1940 and over the next three months

site surveys progressed at a rather leisurely pace to extend the West Coast Chain. While a site at Gwaunysgor above Prestatyn was surveyed in April 1940 to cover the approaches to Liverpool, priority seems to have been given to the North Channel (with a CHL at Glenarm and CH at North Cairn) and the Isle of Man (with CHL at Cregneash and CHs at Scarlett Point and Bride). The latter faced eastwards, watching for aircraft overflying northern England and would earn its keep during the devastating Belfast raids of April and May 1941. Following the fall of France, a decision by AMRE taken 27 May 1940, to provide 'priority a.s.a.p' cover for London, Straits of Dover to Humber, Lizard to Bristol Channel, Liverpool to Clyde, Humber to Shetland, meant that eight additional CHs and fifteen new CHLs, plus six 're-sites' Fighter Command permitting), had to be provided 'overnight' or even

TABLE OF RADAR STATIONS WITHIN Nº 9 GROUP FIGHTING AREA

Group✠	Station	Function	AMES No	Type+	Maps 1940	1945*	Remarks
9	ABERLERI	GCI	47G	8/?7/15			C&M 23.8.43
82	BALLYMARTIN	CHL	78A	2		*	C&M 6/44
82	BALLYWOODEN	GCI	29G	7		*	
9	BRIDE	CH		1			
9	BRYNGWRAN	ACH	66	1			To Nefyn 8/40
9	CASTELL MAWR	CHL	67	2			C&M 4/44
9	CREGNEASH	CHL		2/31/52	*	*	
9	DALBY	CH		1			Closed 5/44
9	FORMBY	CHL	64A	2			
82	GLENARM	CHL	2	2/31	*	*	
9	GREAT ORME HEAD	CHL	65B	2/41		*	
82	GREYSTONE	CH	61	1		*	
	GWESBYR	CD/CHL		NT273			Naval
9	HACK GREEN	GCI		7		*	
9	HAWCOAT	CHL		2		*	
82	KILKEEL	CH	78	1		*	C&M 4/44
9	NEFYN	CH	66	1		*	C&M 4/44
13	NORTH CAIRN	CH	60	1		*	
9	PENYBRYN	CHL	66A	2/57		*	C&M 4/44
9	PRESTATYN	CHL	65A	2/57	*	*	C&M 5.44
9	RHUDDLAN	CH	65	1		*	
82	RODDANS PORT	CHL	61A	2		*	C&M 4/44
9	Sᴛ ANNES	GCI	68G	7			C&M 23.8.43
9	Sᴛ BEES HEAD	CHL		2			
9	Sᴛ GEORGE	MRU		9 Mk 1			to Rhuddlan
9	SCARLETT POINT	CH		2			C&M 5/44
9	SOUTH STACK	CHL		76A			2/31/52 *
9	TANYBWLCH	CHL		2			to Castell Mawr
9	TOWER (BLACKPOOL)	CH	64	1			Closed 2/42
9	TREWEN SANDS	GCI	19G	8/7		*	C&M 4/44
9	WYLFA	CH		76 1		*	C&M 4/44

Notes: ✠Ultimate Fighter Command Group.

* 1939/40 and 1945 distribution maps in Jack Gough, *Watching the Skies* (HMSO, 1993), pp.25,27.

+ Type 1 Floodlit EW, 5–13m. Type 2 Beam EW, 1´m. Type 3 COL version of CHL primarily for overseas, but some sets used in UK. Type 7 GCI 'final' state, (the 'Happidrome'), 1´m. Type 8 GCI mobile, 1´m. Type 9 CH mobile, used while main station under construction, 7m. Type 15 GCI, mobile version of Type 7. Type 31 Medium power naval variant (NT 271) coastal watching radar, 10cm. Type 41 Low powered coastal watching radar, doubled for CD/CHL 1´m. Type 52 CHEL, higher powered surveillance radar derived naval NT277 set, 10cm. Type 57 CHL Derived naval NT277 set, 10cm.

Radar stations within Nº 9 Group Fighting Area, including Army and Navy establishments. Among GL units are Nº 4 HAAPC Ty Croes, Nº 7 HAAPC Tonfannau and Nº 4 RAF Regiment, AAPC Towyn

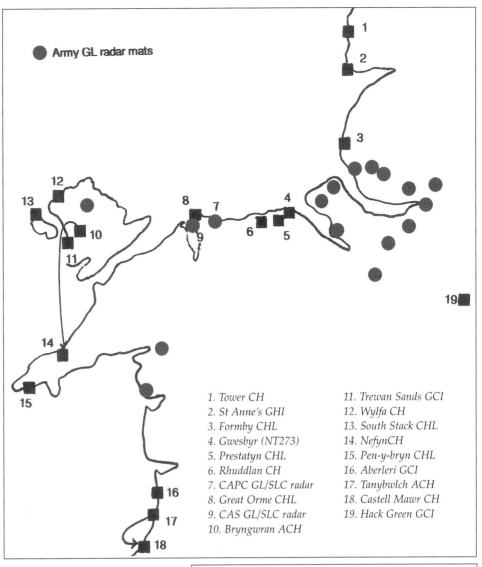

● Army GL radar mats

1. Tower CH
2. St Anne's GHI
3. Formby CHL
4. Gwesbyr (NT273)
5. Prestatyn CHL
6. Rhuddlan CH
7. CAPC GL/SLC radar
8. Great Orme CHL
9. CAS GL/SLC radar
10. Bryngwran ACH

11. Trewan Sands GCI
12. Wylfa CH
13. South Stack CHL
14. Nefyn CH
15. Pen-y-bryn CHL
16. Aberleri GCI
17. Tanybwlch ACH
18. Castell Mawr CH
19. Hack Green GCI

Right: Details of the horse-box trailer used in early experiments.

Below left: Interior of Rhiw receiving station. The 4ft dishes are mounted behind canvas covered windows left. Central recording table in right foreground.

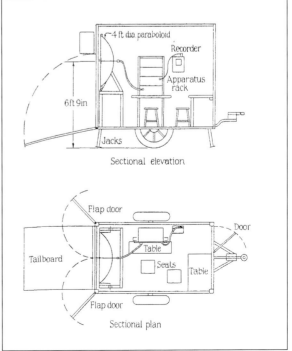

'yesterday'. According to surviving minutes extra cover was needed to meet expected enemy action from as far as Brest in northern France and the possibility of a German invasion of Eire. CH expansion in Northern Ireland was also needed to detect the Focke-Wulf 200-C ('Condor'), the four engined reconnaissance plane for a time known as 'the scourge of the Atlantic', an effective low-level destroyer of shipping, especially when co-operating with U-boats. With a range of 2,000+ miles the Condor, since the fall of France, could take off from Brest or Bordeaux, fly round the British Isles to the westward using the remote Atlantic islands of Rockall and St Kilda for fixes, land in Norway and make the return trip via Mull and along the west coast of Ireland, the following day.

In September 1940, before embarking on his second stint as AOC-in-C Coastal Command, AM Sir Philip Joubert as Assistant Chief of Air Staff (Radio), painted a bleak picture of the chaos facing Nº 60 (Signals) Group. Some 36 CH stations were up and running; the majority of those in the East Coast Chain were 'on final' but only on one wavelength and 'without a buried reserve'. In layman's language 'final' meant buildings were theoretically, if not in practice, protected or semi-sunk, Tx aerials were slung on 350ft steel towers with 240ft wooden Rx towers; range height and direction finding was possible, together with anti-jamming devices; all major equipment was duplicated, preferably underground. Four wavebands were to be used to lessen interference. In the event only two wavelengths were used, the 10–13.5 metres and one around 7 metres; the other two were abandoned. By contrast none of the 14 West Coast Chain were on 'final' but expansion was continuing. In the original January 1940 scheme ACHs were to be provided at each chosen site as the necessary first step in commissioning. A. F. Wilkins, formerly of the NPL, Slough, had surveyed a site on Morfa Rhuddlan in March 1940, but, owing to the dramatic turn of events on the continent and shortage of parts and materials, mobiles were now to be provided to bring forward operating dates; additionally an overstretched AMWD would not have to provide living quarters or mast footings. The ACHs would follow later. Against this chaotic background must be seen the appearance in the first week of June 1940 of a Mobile Radar Unit (MRU) fleetingly known to the records as St George

(Abergele), which held the fort for ten months until CH Rhuddlan (AMES 65) came on stream in April 1941. A 24-hour watch was set up immediately. More accurately the MRU staffed by a Warrant Officer and 22 ORs, RAF, was located in Kinmel at Glan-y-morfa (='edge of the marsh') farm (military Grid Ref. J458983). St George was an AMES Type 9 Mk 1, fully transportable in regulation ten vehicle convoy with trailers with 105ft telescopic wooden aerial masts, self contained with tented accommodation, fields kitchens and workshop, capable of being set up in 12 hours and operating on 7m wavelength. Nothing remains to mark the site, equipment being simply hauled through the farmyard onto the gently sloping field facing Abergele Roads. The RAF crew quitted their tents at the height of winter for the farm outbuildings, never the best solution, as witness the unfortunates on St Twynnell CHL station (Pembroke), billeted in the stables at Stackpole House, which Joubert described as 'filthy and in a bad state of repair'. Conditions at this latter station are perhaps symptomatic of the reigning confusion. St Twynnell had become operational in July 1940, but two months later Joubert rants '… there is no protection, not even sand bags, for the CHL huts which are standing in an open field exposed to enemy fire'. Security was in the hands of ten regular Army under an NCO and thirty-five Home Guard 'of which only three were armed'.

In addition to the Home Chain, Nº 60 (Signals) Group also took over Nº 2 Installation Unit, Special Flight and Special Calibration Unit on 18 April 1940. This had local implications. On 1 July 1940 a Nº 8 Radio Maintenance Unit (RMU) arrived at RAF Speke — designation deliberately misleading, for to this unit devolved the task of building, commissioning and running all the CH/CHL radar stations in the northwest, north Wales, the Isle of Man and Ulster. Essential early calibration work was carried out by the Ansons of Nº 48 Squadron which had arrived at RAF Hooton Park on 16 July 1940. On 31 August Nº 8 RMU moved its HQ to 48 Ullet Road, Sefton Park, Liverpool, later to 'High Lee', Beaconsfield Road, Woolton. Its 'Calibration Flight' continued to be based at Speke. This was a specialist roving unit whose task it would be to fly at known bearings and constant heights, on radial or circular tracks, to

Nº 48 Squadron Avro Anson N9908, Hooton Park, 1940. This aircraft took part in early calibration work along the north Wales coast

The peril of operating sea patrols. Avro Anson K6166 lies in harbour after being towed in by a tanker after ditching.

'calibrate' new stations as and when they were commissioned and at regular intervals thereafter. No two stations were sited the same; each had to be checked individually. and where necessary corrections and adjustments fed into the 'calc.' or 'electrical calculator' ('computer' in today's parlance). Two-way ground-to-air R/T contact was maintained during such acceptance trials, which would continue until a satisfactory performance in terms of bearing accuracy and height finding was achieved, problems of site notwithstanding.

Nº 8 RMU Calibration Flight consisted of a number of impressed civilian Hornet Moths and larger aircraft mainly Blenheims (see table below). The first Hornet Moth (W9389) was already allotted by the time the RMU arrived at Speke. It had simply been flown across the Mersey from where it had been attached to Nº 4 CPF, RAF Hooton Park. On 21 September 1940 the RMU was redesignated, still very much 'under cover', Nº 8 Radio Servicing Section (RSS), on paper boosting its Calibration Flight to 3+1 Blenheim IVs, 1+1 Hornet Moths and 1+1 Rota. In the event, the latter were not supplied, all re-impressed Cierva-30As being allocated to Nº 1448 (Rota) Flight, Nº 74 (Signals) Wing. In February 1941 the RSS would disband into Nº 77 (Signals) Wing. The Calibration Flight was enlarged in November 1942 when it absorbed similar flights of the adjacent Nºˢ 73 and 79 (Signals) Wings but itself would be disbanded on 18 June 1943, its role, with an increased demand for faster more up-to-date aircraft being met by local AAC squadrons such as Nº 577, based at RAF Wrexham.

Some Representative Calibration Aircraft

Nº 8 RMU/RSS (CF)
D.H. 87 Hornet Moth:
W5753
W9389
Blenheim IV:
V5794

Nº 77 Wing (CF)
D.H.87 Hornet Moth:
W5747
W5749
W5778
W5779
X9325
Blenheim IV:
Z6166
Z6167
Z6168
Tiger Moth II:
T6862
D.H. 89A Rapide:
X9457
Airspeed Oxford II:
X7238

Nº 73 Wing (CF)
D.H. 87 Hornet Moth:
W5778
W5779
Blenheim IV:
V5727
Z2601
Tiger Moth II:
T6862
T7613

Nº 79 Wing (CF)
D.H.87 Hornet Moth:
W5747:
W5749
Blenheim IV:
T2004
Tiger Moth II:
T6863
T6863

Calibration of radar instruments along the north Wales coast was not without its dangers, especially when using

Impressed Hornet Moth W9389 (ex-G-ADMT) of the calibration flight Nº 8 RMU. [via R. T. Riding]

impressed, former civil aircraft. Hornet Moth, W5753, ex G-AEKS, had first been registered on 17 July 1936, but had been impressed on 21 January 1940 for work with Nº 4 CPF at Hooton Park. It had missed the great Grandstand fire of 8 July 1940 which destroyed some eighteen impressed aircraft. After Nº 4 CPF was disbanded on 27 May 1940 W5753 followed, via a 3-week stint with the Biggin Hill Cal. Flt the well-worn track of Hornet Moths across the Mersey to Speke. Here it made the standard progression Nº 8 RMU > Nº 8 RSS > Nº 77 (Signals) Wing. On 10 October 1941, piloted by P/O T. M. Calderwood, its duty was calibration with the Chain Home station at Nefyn on the Llŷn Peninsula (Caernarfonshire). On starting the first leg of the calibration course the pilot discovered that the special equipment in the Hornet Moth was malfunctioning. He decided to land and make the necessary adjustments. He selected a likely field at Cefn Ceisiog near the radar station, but as he came over the hedge W5753 began to drift. The pilot decided to go round again, opened up the throttle but failed to clear the far boundary hedge, tipping onto its nose and injuring the pilot. W5753 was damaged beyond economic repair.

In the first instance north Wales RDF stations had to rely on a motley miscellany of target aircraft to calibrate their instruments. While the first calibration test for the CHL station at Gwaunysgor (Prestatyn) — two flights 40 miles at 310° true and reciprocal — were carried out on 26 July courtesy of Nº 48 (Coastal Patrol) Squadron newly arrived at Hooton Park, it was not until 5 and 7 August that subsequent tests could be held. F/Lt C. S. Pollard, station CO, complained bitterly about the difficulty of obtaining aircraft for testing purposes. For a test on 4 September 1940 the station had to make do with a clapped out Fairey Battle of Nº 5 BGS, Jurby, Isle of Man, — 'a plane notoriously poor in its RDF response'. Matters were not helped by there being as yet 'little operational flying 'which could have been used to test the station's performance'. All this would soon change! Reading between the lines better results were being obtained from tracking shipping 40 miles out in Liverpool Bay and the Irish Sea. Representations to 'Western filter room' proved unavailing in producing aircraft. He concludes, 'It seems likely that a combined approach to AMRE and SRS and Nº 60 Group and higher authority is necessary'. 'Western' was Observer Corps Western Area

RAF Nefyn, AMES N° 66

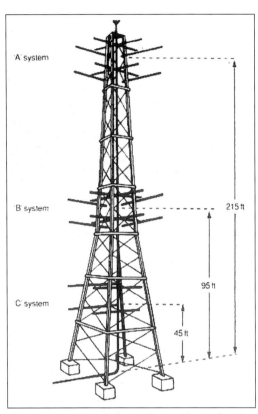

Above: reconstruction of a wooden aerial mast depicting bases and receiving systems A, B and C. Running down the centre of the mast is a lightning conductor and receiver cables.

Above: Electrical sub-station cubicle at RAF Nefyn RDF station. Backdrop is Garn Bochian.

*Above: Standby Set House, RAF Nefyn RDF Station.
[W. Alister Williams]*

*Left:West Coast 'C' type receiver block at RAF Nefyn RDF Station, camouflaged under a mound of earth with the backdrop of Garn Fadryn and Moel Caerau.
[W. Alister Williams]*

*Right: The concrete foot bases for the 240ft wooden receiver aerials at the RDF station on Cefn Leisiog Farm, near Nefyn.
[W. Alister Williams]*

*Stanton semi-sunken air raid shelter, RAF Nefyn,
Army Guard Camp at Giat Goch.
[W. Alister Williams]*

*Left: Former Orderly Room and 'Officers' Ablutions, now
converted into a vehicle garage.
[W. Alister Williams]*

*Right: The officers' mess Army Staff Room adjoining Staff Institute
with water tower, now converted into a modern
bungalow with a watch tower (2005).
[W. Alister Williams]*

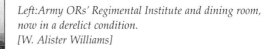

*Left: Army ORs' Regimental Institute and dining room,
now in a derelict condition.
[W. Alister Williams]*

*Right: An 80ft long barrack block at the Army Guard Camp, RAF
Nefyn (AMWD Drawing Nº 9059/40
[W. Alister Williams]*

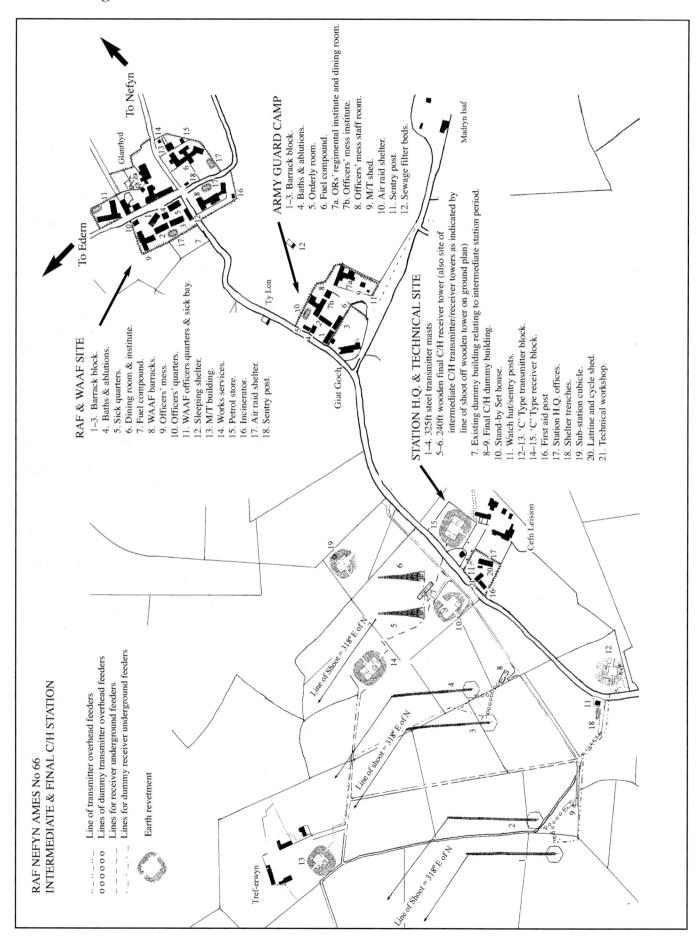

(1937) and Nº 10 Group, Fighter Command (June 1940), joint HQ at Rudloe Manor, Box, Wiltshire, to which RDF plots in a panic situation were being 'told' either instead of, or in tandem with, a putative Nº 9 Group filter room, Barton Hall, Preston. The production of Hornet Moth W9389 for Test 2 (visual circling of station at 1,500ft) and Test 3 (ditto at 500ft) may help date more precisely when the Speke Calibration Flight was 'up and running'

The converse situation existed whereby radar carrying aircraft used ground radar stations to calibrate their AI and/or ASV equipment. This obviated the need for putting up a second aircraft and crew for the purpose. It may also explain why Bristol Beaufighters figure largely in the accident statistics over north-east Wales. Much of the installation and final testing of AI radar was done by Nº 30 MU at Sealand, either on production aircraft straight from the factory or flown in from unit. Thus it was that Beaufighter IIF, R2271, came to a sticky end on 26 April 1941, killing its test crew. Strangely the incident does not appear in Flintshire's Civil Defence log. R2271 had come off the Filton assembly line at the end of March and had been flown to RAF Sealand for the installation of AI radar prior to allocation to unit. On that fateful day it had taken off at 1615hrs, duty — 'test flight'. Pilot was F/Lt N.D.G.B. Woods. Radio/observer for the test was LAC Thomas McKenzie of Nº 30 MU, a radar technician on secondment from Nº 32 MU, St Athan. The weather was fine as they climbed out over the Dee estuary. Testing of AI and radio equipment was accomplished without incident. Problems arose when they were about to re-enter the Sealand circuit. Sgt Edward Hughes, Flintshire Police, takes up the story at this point:

'I was in the yard at the back of the Police Station at Bagillt, when I heard an unusual roar from an aeroplane somewhere in the vicinity. Looking up in the direction from which the sound was coming I saw a plane travelling from a point between Holywell and Halkyn towards the River Dee at Bagillt, and two or three seconds later I saw a second plane about the same point as the first aircraft. This one started to turn over and over and then went into a screaming dive towards the LMS Railway line. There was a very large explosion and a black cloud rose from this area. I went to the scene as quickly as possible on my pedal cycle and found the plane in the back garden at the rear of the 'White Horse' Inn, Bagillt, The aircraft and an unoccupied bungalow near it were ablaze. Time 1705hrs; approximate time of the accident 1655hrs. The flames were so intense it was impossible to rescue the occupants until the Fire Brigade from Flint had put out the fire. The Beaufighter had embedded itself some 14ft into the ground. Firemen and locals worked vigorously until the bodies were extracted from the wreckage. They were then taken to RAF Sealand by local ambulance'.

F/Lt Woods, aged 33 and a science graduate of Liverpool University hailed from Bidston and lies buried in St Oswald's Churchyard, Birkenhead. LAC McKenzie was buried in his native Glasgow.

Some 44 years after it was lost the re-discovery of the wreckage of Avro Anson EG447 of Nº 11 Radio School, Hooton Park, recalled the dangers of radar training over open sea. On 17 July 1944, after the unexplained failure of both engines whilst on an ASV exercise in liaison with the Great Orme CHL station , EG447 was forced to ditch some eight miles off Llandudno. Two of the four-man crew were killed. The wreck of the aircraft was never found, but Civil Defence records note that from 21 July 1944 long shore drift began to cast debris ashore at Colwyn Bay and Pensarn — 'two engine covers, portions of a bomb, chemical tank racks, a spanner etc.'. In August 1989 something snagged the nets of Mr John Povah, fisherman and amateur diver of Rhos-on-Sea, some six miles off Colwyn Bay. On diving to disentangle his nets, Mr Povah rediscovered the mangled remains of EG447, now much the worse for wear after being rolled along the sea bed for half a century by shifting sand banks.

Equally top secret was airborne interception radar (AI). Development had not proceeded as easily as ground based systems, but pressures to equip night fighters with AI equipment had been immense and, with hindsight, rather premature, with too great a gap between ground control and AI performance. Things improved as AI Mk VII and an interim Mk VIII came on stream in 1942, usually as 'cats' eyes' Defiant squadrons converted to the Bristol Beaufighter. On 8 June 1942 Nº 256 Squadron had moved to RAF Woodvale from Squires Gate. They were equipped with Beaufighter IF but in October commenced working up on Beaufighter VIF, gaining proficiency on GCI/AI interception by using any bombers from the OTUs that happend to enter the squadron's airspace on a NAVEX. On 31 October a Brougthon-built Wellington III (BK234) of Nº 25 OTU, Finningley (Yorkshire) had taken off at 1850hrs for such a 'Bullseye' dummy night attack. It was crewed by F/O D. R. Harding and Sgts T. M. G. Grey, S. E. Blackman, J. D. Forsyth and S. G. Cook. Unfortunately, the exercise was tragically terminated when the 'target' was rammed by the 'hunter' over Bangor, Caernarfonshire. Beaufighter IF (X7845) of Nº 256 Squadron was piloted by S/Ldr R. De-W. K. Winlaw with S/Ldr C. T. Ashton on AI. The collision was witnessed and reported by Observers O. W. Owen and T. C. Parry of Bethesda, on duty at B.1 Bangor post, Nº 28–2 Group, ROC. Because of their detailed local knowledge, both men had often assisted in the recovery of aircraft wrecks and bodies of aircrew in Snowdonia. On this occasion they were rather nonplussed when after recovering the bodies, they were excluded from any part in handling the wreckage due, they thought, 'to the high security risk of the RDF/AI equipment'. A special team from 'the Radio School at Liverpool' i.e. Nº 77 Wing made the recovery and nothing was left behind to betray the crash site. The wreckage of the Beaufighter was carted away 'by a firm from Liverpool called LEP Transport', which was the undercover pseudonym for Nº 77 Wing's MT section.

The CH radar worked on wavelengths of around 12m. Aerials were accordingly large and did not produce the narrow 'searchlight' beam, moved about and directed at different parts of the sky as would soon be the general practice. CH aerials were slung between giant supporting towers and invisibly 'floodlit' the area out to sea. All aircraft within the 'illuminated' area were potential radar targets as echoes from each were plotted by the CH RDF system. There was one serious disadvantage to the aerial array system — a

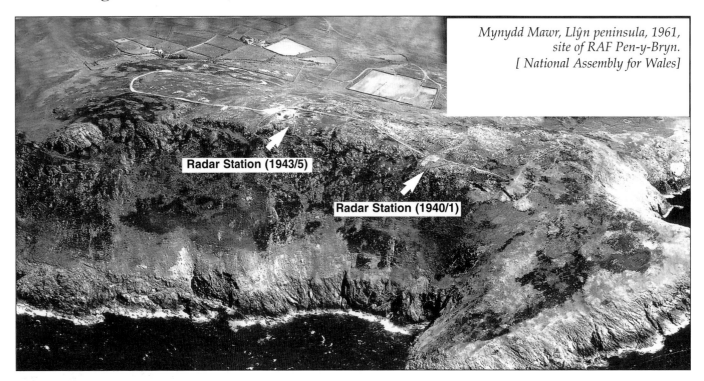

*Mynydd Mawr, Llŷn peninsula, 1961,
site of RAF Pen-y-Bryn.
[National Assembly for Wales]*

Radar Station (1943/5)

Radar Station (1940/1)

RAF Pen-y-Bryn CHL & CHEL AMES Nº 66A, 1940–5
1. AMES type 2, 5 bay aerial array; 2. Tx and Rx operations nissen hut lying within a brick-built
protection wall reinforced with steel bar & concrete; 3. Brick/reinforced concrete generator & stand
by generator house; 4. Latrine; 5. Army guard room; 6. AMES type 14 MkII, naval type, centimetric
radar 'mobile'; 7. Transformer kiosk; 8. Latrine; 9. Radar plinth; 10. Stand by set house; 11. Army
guard/orderly room; 12. Ground anchor rings used for the conveyance of equipment down
 the long, steep gradient.

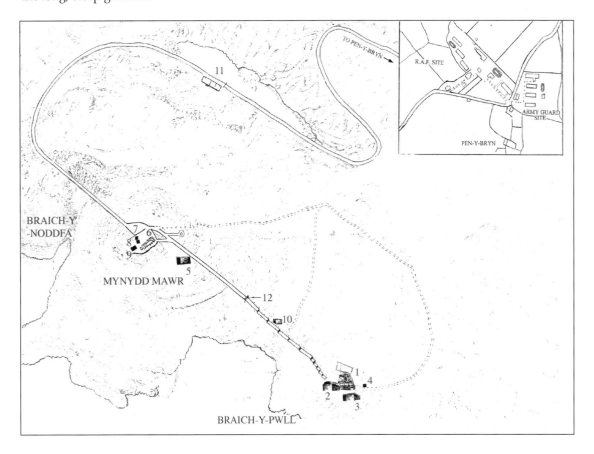

RAF Pen-y-Bryn, CHL & CHEL
AMES 66A, Mynydd Mawr

Left: A converted RADAR plinth at the summit of Mynydd Mawr.
[W. Alister Williams]

Below: The concrete path which leads down from the summit of Mynydd Mawr to the CHL station falls 50 metres in 150 metres.[W. Alister Williams]

Left: A view from the summit of Mynydd Mawr. In the foreground is a plinth footing and in the background, Ynys Enlli (Bardsey Island). [W. Alister Williams]

Below right: On the left hand side of the concrete path is the reserve standby set house. At the end of the patch is the sudden drop to the CHL station. [W. Alister Williams]

Left: The remains of the CHL station. In the foreground is the Tx & Rx operations Nissen hut on the cliff edge and in the background, the standby generator house.
[W. Alister Williams]

The remains of the Tx & Rx operations Nissen hut which lay within a brick built protection wall reinforced with steel bars and concrete.
[W. Alister Williams]

gap occurred in the radiation pattern near ground level; consequently low flying aircraft could not be detected until very close. This was overcome by interpolating low cover CHL stations working in parallel with existing CH stations but on a shorter wavelength. Thus CH Blackpool Tower (AMES 64) was partnered by CHL Formby (AMES 64A), while CH Rhuddlan (AMES 65) teamed up with CHL Prestatyn at Gwaunysgor (AMES 65A and CHL Great Orme Head (AMES 65B)); in Anglesey CH Wylfa (AMES76) (by coincidence < W.gwylfan = 'look out, watch place') worked in conjunction with CHL South Stack (AMES 76A) while CH Nefyn (AMES 66) was in tandem with CHL Peny-y-bryn (AMES 66A). During the Battle of Britain one notes similar hastily added pairings in South Wales e.g. Haycastle (CH) and Strumble Head (CHL); and Warren (CH) and St Twynell (CHL), all either side of Milford Haven. On the Isle of Man, because of technical problems, not in the least severe interference (under certain climatic conditions) from the USA east coast, Cregneash CHL came on stream several months ahead of its parent CH station at Scarlett Point. In the north of the island the CH at Bride seemingly worked alone, but its CHL counterparts are to be looked for on the Lancashire coast at St Bees Head and/or Hawcoat.

At first sight these dispositions would appear to suggest order and method, but such were rare commodities in the early part of the war. In practice the setting up of radar coverage in western regions was accompanied by chaos, lack of co-ordination not so much between Services as between Commands and Groups, duplication of effort and research, and bitter infighting between Ministries, Committees, and individual scientists, compounded by rapid advances in radio/radar technology which frequently rendered plans for radar stations obsolete even before they left the drawing board or enforced changes to aerial configuration even as sets were up and running. Indeed, from the few surviving records relating to CHL Prestatyn, where there were always 'scientific observers' — Messrs F. Kay and G.R..Bacon — from Worth Matravers on post reporting to their superintendent, Dr A. P. Rowe at the AMRE/TRE, one gains the impression that many, if not all, north Wales radar stations were also experimental even as they filled an

operational role.

CH stations were normally sited near the coast, preferably with flat or gently sloping terrain on the seaward side. Even so the reflective nature of the ground produced 'clutter' on screen, hence the need for stations to be calibrated on an individual basis. The one good thing to come out of the 1940 'panic' situation was that the cumbersome procedures of the Defence Act of 1842 which regulated the compulsory purchase of land by the military were swept away. The Emergency Powers (Defence) Act, 1939, permitted the requisitioning of land and buildings 'by a competent authority', not always with the success anticipated. One thinks immediately of the proposal in September 1940 to turn Blackpool Tower into a CH radar station, with Tx arrays on the N, S and W faces and a single dipole cross at 485ft. Initial work at 'RAF Tower' (AMES No 64) began in February 1941, handicapped by the fact that there were no accurate drawings of the Tower available. In June 1941 the MB2 transmitters began to arrive in sections, with strict orders that they were to be moved into the Tower during the early hours of the morning, protected from curious or prying eyes as they were moved through the public parts of the building — a vain exercise in secrecy, since it had been agreed that all aerials and transmission lines would be handled by the Tower riggers. The Tower Company had even acquiesced to the suggestion that the top should be cut off to make way for a CHL station. Fortunately for today's aesthetic townscape the idea was vetoed by the AMWD, while the respective merits of Gwrych Castle, Abergele, or the sand dunes at Formby for a sea-level 'shoot' were being examined. Gwrych is mentioned by name, but the four-figure military map reference (J.3799) refers to a kilometre square which includes Llanddulas. As it was the Tower scheme was short lived. The preparation of working drawings had revealed that the Tower's orientation 'was two degrees anticlockwise out of true NE–SW heading'. This may have accounted in part for the 'unacceptable' levels of receiver interference and large bearing errors noted throughout July during work-up — apart from the static generated by the fun-fair at the foot! The problems continued, defeat was conceded and in February 1942 the

Great Orme, Llandudno. A: Location of the Second World War Chain Home Low station and AMES type 31 coastal defence radar.
B: Llandudno Coastal Artillery School (Army gun laying radar).

decision was taken to close RAF Tower down.

More successful was simply affixing an aerial on the roof of a requisitioned building — as on a hotel in Llandudno — and lo! CHL station Great Orme's Head was born. With equal facility the RAF, on grounds of secrecy, evicted the Royal Artillery detachment from 'Stella Maris', an eighteen room flat-roofed building in the sand dunes at Formby, nerve centre of a gunnery range out into Liverpool Bay. Internal modifications were made, a hand operated single broadside aerial erected on the 50 x 30ft flat roof — and AMES 64A was established, from the outset passing its plots directly to Barton Hall, Preston, filter room independently of its CH station on Blackpool Tower. The days of the Army's artillery range at Formby were numbered anyway, since the 'fall of shot area' was now a major marshalling and dispersal point for Atlantic convoys, but ready surrender of the dunes to the RAF police dogs coincided with a rationalisation of Royal Artillery training and experimental provision in the NW and north Wales, with the transfer of the RA's Coast Artillery School from Shoeburyness to the NW tip of Great Orme Head, becoming operational on 24 September 1940 with Searchlight and Wireless Wings (a euphemism for CD and GL radar) following in October and December 1940

AMRE scientists pinpointed likely sites for radar stations by the simple method of examining the one-inch OS map and marking off flat coastal areas that hopefully would be free from reflective clutter. Rough rules of thumb were: the higher the station the greater the range at which incoming aircraft were detected; and the smoother the fall of land in front and to the sides of the aerial displays the more accurate height and direction finding. But this was easier said than done! Scarlett Point never did solve its 'clutter' problem before its closure in May 1944. Glenarm had been pronounced operational as from 15 July 1940 yet in September was still bugged by echoes from the Isle of Arran and the mainland of Scotland, while Prestatyn's early history was plagued by interference not only from 'seaclutter' (dominant waves), but also by the bulk of the Great Orme in one direction and the Lancashire coast ('much chimneyed') and Blackpool Tower in the other. In general, areas below 50ft OD were avoided owing to the risk of flooding. Selected areas were then visited and field walked, noting accessibility, or lack of it, to the national electricity grid, pencilling in potential sites for transmitting and receiving towers, Rx and Tx blocks, generator houses, stand-by sets, buried reserves and all the necessary infrastructure of admin. and guard huts, dog compounds and the like. In practice speed was not possible, there being too many fingers in the one pie and overriding everything the overwhelming need for secrecy. AMRE had to approve technical aspects of the site; AMWD had to oversee land acquisition, the laying on of essential services, arranging for test drilling for foundation and anchor blocks for towers and masts, etc.; Signals were responsible for the installation of

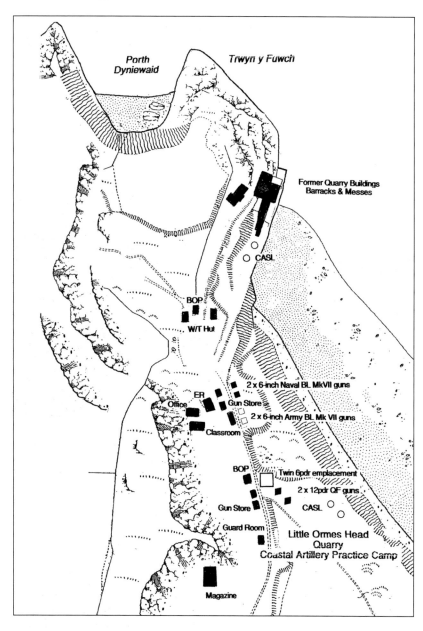

The CAPC & CASL at the Little Orme Quarry, Llandudno. A necessary adjunct to the Royal Artillery School which moved to Llandudno in September 1940. There was also a gunlaying radar on this site. [Detail inserted on a 1912 base map (25-inch sheet), Caernarfonshire 11.14/ by kind permission of the Ordnance Survey.]

equipment and the Post Office for outside telephone lines — all subject to the approval (or veto) of Fighter Comand who would ultimately administer the stations.

Desk-top evaluations and field walking were not always infallible. To ignore local knowledge and advice could lead to problems as witness the enforced migration following flooding of the VHF radio and radar station originally established behind the spit on the tidal flood plain of the Ystwyth at Tanybwlch, south of Aberystwyth, to Castell Mawr, a hill-fort or Iron Age enclosure at Llanrhystud where the Wyre and Wyre Fach flow into Cardigan Bay. This CLH station was short-lived, closing in May 1944 With an even briefer existence, north of Aberystwyth, was the GCI station at Aberleri (originally parented by RAF Valley but closed and put on ''Care and Maintenance' w.e.f 23 August 1943). There is very little left of GCI Aberleri having started life as an emergency mobile unit (Type 8) in 1942. Whether it made the transition to the 'Final' form (Type 7) is uncertain from surviving 'archaeology' or lack of it — Borth spit does not lend itself to semi-sunken installations It probably improved no further than a fully mobile Type 15. Whatever, both scanned the Irish Sea off the west coast of Wales, a very busy quadrant of air space since the opening of aerodromes at Aberporth,

The sea area off Rhos-on-Sea from the CAPC at the quarry on the Little Orme.

The view from the former CAPC and CASL looking toward Trwyn y Fuwch and the Little Orme Quarry.

Great Orme CHL Radar Station, Llandudno (AMES 65B)

The Great Orme Hotel, home to a Second World War radar station. The extended area in front of the hotel was covered with hutted accommodation

Right: Great Orme Hotel with the common to T & R power turned aerial array on the roof. [PRO Avia 7/320]

Below left: Looking at the site of the AMES Type 3 Coastal Defence Radar (medium power).

Below right: Coastal defence Radar [RAF Museum, Hendon]

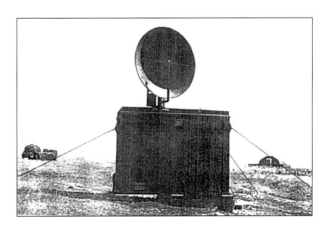

AMES N° 64 CHL station, Formby. Built in June 1941 to provide coverage down to 500ft at the mouth of the Mersey. The building is called 'Stella Maris' and lies in the sand dunes on the Formby coast. Radar aerial just visible on roof top.

Tywyn, and Llanbedr. But during the *Blitz* Cardigan Bay was also much frequented by *Luftflotte 3*. Its bombers used the lighthouses and unblacked-out towns of the Irish Republic as navigational aids before turning east over the Welsh mountains to Midlands targets. Even the Admiralty, who perhaps should have known better, could miscalculate. As noted earlier the Navy maintained an operational presence at the radar station on the Great Orme. In the Spring of 1944, in its U-boat 'snorkel-hunting' period it was decided to site a MRU as near sea level as possible — a 3cm set with its aerial dish mounted on the trailer roof, about ten feet above the ground. To make the sea-level 'shoot' even more effective a bulldozer was used to scoop out a deep trench in the Morfa, into which the trailer was towed — above the HWM normal tides of course. All went well during the summer, but the first abnormally high Autmn tides filled the trench, submerging the trailer in some six foot of water, ruining valuable electronic equipment with sand and salt!

Occasionally the Air Ministry's left hand did not know what the right hand was doing. Early in 1940 an 'Advanced' Chain Home (ACH) station had been erected at Bryngwran, some eight miles SE of Holyhead on the A5. It was a dry land site, with a line of 'shoot' across the overdeepend seaward end of a sunken river valley (Tywyn Trewen), infilled with drift and blown sand, and beyond into Caenarfon Bay where the *Luftwaffe* were very busy. In this instance 'Advanced' signified an initial, experimental stage, compared with sucessive 'Intermediate' and 'Final' stages of development. The Bryngwran ACH had wooden huts exposed to air attack, with no camouflage or blast protection, 70 and 90ft towers, mobile or experimental equipment, but no height finding — ideally placed one would have thought in a reporting context for N° 9 Group Fighter Command. and the new Rhosneigr (Valley) Sector that became operational

on 1 April 1941. But in the middle of 1940 contractors appeared on site to begin the construction of a new aerodrome at Rhosneigr less than a mile away. Someone, somewhere, decided that the one installation might interfere with the other. Consequently, in August 1940, Bryngwran ACH was moved lock, stock and barrel across the water to Nefyn on the Llŷn Peninsula, sending its first plots into Barton Hall in August 1940, along with the CHLs at Glenarm, Cregneash, Prestatyn, and the CHs at Bride and Scarlett Point. During the move from Bryngwran the opportunity was seized to replace the 70ft guyed masts of the ACH station with 105ft masts. This was to meet complaints from Fighter Command that height reporting by the ACH was deficient. More accurately the new mast was was constructed to a height of 87ft and a height aerial stuck on the top. There was only one problem. As an interim (?false economy measure), the upper steel guy wires, allegedly to eliminate possible electrical distortion on tube, were replaced by hempen rope stays. This made the masts unstable in highwinds; in the first November gales the Nefyn masts were blown down overnight, along with those at Bride, Scarlett and North Cairn. The reporting capabilities of N° 9 Group filter room were seriously impaired almost as soon as it opened for business! Fortunately, perhaps, the Battle of Britain had ended, according to British reckoning, on 31 October.

Again this raises interesting questions of paper chronology. Most RAF sources give 8 August 1940 as the date for the formation of N° 9 Group. Yet on 15 September N° 9 Group was no more than a pencilled memo on a Bentley Priory ORBAT. The name of its AOC, AVM W.A. McLaughty, DSO, MC, DFC, was duly promulgated on 16 September. On 9 September as Air Commodore McClaughty, then SASO at N° 12 Group, he had chaired a vital meeting at Barton Hall to set up a Group Communications and Operations Room without which nothing could be done. The GPO promised dedicated telephone lines within 3–8 weeks; however, all this notwithstanding, some sort of independent reporting system must have been in place several weeks earlier — plots from CH North Cairn and other radar stations were being told to a N° 9 Group Filter Room, Barton Hall as of 0900hrs, 13 August 1940, even though the Operations Room along the corridor was not operational.

Two basic criteria for the location of CHL stations seem to have been complete isolation and inaccesssibily, which while ideal for maintaining a curtain of secrecy was counter productive in terms of productivity, efficiency and morale. In September 1940 the Inspector General, ACM Sir Edgar Ludlow-Hewittt (ex-AOC-in-C Bomber Command) rightly exploded, highlighting problems of getting labour and materials to such outlandish sites. At Hayes Castle Cross only one wooden mast had been erected, yet German bombers were overhead. Huts were ready yet mobile gear was still in lorries and trailers. Workmen everywhere knocked off Saturday and went home until the Monday morning. Many stations had no proper water supply and other niceties that made life bearable were missing — 'no steel helmets, respirators, gum boot, sou'westers or accommodation for the Army guard. But the worst condemnation was reserved for the habit, common to all services of giving the 'dirtiest jobs' to the most inexperienced. Ludlow-Hewitt rumbles on: 'At Cregneish the CO, a pilot officer, is very young and inexperienced, and not a capable person fit to run an isolated station of this kind. I would suggest the training of these officers should be done by an older commanding officer at one of the established CH or CHL stations'. Ouput from the station was obviously affected — 'range is irregular and plots are lost as close as 30 miles … and on a test run on 4 October (1940), nothing was seen at all with plotting inconsistent and aircraft disappeared unaccountably'. One can imagine the petrified state in which a callow youthful RAFVR P/O would find himself after a confrontation with an acerbic all-knowing, all-seeing Inspector-General, who as 'next to God himself', did not tolerate fools gladly.

Hopefully such a cringing state of affairs was not universal. The CO at CHL Prestatyn was F/Lt (RAFVR) rank, reporting to S/Ldr ranks at AMRE/TRE, N° 60 (Signals) Group and N° 77 (Signals) Wing. One wonders what either Joubert or the Inspector General actually made of 2/Lt H.B. Wood, US Army Signal Corps, who, albeit only for two weeks, was given command of Formby CHL (AMES 64A) or of the Naval radar station at Gwesbyr, Llanasa, Flintshire, perched high on the end of the Clwydian Range, overlooking the approaches to the mouths of the Dee and Mersey. This had become operational by 31 December 1942; but it had a short life, with orders to close down being issued by the Admiralty in October 1944, potential coastal and surface watching duties as the Navy proceeded with the clearance of minefields after the cessation of hostilities, notwithstanding. Gwesbyr, located on the wettest, muddiest, windswept spot in the UK (preparation of site was done by Italian POWs which might explain the discomfort experienced!), was essentially a surface watching radar, used to plot shipping in and out of the Mersey, to watch for submarines and to give warning of ships straying out of swept channels and into minefields. It this respect it lessened the mundane routine 'watching' burden of RAF Prestatyn. Being a 'dedicated' Naval station Gwesbyr was able to carry on its work round the clock, whereas Prestatyn was only able to plot shipping when there was no significant aircraft movement in its vicinity. A simplified layout of the station survives in the PRO amongst 'RDF stations for mine detection, 1941–1943.' which may hint at Gwesbyr's proper role in Admiralty eyes. Gwesbyr ran a Type 30 CD/CHL centimetric radar (1´m) which had a 4ft 6ins parabolic dish aerial housed in a perspex 'lighthouse', the remains of which Naval Type 273 operations room still stood on site in 1996 where attached images were taken, along with remnants of the office, stand-by generator house, and fuel oil store. As far as is known there were only four other such stations in the UK, all of which were in northern Scotland. In the early months N° 77 (Signals) Wing posted RAF technicians to Gwesbyr, and from Wing correspondence we learn: 'the personnel including the officer commanding are WRNS ratings with the exception of the one male radio mechanic, who it is understood will be replaced by a WRNS mechanic

in the near future. The station will then be manned entirely by women, an experiment that will be watched with interest by the RAF authorities'.

In April 1951, after a long struggle to evict 'squatters' or displaced persons, the former Gwesbyr radar station was taken over by the Royal Observer Corps as post 19/G.4. Mostyn ROC post, established in October 1937 as 7/H.3 for some reason made the move, apparently without name change until 1953, when it was re-christened 'Prestatyn', equally incongruous! Geographically it became a little sounder in January 1961, when the Gwesbyr post was again moved, up the hill to Gwaunysgor (but just within the Prestatyn parish boundary) and into the newly commissioned underground monitoring post outside the gate and perimeter fence of the Second World War CHL and Cold War ROTOR station. It survived sundry regroupings and internal re-organisation as 17/N.4 (1966) and 17/C.2 (1968) and 17/20 (as of ROC 'Stand-down', 1991).

Both Joubert and Ludlow-Hewitt had bees in their bonnets about camouflage, or lack of it, at radar stations, an obsession no doubt stemming from the destruction wrought on the East Coast Home Chain during the Battle of Britain. But how they envisaged radar masts should be made invisible is not made clear in their reports, but efforts were obviously made; skirts of heavy wire mesh, interwoven with scrim, were slung from the lower parts of masts, hiding some of the Tx and Rx blocks. But they only succeeded in increasing 'clutter' echo or interference. The differing layout of the West Coast stations may give some further guidance, relying as they did upon dispersal, as the best means of camouflage. Our images of what remains (in 1996) of Rhuddlan CH station and domestic camp (AMES 65) serve to qualify. It is evident from the minutes of a meeting held on 21 February 1941 that the main discussion revolved around the 'camouflage problem', which had a knock-on effect, causing hold-ups to the final commissioning of the West Coast Chain as individual site plans were continually being altered. It was resolved that the layouts of the outstanding thirty West Coast sites should be standardised so that progress could be made.

Joubert himself was called to account in a series of meetings of the RDF Chain Committee during May 1941, the Secretary of State for Air in the chair. On 22 May Joubert had to admit that 'the active liaison between branches which had been hoped for had not materialised'. The newly appointed deputy Director of Signals was even more blunt, blaming defective planning, which gave too optimistic a picture of prospects, and set up a timetable that in practice was impossible to fulfil'. The AMWD, tasked with reconciling an over-ambitious construction plan with the resources available, wholeheartedly 'agreed'. One suspects that Churchill, who had enthusiastically embraced the new radar technology may have squirmed in his seat on reading this. (Later Sir) Robert Watson Watt stated that 'branches should not accept work if they regarded it as unpracticable'. At the fourth meeting on 30 May 1941 Joubert admitted that 'the original schedule for the West Coast Chain was framed without experience of executing a programme of remote sites with full precautions, for camouflage and dispersal; the

AMES No 76, RAF Wylfa, a CHL station. The final type of west coast design located on the northern coast of Anglesey. The cliff site made for greater range and accuracy of shot. [National Assembly for Wales]

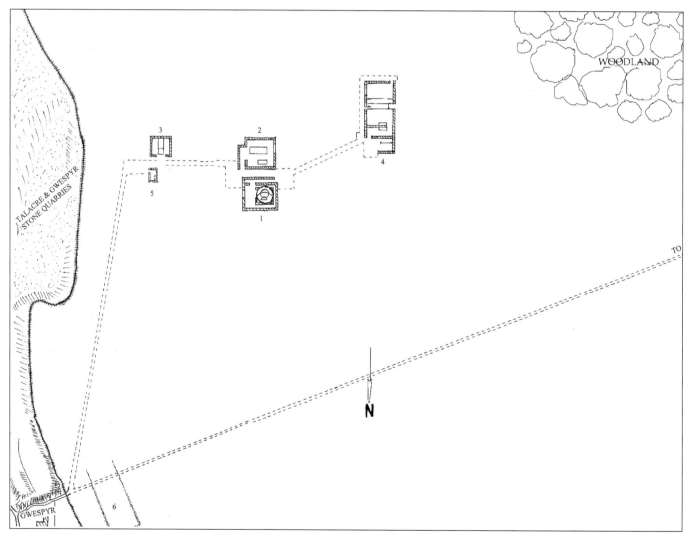

Gwesbyr Royal Naval Radar Station Type T273, 1942/3.
1. Radar plinth building with a perspex dome housing a Type T273 centimetric radar.; 2. Tx & Rx building; 3. Standby generator; 4. Army guard accommodation building; 5. Army sentry box; 6. Bofors ack-ack gun site. This site became ROC post N° 19/G4 in 1953.

Gwesbyr Royal Naval Radar Station

Left: View of the area in front of the radar station looking out over Liverpool Bay. The Second World War air firing range is in the middle of the photograph with Talacre lighthouse on the right.

Right: The transmitter/receiver building (Tx & Rx) is on the right of this photograph. In the centre is the army sentry box and, on the left, the radar plinth building.

Left: The radar plinth building which housed the Type T273 10cm radar which sat on top covered by a perspex dome.

Below, right: A view of the roof of the radar building, the radar dish moved through its axis covered by the perspex dome.

Left: The remains of the army living acommodation at Gwesbyr.

A winter scene at the Second World War RDF station site, RAFRhuddlan AMES N° 65. The long 'pin like' shadows on the left are cast by the 360ft transmitter masts. The shorter 'lattice-like' shadows amongst them are the 240ft receiver masts.
[National Assembly for Wales]

obstacles were not fully appreciated ...'.

One should note that 23 August 1943 was also the closing down date for the GCI station at RAF St Annes, Lancashire (AMES 68G), only opened the previous year. Non-technical personnel were moved to RAF Woodvale and Squires Gate, but radar mechanics and operators were posted to new radar units being formed uner the aegis of 2nd TAF in preparation for *Operation Overlord*. But this is for the future; more narrowly closures in north Wales and the north-west of England are better seen against the gradual wind down of N° 9 Group, Fighter Command, prior to the surrender of operatioal commitments to N°12 Group in August 1944 and disbandment on 15 September 1944.

Also w.e.f. 0900hrs 4 August 1944 Hack Green GCI station, once parented by RAF Wrexham whilst the latter was an operational night-fighter aerodrome, passed under the control of Church Fenton sector, N° 12 Group. As enemy air activity drifted SE, the contraction of N°9 Group and its RDF infrastructure, originally established to fill a specific gap in the air defences of the UK, was perhaps inevitable. Valley Sector had been dissolved as early as 1 November 1943, with RAF Valley passing under the control of Transport Command as the aerodrome became the trans-Atlantic terminal, part of Operation TRANSAT, receiving USAAF bombers en route for operational stations in south-eastern England. By dint of hard bargaining the new arrangements made provision for the accommodation of one nightfighter squadron (N° 125), and ASR detchment (N° 275 Sqn) a Target Towing Flight (N° 1485) and, most importantly for our present purpose from 18 July 1944, a Telecommunications Flying Unit (TFU) to carry out radio and radar research along the north Wales coast. The TFU would be redesignated the Radar Research Flying Unit in 1955.

Expanding on the data given in tabular form at the beginning of this chapter, by the middle of 1944 some 24 stations of the west coast reporting chain had been closed.

On 19 September 1944, despite German rocket attacks in the south-east, the whole of the West Chain, north of St David's Head was abandoned with the exception of three stations retained to give cover for trans-Atlantic aircraft. Elsewhere in the UK 24-hour watch-keeping at radar stations ended in April 1945.

In Wales from the five stations barely operational at the beginning of the war, radar stations by the end of hostilities had peaked at twenty-two, eleven in Pembrokeshire alone, covering Welsh coastal approaches. The figure could be higher if account were taken of poorly documented temporary sites, test areas and MRUs, or if this chapter's brief included Army and Naval installations. There were some ten each of CH and CHL and 10cm (CD/CHEL), plus five GCI stations, seven if once includes Hack Green and Comberton which covered the Welsh border region. Deserted CH stations everywhere quickly lost their curtain aerial arrays. Masts survived a little longer, topped by red warning lights. A vertical aerial photograph (page 88) taken from a Lancaster of N° 90 Squadron, Tuddenham (Suffolk), shows all six masts at Rhuddlan CH still standing on 16 January 1946, with the two 240ft wooden towers casting some remarkable shadows in the low wintry sunshine, but with shadows of the four pencil-thin guyed steel masts not so obvious. By the time the site was overflown again — 13 April 1947, by a PR Mosquito of N° 58 Sqdn, Benson — the four 325ft steel masts had disappeared. The wooden towers were still standing on 3 April 1954 but by 5 March 1962 photo reconnaissance shows no evidence ot towers. The demolition of these landmarks seems to have caused little stir and as far as is known no photographs exist of them lying on their sides, crumpled heaps of steel or splintered feet 'kicking in the air', folorn redundant symbols of the inventiveness of British scientists in the hour of need. But as the accompanying illustrations show, in the 1990s the aviation researcher did not have to look very hard to discover traces of the earth covered, semi-sunk Tx and Rx

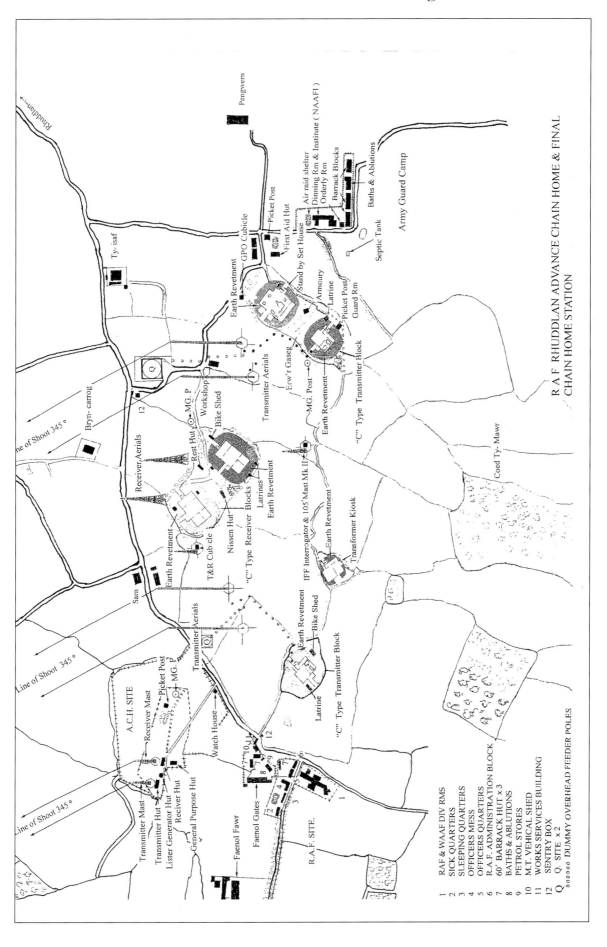

R A F RHUDDLAN ADVANCE CHAIN HOME & FINAL CHAIN HOME STATION

1   RAF & WAAF DIV RMS
2   SICK QUARTERS
3   SLEEPING QUARTERS
4   OFFICERS MESS
5   OFFICERS QUARTERS
6   R.A.F. ADMINISTRATION BLOCK
7   60' BARRACK HUT x 3
8   BATHS & ABLUTIONS
9   PETROL STORES
10   M.T. VEHICAL SHED
11   WORKS SERVICES BUILDING
12   SENTRY BOX
Q   Q. SITE x 2
oooooo DUMMY OVERHEAD FEEDER POLES

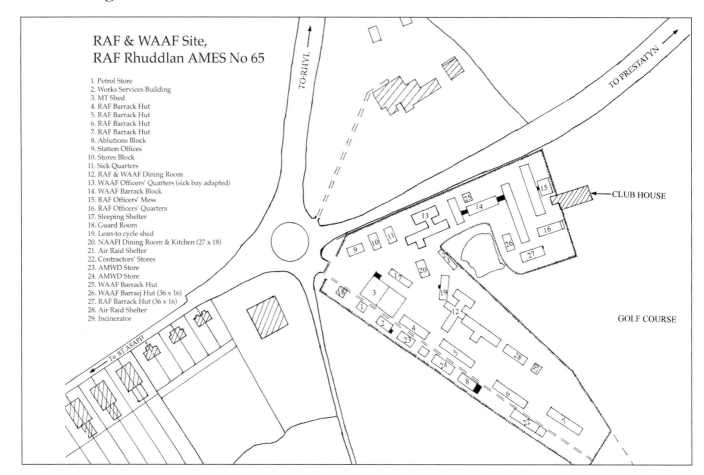

RAF & WAAF Site,
RAF Rhuddlan AMES No 65

1. Petrol Store
2. Works Services Building
3. MT Shed
4. RAF Barrack Hut
5. RAF Barrack Hut
6. RAF Barrack Hut
7. RAF Barrack Hut
8. Ablutions Block
9. Station Offices
10. Stores Block
11. Sick Quarters
12. RAF & WAAF Dining Room
13. WAAF Officers' Quarters (sick bay adapted)
14. WAAF Barrack Block
15. RAF Officers' Mess
16. RAF Officers' Quarters
17. Sleeping Shelter
18. Guard Room
19. Lean-to cycle shed
20. NAAFI Dining Room & Kitchen (27 x 18)
21. Air Raid Shelter
22. Contractors' Stores
23. AMWD Store
24. AMWD Store
25. WAAF Barrack Hut
26. WAAF Barracj Hut (36 x 16)
27. RAF Barrack Hut (36 x 16)
28. Air Raid Shelter
29. Incinerator

TO-RHYL

TO PRESTATYN

CLUB HOUSE

GOLF COURSE

To ST.ASAPH

RAF and WAAF site at RAF Rhuddlan, AMES Nº 65. The camp was located north of the town of Rhuddlan. All that remains today is the main entrance located on the junction of the A525 and A547 on the road from Rhuddlan to Rhyl.

blocks, the miniscule 'camps', and buried reserves etc.

But this was not the end to ongoing radar research in north Wales. Snowdon summit radar station continued to be used by naval research teams (*cf.* pages 68–80). An Admiralty file in the PRO contains summary reports on 'the performance of high power 'S' band radar at high altitudes against low flying aircraft carried out on Snowdon, 1945'. Obviously the research was Navy inspired, but in that the TRE at Defford / Great Malvern 'lent' aircraft for the purpose suggests that RAF scientists also had a professional interest in the outcome of such research.

Left: West coast Type C transmitter block at Rhuddlan.

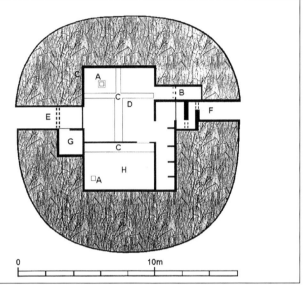

Right: A 'C' type transmitter block plan.
A: roof vent; B: transmission line ports; C: cable duct 80cm deep;
D: transmitter equipment; E: equipment access; F: personnel access;
G: transformer room; H: ventilation equipment; I: earth bank.
[Alan Cleary]

Right: The ventilation equipment room for the Type C transmitter block (shown in the diagram plan as 'H'.)

Left: Interior of a Type C transmitter block showing the room which housed the MB3 transmitter. The recess half way up the wall is where the transmission line passed out through a glass insulated feed-through for connection to the aerial transmission lines. This room is shown in the above diagram plan as 'D'.

Left: A view down the tunnel showing the glass insulated feed-throughs through which passed the transmission lines from the MB3 transmitter which in turn fed radio frequency power to the transmitting aerials.

Right: A reconstruction by Alan Cleary of the transmission lines between aerial and Type C transmitter building. At Rhuddlan the lines passed into the hedgerows to camouflage them.

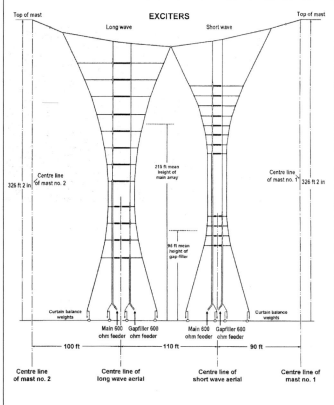

Left and below: The west coast transmitter aerial system slung between two 326ft 2in masts. The active aerial exciters had an identical passive reflector placed behind them which concentrated the transmitted signal in the desired direction. The aerials were designed for two frequencies in the range 22–50mhz.
[Courtesy of Alan Cleary]

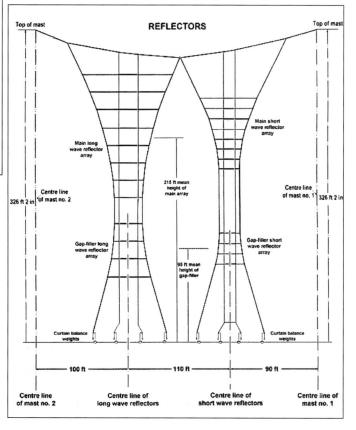

A Mark III interrogator aerial and transmitter cubicle. Rhuddlan had two of these sited just off each transmitting aerial array.

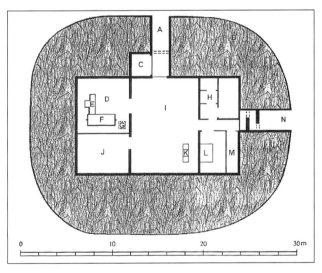

Above: A main aerial halyard anchor block. One of the lucky ones which has survived due to being sited in a hedgerow at Rhuddlan.

Above: A dummy (Q) building at CH Scarlett, Isle of Man, 1942, identical to the two which were sited at Rhuddlan. [James S. Farrior]

Left: Plan of a West Coast receiver building.. A: goods entrance; B: earth bank; C: transformer room; D: switchgear and ventilation system connected to ducting throughout the building; E: pump; F: fliter unit; G: roof vent; H: electrical parts store; I: receiver equipment; J: electro-magnetic calculator; K & L: cable ducts; M: battery room (GPO); N: personnel entrance. [Alan Cleary]

Below left: West coast Type C receiver block (A) at RAF Rhuddlan AMES N° 65. The view shows the personnel entrance with bicycle shed in the foreground.

Below right: West coast Type C receiver block (B) at RAF Rhuddlan AMES N° 65. The view shows the goods entrance.

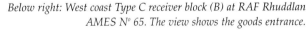

Right: Nissen hut on the receiving block site at Rhuddlan. This type of hut, with its distinctive 'T' shaped door and window combination, was common on radar sites

Below: Concrete receiver aerial footings for the 240ft wooden lattice aerial, a diagram of which appears on **page 74**. *This photograph depicts the Nefyn aerial footing which would have been identical to those at Rhuddlan.* [W. Alister Williams]

These two diagrams depict the range tube which enabled the RDF operator to track both enemy and friendly aircraft.

The diagram on the right shows a display of passive reflection from the targets in response to a high burst of energy from the transmitter.

The diagram below shows a response from an airborne transmitter to its receiver on the RDF station. If an aircraft did not ransmit a signal it was regarded as hostile and the appropriate steps would be taken to intercept it. The system was known as IFF – identification friend or foe. [Alan Cleary]

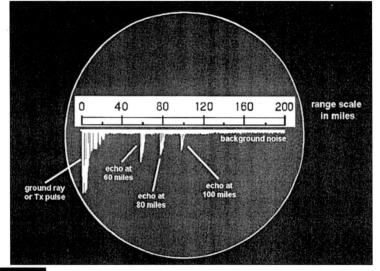

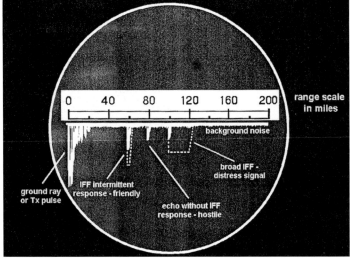

Right & below: The stand-by house at RAF Rhuddlan AMES No 65. In 2005, 64 years after it was buried by a mound of earth to camouflage it, the road stone and earth are removed to reveal basic design features. These two photographs show road stone still embedded in the thick layer of bitumen which waterproofed the structure.

Above right: The interior of the stand-by set house. The plinth in the floor was the bed for the stand-by generator and the pipe on the wall is part of the return water cooling system for the diesel engine. The generation set could provide 11kv for the site.

Above The electrical sub station cubicle. This building would have been completely covered with layers of stone and earth, identical to that of the stand-by set house. Its function was to control the distribution of electrical power from the public 3.3kv line to the technical buildings by way of a three-phase ring main. A transformer in each technical building converted the 3.3kv supply to 230v, single phase and 400v three phase for use across each individual site.

Right: The entrance to the transformer room electrical sub station cubicle.

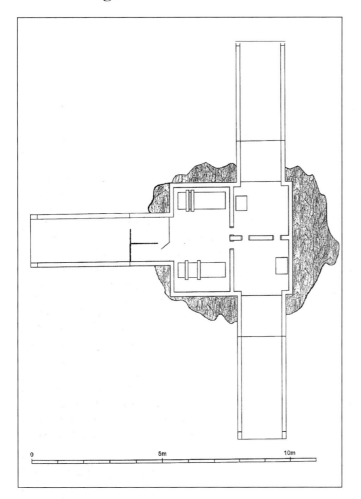

Two surviving examples of Second World War military architecture still surviving at the Army guard camp on RAF Rhuddlan AMES No 65 are the picket post (left) and the first aid hut (right). Left to the elements for 52 years the roofs were still water tight in 1994 when this picture was taken.

The electrical sub station cubicle. [Alan Cleary]

AMES 65A (PRESTATYN CHL)

An far as local historians are concerned RAF Prestatyn is a welcome exception to the norm — unlike most Second World War radar stations it is reasonably well documented.

(a) SITE
After some 65 years the hill site 750ft above Prestatyn, but actually nearer Gwaunysgor village, is still a 'vital point' for telecommunications. The site has been continuously modified over this period, the last phased development being for the 1950s Cold War ROTOR surveillance radar system whose buildings indiscriminately litter the upper (southern) part of the site, and cry out for some sort of interpretation. The massive BT mast with its myriad of antennae and dishes stands where stood the original (1940-41) aerial arrays. By isolating visible traces of the successive 'destruction layers', the present authors have succeeded in producing a number of technical 'period maps' (pages 101–2) which hopefully are self explanatory. One should note, however, the expansion of the domestic side of the compound, both in terms of hutting and fencing brought about the need for high security and problems with billeting and rationing in Prestatyn itself. In July 1940 station complement was as follows:

1 Officer (F/Lt)
1 Sergeant
1 Corporal (Admin.)
1 Corporal (SP/Security)
1 Corporal (RDF Mechanic, Aug. 1940>)
6+ LAC (RDF Mechanics)
12–14 AC (RDF Operators)

These were divided into a 4-watch shift system:

| 1750–2400hrs | A B C D A | | 0800–1300hrs | C D A B C |
| 0001–0800hrs | B C D A B | | 1300–1750hrs | A B C D A |

— which pattern gave each watch a full day off every four days.

Attempts at sabotage were frequent. Between 20 July and 23 October land lines were deliberately cut on four occasions, necessitating a guard posted on the road up the hillside. and the setting up of R/T links. In September, as enemy action over Liverpool was starting at dusk, an adjacent cornfield was set alight. Again, purely by chance, 'Western' filter room, asked for a possible visual identification of an X-raid on its table. The NCO i/c watch climbed onto the gantry with a pair of binoculars and noted a glow emanating from a workmen's hut — a bundle of rags had been laid in the corner and was smouldering, on the point of bursting into flame. An attempt was also made to wreck the relief watch 'carry', midnight relief, by placing large boulders across the unlit path of the vehicle. Such incidents do not surprise the researcher. The pre-emptory requisitioning of Welsh land, without consulting Welsh people and the apparent indiscriminate dumping of military installations into a pacifist Welsh landscape, raised Welsh hackles everywhere and sometimes led to direct protest — as witness the token demonstration surrounding the construction of an aerodrome at Penrhos, Llŷn, in September 1936 — a *cause celebre* then and now. Response to a radar station at Prestatyn was more muted, possibly because of the cloak of secrecy surrounding RDF and Air Ministry Experimental Stations country-wide. It is interesting to speculate, as a novel alternative to the provocation offered by the Warrington and Runcorn conurbations to convert the Ceiriog valley into yet another reservoir complex, how far the erection of another five aerodromes, three artillery practice camps and at least fifteen radar stations in north Wales, contributed to a surge in membership of the Welsh Nationalist Party!

(b) MATTERS TECHNICAL

RDF technology improved by leaps and bounds, driven by the Battle of Britain, the Blitz, and the imminent threat of invasion. In 'safe' back areas, such as north Wales, operational radar stations also doubled up as research and development laboratories until a point was reached that the two functions became incompatible. Research at Prestatyn was seemingly geared to perfecting CHL Tx and Rx aerials; in this Appendix we note the introduction of a dozen or so

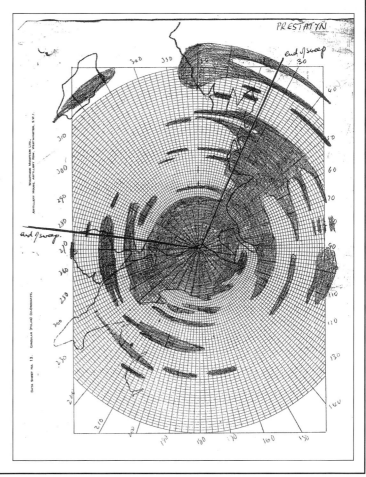

different types within a short period of ten months, before the station standardised on a Common Aerial and VT98 in April 1941. It is the documentation engendered by this research that has made for the rare survival of an RDF file in the Royal Radar Establishment Files at the PRO (AVIA 7/515) upon which much of the preceding chapter and this Appendix is based. The file closes in December 1941, on going research into 'back radiation' being transferred to the TRE. So, equally abruptly, ends our chronological log, the Radar Research and Development Establishment of the Ministry of Supply having no further interest in the day to day running of an exclusively operational radar station.

(c) LOG

13 May 1940
Work began on AMES Prestatyn (Gwaunysgor) 'on a rough hillside with wooden working huts and manually operated aerial array mounted on a timber lattice platform'.

20 July 1940
AMES Prestatyn became operational, 'everything new

Sweep tracing July 1940 for RAF Prestatyn, showing front-looking coverage as far as the Isle of Man and a surprisingly clear back-looking sector, beyond PEs offered by Clwydian Range and Ruabon Mountain (see log for 31 July 1940 and 4 September 1940).

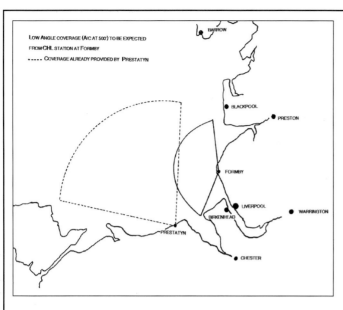

LOW ANGLE COVERAGE (A/C AT 500') TO BE EXPECTED
FROM CHL STATION AT FORMBY

----- COVERAGE ALREADY PROVIDED BY PRESTATYN

Proposal to close RAF Prestatyn in favour of Formby CHL were given short shrift. This map shows why. In April 1941 AMES 65A would achieve a range of 142 miles, 126 miles on average.

and workmen still in the compound'. Aerials — Yagi(T) transmitter, 37ft 5ins from the ground; 4-stack Broadside receiver, 29ft from the ground

26 July 1940
First calibration flights at 500 and 2000ft to 40 miles out by an Anson of No 48 (Coastal Patrol) Squadron, Hooton Park. 'Multitude of permanent echoes in front of station cluttered up screen at ranges less than 20 miles'.

31 July 1940
'Inland-looking' experiments for Fighter Command. 'Not practice of this station to cover inland directions, ... anything under a range of about ten miles is difficult due to permanent echoes ... maximum range observed is 67 miles ... performance over small sector sweeps is fairly satisfactory'.

5 August 1940
Second calibration flight by Hornet Moth W9389 (No.4 CPF) — 'only aircraft available'. Monitored by Dr Taylor for No 60 Group, No 8 RMU and No 10 Group, Box. Tests carried out 'on visual', circling station at 1,500ft.

7 August 1940
Third series of test flights, on visual at 500ft.

8 August 1840
Report demands greater efficiency to overcome 'the permanents' i.e. echoes from the Lancashire coast ('much-chimneyed'). Despite comparative lack of operational flying 'good plots' made from 30-60 miles ... ships have been plotted at 40 miles.

3 September 1940
Changed over to 2 x 2 aerial arrangement Rx on 3 and 4, Tx on 1 and 2; 'receiving more tracks than ever and covering greater area'.

4 September 1940
First day of use of 2 x 2 aerial system. Test flight on bearing 312⁻ true; aircraft seen up to 25 miles, but amplitude poor 'as we only had a Fairey Battle (No 5 BG, Jurby, IoM) a plane notoriously poor in its RDF response'. Blackpool Tower CH signal very strong; 'sea cover into Liverpool poor at this time'. 'Overland looking' is the domain of the ROC but it has been noticed that hostiles at present raiding the North-west seem to come from the back of us'. Certain feeling of impotence therefore, when 'day after day we plot coastals and scarcely ever a hostile'. Permission sought to alter sweep to 145–360–45 'as we will pick up useful tracks at night'. Gwaunysgor (at 750ft OD) may be too high above sea level; some thought given to moving to a station on the Wirral at 300ft OD, or to Gwrych Castle (Abergele) at 560ft OD. The latter 'would give a good low-angle coverage of the sea, while, looking east, the hills of Prestatyn would cut out PEs yet allow aircraft over Merseyside to be detected at a height of 3,000+ft; ultimately advised 'better to stay put' whilst awaiting first reports from Formby CHL even then being erected.

5 September 1940
Tracks plotted in over Anglesey.

6 September 1940
J. R. Ratcliffe (TRE) urges improved performance at Prestatyn. On-site scientific officers given full authority 'to make any changes which are considered necessary. The only provision is that once the work is completed, No 60 Group should be informed of all the changes'. Extra bay of aerials being sent for 2T x 3R; 2T x 2R readings unsatisfactory. Extra scientific officer (Mr Lees from Cromarty CHL) being posted in.

RDF responses from coastal plots in Liverpool Bay, as recorded by RAF Prestatyn during a busy day in September 1940.

7 September 1940
Aerial change to Rx on 1 and 4, and Tx on 2 and 3.

8 September 1940
Tracking report: 2/9 = 32 tracks; 3/9 = 30 tracks; 4/9 = 46 tracks; 5/9 = 27 tracks, all up to 1700hrs. Scientific observer at Barton Hall filter room opines station 'has improved greatly, in fact is as good as Creigneish and Glenarm" N° 8 RMU have assisted with experiments and alterations to aerial arrays.

14 September 1940
Experiments to aerial arrays being carried out in gale-force winds. Five-bay Broadside adopted, receiving on 1,2, and 3; transmitting on 4 and 5

15/16 September 1940
Station off the air for long periods with 'split-motor' trouble.

17 September 1940
Aerial array locked down for a few hours due to gales. Neverthless 40 tracks noted up to 1700hrs.

18 September 1940
Shared test flight with Strumble Head CHL did not materialise, but secured co-operation of IoM-bound Battle. Left Prestatyn on bearing 312° true at 500ft; seen out to 46¹/₂ miles. Still carrying out inland looking experiments with many X

(unrecognised) and hostile tracks being obtained between 2200–2400hrs as far as 60 miles from Prestatyn. Operational performance of the station adjudged 'satisfactory'.

19 September 1940
Extra reflector flaps added by No 77 Wing to 'Modified Birdcage aerial' to overlap dipoles.

23 September 1940
Extra flaps removed and a reflector placed behind the dipoles. 'It was felt that some improvement was apparent. although actual PE diagrams hardly bore this out.'

24 September 1940
CH Westcott, visiting scientific observer, advises increase in number of test flights to test station's performance and readings.

15 November 1940
Audit of October's graphs and logs completed:

Hostile	78	ACCUs	7
X	83	Civil	12
Bomber	45	Unidentified	304
Coastal	365		

19 December 1940

Experiments carried out with a second aerial array 150 yards from the main array, at the same height. [The 'squegging oscillator' of the 1941/2 site map, page 101]

2 January 1941

The scientific observer in the Barton filter room puts Prestatyn's plotting error (after 'cleaning up') at 'less than 2 miles at a range of 70+ miles'. Although overland looking 'is and has been carried out successfully, this is now discouraged by the filter room on the grounds that co-ordination with the Observer Corps is poor'. Hostiles have been detected at a range of 60 miles at 15,000ft east of Liverpool. Station begs to be allowed to continue looking inland 'in any case during the night when aircraft in the sea sector are rare'. Aerial array now 'Mixed Broadside', three receivers and two transmitters, with centre of array 780ft OD.

25 April 1941

Conversion to common aerial and VT98 completed. Great improvement in range, signal strength, response 'noise'; test flight (by Blenheim at 5,000ft) awaited as and when Creigneish back on air, using same flight to calibrate both stations. Best range to-date is 142 miles 'but an average of 126 miles is more to the mark'.

5 May 1941

Major breakdown during operational sweeps, lasted 36 hours; Nº 77 Wing brought into help. Matters exacerbated by phone lines down at the same time. Station had been monitoring raids on Liverpool and 'this really upset the whole system in our sector. Motor transport sent at high speed to all local units for spares to get Prestatyn on the air'.

6 May 1941

Station back on line late afternoon.

16 May 1941

PPI tube now in use. Average of 100 tracks a day; but problems of getting information to Preston filter room. Great need for own dedicated phone line; at present plots 'told' via Rhuddlan CH.

Tracks plotted during month:	1 May	145
	2 May	109
	3 May	161
	4 May	76
	5 May	108
	6 May	117
	7 May	170
	8 May	153
	9 May	117
	10 May	76
	11 May	98
	12 May	62
	13 May	45
	14 May	99
	15 May	204
	16 May	122

6 June 1941

Station audit: increase in range 'striking'; best to date 147 miles; ships plotted at 35 miles; speed of plotting limited by having to share a line with Rhuddlan CH. Some new PEs apparent. Over 100 tracks a day plotted on average.

21 December 1941

Owing to increasing difficulty of doing research work on an operational station, experimental work at Prestatyn ceases. Experiments in 'back radiation' transferred to TRE Worth Matravers.

We take leave of Prestatyn where the aerial array is still turned manually. It has its advantages — greater accuracy and precision — as the aerial array could be 'inched' through the full 275° –25° of the sweep.

AMES 65A (PRESTATYN CHL)

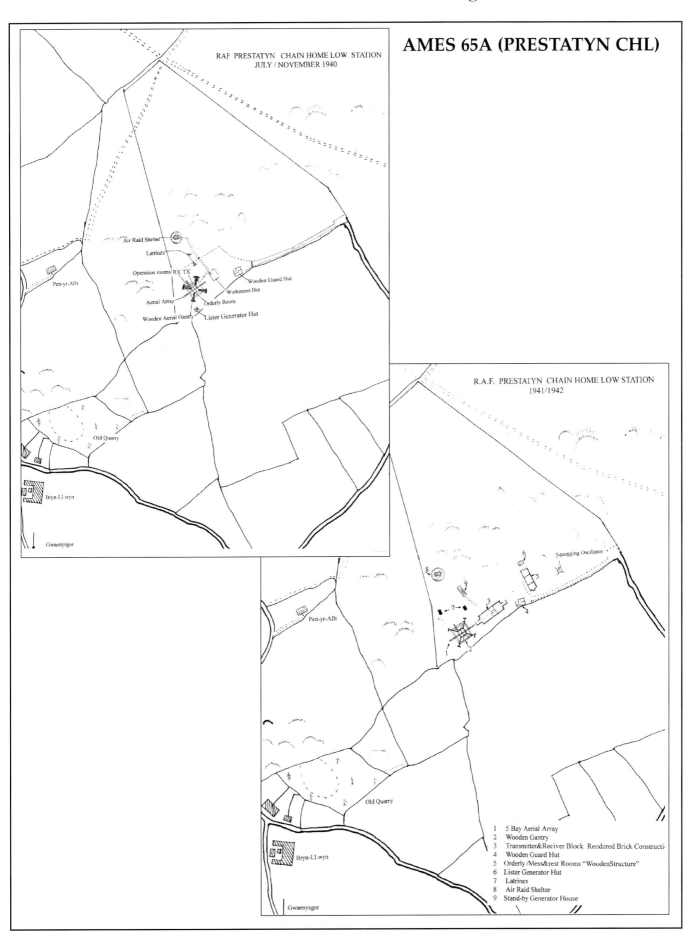

RAF PRESTATYN CHAIN HOME LOW STATION
JULY / NOVEMBER 1940

Air Raid Shelter
Latrines
Operation rooms RX TX
Wooden Guard Hut
Aerial Array
Workmens Hut
Orderly Room
Wooden Aerial Gantry   Lister Generator Hut
Pen-yr-Allt
Old Quarry
Bryn-LLwyn
Gwaenysgor

R.A.F. PRESTATYN CHAIN HOME LOW STATION
1941/1942

Squegging Oscillator
Pen-yr-Allt
Old Quarry
Bryn-LLwyn
Gwaenysgor

1   5 Bay Aerial Array
2   Wooden Gantry
3   Transmitter&Reciver Block Rendered Brick Constructi
4   Wooden Guard Hut
5   Orderly /Mess&rest Rooms "WoodenStructure"
6   Lister Generator Hut
7   Latrines
8   Air Raid Shelter
9   Stand-by Generator House

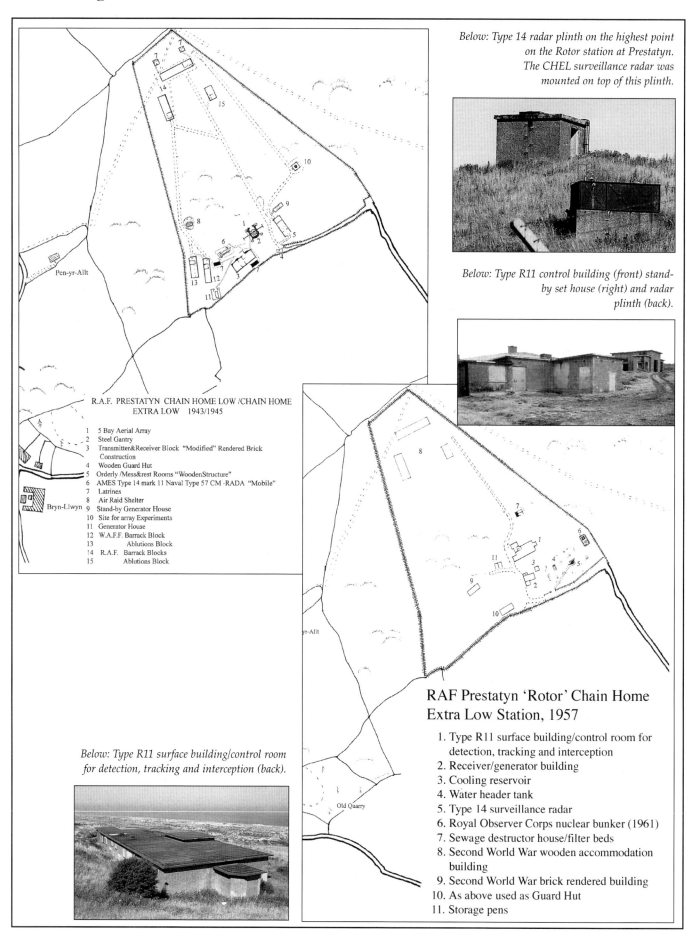

Below: Type 14 radar plinth on the highest point on the Rotor station at Prestatyn. The CHEL surveillance radar was mounted on top of this plinth.

Below: Type R11 control building (front) stand-by set house (right) and radar plinth (back).

Pen-yr-Allt

R.A.F. PRESTATYN CHAIN HOME LOW /CHAIN HOME EXTRA LOW   1943/1945

1   5 Bay Aerial Array
2   Steel Gantry
3   Transmitter&Receiver Block "Modified" Rendered Brick
     Construction
4   Wooden Guard Hut
5   Orderly /Mess&rest Rooms "WoodenStructure"
6   AMES Type 14 mark 11 Naval Type 57 CM -RADA "Mobile"
7   Latrines
8   Air Raid Shelter
9   Stand-by Generator House
10 Site for array Experiments
11 Generator House
12 W.A.F.F. Barrack Block
13   Ablutions Block
14 R.A.F. Barrack Blocks
15   Ablutions Block

Bryn-Llwyn

Below: Type R11 surface building/control room for detection, tracking and interception (back).

RAF Prestatyn 'Rotor' Chain Home Extra Low Station, 1957

1. Type R11 surface building/control room for detection, tracking and interception
2. Receiver/generator building
3. Cooling reservoir
4. Water header tank
5. Type 14 surveillance radar
6. Royal Observer Corps nuclear bunker (1961)
7. Sewage destructor house/filter beds
8. Second World War wooden accommodation building
9. Second World War brick rendered building
10. As above used as Guard Hut
11. Storage pens

Old Quarry

RAF PRESTATYN CHL STATION
Experimental aerial arrangements, July 1940–December 1941

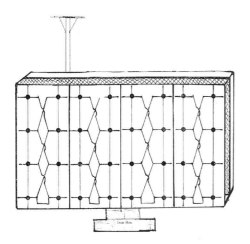

Nº 1 Array (left)
*July 1940. First aerial array, Yagi Tx aerial.
Yagi transmitter, 4 x receiver broadside, chicken wire reflector frame. The array was mounted in a wooden constructed 'bird cage'.*

Nº 2 Array (right)
1 September 1940. Second aerial array. This was the '2x2 system' which transmitted on 1 and 2 and received on 3 and 4..

Nº 3 Array (right)
Between 3 September and 14 September a trial change to transmitting on 2 and 3 and receiving on 1 and 2 was carried out. Chicken wire reflector frame. The Yagi aerial has been dispensed with.

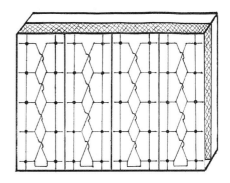

Nº 4 Array (left)
14 September 1940. Fourth aerial array. On this date the station switched to a 5 bay broadside. The reflector did not overlap the dipoles. Bays 4 and 5 are the transmitters and 1, 2 and 3 the receivers.

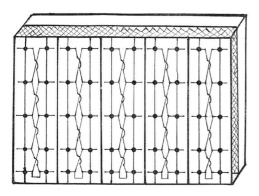

Nº 5 Array (right)
The introduction of the Common Aerial at Prestatyn on 25 April 1941, was no surprise, as the station was already operating a 5 Bay Broadside Aerial Array, wuth T-R Switching before this date using the VT 58 Transmitting Valve, which gave an output of 80kw, but it was the introduction, on the same day, of the VT98 UHF Pulse Transmitting Thoriated - Tungsten Filament Triode Valve in the same structure, which gave a two-fold increase in emission on half filament power. This raised eyebrows at Prestatyn. Overnight, it changed the station's ability to bring in tracks and improved range to an all-time high, as reported by F. Kay, technical officer to his superiors at at the Technical Research Establishment.

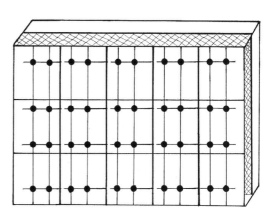

Nº 6 Array (right)

19 September 1941. Sixth aerial array. This was the first experiment whereby flaps were added to the reflector to overcover the dipoles.

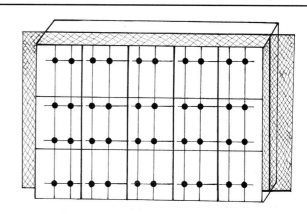

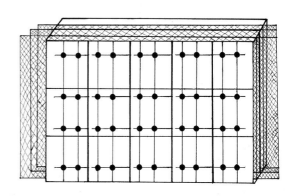

Nº 7 Array (left)

23 October 1941. Seventh aerial array. On this date the flaps were removed and an extra reflector installed behind the dipoles. The experiments with the reflectors and flaps were done with a squegging oscillator placed some 150 yds away from the main aerial array. The oscillator was placed at the same height as the main array.

Nº 8 Array (right)

December 1941. Eighth aerial array. This system has three reflectors, each with side flaps. This gave the best results during the experimental period but, after careful consideration, it was felt that a two reflector system, placed at the optimum spacing would give Prestatyn a workable system.

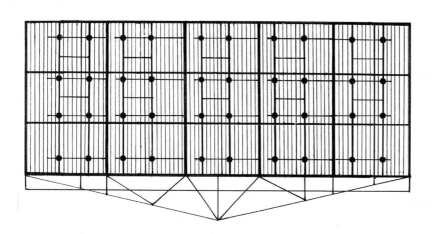

Nº 9 Array (left)

The ninth aerial array, as at 31 December 1941. It consisted of five bays with four tiers of full diploes set on an overlapping single frame Wire Mesh Reflector. The array at this time was still hand turned.

6. Secret Starfish

The air war in north-east Wales and Shropshire border country had two sides — one furtive and clandestine, and one highly visible. As intimated in the preceding pages, the location of decoys was shrouded in such secrecy and subject to a smoke-screen of disinformation so dense that, half a century later, it is virtually impossible to discover anything concrete about them. Not even the Imperial War Museum can produce a representative photograph of these deception measures! So 'hush-hush' were they that decoys were rarely, if at all, photographed for record purposes.

In his history of the Second World War Churchill reveals how, for the crucial period whilst boffins struggled to overcome technical problems in countering the new German navigational beam known as the 'X-System' (*X-Verfahren*), this country's night defences relied heavily on decoy fires, 'often with remarkable results'. Even while counter-measures had yet to be refined, from the settings of the beams and the time at which they were deployed, RAF Intelligence could reasonably forecast target, time, route and height of attack. But as Churchill ruefully admits: 'Our night fighters had, alas, at this date neither the numbers nor the equipment to make much use of this information'. The war was now entering its 'high technology' phase. But the realisation that, eighteen months into hostilities, ground defences were relying on something straight out of a Spanish Armada scenario, comes as something of a shock to local historians.

As attrition set in, as the tempo of *Luftwaffe* attacks increased, as losses of pilots and aircraft piled up, as airfields were put out of commission, as fliers neared exhaustion point, something had to be done to relieve the pressure, to dilute the enemy offensive, however marginally. Hence the use of decoys, especially at night when radar, the (Royal) Observer Corps and other defensive measures were least effective. To give Colonel Turner as free a hand as possible — and to preserve secrecy — his 'Department' was detached from the normal chain of command. Churchill, a firm believer in deception and 'cloak and dagger' stuff, personally monitored with great satisfaction the spread of decoys throughout the land.

The early decoys were largely military, spawned of the Battle of Britain, protecting Fighter Command airfields in southern and eastern England. 'Key Point' decoys evolved to cover factories, public utilities and establishments of national importance. In passing, it should be noted that the *Decoy Farm* in Marlston-cum-Lache [*SJ381628*] just over the Flintshire border is not called after the Vickers Armstrong and RAF Hawarden decoys set up a mile or so to the west. The farm-name has a respectable pedigree going back to at least 1633! But following the bombing of Coventry on 14 November 1940 — the same night that RAF Hawarden was raided for the first, and only time — the decision was taken to provide decoy fires about those cities strategic to the nation's war effort. By December a total of eighteen 'Starfish' protected Crewe, Derby, Sheffield, Birmingham. Coventry and Bristol, each straddling approach routes initially favoured by enemy aircraft. The small numbers provided indicate the pressure that was being put on Colonel Turner's slender, finite resources. Following the mauling of Liverpool and Manchester over the Christmas period 1940, the first decoys were provided for the manufacturing towns of the industrial north-west, especially those along the axis of the Manchester Ship Canal. They would be continually added to until May 1943, by which time Liverpool had 28 decoys on 14 sites, Manchester 10, and Warrington, Crewe and Northwich three each. Included in Liverpool's total were the so-called 'Strategic Starfish' decoys way out at Llanasa, Llandegla and Fenn's Moss. Fortunately for the researcher the last three are reasonably well documented, especially in the way of oral testimony from those who served on them or assisted in their construction.

Focussing on that at Fenn's Moss, one is immediately confronted with problems of chronology, with evidence for at least two, possibly three, decoys on the Moss, but with little to suggest which came first or, indeed, whether they functioned together or separately. Because of the incompleteness of official records the researcher starts with the fact that some sort of decoy was in place by 15 September 1941, but from other evidence immediately has to acknowledge that they were probably *in situ* some twelve months earlier.

The first series of 'special fires' were simple affairs, possibly associated with Colonel Turner's early 'experimental' phase and at his suggestion installed to 'upgrade' and lend much needed credence to RAF Shawbury's shambolic and short-lived decoy. Had the latter been attacked the provision of 'fire damage' would have improved the deception and have given the German pilot the satisfaction of seeing splendid fires raging in the wake of his attack.

In the centre of the Fenn's Moss [*SJ493365*] at what used to be known as the Fenn's Wicket portable fire baskets were set up on 4-inch concrete slabs 4–5ft square. Two blocks yet survive, devoid of any superstructure. Others existed but have been removed to facilitate peat digging or to fill pot-holes. These giant braziers were filled with scrap timber, weathered blocks of peat, old tyres, felting, brushwood and creosote etc. scrounged from neighbouring farms and garages. The fires were ignited by electrical incendiary devices. Hopefully flames escaping into the darkness over Bronington would have been impressive enough to convince an enemy aircrew that they had hit a fuel tank, hangar or dispersal on the makeshift airfield that was for the moment Shawbury's decoy.

Whether these particular 'basket fires' continued in use after the abandonment of Shawbury's decoy in August 1940 is not known. Since they were supplementary to the 'Q' lights, probably not. However, since the more complex 'Strategic Starfish' units were erected barely 100 yards away, the 'baskets' may have been incorporated into that set-up.

Out of the Fenn's and Whixall Moss Oral History Project 1995, sponsored by Clwyd Archaeological Service, has emerged information relating to a possible second 'basket-type' decoy somewhere to the rear (west) of Moss Cottages, Whixall [*SJ504365*]. Although at first sight rather too close to habitation and enclosed crofts on the edge of the Moss, there is sufficient detail to give credence to the oral evidence.

This second set of fires comprised 'crates' set upon a concrete base and holding a bed of peat, combustible and slow burning in itself. On this was piled, *inter alia*, metal shavings and filings. Above this, on tubular steel scaffolding was a drum of diesel or 'some other fuel'. Such is the detail absorbed and filed away by Alf Hamer, a peat cutter on temporary release from the Army. He had served with the King's Shropshire Light Infantry and the 2nd Bn. Herefordshire Regiment at Camberley, Horsham, Cromer and Bognor Regis during the Battle of Britain and the initial invasion threat. In other words a military head on rustic shoulders, quite capable of appreciating the strategic significance of these supposedly 'top secret' contraptions on the Moss.

Local tradition links this second set of fires with 'Marchwiel ammunition factory', otherwise the Royal Ordnance Factory east of Wrexham in Isycoed parish, which came on stream early in December 1940. However, as noted earlier, the ROF had its own 'QF' decoy on the Worthenbury/Shocklach border. It was abandoned on 29

October 1943. 'Basket fires' would burn for about an hour and their ignition would be staggered to cater for successive waves of enemy aircraft whose presence over target could last for anything up to four or five hours. The adding of metal filings to the combustibles would affect the colour of the flames according to the deception intended. Thus iron shavings would burn with a bluish tinge, simulating poorly blacked out foundries or furnaces. The raised fuel tanks on scaffolding might also suggest the presence of troughing for water flushes, which when mixed with the burning oil would cause explosive bursts of flames, simulating the dropping of an oil-filled *Flammenbombe*, at 250 and 500kg the largest German incendiary bombs.

In March 1942 both of the above mentioned decoys would be superseded by the establishment of a 'Strategic Starfish' on the Moss [*SJ494368*], not far from the original 'basket fires' and just beyond the southern boundary of the bombing range. It is the only decoy site for which some documentary and cartographic evidence exists to support testimony on the ground. Apart from a couple of drainage ditches dug in connection with current conservation work, this particular corner of Section 4 (or Canal Section) has for some hitherto unexplained reason not been cut for peat and vegetation-wise stands out as distinctive patch of Moor Grass only slowly being colonised by heather and bracken.

North-east Fenn's Moss, showing the Strategic Starfish site and later 'train busting' gunnery target. [National Assembly for Wales]

Concrete base for an early 'basket fire' decoy (1942) on Fenn's Moss.

Turner's secret school at Hook near Goole. Sergeant Vaughan reported directly to the decoy 'area' Flight Lieutenant at Tern Hill Sector HQ, but for routine administration, supplies and inspections etc. the unit's parent station was RAF Tilstock. In practice theirs was a monotonous but essential task, with daylight hours spent in checking generators, wiring, detonators, igniters etc. and then at night sitting back waiting for something to happen.

The 'Strategic Starfish' was controlled from the duty crew-room, otherwise a half Nissen hut not exactly shrapnel proof — 1,000yds away beyond the last habitation in Moss Lane, on the Whixall/Shropshire side of the border [SJ499364]. Its concrete base, used occasionally for the stacking of peat, is still visible, but its walls, some six courses high, and roof have been knocked down for in-fill and fencing. However, the battery storage hut (it looks more like a forlorn latrine!) still stands albeit minus its door and corrugated asbestos roof.

From this command 'bunker' electric wires ran out to the Starfish. Fires would be detonated to order by dialling the appropriate number and pressing a switch. Each evening a priority call was put through to the Air Ministry giving details of cloud amount and height, wind speed, visibility, and other information that might have had a bearing on the effectiveness, or otherwise, of a decoy fire. Someone would then await the instruction via Tern Hill (later Atcham) Sector Control (Nº 9 Group, Fighter Command), to light up selected fires. Before a land line was run to the command bunker this posed something of a problem, with a corporal having to ride into Whixall (Welsh End) to use the phone at 'The Waggoners'. This was also used by the bombing range 'HQ staff' and some conflict of interests arose. Time was of the essence and the messenger had about two minutes to get back to the control room with the order to light up. Matters were eased somewhat when the RAF commandeered Manor House telephone and set up a continuously manned 'signals centre-cum-guardroom in the sitting room. Mr Herbert Beckett, a successful market gardener, was allowed just two minutes to make private or business calls!

Making allowances for the natural accretions of 50 years it is still possible to discern a raised access 'path' opening out onto a 'square' where presumably materials were assembled for the maintenance and restocking of the decoys.

A vertical aerial photograph (page 106) taken in 1946 still shows, radiating out from the 'square', the bases or remnants of at least eleven multi-unit combustion sites. These have been tentatively plotted in map form. Their disposition clearly suggests streets of terraced housing in a city suburb rather than some industrial complex. Nothing is shown on later photographs taken between 1983 and 1994. This is hardly surprising. A geophysical survey or a sweep with a metal detector might reveal something still existing beneath the peat. Each base carried two-tier shelving some 4ft wide, and over 6ft long, carrying a double row of sacks stuffed with sawdust and wood shavings soaked in creosote. Each was screened from prying eyes by a light framework of scaffolding and sackcloth that blended well with the purples and browns of the moss. Strangely, recalling the tight security that prevailed elsewhere, construction was largely undertaken by peat cutters pulled off the Bettisfield section of the Moss. Possibly this was because they were more familiar with the peaty terrain and the working of the peat tramway used to get materials from the Manor House wharf to the decoy site. They were, however, denied the use of the Simplex locomotive and trucks had to be manhandled along the track. The whole lay-out was arranged and wired so that units could be fired individually or together or holding some in reserve so that the decoy could be fired on successive nights should the need arise.

The original 'basket fire' sites required only two trained men to throw switches to create instant 'fire damage'. The more elaborate 'Strategic Starfish' was operated by a squad of nine under a sergeant, the latter billeted in Fenn's Bank. All these 'general duties' men had special training in simple camouflage techniques and the use of decoys at Colonel

Very much the same scenario was followed in the establishment of a 'Strategic Starfish' decoy in and above an abandoned sandstone quarry on Llandegla Moors some seven miles northwest of Wrexham [SJ222535], its existence unsuspected by a public at large, even to this day. Its fires were only visible from the air or from the adjacent summits of Moel Garegog and Cyrn-y-Brain. Again the historian is helped by the oral testimony of two former airmen, LAC Alan Bates a General Duties 'bod', and Cpl Ernest Dyer, electrician by trade. The latter was also involved with the commissioning of the Hack Green decoy, one of Crewe's two protecting 'Starfish' sites [SJ658476 Centre]. Of all the RAF installations in Wales and the north-west only operational

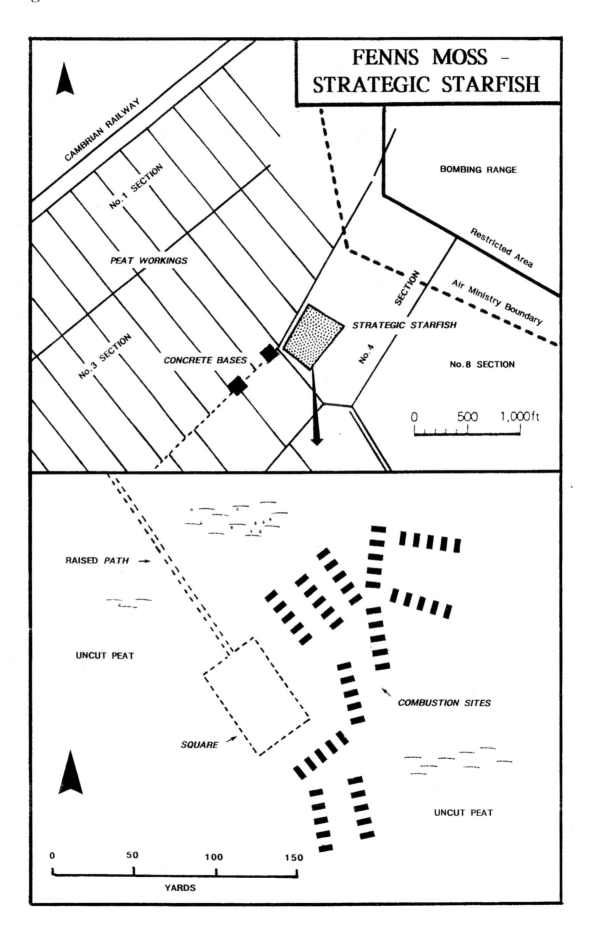

Battery Room to Fenn's Moss Strategic Starfish, 1995. The base of the command bunker is immediately to the rear of this building.

airfields seem to have warranted their own decoys. Cpl Dyer will be met with again as he nightly speeds through the country lanes south of Farndon with RAF Wrexham's mobile homing beacon.

Of the decoys treated in this present volume, the history of Starfish N° 5(b) at Hack Green, south of Nantwich, Cheshire; an ironic twist, since this particular decoy was amongst the shortest lived. The information has been obtained through the good offices of Mrs Peggy Furber, Audlem, whose family farmed Austerson Hall during the critical period two sets of decoys were established on her land. Twice the Furbers were given the opportunity to leave their farmhouse. Twice they refused, accepting compensation for land lost to farming but then living uneasily for some fifteen months waiting to be bombed, an apprehension shared by RDF technicians billeted at the Hall. The first decoy at Hack Green, ultimately one of two for Crewe, was a tentative offshoot of the Home Office or Ministry of Home Security forays into the murky waters of defensive deception. In June 1940 MoHS camouflage technicians and artists made night flights over Crewe to record impressions of industrial area and railway marshalling yard lighting under current blackout conditions, returning to the Civil Defence Camouflage Centre at Leamington Spa to conduct experiments with lights and fires.

These were completely separate from Colonel Turner's work on QF decoys. 'Special fire' or Starfish N° 5(b) first appears on Colonel Turner's running schedule for 1 August 1941, its counterpart at Chorlton (SF.5a), five miles further east, on 15 July 1941. The low serial numbers demonstrate the perceived urgency behind the need to provide Crewe with SF decoys and the early stage at which Colonel Turner's Department became involved in their running. But it was all for nothing; within twelve months both decoys at Hack Green would be abandoned as the RAF radar station undergoing yet another tranformation and upgrading in the fields west of Coole Lane expanded too near the new QF site for comfort; many of the RDF operators were actually billeted, and an orderly room set up, in Austerson Hall and outbuildings. As pressure on space increased, a separate hutted orderly room was erected in the 'Big Yard'. The radar station would eventually blossom into Hack Green GCI, becoming operational within N° 9 Group between 14–23 July 1941, but before then the site was home to an AMES Type 8C 'Intermediate' — XI, semi-static, theoretically 'transportable' but having its 35ft aerial system mounted on a gantry and operations and transmitter rooms hutted.

Having a vested interest in marshalling yards vital to its supply system, the Army was first into Hack Green with a 'dummy' marshalling yard At Austerson, mimicking the real thing at Crewe. Peggy Furber's description of 'small chicken

coops on 10-ft high poles' resolves itself into a series of shielded lights, arranged in two straight rows to represent railway tracks, all very basic — the later addition of signal lights and a 'loco-glow' were probably Colonel Turner refinements. The semi-sunk control bunker still stands to the rear of the farm house. According to Peggy Furber personnel were 'Army', with whom there was no social intercourse at all — 'very, very, secretive and uncommunicative, even more so than the RAF types in the house!' This raises the question of telephones and control. Or did the site NCO have the discretion to light up when he believed Crewe to be under attack? — as on the night of Wednesday 9 October 1940, or that most fatal Thursday, 14/15 November.

On 24 November 1940, following the devastation of Coventry ten days earlier plans were approved to build emergency 'first degree' QF decoys ('crashdecs') for seven more vulnerable towns and cities in addition to Coventry and Birmingham each of which had received — by a miracle of panic-driven co-ordination — three QF decoys over the week-end beginning Saturday 23 November. They were to be Sheffield, Manchester, Derby, Crewe, Bristol, London and Middlesborough in that order. There was little subtlety involved with siting and operation of this early batch of 'special fires' — a pity in many ways, as the Hack Green Starfish was responsible for much pollution of water courses and the River Weaver. They were placed in the anticipated path of bombers making for West Midlands targets and on learning from Enigma intelligence the orientation of German navigational beams for a particular night's sorties, would be ignited in advance of approaching enemy aircraft on the off-chance of attracting bombs from vital areas, expecially as Colonel Turner opined '... by those pilots who viewed with some distaste the anti-aircraft barrage in front of them ...' Well might *Luftwaffe* aircrews worry. Within 2nd AA Corps command Crewe had its own GDA with sectors manned by two HAA regiments (N°s 1 and 106), two LAA regiments (N°s 45 and 63) and three SL regiments (N°s 61, 78 and 83).

Once the initial shock waves from Coventry had subsided there was a pause for breath and a re-think. Priorities were re-arranged to spread scarce resources more evenly among probable targets, The planned three sites for Crewe were reduced to two, one at Chorlton and the second at Hack Green, while Manchester would be provided with nine sites

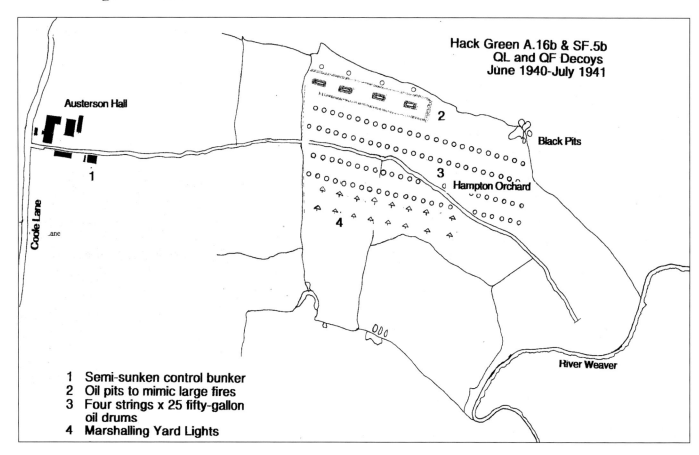

Hack Green A.16b & SF.5b
QL and QF Decoys
June 1940–July 1941

Austerson Hall

Cooke Lane

Black Pits

Hampton Orchard

River Weaver

1   Semi-sunken control bunker
2   Oil pits to mimic large fires
3   Four strings x 25 fifty-gallon
    oil drums
4   Marshalling Yard Lights

Below: Control Bunker, Hack Green QF site. Possibly a one off, this design shows every sign of haste in siting and construction materials — sunk into the side of a drainage ditch — door lintels at ground level — no wonder it flooded!.

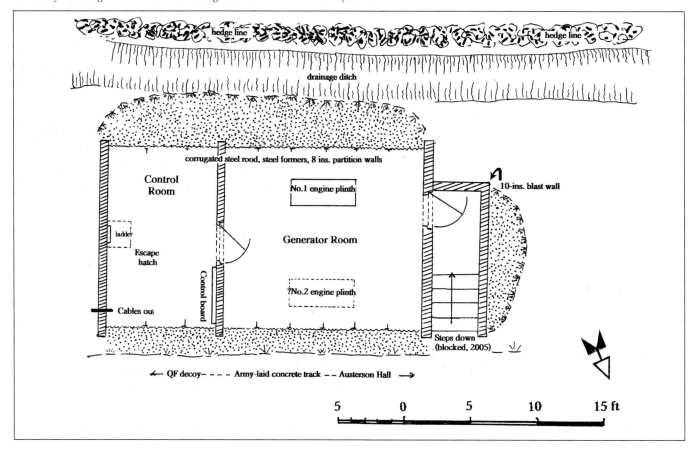

hedge line   hedge line

drainage ditch

corrugated steel rood, steel formers, 8 ins. partition walls

Control
Room   No.1 engine plinth   10-ins. blast wall

                              Generator Room

ladder

Escape
hatch

Control board

?No.2 engine plinth

Cables out

Steps down
(blocked, 2005)

← QF decoy– - - – Army-laid concrete track - - Austerson Hall →

5   0   5   10   15 ft

Hack Green QF Site

Left: Entrance to Hack Green Control Bunker, semi-sunk. The floor lay below the water level in the adjacent ditch.

Below: Control Bunker at Hack Green, May 2005. Taken from the drainage ditch that plagued the site.

Above and right: The concrete road built by the Ministry to convey materials across the water-logged fields from the bunker to the Starfish site.

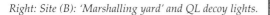

Above: Hampton Orchard, a 100-acre field-site (A): oil pits and oil drums of the QF decoy.

Right: Site (B): 'Marshalling yard' and QL decoy lights.

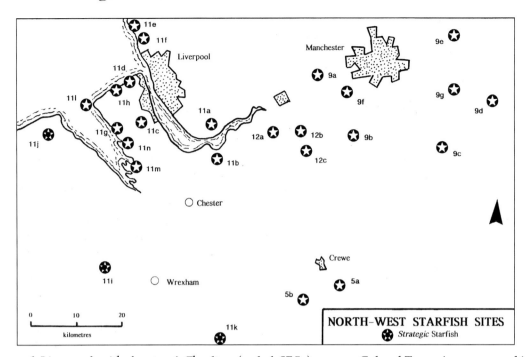

NORTH–WEST STARFISH SITES
✴ *Strategic* Starfish

and Liverpool with fourteen! Chorlton (coded SF.5a) was operational by 27 November 1940; Hack Green (coded 'b') by 3 December. Hack Green was chosen because Austerson Hall had already been reconnoitered for a QL site and had good roads for supplying fuel. The Army had laid a concrete road over part of the farm track leading to the river. Because of the time element and supply problem there was no question of using standard QF equipment. A fuel oil mix was decided upon — 400 gallons crude oil to 100 gallons of petrol. Shellmex, Ellesmere Port, arranged the issue of drums of crude and petrol from their Crewe distribution depot. Gangs of local authority workmen, under the direction of a couple of RE officers from Western Command HQ, Chester, descended upon Hampton Orchard, a 100-acre field at Austerson Hall, and dug four large pits each holding 500 gallons of oil/petrol mix and buried 50-gallon drums in the earth, 4 strings by 25 drums, the one end cut off and sunk with only the neck of the drum above the ground. After a messy filling operation pits and drums were covered with pieces of roofing felt, both to keep the weather off whilst dormant and, when lit, to give the impression of 'spluttering fires'. Although pits and drums were fired by their own igniters,they were wired up to burn in multiple groups, in relays to give a longer burning time. Peggy Furber recalls 'canvas screens' along just one edge of the river path that bisected the site, perhaps not so much to hide the drums from prying eyes as to reflect the flames and suggest containment within non combustible walls. The exact number and arrangement is known because the Furber family had the choice of filling them in when the field was released for agriculture or lifting each one. They opted for the latter, filling some of the drums with concrete to make a river wall to contain erosion by the river Weaver which flows just below the decoy site. The commissioning of SF.5b marked the end of A.16b. Army personnel left, the control bunker was rewired for QF; RDF personnel moved into purpose-built accommodation on their radar station, and

Colonel Turner's men moved into the Hall. SF.5b remained a basic site with minimal staffing — two airmen, a telephone and a shelter were all that was needed; there would be no enlarging of crews that came with refinement of tactics and the introduction of specialised variants of decoy fires. The site had closed by 15 July. It was lit three times during March 1941, and twice during April, but neither decoy nor the surrounding area received any bombs to suggest that SF.5b was doing its work. But with the IAZ blazing merrily away four miles to the north advertising the true position of the target, it must have been obvious to *Luftflotte 3* bomber crews that the fires did not 'belong'; if Crewe's gun batteries had concentrated their fire over the Starfish site the results may have been vastly different but such co-operation was for the future.

Official records have the Llandegla decoy operational as from 1 October 1941, from inception differentiated, along with those at Llanasa and Fenn's Moss, as a 'Strategic' Starfish for Liverpool, but this date can only represent the take-over of the site on the north flank of Moel Garegog by Colonel Turner's department. Before that date, the decoy was the responsibility of the Army, more particularly the Home Guard. When HQ Western Command, Chester, first mooted Llandegla Moors for the establishment of a primitive QF decoy they found a willing participant in Captain G. P. Dewhurst of Bodidris Hall, who owned the shooting rights on the mountain. He was also, before battalion structure was introduced, commander of Zone 3, Denbigh Group, the LDV. Sappers from Chester bull-dozed an access track up the hill side and deepened a shallow quarry in which was placed a half-Nissen hut which was to serve as a control bunker and 'safe reserves' for the decoy crew. As at Hafod on Minera Mountain, the fire pans consisted of little more than drums of creosote and other inflamables set up ready to ignite, which they were on the night of Saturday 31 August 1940, taking their cue from the fires on Esclusham Mountain. The latter, despite stirling efforts at replenishment during the previous two days were beginning to wane — the Wrexham area had been stripped of virtually everything combustible. Moel Garegog, a last minute reserve, as it were, was set ablaze. Pentre Uchaf and Pentre Isaf farms received near misses from HE bombs. The fire pans were re-lit the following night and HE bombs fell around the Rhydtalog cross roads and the A5104 was reduced to single line traffic because of bomb craters and a burst water main. The last time Moel Garegog went up was on 5 September, not so much a deliberate act of torching the fire pans, but a last spasmodic flare up in a stiffening breeze of already smouldering gorse and bracken. It was not as if Liverpool was the *Zielpunkt*; German bombers were ranging widely across the Midlands, Manchester and Liverpool conurbations exposing 'the pitiful inadequacies of the British night defence system'. Tafarn-y-gath on the A525 duly received an opportunist *Flammenbombe* which in turn attracted a last flurry of HE bombs and IBs on the surrounding hills out towards Acrefair and Penycae with some UXBs at Ponciau, which could not be cleared for three weeks, such was the backlog following the efficacy of Wrexham's primitive Army decoys. A Llandegla decoy would be lit again on 20 October 1941, attracting a parachute mine to Pendinas, causing serious damage to several farms — Tan-y-graig, Hafod-dafalog and Ddol-ddu, and injuring two people. But, by this time, the decoy was a vastly different beast, having received a Colonel Turner 'make-over' and now covered several square miles of moorland and from its qualifying epithet 'strategic' presumably doing its best, in a more sophisticated fashion, to replicate a piece of Merseyside. Alan Bates takes up the story.

LAC Bates was posted to RAF Wrexham the same time as the opening up party — 9 June 1941 — and was immediately sent on a 'decoy familiarisation course' at Hook, Humberside. He arrived back at Wrexham to join a special 'decoy unit' made up of a sergeant, two corporals and fourteen other ranks, under the command of F/Lt Batchelor. Nominally attached to RAF Wrexham for matters of supply and personnel — pay, health, discipline etc. — operationally the unit came under the direct control of N° 9 Group HQ, Preston via Sector HQ Tern Hill (later Atcham).

Secrecy was paramount. The 'Starfish' crews themselves did not know exactly what they were decoying and locals had even less of an idea of what they were up to. There was a tented searchlight unit at Pen-y-bont [SJ246534] on the B5430 Four Crosses–Rhydtalog road with either an orbit beacon or homing light, and even they were left in the dark was to what was happening beyond the Nant-y-ffrith Reservoir! Until the decoy unit got their own Nissen huts in the 'quarry', men were billeted about nearby villages — Bwlchgwyn, Gwynfryn and Coedpoeth — being picked up each day by unit truck. For the moment this was an unexpected luxury, but it had its drawbacks. Number, rank and unit were not used on incoming or outgoing mail; letters were collected from Bwlchgwyn post office, and the Official Secrets Act and censorship curtailed 'talking shop' with relatives and/or over-curious landladies.

It took a Manchester firm of contractors and their Irish navvies just two weeks to re-align the track to the quarry

from the A5104, to build a picket post, and to 'skin' and prepare an area of moorland above it. Their tented camp was self-contained for catering and boozing purposes — the tiny 'Liver Inn' at Rhydtalog could just not have coped! A specialist engineering firm from Birmingham was responsible for the erection of the actual decoy. This comprised eight steel pans or troughs, each 35–40ft long, fired by wood, coal and/or heavy fuel oil. Above these a fine mesh grille carried brass pairings which would lend colour to the flames. The contents of the pans were detonated electrically from the control room (a half-Nissen) in the quarry. An ordinary GPO telephone was used to dial any number 1–8. At the same time a firing button was pressed to blow the selected pan. Simultaneously a small detonator blew a valve of the 200-gallon paraffin tank which stood on scaffolding some 20ft above each pan, with remarkable results! Electrics were checked daily, despite being snowed up several times during the winter of 1941–2, when the caterpillar tractor from Llandegla sawmills was requisitioned to get onto the moors.

Initially HQ and orderly room were set up at Rhydtalog, the nearest hamlet to the decoy. It was in a ground-floor room of a large house across the road from the 'Liver Inn'! Here was located the only telephone for miles. There were unexpected perks, such as a maid bringing in tea and toast to the duty crews early each morning. There was real regret when the move was eventually made to quarters in the quarry! The latter was inevitable and certainly eased the wheels of the war machine. Firstly it obviated the desperate cycle ride in the dark from Rhydtalog to the decoy with orders to 'light up'. Secondly, in an era of small rural manual exchanges, it got rid of the confusion' that sometimes occurred, with a puzzled postmistress at Llandgela getting an order to ignite — whether for real or in practice something of which she knew absolutely nothing, despite the decoy being only 1½ miles away!

A similar Fred Karno arrangement seems to have pertained at the third 'Strategic Starfish' site at Llanasa [SJ096824] on the seaward end of the Clwydian Range. Less is known of this decoy. Mr John Mason, Prestatyn, can remember it comprising 'big square stacks of tyres, oil drums, electric wires and creosote-soaked timber'. At least duty crews had a shrapnel proof bunker, possibly deemed advisable because of its rather exposed position *vis-à-vis* the Talacre air-to-ground gunnery range and the Gwaunysgor CHL station. But there may have been another reason, more obvious then than now. There was, according to many people, 'some sort of rocket projectile weapon' on site. Opinion then differs as to whether it was real, i.e. an outlier to Merseyside's AA defences, or was a fake. If the latter it hints at the Llanasa decoy being rather more than a simple 'Starfish'. Be that as it may, as John Mason recalls, '… the trouble was, to get the signal to fire, an airman had to cycle a very rough 1½ miles to Llanasa every night from the Nissen hut situated above a conifer wood near a ruined keeper's cottage, along a muddy, rutted lane, to phone London for instructions from the public phone box'.

Strangely, for something some 41 miles as the Heinkel flies from the port, the Fenn's Moss 'Starfish' was a

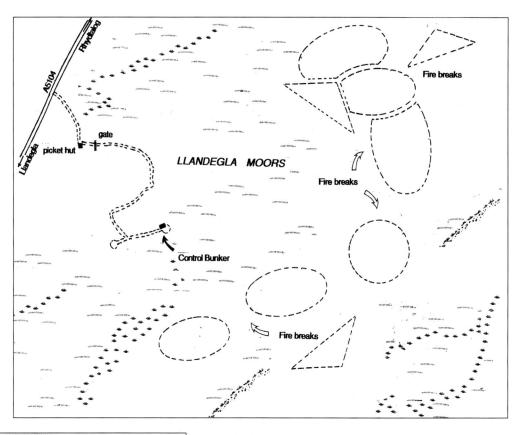

Above: Llandegla Strategic Starfish SF11 (j). Decoy for Liverpool, final layout. Despite much interference in laying out ranges for a gun club, fire breaks can be fairly easily recovered.

Left: The original approach track and gateway to Llandegla Starfish, is really suitable only for pack animals.

Above: Site of the Second World War Starfish at Llandegla. A semi-sunken Nissen hut served as the control bunker against the cliff face, top left of the hard standing.

Left: The flattish area of desolate moorland provided an ideal site for Llandegla's decoy fires. A triangular fire break strip is discernible left centre.

Liverpool decoy (as were also Llandegla and Llanasa) deliberately placed so that enemy aircraft had to fly over it on their way to attack the port. Theoretically, when flares/incendiaries were dropped on the actual target, they would be immediately extinguished and, at the same time, fires lit at the Starfish site. By reproducing the effect of a target being bombed it was hoped that follow-up waves would see the 'Starfish' before the real target and be encouraged to waste bombs on the peat moss. However, such conditions were rarely met with in practice. Liverpool's hard-pressed fire fighters never won the race to extinguish early pathfinder fires. Indeed, when Liverpool burned, as in the May 1941 *Blitz*, incoming bombers at high altitude could see the red glow that was a burning city from as far off as London. Under such conditions even the most sophisticated decoy would be useless.

What intrigues the researcher, however, is the differentiation of the Fenn's Moss, Llandgela, and Llanasa 'Starfish' sites as 'strategic', the only three of some twenty-eight 'Starfishes' that protected Crewe, Northwich, Manchester and Liverpool, to carry that *soubriquet*. The three are near enough in a diagonal line and a possible explanation may have something to do with the ability of British boffins to 'bend' the German navigational beams. Thus, as a raider would be expecting to pick up flares or fires illuminating, say, Crewe, Bromborough and Birkenhead, its crew would see fires at the three 'Strategic Starfish', two along the Dee estuary which was often confused with that of the Mersey. Unfortunately, with pertinent documents in the PRO missing, one may never know the exact contribution made by these remote corners of Denbighshire and Flintshire to eventual victory in the night skies over north-east Wales and north-west England.

It should be remembered that in the early part of 1941, when decoys were reaching their maximum extent, night attacks on Britain were expected to continue at an infinite crescendo — one has only to recall the 7-day *blitz* on Merseyside in May 1941 that almost brought the port to a standstill and how, thankfully but inexplicably, the merciless pounding ceased on the eighth night. Only after Hitler invaded Russia on 22 June 1941 would air raids gradually die away and stop. But this is with hindsight.

Until the penny dropped boffins continued to strive to improve the measures and devices by which the nation had hitherto survived, and to develop new ones, notably radar in all its applications. Labour, material and manpower continued to be made available for decoys spurred on by costly raids on ports and cities. But even as the network of decoys reached saturation point the threat from the sky they were designed to meet suddenly came to an end. Yet such would be the uncertainty that for another 18 months, as the incidence of air raids over the north-west and north Wales dwindled — the last bombs fell in Flintshire on 11 January and the last 'All Clear' sounded over Merseyside on 9 August 1942 — the Welsh 'Starfishes' continued to be manned. That at Fenn's Moss was finally abandoned on 30 September 1943, but that on Llandegla Moors not until 30 December.

Inevitably there will be those who will underrate the military value of these decoys. Their true worth could only have been proved by major trial. Sergeant Vaughan and his men in their control 'bunker' down the Moss Lane at Whixall were ready and willing. Fifty years later, perhaps, one can only be thankful that events did not come to this pass.

But even before the 'Starfish' fires were dismantled their part of Fenn's Moss was put to other uses by the RAF — as an *ad hoc* specialist gunnery range. About 700 yards down the peat 'stackway' or tramway track-bed towards Oaf's Orchard [SJ486363] Sgt Vaughan's squad erected a static mock-up of a railway train. The full-scale model was made up of galvanised sheeting attached to a tubular frame and painted on both sides to simulate a locomotive and carriages. It could therefore be approached from any direction.

This target provoked and disturbed local inhabitants, especially smallholders with livestock, than any other military installation on the Moss. '… these blasted fighter planes, they'd drive you mad coming over with them practising shooting trains and railway engines up in France, see ….' A typical comment (minus expletives) — and this despite camera or ciné-guns being used. When developed the film would reveal accuracy, opening and closing ranges, length of burst etc. Such details would be compared with the pilot's oral or written version of his 'shoot', which often entered the realms of near fiction! Day in, day out, weather permitting, as the build-up to D-Day gathered momentum, planes came screaming in, hedge-hopping across the Moss, usually from the direction of Morris' Bridge [SJ494354]. Major culprits were the Allison-engined North American Mustangs of N° 41 OTU and N° 3 Tactical Exercise Unit from RAF Poulton as they trained up for their cross-Channel sweeps and armed tactical reconnaissance and ground support rôles. These were essential preliminaries before moving on to Andover for a week's 'live' practice on Salisbury Plain.

Had any incensed Whixall smallholder been in the habit of taking the numbers of offending aircraft he would surely have noticed, between March 1944 and February 1945, a constantly recurring BR372. The latter had come off the assembly line in April 1942 as a standard version of a Mark IV photographic reconnaissance Spitfire but it was immediately hi-jacked by the Controller of Research and Development (CRD) as an experimental aircraft. The RAF had been clamouring for some form of air brake to assist Spitfires decelerate and not overshoot during combat. After being fitted with double trailing edge braking flaps, one section moving up, the other down, by Heston Aircraft, BR372 underwent trials at the Royal Aircraft Establishment (RAE), Farnborough. In July 1943 it was returned to Heston Aircraft for the installation of upper surface dive brakes and for other drag reduction modifications. In October BR372 was returned to the RAE for further, successful, trials. Dive brakes were always used with flaps and although deceleration could peak at 5G at 400mph, pilots reported targets could be kept in gun-sight during combat manoeuvres. From March 1944 BR372 underwent service trials under the auspices of the Air Defence Development

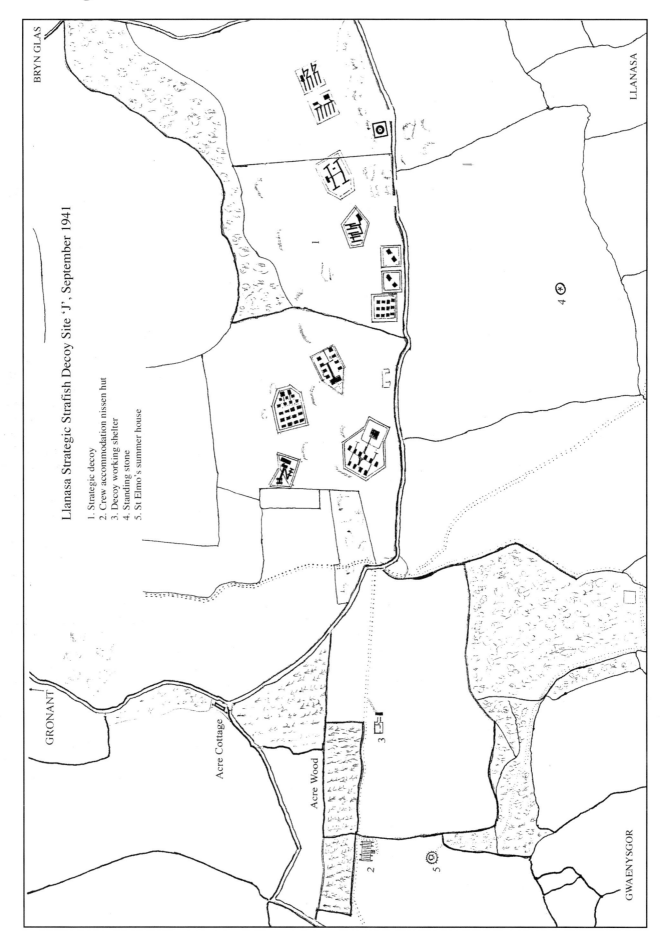

Llanasa Strategic Strafish Decoy Site 'J', September 1941

1. Strategic decoy
2. Crew accommodation nissen hut
3. Decoy working shelter
4. Standing stone
5. St Elmo's summer house

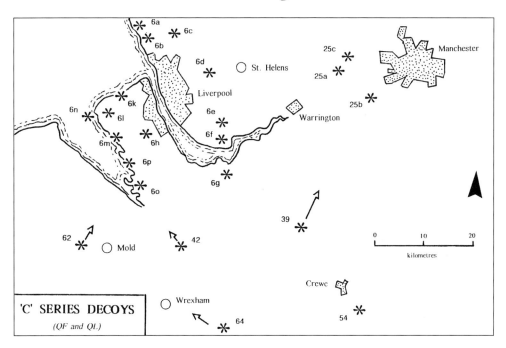

'C' SERIES DECOYS
(QF and QL)

Unit, Boscombe Down, but until February 1945 field trials were actually held at Nº 61 OTU, Rednal, on both the Baggy Moor and Fenn's Moss ranges, the latter particularly after BR372 had been converted into an *ad hoc* fighter-bomber with the fitting of fuselage bomb racks. The Spitfire's dive bombing trials, squeezed in between the practice bombing runs of the never ending stream of learner aircraft from the bomber OTUs, proved the success of the specially strengthened flaps in steepening dives onto ground targets. BR372 was flown up to Eshott, Northumberland, on 8 February 1945 for further trials with Nº 57 OTU. It is doubtful if its presence was missed in the general cacophony that daily surrounded the Fenn's Moss range.

Between April–July 1945 the final users of the range were the Spitfires Vs and IXs of Nº 58 OTU, the last training unit at Hawarden and Poulton, producing fighter-bomber pilots for *Rhubarbs*, *Rodeos* and *Circuses*. While finding and shooting-up the Fenn's 'train' was an integral part of intensive, low-level navigational exercises, it should be remembered that during their course pilots had also to drop at least sixteen practice bombs on the adjacent Fenn's bombing range so that the two exercises may have been linked. Surprisingly, despite adding to the congestion of the middle Dee low-flying area, there were in these latter months no accidents whilst this particular range was in use.

On grounds of accuracy, perhaps, this might be re-phrased to read '… no accidents on this particular range …', for after September 1943 there is a subtle, yet discernible, shift in emphasis in Nºs 41 and 58 OTUs' aircraft crashes to the Whitchurch–Malpas area. The most spectacular was the fate of Spitfire IX NH437 of Nº 58 OTU, which on Wednesday, 30 May 1945 had just shot up 'the train' on Fenn's Moss. At full throttle and still at tree height the Polish pilot, Sgt W. Polowancywk, adrenalin flowing, decided to beat up a moving target, namely a three-tonner travelling from Nº 5 MT Squadron, Liverpool, to RAF Tilstock along the A41 at Edge Green north of Malpas. He completely

misjudged his attack and hit the lorry. NH437 carried on across the road, tore through a couple of hedges and ploughed up a field before coming to rest, a tangled wreck. Miraculously, Polowancywk was not killed, though critically injured. Unfortunately, two airmen in the rear of the lorry who had stood up to get a better view of the assault, were killed instantly. One of them, F/Sgt L. A. Broadstock, lies buried in the Commonwealth War Graves Cemetery at Blacon, Chester.

For those with a technical bent some further research might profitably be made into why so many of the Allison-engined Mustangs from Nº 41 OTU suffered glycol (coolant) leaks, blocking vision and filling cockpits with deadly fumes, again with a suspicious concentration of such incidents in the Whitchurch area — as well as on the Talacre air-to-ground gunnery range!

The end of hostilities in Europe immediately reduced the demand for fighter pilots. Nº 58 OTU closed down on 20 July 1945 with the passing out of Nº 6 Course. An unaccustomed silence descended upon Fenn's Moss, broken only by the occasional drone of high flying bombers and the crump of practice bombs on the N.E. Fenn. Even this ceased on 10 August 1945; as noted in Chapter 3, the bombing range would be reactivated between 1949 and 1953, since when, on the Moss, aquatic beetles, dragonflies, heath butterflies, raft spiders, bush-crickets and caddisflies regrouped. But the military onslaught upon their environment was as nothing compared with the threat posed by mechanisation of traditional sod cutting techniques and a more intensive exploitation of the Moss that occurred between 1968 and 1989.

Decoy Sites Nº 9 Group Fighting Area

Subsequent entries in italics indicate changes in either name, number, function or status.

Date	Serial	Parent Station	Decoy	Type of Decoy	Map Ref (War Rev.)	NGR
'N' Series						
1/8/41	N.24	Ditton Priors	DP.1 Neenton	QF.C.FI	71/105099	SO651889
12/3/42	N.29	Stretton	ST.1 Budworth	Q	44/170016	SJ705806
22/8/43			*ST.1 Budworth*			*Abandoned*
* Naval establishment						
'A' Series						
1/8/41	A.10	Donnington	Kinnersley	QF.QL	61/135393	SJ677183
1/1/42		(a) Kinnersley				Tfrd to 124Q
		(b) Shefiff Hales		QF.QL	61/198327	SJ741120
1/3/42	A.43	Harlescott	Withington	QF	61/006353	SJ548142
30/11/43						*Abandoned*
1/8/41	A.34	Mold	Cilcain	QF	43/635850	SJ172635
1/5/43						*to 'C' Series C.62*
1/8/41	A.36	Marchwiel	Worthenbury	QF	51/905683	SJ444471
1/5/43						*to 'C' Series C.64*
1/8/41	A.40	Ironbridge	Leighton	QF	61/082267	SJ624057
1/5/43						*to 'C' Series C.68*
* Army establishment						
'F' Series						
11/8/41	P.5	Stanlow	Ince	OF	43/935978	SJ471766
* Petroleum (oil refineries etc.)						
STARFISH SITES (inc. STRATEGIC STARFISH)						
1/8/41	SF.5	Crewe	(a) Chorlton		52/197715	SJ736504
			(b) Hack Green		52/124682	SJ632473
1/8/41	SF.9	Manchester	(a) Chat Moss		36/161166	SJ695957
1/5/43			*(a) Chat Moss*			*'C' Series C.25(a)*
1/8/41			(b) Tatton Park		44/231031	SJ765823
			(c) Park Moor		45/434011	SJ969805
1/3/42			*(c) Park Moor*			*Abandoned*
			(d) Chunal Moor			*Abandoned*
1/8/41			(e) Mossley		37/464223	SD996017
			(f) Carrington Moss		36/219128	SJ753919
1/5/43			*(f) Carrington Moss*		*'C' Series C.25(b)*	
1/8/41			(g) Ludworth Moor		37/468113	SK002908
1/3/42			*(g) Ludworth Moor*			*Abandoned*
1/8/41	SF.11	Liverpool	(a) Hale		43/920046	SJ454833
			(b) Ince		43/936979	SJ472767
3/3/42			*(b) Ince*		*Transferred to 'P' Series P.5*	
1/8/41			(c) Brimstage		43/762047	SJ297833
1/3/42			*(d) Wallasey*			*Abandoned*
21/4/42			(e) Formby		35/752263	SD284048
			(f) Little Crosby		35/775231	SD307017
			(g) Heswall		43/709039	SJ245826
			(h) Morton		35/713123	SJ247909
			(i) Llandegla (Strategic Starfish)		51/683750	SJ222535
31/12/43			*(i) Llandegla*			*Abandoned*
1/10/41			(j) Llanasa (Strategic Starfish)		42/562038	SJ096821
15/9/41			(k) Fenn's Moss (Strategic Starfish)		51/952578	SJ491365
30/9/43			*(k) Fenn's Moss*			*Abandoned*
1/1/42			(l) Little Hilbre		35/655090	SJ189872
			(m) Burton Marsh		43/752963	SJ286749
			(n) Gayton		43/734010	SJ269796
1/8/41	SF.12	Warrington	(a) Hatton		44/059031	SJ594821
			(b) Appleton		44/107032	SJ643821

Date	Code	Airfield	Location	Type	Grid	Grid
5/2/42			(b) Appleton			*Abandoned*
1/8/41			(c) Arley		44/133004	SJ669793
1/8/41	SF.32	Stoke	(a) Caverswall		52/392657	SJ931452
			(a) Caverswall			*Abandoned*
			(b) Swynnerton			*Abandoned*
1/8/41			(c) Keele		52/273638	SJ813430
			(d) Beech		52/315577	SJ855371
20/6/43			*(d) Beech*			*Abandoned*
1/8/41	SF.37	Northwich	(a) Bostock		44/151901	SJ686693
			(b) Little Budworth		44/073860	SJ610650

'M' Series*

Date	Code	Airfield	Location	Type	Grid	Grid
1/8/41	M.2	Boulton Paul Wolverhampton	Coven	DB.S.QL	61/351266	SJ894058
18/6/42						*Dismantled*
1/8/41	M.4	Arm. Whitworth Baginton	Leamington-Hastings	DB.QF.QL	73/914879 (also SF.7(a) Coventry)	SP452680
15/9/41				*DB.QF.QL.Q*		
18/6/42						*Dismantled*

* Miscellaneous (dummy buildings etc.)

DECOY SITES ('Q' AND 'QF' AIRFIELDS)

Date	Code	Airfield	Location	Type	Grid	Grid
1/8/41	71	Tern Hill	Chipnall	Q	52/181534	SJ721326
12/8/42				Q/T		
30/11/43						*Abandoned*
1/6/41	72	Shawbury	Withington	Q	61/181534	SJ548142
12/8/42			*(see A.43)*	Q/T		
22/1/42				QF.Q		
30/11/43						*Abandoned*
1/8/41	98	Honiley	(a) Wolverton	Q	82/670820	SP218616
1/1/42			*(a) Wolverton*	Q/D		
1/8/41			(b) Wotton Wawen	Q	82/582815	SP129611
12/8/42			*(b) Wotton Wawen*	Q/D		
30/11/43			*(b) Wotton Wawen*			*Abandoned*
1/8/41	102	Cranage	Betchton	Q	44/248811	SJ787602
12/8/42				Q/T		
30/11/43						*Abandoned*
1/10/41	124	High Ercall	Kinnersley	Q	61/132392	SJ673182
12/8/42				Q/T		
30/11/43						*Abandoned*
11/11/41	134	Penrhos	Porth Ceiriad	Q	49/779575	SH319250
12/8/42				Q/T		
30/11/43						*Abandoned*
11/11/41	135	Valley	Newborough	Q	41/874861	SH411637
12/8/42				Q/D		
30/11/43						*Abandoned*
1/11/41	136	Wrexham				
15/11/41		Wrexham	Minera	Q	51/715699	SJ255486
12/8/42				Q/D		
30/11/43						*Abandoned*
	153	Sealand (see 205)				
12/8/42	155	Atcham	Cressage	Q/D	61/044229	SJ587019
	157	Hawarden (see 207)				
20/3/42	164	Woodvale	Great Altcar	Q	35/797290	SD329076
12/8/42				*Q/D*		
1/8/41	205	Sealand	Puddington	Q.QF	43/777947	SJ313734
15/12/41	153					
2/8/42				Q/T		
22/11/42				*Starfish. Q*		
1/8/41	207	Hawarden (Vickers)				Tfrd to C.42
15/12/41			Bretton	Q.QF	*Transferred to C.42*	
1/1/42	*207*	*Hawarden*	*Bretton*	*QF (RAF)*	*Transferred to C.42*	
	157	*Hawarden (Vickers)*	*Bretton*	*Q (see C.42)*	*43/830843*	*SJ366629*

22/11/42	*207*	*Hawarden*	*Bretton*	*Starfish*	*Transferred to C.42*	
1/8/41	210	Cosford	Boningale	QF	61/271227	SJ814019
31/12/43						*Abandoned*
20/3/42	226	Woodvale	Great Altcar	Q	35/797290	
12/8/42				*Q/D*		

'C' SERIES (CIVIL QLs and QFs)

1/5/43	C.6	Liverpool	(a) Formby	QL*	35/752263	SD284048
			(b) Little Crosby	QL*	35/775231	SD307017
			(c) Lydiate	QL/QF	35/814251	SD347038
1/11/41			(d) Knowsley	QL	35/88167	SD421955
1/5/43				QL/QF		
1/5/43			(e) Halewood	QL/QF	35/927078	SD461866
1/1/42			(f) Hale	QL*	43/920046	SF454833
1/5/43			*(f) Hale*	*QL/QF*		
			(g) Ince	QF*	43/936979	SJ472767
			(h) Brimstage	QL*	43/762047	SJ297833
			(k) Moreton	QL*	35/713123	SJ247909
			(l) Hoylake	QF	35/695096	SJ229882
			(m) Heswaft	QL*	43/709039	SJ245820
1/1/42			(n) Little Hilbre	QL*	35/655090	SJ189872
			(o) Burton marsh	QL*	43/752963	SJ286749
			(p) Gayton	QL*	43/734010	SJ269796

* see also Starfish sites (SF.11)

1/5/43	C.25	Manchester	(a) Chat Moss	QL*	36/161166	SJ695957
			(b) Carrington Moss	QL*	36/219128	SJ753919
			(c) Astley Moss	QL/QF	36/186190	SJ719981

* see also Starfish sites (SF.9)

1/5/43	C.35	Stoke on Trent	(a) Caverswall	QL*	52/392657	SJ931542
			(b) Swynnerton	*QL**		*Abandoned*
			(c) Keele	QL*	52/273638	SJ813430
			(d) Beech	QL	53/315577	SJ855371
20/6/43			*(d) Beech*			*Abandoned*

* see also Starfish sites (SF.32)

1/5/43	C.39	Northwich	(a) Little Budworth	QL*	44/073860	SJ610650

* see also Starfish sites (SF.37)

1/5/43	C.42	Hawarden (Vickers)	Bretton	Q/QF	43/830843	SJ366629
					(see also Decoy site 207)	

1/5/43	C.54	Crewe	Chorlton	QL*	52/198713	SJ736504

* see also Starfish sites (SF.5)

1/5/43	C.62	Mold	Cilcain	QF*	43/635850	SJ172635
18/5/43			*Cilcain*			*Abandoned*

* see also 'A' series (A.34)

1/5/43	C.64	Marchwiel	Worthenbury	QF*	51/905683	SJ14171
29/10/43			*Worthenbury*			*Abandoned*

* see also 'A' series (A.36)

1/5/43	C.68	Ironbridge	Leighton	QF*	61/082267	SJ624057

* see also 'A' series (A.40)

1/10/41	C.80	Dolgarrog	Rowlyn	QF	42/295895	SH742675
1/5/43			*Rowlyn*			*Abandoned*

7. Four into one will go!

As this chapter's title indicates, it is difficult to categorise aerodromes in north-east Wales and borders in simplistic terms. Being generally 'back area', save for the period June 1940–August 1942, airfields here carried out several functions at any one time, housing units that existed uneasily side by side, often getting in each other's way, and giving rise to bitter verbal exchanges at ministerial, if not grass roots, level. The researcher has problems in differentiating which unit is the principal 'occupier' and which enjoyed 'lodger' status at any given time. RAF Hawarden is a case in point. Today, as Hawarden Airport, it is barely recognisable as an early Second World War aerodrome. The continued expansion of BAe Systems and Airbus UK has seen to this. Indeed at the time of writing the whole of the former OTU (N° 4) site, both technical and domestic areas,, has been razed to house the production line

and support factories for the wings of the Airbus A380 'Super Jumbo' jet, which, assuming environmental and dredging problems are overcome, will begin their journey to France via the River Dee and the port of Mostyn. 'Temporary' wartime hutments have long gone, but elsewhere hangars and 'permanent brick' buildings yet linger on, recycled in many guises, so that with a discerning eye and the obligatory security passes, it is still possible to absorb something of the atmosphere of a busy wartime training and MU/ASU airfield. No apology is offered, therefore, for breaking historical narrative of this chapter with illustrative digressions into the realm of airfield archaeology, There is no better place with which to start than the runways! The peri-track has been retained and is very busy but the typical triangular layout has been much modified. Runways 3/6(32/14) and 1/4(19/01) have vanished; N° 2/5(30/23) remains having been lengthened and widened to cater for the daily visits of the giant SATIC 'Beluga' super-transports. Yet despite the enormous technological leap into a new millennium, all aircraft movements are still controlled from what is basically a Second World War watch/met. office or control tower, 518/40, 8936//40 pattern, re-clad and with modern VCR up top, and crammed full, of course, with more up-to-date hi-

RAF Hawarden showing the various units involved with the aerodrome. Part AMWD drawing 1883/45.
[Crown copyright, RAF Museum]

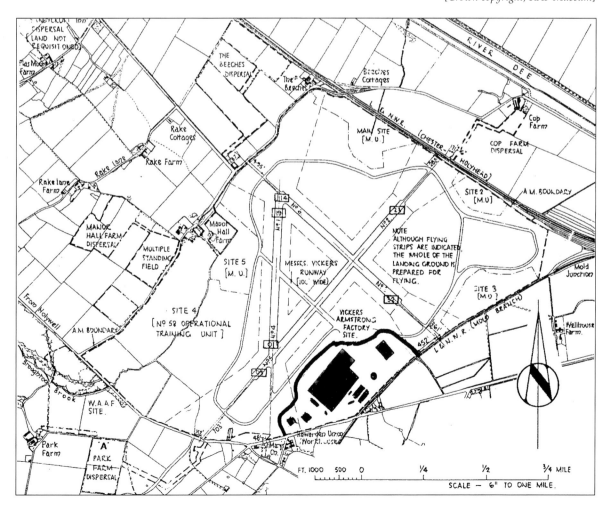

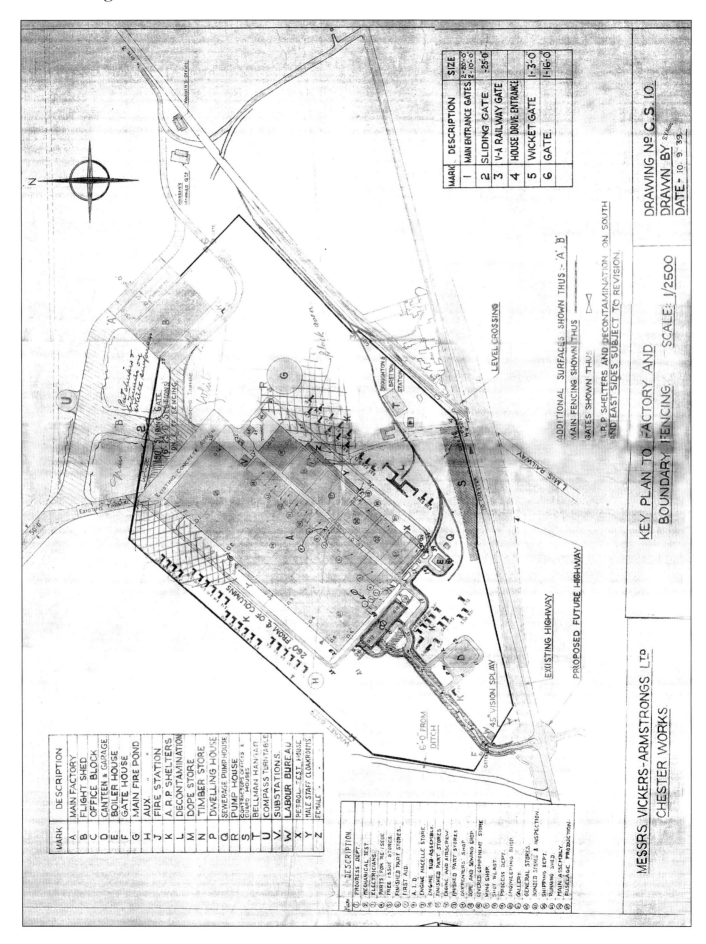

Facing page: Contractor's plan of the Vickers/MAP factory, Broughton, Flintshire, dated 10 September 1939. Produced for improving camouflage and a proposed diversion of the A55 (which was never implemented).

tech gadgetry than existed in 1940.

As already noted in Volume 2 of this present history, first on site was the Vickers Armstrong-managed but MAP-owned shadow factory, earmarked initially for the assembly of Wellington bombers. Ground works and construction commenced on 14 December 1938, the main contractor being Sir William Arrol & Son, Glasgow, builders not only of the Tower and Forth Bridges, but also, in 1924–26, of the Queensferry road bridge which carried the A540(T) across the Dee. The factory officially became fully operational in September 1939, although the first Wellington I, (L7770), had rolled out of its stop-gap Bellman hangar on 2 August 1939 and, not without some difficulty, had managed to take off from the notoriously soggy landing ground, en route to Weybridge for flight testing and acceptance. The short (700yds) runway still known as the 'Vickers Track' would not be laid until late 1940, post 18 September to be more precise, this being the date of the earliest extant *Luftflotte 3* aerial reconnaissance photograph of the aerodrome. On the same date *Luftwaffe* Intelligence had also secured detailed studies of John Summers's steelworks at Shotton and RAF Sealand. Ten days later their PR aircraft had added RAF Tern Hill and RAF Wrexham, the former in the throes of botched camouflage and decoy initiatives which left nothing to the imagination, the latter not even built but with Borras Lodge being used as a much needed RLG, currently home to N° 5 SFTS, Sealand

The early morning reconnaissance, as was the custom, was followed by an evening raid, with the Hawarden 'Battle Flight' being in action for the last time, claiming a dubious Dornier Do215. The existence of this particular image (one of several of 'Adolf's holiday snaps' taken locally — RAF Sealand and John Summers's Steelworks, Shotton were also photographed the same month, possibly on the same sortie), scotches speculation by some local historians that that the *Luftwaffe* was rather slow in latching on to the existence of Hawarden aerodrome. '*Broughton Nachschubslager*' (literally ''reserve/replacement [aircraft] depot') is a fair approximation to an ASU/MU so that the airfield seems to have appeared on enemy intelligence maps some two years before Hawarden was shown on RAF aviation charts — 1942 according to RAF Museum map holdings. Consequently one might interpret the fall of bombs on other occasions — e.g. 20 August, 30 August, 9 September, 28 September, 28 November 1940 — all too easily dismissed as bomb loads jettisoned haphazardly by fleeing enemy aircraft, as serious attempts to 'clobber' the airfield as a secondary target to Merseyside. The 28 November 1940 raid was also 'one of the worst nights' in Chester's brief encounter with the *Luftwaffe*, the city boundary at Saltney being barely two miles from the aerodrome.

In May 1936 the Air Council had embarked upon a gradual re-structuring of RAF Home Commands to produce an organisation in peace time that conformed as closely as possible to that visualised for war. Maintenance Command was duly formed on 1 April 1938, setting up HQ at RAF Andover. It took over executive control of all UK-based Maintenance Units. Prior to that date most of the Maintenance Units had been administered by Training Command. The new Command was organised into four groups, N°s 40–43, each Group devoted to a specific function. N° 41 Group, also with HQ in Andover, but with a Midland regional HQ 'hut' on the Vickers site at Hawarden, became operational on 3 April 1939, controlling, initially, eight MUs including N° 19 MU at St Athan and N° 36 MU at Sealand (redesignated N° 47 MU w.e.f. 1 May 1940). Ultimately N° 41 Group controlled some 26 MUs with the addition locally of those at Shawbury, High Ercall, Lichfield and Hawarden, a westwards locational drift, to lessen the impact of enemy attack. Nevertheless, we will notice later in this present volume that Hawarden was bombed once — on the night of 14th November 1940 as an alternative target to Coventry! N° 41 Group was responsible for for the reception, storage, maintenance and delivery by air of all new and reconditioned aircraft to RAF units; but, while being administered by Maintenance Command, was under the technical direction of the Ministry of Aircraft Production, hence possibly, in addition to the availability of land, the decision to place N° 48 MU next door to the Vickers Armstrong factory. It was also within easy reach of the Packing Depot at Sealand. Geographically the ASUs were so distributed that each unit could take the load off the depot to its north and south should necessity arise in the event of dislocation by air attack.

The *Luftwaffe* reconnaissance photograph clearly shows the stages by which Hawarden aerodrome was developing. The Vickers /MAP factory flight shed, canteen block (with vehicle park under) and main factory, fronted by the admin. block, are clearly in evidence as bombing target 'C', despite strenuous efforts to camouflage the distinctive 'Northern

The unofficial insignia of N° 48 MU, drawn by Harry Phipps.

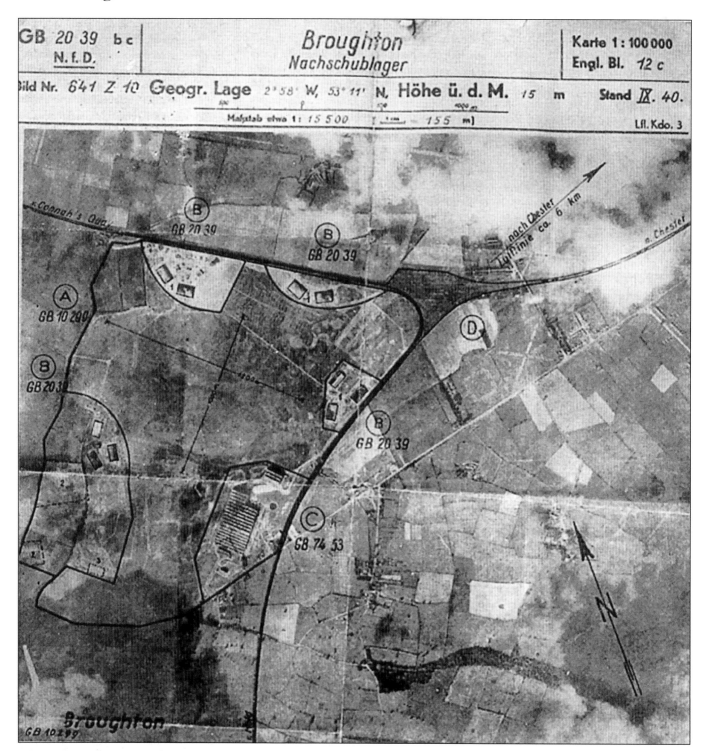

A Luftflotte 3 bombing target aerial photograph of Hawarden aerodrome, taken
18 September 1940 by a specialist Kommando recce unit.
'A' target — MU dispersal;
'B' targets — MU sites;
'C' target — Vickers/Map factory, Broughton;
'D' target — Mold Junction marshalling yard.

Aircraft, aircraft, everywhere — RAF Hawarden in January 1947, a glorified 'knackers yard'. Former OTU left centre; MU sites and dispersals top and left; Vickers/MAP factory still with wartime camouflage, bottom centre. [National Assemby for Wales]

Light' roof. Construction scars and hard standing about the flight shed have yet to be lessened by grassing and the application of a bitumen and clinker covering, the latter obtained from the Buckley brickworks. Water is impossible to camouflage and the circular main 'fire pond' is a dead give away. Paradoxically the grass covered ARSs either side of the main factory produce distinctive linear 'crop marks' for the roving 'eye in the sky'.

The ASU sites have been lumped together as target 'B'. On the Main Site (north end of field) the 'J' and 'K' type hangars are up and in use. Ground works suggest either preparatory work for a third hangar (which in the event did not materialise) or the sinking of the 18,000-gallon bulk petrol installation. Alongside, to the east of Manor Hall Lane, target 'A' is a dispersal field, predecessor of the more extensive dispersal area at 'The Beeches' that would emerge, complete with 'fry-pan' hardstanding and a blister and super-Robin hangars, on the west side of the lane. Site 2 with its 'K' type, and Site 3 with its 'L' type hangars blend more securely into the landscape and have obviously been finished first, prior to the current growing season. The ATA aircraft shed and Robin hangar have yet to materialise. On the west side of the airfield, the MU Site 5 target area, with its three 'L' type aircraft sheds (two up, one under erection), has been extended southwards to take in what would become N° (5)7 OTU site. Although no buildings are yet in evidence something was going on here according to *Luftwaffe* Intelligence; three subsidiary targets are highlighted by pecked lines, including (a) the putative sergeant and WO pilots' quarters, (b) parade ground, NAAFI, and airmen's barracks and (c) the southernmost, and first of six 'T2' hangars, although with the eye of faith one might discern the the blacked out footings of four more. Although N° 7 OTU had been formed in June 1940, and was officially the occupying unit with the MU as 'lodger', at the time of the reconnaissance photo the OTU was entirely tented (including Station HQ), fed by field kitchens and transported in rota to RAF Sealand for weekly bath nights. As winter closed in and the aerodrome reverted to an estuarine salt marsh, desperate measures were called for. Hawarden Castle was requisitioned as an officers' mess, surrounding villages were scoured for airmen's billets, the MT offices were transferred to Manor Hall Farm outbuildings, and giant aircraft packing cases were scrounged from RAF Speke for flight offices etc. In September 1940 Hawarden aerodrome is still all-grass, but German Intelligence has dutifully marked out two most important landing strips, that N-S at 1,000m and that W–E at 1,200m. By coincidence the arrows coincide with later runways 23/05 and 14/32 respectively.

N° 48 MU, Hawarden, became operational on 6 March 1940, but as part of a decentralisation programme, theoretically making for greater efficiency and speedier turnround of aircraft, became vested in N° 51 (Maintenance) Wing (Midland) on 21 April 1941. The latter had inherited its HQ at Broughton Hall from N° 9 (S)FPP. It has long been demolished, but lay immediately south of Hawarden aerodrome. In addition to the aforementioned ASUs the Wing also controlled N° 24 MU at Tern Hill/Stoke Heath and

the SLGs at Hodnet, Brockton, Weston Park, Hardwick Park and Teddesley Park.

N° 48 MU ran several communications aircraft for ferrying Broughton Hall officers about their region and to and from Andover as well as collecting delivery pilots. An impressed Miles Whitney Straight (AV970), Hornet Moth (W9386), and a Stinson Reliant (BS803) — cabin monoplanes for absolute comfort — a Miles Magister (N3851), an Avro Anson (PH856 '3D-D'), an Airspeed Oxford (NJ280 '3D-F') and Percival Proctor (DX190 '3D-H') are amongst those CF aircraft logged at N° 48 MU Hawarden between September 1940-November 1943. Aircraft codes were allocated to ASUs at Shawbury (L4), High Ercall (Q7) and Stoke Heath (4U), but there is no evidence of use. As from 1 February 1940 N° 41 Group also became responsible for the allotment of 'non-effective' aircraft, other than those resulting from accidents, which were beyond repair to ground instruction frames, to ATC squadrons, and to more realistically garnish decoy sites, the latter being particularly supplied by N° 24 MU, Tern Hill.

For seven months, until the aerodrome had operational functions thrust upon it, out of necessity from its strategic position within N° 9 Group Fighter command territory, stabling day and night fighter units for the defence of Birmingham and the north-west, N° 29 MU at High Ercall seemed to have been that rare bird, a self contained ASU with its own landing ground. Single-user occupation of an airfield was an extravagance that the RAF could ill afford, especially since, by the time N° 29 MU opened for business on 1 October 1940, wiser counsels had prevailed at the Air Ministry and from the start High Ercall was provided with concrete runways. ASU sites, sub-units and dispersals, including MAP dispersals, are located on and around the northern edge of the airfield while operational/OTU technical site (with its T2 hangars), fronted by control tower and squadron offices, and dispersals with overblisters, backed by the statutory rash of some thirteen RAF and WAAF communal sites, are grouped nicely about the southern perimeter of the airfield and despite the time lag involved, indicate a planned multi-use from the outset. One might argue that the provision of runaways at High Ercall was a one off special dispensation in anticipation of an expected influx of American aircraft, which in the event did not materialise. Whatever, the runways were the envy of units based on traditional all-grass airfields, unserviceable for long periods during the harsh winters of 1940 and 1941. The table on page 135 emphasises the short term value of the airfield other than as an aircraft storage facility.

There had been an 'all change' at Tern Hill in November 1940. N° 5 SFTS managed to survive the flooding in the wettest winter of the war by farming flights out as far afield as Bassingbourn, Driffield and Cosford. Tern Hill had become as N° 9 Group Sector station w.e.f. 1.12.40, initially as a satellite to Speke but independently operational on 23 December 1940. It now housed N° 306 Squadron's Hurricanes, and if the landing ground there became untenable arrangements were made for the squadron to use High Ercall until the water table at Tern Hill had dropped sufficiently. After slumming it on a north Shropshire raised

RAF Hawarden

Aircraft shed Nº 1, a type 'L', former MU Nº 2 site, now in use by the Hawker fuselage assembly plant.

Right: Aircraft shed Nº 2. A type 'L', ex-MU Nº 2 site, also now used by the Hawker assembly plant.

Left: An abandoned aircraft, DH.112 Venom FB50 ex-Swiss Air Force (J-1601), refurbished for air show displays 1984, crashed on take-off at Hawarden 7 July 1996, still there in early 2004.

Right: The Fire Practise Area ex-MU Nº 3 site, which was a cannon range in 1940.

bog, the refinements of concrete runways took some getting used to. On 1 February 1941, whilst landing at High Ercall, P/O Jan Artur Czapiewski rolled his Hurricane (V6986 'UZ-Z') off the end of the runway and stood it on its nose. No 13 Squadron's Lysander IIIs were refugees from Hooton Park for a shortwhile in February 1941, exchanging the guns of No 63 AA Regiment (4th AA DIvision) for those of No 45 Regiment (11th AA Division). On 10 April 1941 High Ercall aerodrome became a No 9 Group night fighter airfield in Tern Hill Sector (Atcham Sector from September). The list of operational units is one of units forming, working up, gaining experience in the defence of Liverpool and Manchester before being thrown to the lions in the south of England.

The large and complicated ASU at High Ercall was investigated, planned and commenced early in in 1938, a relatively slack year for airfield construction. The preparation of design, constructional and contract documents for the Hawarden ASU was a more urgent affair, beginning in January 1939, hard on the heels of the Vickers

Armstrong contract. In lay out of both aerodromes have certain features in common which is not suprising since, in the interests of economy and speed, plans, drawings etc. used earlier at Tern Hill, Shawbury, and elsewhere, were recycled as standard, off the peg facilities.

Although the airfield was still a construction site and a winter quagmire, the first aircraft for storage at No 48 MU started to arrive in April 1940. The problem of flooding at Hawarden was perennial. Writing in 1945 First Officer E.C. Cheesman, ATA, recalls the jockeying to be able to land on the 'Vickers track': '… this was so placed that the approach from one end lay between two large hangars. Ferry pilots landing fast fighters would pray that the aerodrome gates at the start of the runway might be open, so that they could come in even lower and thus gain another hundred yards in which to pull up'. It should be recalled that the ASU was responsible for acceptance checks and the installation of radio and RAF -pattern equipment and flight testing before aircraft were issued to operational units. The first 'L'-type hangars on Nos 3 and 5 Sites had been completed by June

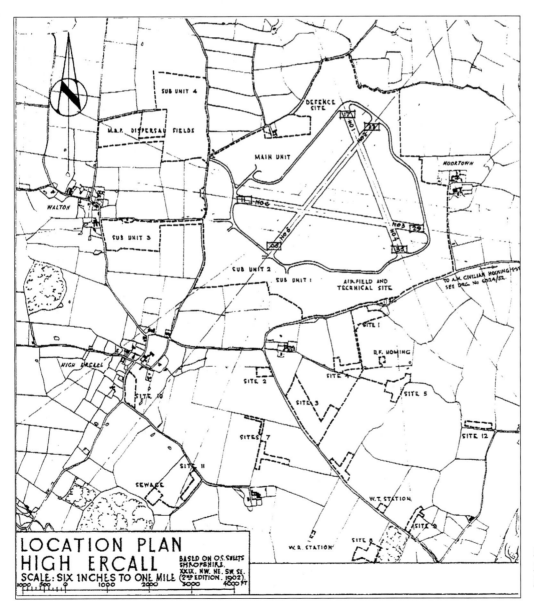

Part of AMWD drawing No 2152/45. [RAF Museum, Hendon]

1940 and, on paper, the ASU was 'full', with 14 Wellingtons, 9 Lysanders, 7 Herefords, 2 Bothas and one each of Henley, Magister and Miles Falcon. But then Hurricanes started to arrive and the twin-engined medium bombers had to be picketed outdoors. In the early years of the war this simple process was complicated by rules and regulations designed to lessen the impact of expected air raids and/or sabotage. As noted elsewhere the ASU Main Site was bombed and strafed on 14 November 1940, two bombs penetrating the roofs of both the 'J' and 'K' type hangars, exploding inside and destroying three Magisters, the 'Broughton Wellington' (just purchased by Vickers MAP employees for £15,000) and damaging two dozen other miscellaneous, mainly obsolescent, aircraft. This was the only raid suffered by RAF Hawarden and with hindsight such dispersal precautions as were adopted proved very extravagant in land consumption. However, AMWD maps of Hawarden, in the period before runways were constructed, are endorsed: 'Although flying strips are indicated the whole of the landing ground is prepared for flying'. Bearing in mind the conflicting interests of MAP factory, an ASU, an OTU and the ATA ferry pool 'parking conditions' imposed on the first two would have quickly sterilised the central grass area of the aerodrome and seriously hindered flying operations especially when there was not a stick of natural vegetation - copses, hedgerow or ancient parkland-trees to provide concealment:

(a) 100 yards to be allowed between individual aircraft in the open —
(b) reduced to 50 yards if aircraft were adequately concealed or camouflaged.
(c) aircraft of one type to be dispersed over at least four sites.
(d) 'scarce' or (valuable' aircraft (Hurricanes and Spitfires) to be distributed over as many hangars and dispersals as possible, maximum three on any one site.
(e) a maximum of 30 aircraft in camouflaged 'L' type hangars, 15 if uncamouflaged.
(f) a maximum of eight aircraft in uncamouflaged 'J' and 'K' types.
(g) dispersals or parks in the open to be al least 400 yards from 'L'-hangared ASU sites
(h) dispersals to be at least 800 yards from each other and —
(i) not too big — no more than 200 yards across in any direction.

The vertical aerial photograph of Hawarden aerodrome, taken in January, 1947, illustrates perfectly what happened after January 1944 when dispersal restrictions were relaxed on aerodromes in rear areas. The very dense carpets of aircraft reflect the airfield's final function as a glorified 'knacker's yard' dismantling war surplus aircraft and reducing airframes 'to produce'. As it was in 1940 dispersals were located immediately outside the perimeter fence for ease of access to the flying ground, but maximum airfield efficiency was reduced by the hardcore access tracks which proved useless with the advent of heavier aircraft. Parallel with the provision of runways and peritrack, dispersals were provided with hardstandings of various types off concrete access tracks — 'frying pan' of mixed diameters, 'finger' and star-shaped multiples, as noted in the accompanying aerial photographs of the ASU Main Site and

OTU frontage. The dispersals were located on Manor Hall Farm, The Beeches, Park Farm and Gop Farm. Using the latter was a risky business as aircraft were towed over an accommodation crossing on the main Chester–Holyhead railway line! The furthermost dispersal was that at Sandycroft, a mile or so along the B5129 Queensferry road. By coincidence, as seen in Part 1 of this history, this field had been one of Thomas Murthwaite Dutton's flying fields and had seen a RNAS/RFC presence in 1915 as well as being used as a RLG to Shotwick aerodrome. But here, in 1941, twelve Super Robin hangars were erected, initially supplied, in the manner of civilian contractors, without their doors! These were exclusively to house valuable fighters, distanced as far as logistically possible from the main ASU site which, it was anticipated, would be the first to be bombed. Spitfire and Hurricanes were towed along the B5129 with their wings on and care had to be taken to trim hedges and move telephone and electric poles along the road verges. But even these were insufficient and recourse had to be made to SLG as far afield as Bodorgan/Aberffraw, Anglesey (as from 1.4.41>), and Tatton Park, Cheshire (11.8.41>). The use of grass aerodromes at Elmdon (now Birmingham Airport) and Ansty in the Midlands was short lived and ill-conceived as Bothas and Herefords ferried out here tended to sink without trace in the winter muds and could not be retrieved until the landing strips had dried out in the May or June, unless dismantled and removed by road.

All these aircraft pouring out of the factories needed ferrying to and from ASUs/MUs and thence to units. Researching the third occupation element shoe-horned into Hawarden aerodrome immediately becomes rather complicated, as judged from the small table given on page 135; one has to carefully differentiate between (Service) Ferry Pools, RAF Aircraft Delivery Flights and the largely civilian-manned ATA. By late 1939 much of the task of ferrying within the UK had fallen to the Air Transport Auxiliary (ATA). This latter organisation, with HQ at White Waltham (Berkshire) was founded in August 1939 at the instigation of Gerard d'Erlanger, a director of British Airways, with the concurrence of the then Director General of Civil Aviation, Sir Francis Shelmerdine. Initially some thirty professional and 'amateur' pilots, holders of 'A' or 'B' licences, were invited for induction and 'flight-testing'. Two ranks were created, Second Officer for those limited to flying light single-engined aircraft and First Officer for pilots with over 500 hours experience able to handle twin-engined aircraft. Control of the ATA became vested in MAP and the every-day running of the organisation in BOAC. Hawarden had become a clearing house not only for locally assembled Wellingtons but also for the Blenheims produced by Rootes at Speke and the Hampdens from English Electric at Preston. Small wonder that the first ATA 'branch' established outside White Waltham, was set up at Hawarden. 'C' Section, N° 3 FPP, opened for business on 1 April 1940, with seventeen pilots and four superannuated Anson aircraft (K6302, K6323–K6325) commanded by Captain Walter Leslie Handley, and, after the latter's death in a flying accident in November 1941, by Commander Sydney Watson Ogden. Apart from re-numbering in the November, N° 3 FPP would

The Broughton Wellington.
— 7th. Nov. 1940. —

The 'Broughton Wellington', (R1333), so christened on 6 November 1940. Note the Welsh dragon emblem below the cockpit.
[Vickers Armstrong]

Above and left: HM King George VI and HM Queen Elizabeth visit the Vickers plant at Hawarden on 15 July 1942, escorted by Bernard Duncan, Superintendent. The Wellington III (BJ708) in the background would be lost on a raid to Kassel on 27/28 August 1942, flying with Nº 75 Sqn, Mildenhall.
[Vickers Armstrong]

RAF Bodorgan, Anglesey. Between 1 April 1942 and 30 December 1944 fields surrounding this all-grass airfield served as a SLG (Nº 15) to Nº 48 MU, Hawarden.

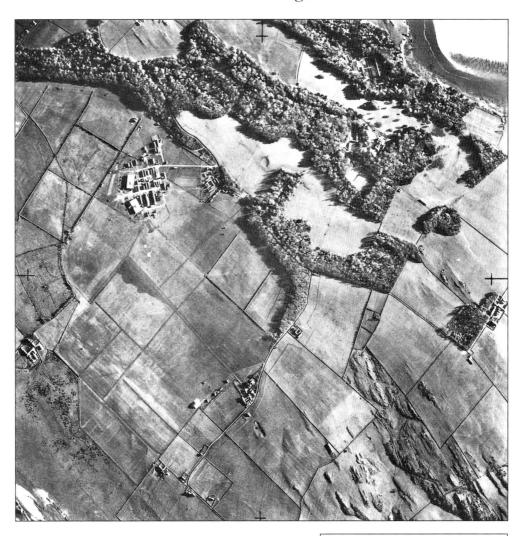

Right: The Bodorgan pillbox layout.
[Mike Osborne]

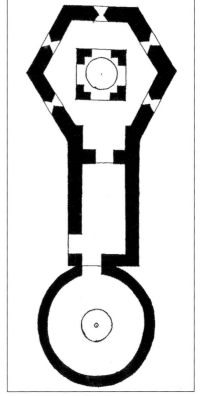

Below: At the entrance to RAF Bodorgan is a unique hexagonal combination pill box and 'instrument tower' with a LAA pit and shelter.

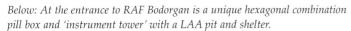

Caricature of Walter Handley, commander of Nº 3 Ferry Pilot Pool, relating to his days as a TT rider.

(R5932), the latter replacing X7354 lost on a return ferry crew pick-up in the blizzard that struck on 'Black Friday', 7 December 1941, which, as seen elsewhere claimed no fewer than five Spitfires of Nº 57 OTU). Another ADF pilot was killed when Spitfire P8661 crashed at Llanfair PG, Anglesey on 24 November 1941, following engine trouble and a fire whilst being ferried to Nº 350 (Belgian) Squadron then forming at Valley. Nº 3 ADF transferred to High Ercall on 10 January 1942, being finally disbanded in November 1943.

The fourth occupant of RAF Hawarden, and the one which gave most trouble space-wise was Nº 7 OTU formed on 15 June 1940, initially as a fighter pilot training unit within Nº 13 Fighter Group, with a paper establishment of 25+8 (spare) Spitfires, 14+5 Hurricanes and 13+4 Masters. By August 1940 it was specialising in Spitfires (45+13) with 13+4 Masters and 4+2 Battle TTs. As seen elsewhere in this narrative, until Nº 9 Group, Fighter Command became operational and got its act together the OTU's Spitfires, provided, August-September 1940, a 'Battle Flight' armed and at instant readiness in the defence of Merseyside and north-east Wales. It met with considerable success, but this was not sufficient to prevent Lord Beaverbrook, newly appointed Minister of Aircraft Production (MAP) making a serious effort to evict the new fighter OTU from the airfield 'Learner drivers' were cluttering up the landing ground at the very period production of Wellingtons at Vickers Armstrong was beginning to pick up speed, and when an additional facility for the assembly of American aircraft was in the pipe line. As things turned out, the latter would be concentrated at Speke. Beaverbrook also feared that the presence of a fighter OTU would automatically increase the chances of his factory being bombed. He was nearly right. In the first Report of the Directorate of Camouflage (August/September 1940) camouflage of the MAP factory was described as 'fairly successful' and this is borne out by contemporary reconnaissance photographs. More ambiguously in 'Government-speak' or gobbledygook of the time, the RAF buildings were described as 'non conspicuous', although *Luftwaffe* Intelligence had no difficulty in highlighting the ASU hangars as potential targets. The landing ground was 'conspicuous' —not surprising when contractors were still on site — and the aerodrome itself 'easily located by landmarks'. MAP also

remain at Hawarden for the duration of the war, becoming the largest FPP in the ATA, even spawning a sub-pool (later Nº 14 FPP) at Ringway in January 1941, and was the last but one to close down after the cessation of hostilities. The Battle of Britain put the ATA under great pressure especially in the heavy movement of replacement fighters from MUs to operational units. Following a post-mortem ferrying at Hawarden was strengthened by the arrival on 11 October 1940 of 18 officers and 61 airmen of 'B' Flight, Nº 4 (Service) Ferry Pool, Kemble. They were billeted at Broughton Hall and their four Ansons (R9763, R9764, R9765, R9771) hangared in one of the 'L' types on Nº 5 Site.

This service element was not long at Hawarden. Although becoming a (Service) Ferry Pilots Pool (Nº 9 (S)FPP) in its own right, it was disbanded on 10 February 1941, or as official records euphemistically put it 'absorbed by HQ Service Ferry Pools'. However, one notes on 7 April 1941 the formation at Hawarden of Nº 3 Aircraft Delivery Flight, one of four tasked with the responsibility for the delivery of fighter aircraft to unit within their respective Fighter Groups, Nº 3 ADF to squadrons in Nºˢ 9 and 12 Groups. F/Lt H.L. North commanded, with a strength of six pilots, eight ground crew and a Dominie

Avro Anson N4877 which served with Nº 3 Ferry Pool at Hawarden.

Officers and other ranks, Nº 57 OTU, Hawarden. [RAF Museum P5103]

had some peculiar objection to night flying on the part of the OTU, a trivial point, met by transferring night flying to Cranage, Cheshire, where detachments of Nº 5 SFTS, Sealand, were already slumming it for night flying instruction. This move was not so much to placate Beaverbrook as to escape Hawarden's legendary winter mud. Sir Archbald Sinclair, Secretary of State for Air, rejected Beaverbrook's arguments out of hand. The time was most inopportune — the middle of the Battle of Britain — 'I'm afraid it is quite impossible for us to vacate Hawarden. It is one of the fighter OTUs and is absolutely essential at the present moment. There is no other place suitable for this purpose. It may be that in the future we shall be able to provide another aerodrome but all the indications are that we shall have largely to increase the number of OTUs next year. Consequently I am unable to see my way clear to giving any undertaking to vacate. Incidentally we have spent many thousands of pounds in providing accommodation at Hawarden for an OTU. We cannot afford to see this standing empty at a time when we are very short of winter accommodation' — a tongue in cheek assertion unrecognisable by those hundreds of airmen who had to spend the winter of 1940–41 shivering in tents and packing cases, surrounded by acres of mud and water.

Four more OTUs would indeed be formed in 1940 and three in the early part of 1941. It would appear that Beaverbrook finally got his way when, on 10 November 1942, Nº 57 OTU left Hawarden to become the first occupants of a 'temporary' Nissen-hutted, and as yet unfinished aerodrome newly laid out at Eshott in the wilds of Northumberland. However, his satisfaction could not have lasted long as Nº 57 OTU's Spitfires were replaced on 18 November 1942 by another 60-odd 'learner' aircraft — the tactical reconnaissance Mustangs, Tomahawks and Hurricanes and sundry Harvard TTs of Nº 41 OTU, an Army Co-operation unit from Andover. Congestion at Hawarden would be eased somewhat by the opening of RAF Poulton, between Chester and Wrexham, as a satellite in March 1943. Tentative moves to secure RAF Sealand as a second SLG

were scotched out of hand as being logistically impossible.

To understand the establishment of Nº 7 OTU in June 1940 one must consider the background, a quickly changing scenario, to fighter pilot training at the outbreak of war. Within Fighter Command, in January 1939, plans were set afoot to shift the burden of giving advanced continuation training and operational experience to fighter pilots who had completed their training at a FTS, from the individual operational squadron to which a pilot had been posted, to 'Group Pools', that is, pilots and aircraft withdrawn from the battle order specifically to undertake the further training of new pilots. As so often the case in the hurried expansion of the RAF, resources proved very inadequate. Anyway Nᵒˢ 10 and 13 Fighter Groups were formed too late for such plans to take effect. In practice only Nº 11 Fighter Group Pool got off the ground at Andover, being equipped with eleven Hurricanes and 22 Fairey Battles, the latter almost obsolescent but providing essential single-engine handling experience on the Rolls-Royce Merlin engine. On 1 July 1939 the fighter pool moved to St Athan, where, on the outbreak of hostilities, six Hurricanes, piloted by instructors, became operational within Nº 10 Group as an additional fighter defence for South Wales, very much on the same lines as the 'Battle Flight' established at RAF Hawarden in north Wales. Owing to pressures on St Athan which also housed a large ASU (Nº 19 MU), a School of Technical Training and a refugee School of Air Navigation, the fighter tuition pool was transferred to Sutton Bridge on 9 March 1940 becoming Nº 6 OTU in the process.

It goes without saying that OTUs, as 'post-graduate' units as it were, embodied valuable reserves of experienced instructor aircrew and ex-operational aircraft. In the early years of the war, especially when invasion threatened, it was planned to realise the potential of these assets should a crisis demand it. The two tables below show that, differing from local bomber OTUs at Tilstock and Sleap, where aircrews and aircraft regularly re-inforced front-line squadrons on 'Thousand Bomber' raids, the fighter OTUs were scheduled to be mobilised as additional operational squadrons in their

Fighter OTUs and the Invasion

Unit	Station	Shadow Squadrons
52 OTU	Aston Down	Nos 551 & 552 Squadrons
53 OTU	Heston	Nos 553 & 554 Squadrons
55 OTU	Usworth	No 555 Squadron
56 OTU	Sutton Bridge	Nos 556 & 560 Squadrons
57 OTU	Hawarden	Nos 557 & 560 Squadrons
58 OTU	Grangemouth	Nos 558 &563 Squadrons
59 OTU	Crosby-on-Eden	Nos 559 & 564 Squadrons
61 OTU	Rednal	Nos 561 & 565 Squadrons

Composition of 'Shadow' Squadrons

Shadow Sqn From	Aircraft		War Station
551	52 OTU	18 Spitfires	Colerne
552	52 OTU	18 Spitfires	Colerne
553	53 OTU	18 Spitfires	Church Fenton
554	53 OTU	18 Spitfires	Church Fenton
555	55 OTU	18 Hurricanes	Turnhouse/Ouston
556	56 OTU	18 Hurricanes	Peterhead/Ouston
557	57 OTU	18 Spitfires	Newcastle
558	58 OTU	18 Spitfires	Turnhouse
559	59 OTU	18 Hurricanes	Newcastle
560	56 OTU	18 Hurricanes	Peterhead
561	61 OTU	18 Spitfires	Woodvale
562	57 OTU	18 Spitfires	Newcastle
563	58 OTU	18 Spitfires	Turnhouse
564	59 OTU	18 Hurricanes	Newcastle
565	61 OTU	18 Spitfires	Woodvale

Right: Spitfire II P7296, Battle of Britain veteran with Nº 206 Sqn, came to Nº 57 OTU on 27 March 1942.
[RAF Museum Ref: P5112]

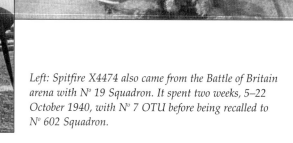

Left: Spitfire X4474 also came from the Battle of Britain arena with Nº 19 Squadron. It spent two weeks, 5–22 October 1940, with Nº 7 OTU before being recalled to Nº 602 Squadron.

own right, with 'shadow squadron' numbers and war stations allocated as shown.

N° 12 Fighter Group Pool was planned for the summer of 1939 at Hucknall with a roster of fourteen Hurricanes and seven Battles, but the speed of political events meant that it did not get beyond the drawing board. Something was salvaged from the chaos though, and a scratch flight was assembled at Aston Down with a motley collection of Gladiators (11), Harvards (7) and Blenheims (3). With an increased establishment of antiquated and/or war weary aircraft it would become N° 5 OTU on 6 March 1940, specialising in Hurricane tuition.

In the reassessment of air defence strategy N° 13 Fighter Group had been formed on 15 March 1939 for the defence of northern England and Scotland. This was cutting it fine. It became operational on 24 August 1939. Not surprisingly, with such an unfortunate time lag, the Group Pool it was supposed to administer, and which had been pencilled in for RAF Yeadon since 11 January, failed to materialise. But on 15 June 1940, three months exactly after the other fighter groups, N° 7 OTU was established within N° 13 Group at Hawarden. Initially the new unit was intended to have a complement of 25+8 Spitfires, 14+5 Hurricanes, and 13+4 Masters. The OTU was to administer Hawarden aerodrome, with N° 48 MU as lodger. The first 'notifiable' accident was not long coming. On 19 June 1940, Sub/Lt K. D. Marks, Fleet Air Arm, was killed when his Hurricane (P2566) stalled off a steep turn and dived into the ground at Brynford near Holywell. This was the only fatal accident that month, but July saw nine aircraft severely damaged or wrecked, two Spitfires, a single Master but six Hurricanes, three of them (L1791, L1870, L1989) with Belgian pilots crashing at the same time, making 'wheels-up' landings in a rough 'Vic'-formation between Erlas and Common Wood, Holt, whilst possibly attempting to 'beat up' the N° 5 FTS RLG at Borras Lodge. In the last four months of 1940 matters got worse, with 23 aircraft seriously damaged (18 Spitfires, 4 Masters, one Battle) and 22 wrecked/written off (including 16 Spitfires). At this time conversion courses at Hawarden had been reduced to two weeks in a desperate attempt to meet the shortfall of pilots in operational squadrons at the height of the Battle of Britain. Pilots left N° 7 OTU with as little as 10 hours logged 'on Spits', insufficient perhaps even for the tactics of the defensive warfare then being waged in the skies over Britain, and failing entirely to inculcate the basic tenets and skills of operational flying. In 1941, with pressure lessened, courses would expand once more to six, even seven, weeks with new intakes of 45 pupils reporting every three weeks. Not that 'learners' necessarily became more careful. In 1941 N° 57 OTU wrote off two Masters and destroyed 43 Spitfires with a further 35 Spitfires seriously damaged!

RAF Units, High Ercall (1941–3)

Unit	In	From	Out	To	Aircraft type
29 MU	01.10.40	Formed	01.03.57	Disbanded	
68 Sqn	23.04.41	Catterick	08.03.42	Coltishall	Blenheim If, Beaufighter If
255 Sqn	02.03.42	Coltishall	06.06.42	Honiley	Beaufighter If
257 Sqn	08.06.42	Honiley	21.09.42	Exeter	Hurricane I, Typhoon Ia, Ib
1456 Flight	06.06.42	Honiley	02.09.42	Re-designated	Havoc I
535 Sqn	02.09.42	ex 1456 Flight	25.01.43	Disbanded	Havoc, Boston Turbinlites
247 Sqn	21.09.42	Exeter	26.02.43	Middle Wallop	Typhoon Ib
41 Sqn	25.03.43	Llanbedr	12.04.43	Hawkinge	Spitfire XII
60 OTU	17.05.43	Formed	11.04.45	Disbanded into 13 OTU	Mosquito
USAAF (June–December 1942)					
309 FS (31 FG)	11.6.42	USA	4.8.42	Westhampnett	Spitfire V
92 FS (81 FG)	8.10.42	USA	12.12.42	?	Airocobra

Aircraft Ferrying Units, Hawarden

Unit	In	From	Out	To	Aircraft type
3 FPP Section 'C'	01.05.40	White Waltham	05.11.40	Renumbered	Anson, Proctor, Argus, Moth, Oxford
3 FPP	05.11.40	ex Section 'C'	30.11.45	Disbanded	Anson, Harvard, Argus, Courier
4(S) FPP 'B' Flt	11.10.40	Netheravon	01.11.40	Renumbered	Anson, Dominie
9(S)FPP	01.11.40	ex 4(S)FPP 'B' Flt	10.02.41	Absorbed HQ	Anson
(S)FPP, 3 ADF	07.04.41	Formed	10.01.42	High Ercall	Dominie, Anson, Moth, Oxford

On 13 July 1940 Nº 7 OTU passed, along with Nº 5 OTU under the control of No 10 Fighter Group. (It should be recalled that Nº 9 Fighter Group, although formed on 9 August 1940 for the defence of NW England, did not become operational until 1 December 1940). Whilst under Nº 10 Group control, the decision was taken that Nº 7 OTU should standardise on Spitfire training and by August held a revised stock-in-trade of 45+15 Spitfires, 13+4 Masters and 4+2 Battle TTs. On 16 December, because Nº 10 Fighter Group had its hands full running some 11 operational squadrons from 7 aerodromes in defence of the SW ports and Channel convoys, it surrendered its responsibility for fighter pilot training to a specially constituted Training Group in Fighter Command — Nº 81, which had its original HQ at RAF Sealand. On 21 December 1940 existing OTUs were renumbered by adding '50' to the existing number, thus Nº 7 OTU became Nº 57 OTU. Whilst at Sealand Nº 81 Group HQ ran two Magisters (T9828, T9829) and an impressed Miles Falcon Major, X9300 (G-ADHI) for communications purposes, stabled in the same hangar as Magisters N3954 and N3995, both of Nº 5 SFTS CF. HQ Nº 81 Group would move to Tallow Hall, Worcester on 22 December 1941.

Right: The burnt out remains of Heinkel 111P of KG27 based at Rennes, lying at Border House Farm, Saltney after being shot down by Sqd. Ldr J. S. McLean, W/Cmdr Hallings Pott and P/O P. Ayerst on 14 August 1940.

Left: A Ju88 of 3/Aufkl.Gr.123 lying in the Clywedog valley, the victim of Sgt L. S. Pilkington from Nº 7 OTU's Battle Flight, 7 September 1940.

Right: Spitfire R7058 carried the name of R. J. Mitchell, the man who designed the type. It came to Hawarden on 26 July 1941 by way of Nº 403 Squadron. Whilst out on an exercise on 18 November 1941, the engine failed and the pilot was forced to land at Belton Farm, Whitchurch, Shropshire. It was later reduced to an instructional airframe.

RAF Hawarden, Nº 48 MU, Site Nº 2

Left: Nº 2 aircraft shed, a type 'K', now part of Raytheon Aircraft Services Ltd and Raytheon Systems Ltd.

Below: Former wardens' office and cycle park.

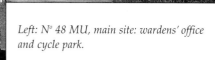

Left: Nº 48 MU, main site: wardens' office and cycle park.

Below: Main workshop, c.2004.

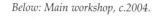

Left: Nº 1 aircraft shed, main site Nº 48 MU. Now occupied by Hawarden Air Services..

Nº 48 MU, Site Nº 5

Right: Wardens' office and cycle park.

Below: Transformer kiosk.

Above: Nº 2 aircraft repair shed, 'L' type office area.

Left: Nº 1 aircraft repair shed, 'L' type.

Right: Nº 1 aircraft repair shed, 'L' type, looking south.

Left: Former service housing estate, built on Manor Hall Farm dispersal area.

Below: Former officers' mess Nᵒˢ 7/57 OTU, c.2000.

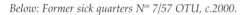

Below: Former sick quarters Nᵒˢ 7/57 OTU, c.2000.

Below: Home to Nᵒ 2247 (Hawarden) Squadron Air Training Corps. Situated in the area in which the institute and barracks huts once stood..

Left: The crest of Nᵒ 2247 (Hawarden) Squadron Air Training Corps.

RAF Hawarden, Site Nº 4 (OTU)

Right: Site 4. P.S. tank on a 50ft tower. Pump house and reservoir, c.2000.

Right: The original Second World War control tower, 518/40 pattern, at Hawarden now lies beneath new cladding and VCR cupola, c.2000.

Left: The fire tender shed with its new cladding, c.2003. In the background the new Airbus A380, West factory starts to take shape.

Right: The petrol installation (aviation), 24,000 gallons.

RAF Hawarden, WAAF Site

Above: All that remains of the WAAF site today is this sewage filtration plant.

Right: The Hawarden Estate 'bottom' lodge entrance to the WAAF camp on the B5125.

Aircraft Losses and Accidents from Nº 7 OTU & Nº 57 OTU, 1940

19.06.40. Hawker Hurricane P2566. Dived into the ground Brynford, Holywell Pilot K. D. Marks killed.

20.06.40. Supermarine Spitfire Mk L P9542. Flying accident at Hawarden.

28.06.40 Fairey Battle R7375 Engine failure after take-off from Hawarden pilot belly-landed aircraft at Buckley, Flintshire.

02.07.40. Supermarine Spitfire Mk I R6607. Flying accident at Hawarden.

15.07.40. Spitfire Mkl K9790. Crashed on landing Hawarden. Pilot injured

18.07.40. Hurricane Mk I, N2478. Crashed in a forced landing Hawarden. Sgt D. D. S. Edgar injured (see also 13.09.40.).

20.07.40. Hurricane Mk I, 1.P3829. Forced to land on beach at Prestatyn. Pilot injured.

22.07.40. Hurricane Mk I, L2020. Crashed on landing at Hawarden. Pilot injured.

24.07.40. Miles Master. N7834. Pilot injured.

25.07.40. Hurricane Mk I, L1989. In formation, crashed Commonwood, nr. Wrexham. Pilot injured.

25.07.40. Hurricane Mk I, L1 791. In formation, crashed Commonwood, nr. Wrexham. Pilot injured.

25.07.40. Hurricane Mk I, L1870. In formation, crashed Commonwood, nr. Wrexham. Pilot injured.

09.08.40. Spitfire Mk I, N.3034. Heavy landing Hawarden. Pilot injured.

14.08.40. Spitfire MkI, K.9876. Damaged tail unit landing Hawarden. Pilot injured.

28.08.40. Spitfire Mk I, L1060. Dived into beach at Hoylake, Cheshire. Pilot Officer W.B.Macassey killed.

31.08.40. Spitfire Mk I, K99 18. Collision with Master N7967 Hawarden. Pilot injured.

31.08.40. Miles Master N7967. Collision with K9918, Hawarden. Pilot Injured.

05.09.40. Spitfire Mk I, K9857. Flying accident on approach Hawarden.

06.09.40. Spitfire Mk I, K9976. Damage force-landing on beach Prestatyn. Pilot Injured.

09.09.40. Miles Master Mk I, N.7967. Spun into ground at Northop, Flintshire. P/Os Stephen Body and W. G. Rees both killed.

12.09.40. Spitfire W. I. K.9981. Forced to land and crashed at mouth of Dee Estuary. Pilot injured.

13.09.40. Spitfire Mk I, X4159. Dived into the ground Tattenhall, nr. Chester. Sgt D. D. S. Edgar killed.

14.09.40. Spitfire Mk I, R6911. Flying accident Hawarden.

14.09.40. Spitfire Mk I, K9967. Crashed on landing at Hawarden. Pilot injured.

18.09.40. Spitfire Mk I, N3269. Flying accident at Hawarden. Pilot injured.

21.09.40. Spitfire Mk I, N328 1. Flying accident Sealand. Pilot injured.

21.09.40. Spitfire Mk I, K9995. Hit mud flats low flying Dee Estuary. Pilot injured

21 09.40. Spitfire Mk I, K9984. Not known. Report says Hawarden. Pilot injured.

21.09.40. Spitfire Mk I, R6917. Flying accident.

22.09.40. Spitfire Mk I, K.9934. Flying accident Hawarden. Pilot injured.

24.09.40. Spitfire Mk I, P9543. Flying accident Hawarden.

25.09.40. Spitfire Mk I, K992 1. Undercarriage collapsed landing at Hawarden.

25.09.40. Spitfire Mk I, K9979. Damage on landing Hawarden. Pilot injured.

04.10.40. Spitfire Mk I, K9874. Flying accident (Queensferry) to instructional frame. Pilot injured.

05.10.40. Spitfire Mk I, K9873. Made forced landing Sealand. No injury recorded.

12.10.40. Spitfire Mk I, P9329. Forced to make emergency landing Broughton. Pilot injured.

12.10.40. Spitfire Mk I, P9332. Forced landing Hawarden. Pilot not known.

12.10.40. Spitfire Mk I, P9327. Forced landing Bryn Gwenallt, Abergele. Pilot killed

16.10.40. Spitfire Mk I, N305 1. Crashed on take off Hawarden. Pilot injured.

18.10.40. Spitfire Mk I, N3067. Overshot landing Hawarden. Pilot injured.

21.10.40. Spitfire Mk I, N3235. Crashed in a forced landing Carmel, Flintshire. Sgt Stanley Smith killed.

21.10.40. Miles Master I. N7836. Stalled, crashed North Wingfield, nr. Chesterfield. Pilot killed.

28.10.40. Spitfire Mk I, K9801. Flying accident Hawarden. Pilot injured.

29.10.40. Spitfire Mk I, N3050. Forced landing Maudley Bridge, Chester. Pilot injured.

31.10.40. Spitfire Mk I, K9829. Flying accident Hawarden. Pilot injured.

06.11.40. Spitfire Mk I, X4103. Flying accident. Pilot not known.

11.11.40. Spitfire Mk I, R6754. Crashed on landing Hawarden. Pilot injured.

13.11.40. Spitfire Mk I, N3072. Crashed on landing Hawarden. Pilot injured.

15.11.40. Spitfire Mk I, K9983. Stalled on landing at Speke. u/c collapsed.

16.11.40. Spitfire Mk I, K9800 Flying accident Hawarden. Pilot not known.

23.11.40. Spitfire Mk I, N3037. Forced to land Hawarden. Pilot injured.

26.11.40. Fairey Battle, L5716. Engine failure crash landed nr. Hawarden. Pilot injured.

26.11.40. Miles Master, N7839. Crashed on take off from Speke into River Mersey. Pilot injured.

10.12.40. Miles Master, K9851. Flying accident Sealand. Pilot injured.

16.12.40. Miles Master, L l049. Crashed in forced landing Speke. Pilot injured.

17.12.40. Miles Master, P9541. Crashed in forced landing Speke. Pilot injured.

20.12.40. Miles Master, N7965. Lost on Navex, crashed into sea at Hoylake, Cheshire, attempting landing on beach. P/Os H. E. Hooker & P. B. Coleman killed.

24.12.40. Miles Master, P9490. Flying accident Hawarden. Pilot injured.

28.12.40. Miles Master, K9921. Not known

1941

13.01.41. Spitfire Mk I, K9789. Flying accident Hawarden. Pilot injured.

18.01.41. Spitfire Mk I, K9921. Flying accident at Hawarden. Pilot injured. Aircraft repaired.

19.01.41. Spitfire Mk I, N3065 Flying accident at Hawarden. Pilot injured. Aircraft repaired.

01.02.41. Spitfire Mk I, K9890. Landed on sandbank off Hooton Park. Pilot okay.

06.02.41. Spitfire Mk I, L1028. Flying accident Hawarden. Pilot injured.

10.02.41. Spitfire Mk I, K9835. Forced landed Rhos-On-Sea. Pilot injured.

11.02.41. Spitfire Mk I, L1042. Forced landed Common Wood, Wrexham. Pilot injured.

01.03.41. Spitfire Mk I, R6927 Flying accident Wrexham. Pilot injured.

01.03.41. Spitfire Mk I, N3250. Flying accident Hawarden. Pilot injured.

02.03.41. Spitfire Mk I, K9840. Flying accident Denbigh. Sgt N. R. Mansell killed

02.03.41. Fairey Battle, L5709. Aircraft hit obstruction on take-off and elavator jammed, aircraft stalled and crashed at Hawarden.

03.03.41. Spitfire Mk I, N3245. Flying accident Hawarden. Pilot injured.

04.03.41. Spitfire Mk I, K9953. Flying accident flolt Lodge Wrexham. Pilot injured.

13.03.41. Spitfire Mk I, L1034. Abandoned Beaumaris, Anglesey. Pilot injured.

13.03.41. Spitfire Mk I, X4175. Flying accident Hawarden. Pilot injured.

14.03.41. Spitfire Mk I, N3034. Flying accident Hawarden. Pilot injured.

16.03.41. Spitfire Mk I, K9847. Damage on take off Wrexham. Pilot injured.

20.03.41. Spitfire Mk I, K9829. Flying accident Hawarden. Pilot injured.

27.03.41. Spitfire Mk I, K9900. Undershot landing Wrexham. Pilot injured.

27.03.41. Spitfire Mk I, K4421. Structural failure in flight Northop. P/O Percival Sloan killed.

28.03.41. Spitfire Mk I, K9824. Flying accident Hawarden. F/Lt L. W. P. Brown killed.

04.04.41. Spitfire Mk I, K9996. Flying accident Wrexham. Pilot injured.

07.04.41. Spitfire Mk I, P9326. Flying accident Hawarden. Pilot injured.

09.04.41. Spitfire Mk I, N3250. Flying accident Tattenhall. Sgt Robert Burton killed.

13.04.41. Spitfire Mk I, K9991. Took off with propellor in 'coarse pitch', crashed Sealand.

15.04.41. Spitfire Mk I, K9825. Flying accident Hawarden. Pilot injured.

16.04.41 Spitfire Mk I, K9857. Flying accident Chester. Pilot injured.

16.04.41. Spitfire Mk I, X4475. Abandoned, lost near Ilkley, Yorkshire Pilot injured.

25.04.41. Spitfire Mk I, K9972. Forced to land on beach at Rhyl due to fire. Pilot injured.

02.05.41. Spitfire Mk I, L1009. Engine failed, undershot landing Sealand. Pilot injured.

08.05.41. Spitfire Mk I, X4179. Swung on landing hit over-blister hangar at Wrexham.

08.05.41. Miles Master, N7840. Crashed in a flying accident. Pilot not known.

09.05.41. Miles Master, L1024. Flying accident Hawarden. Pilot injured.

10.05.41. Miles Master, N3169. Flying accident Hawarden. Pilot injured.

12.05.41. Spitfire Mk I, K9895. Undercarriage collapsed on landing Sealand.

16.05.41 Spitfire Mk I, K9908. Flying accident crashed Abergele. Pilot injured.

17.05.41. Spitfire Mk I, N3046. Ran out of fuel crashed Sealand. Pilot injured.

26.05.41. Spitfire Mk I, R6834. Flew into mountain in cloud, Dolwyddelan, Blaenau Ffestiniog. P/O J. T. Brown killed.

04.06.41. Spitfire Mk I, R6887. Collision with Tiger Moth R.A.F. Sealand. Pilot injured.

08.06.41. Spitfire Mk I, K9994. Hit sea, forced landing on beach Prestatyn. Pilot injured.

16.06.41. Spitfire Mk I, X4600. Crashed on take off Wrexham.

17.06.41. Spitfire Mk I, L1088. Hit hangar on take off Hawarden. Pilot G. R. Cushion killed.

21.06.41. Spitfire Mk I, R7018. Tyre burst on take off Wrexham. Pilot injured.

01.07.41. Miles Master Mk I, N7833. Hit tree at Mill Lane, Upton, Chester, then crashed into house killing P/O J. L. Milmine & Sgt H. A. Womack.

02.07.41. Spitfire Mk I, X4425 Practice scramble Wrexham. Pilot injured.

03.07.41. Spitfire Mk I, K9894. Forced landing Hawarden. Pilot injured.

03.07.41. Spitfire Mk I, K9892. Flew into mountain in formation Minera. Baron René Joseph Marie Ghislain Gerrard Del Marol killed.

03.07.41. Spitfire Mk I, X4167. Marie Jules Dhpiet-de-Beco killed.

05.07.41. Spitfire Mk I, X4274. Forced landing, undercarriage collapsed Llanasa. F/Sgt Czezowski injured.

10.07.41. Spitfire Mk I, R6601. Crashed due to engine failure (Two Mills, nr. Chester). Sgt P. R. Nickerson killed.

10.07.41. Spitfire Mk I, P9436. Forced to land Caerwys Racecourse, Flintshire. Pilot injured.

18.07.41. Spitfire Mk I, P9519. Forced to land at Hawarden. Pilot injured.

20.07.41. Spitfire Mk I, K9895. Mid-air. collision. Both dived into the ground at Rossett, Denbighshire. Sgt Pilot R. J. Kempling killed.

20.07.41. Spitfire Mk I, K9821. Mid-air. collision. Both dived into the ground at Rossett, Denbighshire. Sgt I. R. A. Beaton killed.

23.07.41. Spitfire Mk I, L1070. Flying accident. Pilot inured.

25.07.41. Spitfire Mk I, N3034. Forced to land Llanfair T. H. Pilot injured.

28.07.41. Spitfire Mk I, N3062. Dived into sea Caernarfonshire. Sgt W. M. Scott killed.

30.07.41. Spitfire Mk I, K9996. Crashed on take off Hawarden. Pilot injured.

04.08.41. Defiant Mk I, K7000. Crashed on take off Hawarden. Pilot injured.

05.08.41. Miles Master, N7840. Pilot killed.

07.08.41. Spitfire Mk I, X4169. Crashed in a forced landing Prestatyn. Pilot Officer J. W. Carr killed.

11.08.41. Miles Master, N7837. No details, but written-off after flying accident.

11.08.41. Spitfire Mk 1, N3123. Flying accident Kinnerton. Sgt Pilot C. E. Brown killed.
12.08.41. Spitfire Mk I, Ll043. Crashed on approach to Hawarden. Pilot killed.
20.08.41. Spitfire Mk I, P9335. Undercarriage damaged RAF Wrexham.
22.08.41. Spitfire Mk I, R7018. Mid-air collision, crashed Balls Wood Quarry, Rossett, killing P/O A. W. Parks (from South Africa).
22.08.41. Spitfire Mk I, R1082 Mid-air collision crashed Bagillt, Flintshire. Pilot Officer R. D. Grozier (RCAF) killed.
26.08.41. Spitfire Mk I, K9998. Crashed on landing Hawarden.
26.08.41. Spitfire Mk I, L1004. Engine overheated Wrexham. Pilot injured.
28.08.41. Spitfire Mk I, L1065. Flying accident Hawarden.
04.09.41. Spitfire Mk I, K9824 Delivery flight. Pilot injured.
11.09.41. Spitflre Mk I, N3269. Overshot at Ternhill, Shropshire. Pilot injured.
12.09.41. Miles Master, T8885. Crashed on take off at Hullavington. Pilot not known.
20.09.41. Spitfire Mk I, X4653. Aircraft dived into the sea at Rhyl. Pilot killed.
20.09.41. Spitfire Mk I, R6973. Force landed due to engine failure Wrexham. Pilot injured.
21 .09.41. Spitfire Mk I, K9995. Hit mud flats in Dee Estuary low flying. Pilot injured.
26.09.41. Spitfire Mk I, X4343. Flew into mountain in Snowdonia. Sgt N. A. Mowat Killed
01.10.41. Spitfire Mk I, L1030. Forced landed Bretton, Flintshire. Pilot injured.
10.10.41. Miles Master, N7966. Wrecked in an accident. Written-off, no further details.
25.10.41. Spitfire Mk I, L1070. Crashed on landing Hawarden. Pilot injured.
28.10.41. Miles Master, T833 1. Crashed. Pilot not known.
02.11.41. Spitfire Mk I, P9559. Mid- air collision. Crashed Kinmel Estate, Abergele. P/O H. W. Pronk killed.
02.11.41. Spitfire Mk I, N3066. Mid-air collision. Crashed Kinmel Estate, Abergele. Sgt H. W .Morau killed.
07.11.41. Miles Master, T8502. Hit obstruction on runway Rednal. Pilot injured.
11.11.41. Spitfire Mk I, L1080. Undershot landing Wrexham. Pilot injured.
16.11.41. Spitfire Mk I, X4713. Aircraft hit Ruabon Mountain. Sgt Cyril Coocks killed.
18.11.41. Spitfire Mk I, R7058 (named after R. J. Mitchell). Flying Accident at Whitchurch, Shropshire. Pilot injured.
21.11.41. Spitfire Mk I, N3054. Flying accident Hawarden. Pilot injured.
23.11.41. Spitfire Mk I, N3269. Fire on apron Hawarden. Pilot injured.
23.11.41. Spitfire Mk I, X4850 Flying accident Hawarden. Sgt G. A. Wither killed.
02.12.41. Spitfire Mk I, X4789. Crashed due to icing up Wrexham. No injury.
06.12.41. Spitfire Mk I, P9434. Dived into the ground at Picton. Sgt Lee killed.
07.12.41. Spitfire Mk I, L1005. Aircraft was abandoned by pilot over Pontesbury. Pilot injured.
07.12.41. Spitfire Mk I, R7140. Aircraft dived into the ground at Chester. Pilot A. C. Bower killed.
07.12.41. Spitfire Mk I, L1042. Aircraft dived into the ground at Picton. Pilot killed.
07.12.41. Spitfire Mk I, R7126. Parkgate Road, Chester. Sgt S. W. Bradshaw killed.
07.12.41. Spitfire Mk I, P9446. Aircraft forced landed Bratton RLG, Shropshire. Pilot injured.
13.12.41. Spitfire Mk I, X4899. Flying accident crashed Plaswinter, Flintshire. Pilot J. S. Bird killed.
14.12.41. Fairey Battle, L5706. Landed with undercarriage unlocked at Hawarden, repaired on site.
16.12.41. Spitfire Mk I, L1049. Crash landed at Speke aerodrome. Pilot injured.
21.12.41. Spitfire Mk I, R7062. Wrecked in a flying accident at Hawarden. Pilot injured
24.12.41. Spitfire Mk I, R7193. Flying accident Hawarden. Pilot injured.

1942

06.01.42. Spitfire Mk I, N3221. Flying accident Hawarden. Pilot injured.
26.01.42. Spitfire Mk I, K9863. Collision with X4164, crashed Welshland Sett Bees Nurseries. S/Lt L. S. F. Ricard Cordingsley killed.
26.01.42. Spitfire Mk I, X4164. Collision with K9863, crashed Welshland Sett Bees Nurseries. P/O R. Sowalskie killed.
06.02.42. Spitfire Mk I, K9942. Ground accident Hawarden. Pilot injured. Now at RAF Museum, Hendon.
13.02.42. Spitfire Mk I, R6829. Crashed at Queensferry. Pilot Douglas Ernest Charles Coleman killed.
14.02.42. Miles Master Mk I, T8635. Dived into the ground at Mold, Flintshire. Pilot unknown.
20.02.42. Spitfire Mk I, R6892. Caught fire and crashed at Queensferry. Pilot injured.
27.02.42. Spitfire Mk I, X4388. Crashed in a forced landing Queensfeny. Pilot injured.
14.03.42. Spitfire Mk I, P9494. Mid air collision with X4270 in the vicinity of Hawarden. Pilot unknown.
14.03.42. Spitfire Mk I, X4270. Mid air collision with P9494 in the vicinity of Hawarden. Pilot unknown.
16.03.42. Spitfire Mk I, X4605. Mid air collision with AR212 near Chester. Pilot injured. Survived and crashed later on 10. 10.42.
16.03.42. Spitfire Mk Ia, AR212 Mid air collision with X4605 near Chester. P/O S. W. Steenson killed.
17.03.42. Spitfire Mk I, X4838. Hit at dispersal by P7549.
17.03.42. Spitfire Mk IIa, P7549. Pilot survived but crashed later 16.08.42.
28.03.42. Miles Master Mk III, W8640. Wings came off in dive. Crashed at Tyn-Twll Farm, Holt Road, Wrexham. Sgt Pilot Ronald Lewis York (instructor with N° 57 OTU) and pupil pilot Basil Ewart Hopkins both killed.
29.03.42. Spitfire Mk I, P7438. Aircraft forced landing Boderyn Cross Roads, Abergele. Pilot survived.
30.03.42. Spitfire Mk I, R7117. Flying accident Mancot. Pilot injured.
31.03.42. Spitfire Mk I, R7138. Ground accident Hawarden whilst landing. R7138 hit X4611. Pilots injured.
31.03.42. Spitfire Mk I, X4611. Ground accident Hawarden. At dispersal, hit by R7138 as landing.

05.04.42. Spitfire Mk I, X4239. Flew into Cwm Barlwyd, Snowdonia. American D. A. Brown killed.
05.04.42. Miles Master Mk I, T8364. Crashed in a forced landing at Withington cross roads, Haughmond Hill decoy, nr. Shrewsbury. Pilot injured.
08.04.42. Spitfire Mk I, R6686. Mid air collision Wellington L7818 from N° 15 OTU and crashed at Cold Ashton, Gloucestershire.
11.04.42. Spitfire Mk I, P7990. Crashed at Gronant, Prestatyn, Flintshire. P/O James Patrick Considine (American, RAF) killed.
02.05.42. Spitfire Mk I, X461 I. Collision, landing in bad visibility R7138 hit X4611 . Pilot unknown.
02.05.42. Spitfire Mk I, R7138. Collision, landing in bad visibility. Pilot injured.
08.05.42. Spitfire Mk I, K9864. Mid-air collision with R6769 over Dee Estuary. K9864 crashed in a force-landing on mud banks at Flint. Pilot injured.
08.05.42. Spitfire Mk I, R6769. Mid-air collision with K9864. Landed safely at Hawarden.
11.05.42. Spitfire Mk I, R7160. Crashed on landing at Hawarden. Pilot injured.
16.05.42. Spitfire Mk I, P9429. Flying accident Hawarden. Pilot not known.
29.05.42. Spitfire Mk I, R7257. Caught fire in flight. Crash landed Alton Street, Crewe, Cheshire. Pilot injured.
29.05.42. Spitfire Mk I, K9975. Dived into the ground at Sealand. Pilot Joseph Thomas Parrott killed.
29.05.42. Spitfire Mk I, X4604. Flying accident as above Hawarden. Pilot injured.
02.06.42. Spitfire Mk I, P7368. Hawarden landing accident. Pilot injured.
05.06.42. Spitfire Mk I, X4779. Engine failure, belly landed on sands off Hoylake, Cheshire. Pilot injured.
15.06.42. Spitfire Mk I, P7899. Engine failure crash landed on beach West Kirby, Cheshire. Pilot injured.
25.06.42. Spitfire Mk I, P8017. Flying accident Hawarden. Pilot injured.
28.06.42. Spitfire Mk I, P9334. Bent prop on landing. Pilot injured.
06.07.42. Miles Master Mk I, V8589. Engine failure, crashed Lower Kinnerton, Cheshire. Pilot injured.
25.07.42. Spitfire Mk I, P.8175. Crashed in a forced landing Huxley, Cheshire. Pilot injured.
04.08.42. Spitfire Mk I, N3035. Flying accident Hawarden. Pilot not known.
10.08.42. Spitfire Mk I, N3276. Stalled and crashed into River Dee, Saltney.
14.08.42. Spitfire Mk I, X4186. Mid air collision with AR252, crashed Broughton. Sgt Arnold Page killed.
14.08.42. Spitfire Mk I, AR252. Mid air collision with X4186. Sgt Sylvio Jules Palandri killed.
14.08.42. Spitfire Mk I, P7893. Forced landing near Chester. Pilot injured.
15.08.42. Spitfire Mk I, R6989. Struck tree whilst making forced landing Holywell, Flintshire. Sgt Stanley Coates killed.
16.08.42. Spitfire Mk I, P7549. Mid air collision with P7598 over Higher Kinnerton, Cheshire. Sgt Robert Ian Darg Forsyth killed.
16.08.42. Spitfire Mk I, P7598. Mid air collision with P7549. Sgt John Lawrence Brophy killed.
21.08.42. Spitfire Mk I, P7564. Crashed in a forced landing Beeches Farm, Hawarden. Pilot injured.
22.08.42. Spitfire Mk I, R7018. Mid air collision with L1082 crashed at Rossett. P/O A. W. Parks killed.
22.08.42. Spitfire Mk I, Ll082. Mid air collision with R7018 crashed at Bagillt, Flintshire. P/O R. D. Groxier killed.
23.08.42. Spitfire Mk I, P8343. Flying accident Hawarden. Pilot not known.
25.09.42. Spitfire Mk I, X4234. Crashed Alsager and burnt out. Aircraft broke up in air.
07.10.42. Spitfire Mk I, X4030. Ground accident Hawarden. Pilot injured.
10.10.42. Spitfire Mk I, X4605. A presentation aircraft named *Ceylon III*. Dived into the ground at the Boar's Head Inn, Flint. P/O John Alexander Gilbert killed.
14.10.42. Spitfire Mk I, P7533. Caught fire in the air, crashed Parkside, Birkenhead. Aircraft abandoned. Pilot killed.

Above: AR212 was involved in a mid air collision with Spitfire X4605 on 16 March 1942 and dived into Clivedon Road, Chester. [RAF Museum P5104]

Right: Spitfire P9446 after its forced landing at Bratton RLG (near Wellington, Shropshire) on Black Friday, 7 December 1941. [RAF Museum: P5105]

8. Catalina diary

Whereas the history of fighting and training units is dutifully chronicled in a wide range of war diaries, ORBs, ships' books and logs etc., occupying yards if not miles of shelving in the National Archives, relatively easy to access, it is much more difficult for the a researcher to quantify the role played by the myriad of private sector firms, large and small, that underpinned the war effort, processing the raw materials and producing the weapons of war. The preservation of company records is very much a lottery.

Fortunately, while 'archive', space-consuming, dust-accumulating, time -wasting, is a word foreign to the vocabulary of image-polishing company executives, many war-time managers, scientists, superintendents, test pilots and so on, for their own daily reference, kept note books and memoranda, which have survived, albeit haphazardly, and are still coming to light half a century or so after the event. One such is the small accumulation of records which forms the basis of this chapter, shedding light on the unique role played by a large house on the shores of the Menai Strait, north of Beaumaris. Four 'Day Books' (1942–5) covering the movement of launches, cars, lorries, and personnel (workforce and visitors) are perhaps only of superficial interest for our present purpose; it is a potted 'retrospective' diary and a register recording arrivals, departures, engine runs, test flights of aircraft, especially the Consolidated Catalina, which are of greater relevance to any history of aviation in the region. Judging from the use of the first

Saro Beaumaris site 13 August 1945. The original Friars mansion is to the right of the compass circle. The hangar camouflage is pretty convincing. [National Assembly for Wales]

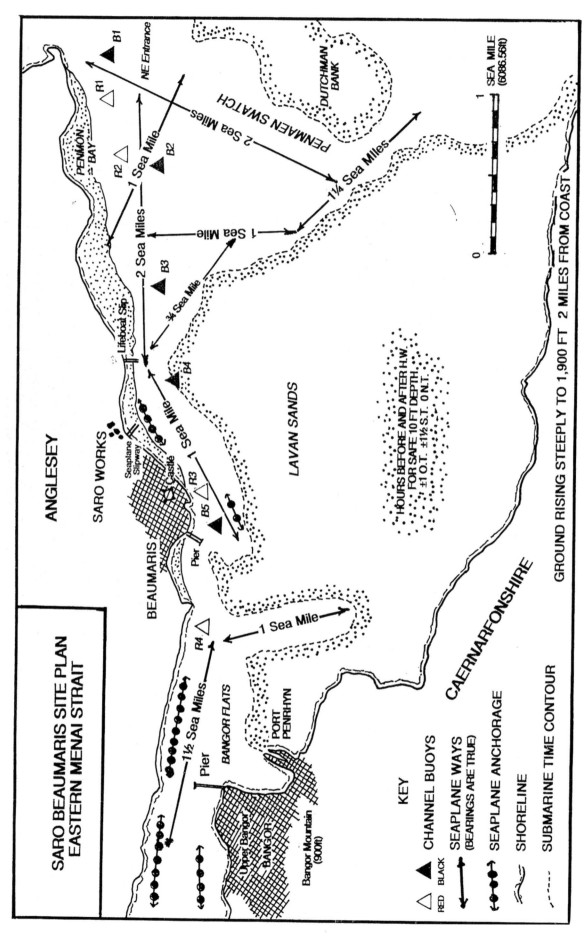

Saro Beaumaris site plan, eastern Menai Strait. The map has been redrawn from an original sea chart by kind permission of Hilary Date.

Catalina flying boats at their buoys below Gallows Point, Beaumaris, 14 January 1945.
[National Assembly for Wales]

person, the 'diary' was typed up by S/Ldr Leslie Ash, Saro test pilot, at the request of Harry Broadsmith who had been general manager at Beaumaris. It now survives, along with day books, Catalina Register and many of the contemporary images seen here, amongst the family papers of the late Ron Adams, former marine superintendent and transport manager at Friars, who from the handwriting kept both day books and register. Ash's diary is the distillation of 'an hour or so free' to rummage through what is (?was) an obviously larger corpus of material 'to see if there is anything of 'snappy' value'. As far as is known to the present writers, a promised follow-up — a selective sifting of the Visitors' Book 'for the names of our visitors who deserve any special mention for some reason or other' does not seem to have materialised. S/Ldr Ash had been a Great War fighter pilot and flew his last aircraft, an Auster IV floatplane, VF517, at Beaumaris in 1946, having logged over 10,000 hours on 100+ different aircraft types.

Saunders-Roe Ltd builder of seaplanes and amphibious aircraft was established in 1928 at East Cowes, Isle of Wight. In the 1930s its reputation was based on the provision of reconnaissance seaplanes for RAF Coastal Command, such as the London, Cloud, and Lerwick. Today, of course the company is no more. Having diversified into small helicopters in 1952 with the take-over of the Cierva Autogiro Company, it was in 1959 itself taken over by Westland Aircraft. Ash's notes hark back to the confused period, August–September 1940 when Saunders-Roe partially relocated to north Wales. This had been brought about by a combination of factors, firstly, the constant disruption of design and development work by air raid alerts, when the Isle of Wight was in the front line of the Battle of Britain, with dog fights overhead, radar stations attacked and often at the receiving end of bombs destined for Portsmouth! Secondly, Saunders-Roe had inherited the production run of the Supermarine Walrus owing to the enormous pressure on

Catalina JX632 on the first of its two visits to Friars, February 1945.

Caernarfon and Dinorwic, since August 1940 refugees from bombed out premises in Croydon, and under contract to MAP for the production of aircraft components for the Wellington, Halifax, Stirling, Defiant - and from now on, assorted sea-planes! As can be seen from the attached aerial views there was plenty of room to erect hangars, workshops, storage sheds etc. Sadly, even as this chapter is being penned (March 2004) much is being swept away in the name of redevelopment. The slipway took some time to construct, and for some three weeks much early modification work had to be carried out afloat as aircraft swung at their moorings. The beaching of Catalina AM267 on 2 May 1941 'the first one on land at Friars' was sufficient a landmark to make the diary.

the latter company's factory space at Southampton, Winchester, Swindon and Castle Bromwich for the production of the Spitfire. Saro would go on to produce 461 Walruses including 191 with wooden hulls replacing the original metal hulls. The diary entry for 13 January 1941 refers, with the first wooden hulled amphibian arriving at Friars for recording and measurement by the design department. On 12 November 1941 The diary reads 'First wooden Walrus X1046 flown at Beaumaris' but according to the records X1046 was a conversion from L2309.

Thirdly, as indicated by a brief entry for 13 February 1941, the Beaumaris facility was to shoulder responsibility for the Consolidated Catalina modification programme. The 50-acre Friars estate NE of Beaumaris, as its name suggests, on or near the site of a medieval Franciscan Friary (1245–1538), offered a secluded site on a sheltered stretch of tidal water, the eastern Menai Strait, affording a four-mile take off and landing run into prevailing SW winds, westwards beyond Bangor Pier almost to Menai Bridge. A little appreciated advantage of settling in at Beaumaris was the proximity to the Hunting Aviation factories at

The over-riding preoccupation with Catalinas stemmed from the Admiralty's search for long range, maritime reconnaissance, anti-submarine flying boats to supplement and eventually replace the undistinguished and short-lived Saro Lerwick. Their choice fell upon the Consolidated PBY-5 (designated 'Catalina I' by the RAF) which had rendered good service with the US Navy since 1936. First deliveries were taken in 1941 (see Appendix and adjoining table). Of the 3,281 Catalinas built in the USA and Canada, some 640 were supplied to the RAF and Commonwealth air forces. Of this latter figure some 310 are generally accepted as undergoing modification at Beaumaris although this does not quite match up to an analysis of the Catalina Register that still survives (see table below), which clearly demonstrates the unevenness of the flow of flying boats arriving at Friars, which led to considerable logistical problems right through to the end.

Because of the non standardisation of equipment between the two countries some modification was needed to

Catalina throughput at Friars according to surviving 'Register'

Month	1941 Mks I–III	1942 I–III	1943 I–III		1944 Mk IV	1945 Mk IV
Jan	-	1	12		6	7
Feb	-	2	4		5	15
March	-	6	7		14	9
April	2	8	2	MkIV	14	1
May	-	6	2	11	8	
June	2	-	-	7	7	
July	2	4		1	10	
Aug	-	11		2	16	
Sept	1	15		9	10	
Oct	-	6		13	10	
Nov	8	10		3	6	
Dec	1	8		2	5	

Catalina Is modified at SARO, Beaumaris 1941–42

Nº	In	Ashore	Out	To

(a) Part batch of 30 supplied March–July 1941

Nº	In	Ashore	Out	To
W8416	10.9.42	11.9.42	1.10.42	Pembroke Dock
W8419	4.6.41	6.6.41	26.6.41	119 Sqn
W8420	12.842	23.8.42	10.9.42	Greenock
W8421	1.3.42	2.3.42	24.3.42	Greenock
W8424	21.4.42	22.4.42	23.4.42	Leuchars

(b) Part batch 20 supplied June–November 1941

Nº	In	Ashore	Out	To
Z2142	19.5.42	19.5.42	10.6.42	Pembroke Dock
Z2143	10.4.42	?	13.4.42	Battery Park*
Z2145	9.7.41	10.7.41	24.7.41	Greenock
Z2146	3.7.41	5.7.41	18.7.41	Greenock
Z2148	17.7.41	17.7.41	5.9.41	Stranraer
Z2151	8.11.41	8.11.41	25.11.41	Greenock
Z2152	11.9.41	2.10.41	3.10.41	MAEE

* the relocated (21.09.39) MAEE at Helensburgh

(c) Part batch 40 supplied March–July 1941

Nº	In	Ashore	Out	To
AH539	29.7.42	30.7.42	16.8.42	Greenock
AH545	13.3.42	14.3.42*	14.6.42	Pembroke Dock (damaged hull slipping buoy)
AH548	10.3.42	10.3.42	4.4.42	Pembroke Dock
AH550	4.5.42	4.5.42	5.5.42	Leuchars
AH564	8.6.41	8.6.41	12.2.44	MAEE
AH565	22.6.41	23.6.41	9.7.41	MAEE
AH567	7.2.42	9.2.42	14.3.42	Pembroke Dock

(d) Batch of 9 supplied November 1941–January 1942

Nº	In	Ashore	Out	To
AJ154	23.11.41	23.11.41	1.12.41	Battery Park
AJ155	18.11.41	19.11.41	5.12.41	Battery Park
AJ156	27.12.41	19.12.41	3.3.42*	Greenock (tail damaged by launch *Saro II*)
AJ157	23.11.41	25.11.41	17.12.41	Greenock
AJ158	25.11.41	25.11.41	17.12.41	Mountbatten
AJ159	25.11.41	29.11.41	23.02.42	Mountbatten
AJ160	10.11.41+	11.12.41	?	Greenock (dates as given in 'Catalina Register', where listed out of chronology)
AJ161	5.1.42	6.1.42	21.3.42	Greenock
AJ162	10.11.41+	10.11.41	7.3.42	Greenock

(e) Part batch 7 Catalin IIs delivered January–April 1941

Nº	In	Ashore	Out	To
AM266	28.04.41	28.04.41	11.06.41	Nº 240 Sqn
AM267	15.04.41	02.05.41	16.05.41	Nº 4 OTU

(f) Part batch 18 Canadian-built Catalina IIas diverted to RAF February–May 1942

Nº	In	Ashore	Out	To
9703*	21.04.42	21.04.42	22.05.42	Nº 209 Sqn
9714*	22.03.42	22.03.42	15.04.42	Greenock
9716*	22.03.42	22.03.42	04.04.42	Nº 240 Sqn
9718*	18.03.42	18.03.42	04.04.42	Greenock
9725*	10.02.42	10.02.42	22.04.42	Greenock
VA703	24.05.42	27.05.42	12.06.42	Pembroke Dock
VA716	24.05.42	26.05.42	15.06.42	Lough Erne
VA718	24.05.42	26.05.42	15.06.42	Lough Erne
VA726	15.04.42	16.04.42	13.05.42	Greenock
VA729	15.04.42	16.04.42	09.05.42	Greenock

* Noted as DA (Direct Arrival) in Register. Being diverted aircraft they arrived with RCAF numeric registration. For RAF purposes the last three digits were prefaced with the letters 'VA', arbitrarily selected some four years before normal allocation reached this point.

Catalina alongside the compass base at Friars.

meet RAF operational demands — to radios, compasses and other instruments, to bomb racks, to machine gun (FP 250 used as a 'gun-bed'), even to hulls (to store RAF-type equipment). One of the first Mark I Catalinas to arrive at Beaumaris, AH564 was retained as the 'DTD' (Directorate of Technical Development) aircraft to trial and fit modifications as became expedient. AH564 touched down on the Menai Strait a on 4 June 1941 and finally left on 12 February 1944, having by then become unrepresentative of later Catalina models then being taken into service. It was replaced by FP260, another MkI Catalina, which outlived its usefulness to the Design Department at Friars after just three months before finding itself returned to MAEE and then to squadron.

Airborne radar (ASV) is noted as being trialled extensively by the '1st crew' under F/Lt Stacey, in February 1942. Trials were successful and an RAF 'fitting party' duly arrived on 29 March. Top secret as radar was, Leslie Ash amusingly refers (2 April 1942) to 'new ASV gear arriving in quantities with special Police Guard etc. etc.' Did this involve the local 'bobby'? The mind boggles! A more powerful, longer range (LRASV) version would come on stream 14 months later, trialled in JX253 and JX 215, which latter arrived at Beaumaris on 4 May 1943 and remained until 8 August 1945 as Saro's current flying test bed or 'CRD aircraft' according to the diary. It was the last Catalina to be cleared. Mark VIII radar followed as from 9 March 1944.

Five months after successful trials were held by

'Direct Arrivals' at Beaumaris

AJ154#	23.11.41	FP107	1.8.42	FP287*	20.12.42
AJ157#	23.11.41	FP191	8.9.42	FP286	20.12.42
AJ158#	25.11.41	FP194	8.9.42	JX313*	15.1.44
AJ159#	25.11.41	FP181	8.9.42	JX290*	23.1.44
9725*	10.2.42	FP185*	8.9.42	JX292	25.1.44
9718	18.3.42*	FP183	8.9.42	JX294*	25.1.44
9716*	22.3.42	FP250	9.11.42	JX315*	8.2.44
9714*	22.3.42	FP249	9.11.42	JX324	20.3.44
9703	21.4.42	FP232	9.11.42	JX593*	29.9.44
FP103*	18.7.42				

(Based on 'Catalina Register" save for # = Ash diary only.   *= also shown in Ash diary)

Catalinas at anchor opposite
Saro Beaumaris.

*Right: Catalina JX246, a Mk IVa, leaving the
water at Saro Beaumaris, September 1943.*

*Below: The beaching party ready. Catalina FP115
ready for towing up the slipway. Above the wing,
to the left of the port engine, is the Beaumaris
lifeboat station. Above the starboard wing other
Catalinas can be seen at anchor.*

Catalina AH545 displays well the Leigh Light and the yagi ASV radar aerial .
[Saunders Roe 220]

May, which left Scottish Aviation in a shambles.

Catalinas destined for Beaumaris were ferried across the Atlantic by (a) a staggered northern route Gander–Reykjavik–Largs, Ayrshire, the last a terminal on the Firth of Clyde operated by Scottish Aviation Ltd., and (b) a more direct southern route via Bermuda and/or Gibraltar. Before the opening of the Largs terminal in December 1942 Trans-At Catalinas made do with SAL's seaplane repair facility at Greenock, before onward transit to Beaumaris. Greenock was the clearance destination for many Beaumaris Catalinas after modification, presumably there to await allocation to a squadron. The Friars Catalina Register records no more than six clearances direct to unit, and all those before May 1942. S/Ldr Ash's diary records the first Catalina arrivals on Menai, from Greenock, on 22 June (AH565, complete with Ferry Command crew) and 3 July 1941 (Z2146, piloted by S.A.L.'s test pilot 'Dutch' Holland), with dedicated Trans-At W/T and R/T stations being set up at Friars on 6 December 1941, followed by a Ministerial conference to iron out problems on 11 December. The northern route was considered the norm by Ash, and movements here receive short shrift in his diary after 23 June 1941. On the other hand he is at pains to record all 'Direct Arrivals' presumably via the southern route individually right through to September 1944. His aircraft registrations diverge somewhat from the Catalina Register so the list given above is a composite one for convenience. It is interesting to note that of the twenty-seven 'Direct Arrivals', for whatever reason they were thus differentiated by Ash, none are recorded in 1943. This does not imply a temporary moratorium on Catalina 'imports' for the Register shows some 77 handled that year. However, as Lend-Lease got into full swing and the Air MInistry grasped at any straw in the wind, there was an increasing tendency for a load of unwanted rubbish to occupy the moorings and hard standings at Beaumaris, causing bottlenecks and backlogs in the smooth handling/processing of Catalinas.

experimental Wellingtons of Coastal Command, discussions were opened at Beaumaris (6 October 1941) re the possibility of installing a 'Leigh Light', an ASV radar guided searchlight, into Catalinas. A further conference, attended by W/Cdr Leigh himself (a well earned promotion under his belt) was held on 28 January 1942. The installation of the Leigh Light involved some wing strengthening. The accompanying individuaL photographs well illustrate some of the modifications made. One experiment, details of which seem to be elusive, is RATOG (Rocket Assisted Take Off Gear), mentioned very late in Ash's reminiscences (23 July 1945) and possibly aborted with the end of hostilities. One dreads to think of the impact of these 'Heath Robinson' packages on the fabric and structure of fully laden float planes that turned the scales at 34,000+ lbs! The concept of 'cartridge initiated acceleration' had been trialled some time (since January/February 1944) in connection with catapult-launched aircraft such as the Hurricane and Seafire. The rockets, 5ins in diameter, 41ins long and carrying some 26lbs of cordite, were fixed,in combinations of two, four or eight, in detachable carriers to wing roots. The theory was to open up the engine to maximum throttle and then fire the rockets, which burnt for four seconds only … with fingers crossed that the rocket exhaust did not set fire to rudder, elevators and doped fabric skin. How these would have functioned in a watery environment is a matter of debate, hence possibly the experiments at Beaumaris.

Initially the Catalina conversion contract was to be shared with Scottish Aviation Ltd, based in a redundant shipyard at Greenock on the Clyde. Ash's diary duly notes (1–4 March 1941), the migration northwards of Saro design staff, including Bridges and Henry Knowler, chief designer . Mr Bridges was to oversee the implementation of Saro designs and modifications at Greenock and Ash records, possibly with some satisfaction Bridges's return with his designs and records to Beaumaris, 'the last man' on 8 May. Their position had become increasingly precarious after the Glasgow and Clydeside *Blitz* was initiated 13 March 1941, with a heavy raid against the shipyards on 7 April followed by a *Doppelgänger* on 5/6 May and a follow-up punch on 7

Admittedly work was piling up and some contracts had to be relinquished or aborted. Imminent in the latter half of 1943 were the Consolidated Coronado and Martin Mariner contracts. Both were American patrol-bomber flying boats in service with the US Navy, but now diverted to the RAF under Lend-Lease and hopefully intended for Coastal Command. Neither model really came up to scratch in terms of handling, range, reliability and workmanship and had a mixed reception. Of an initial order of 100, only ten Coronados were actually delivered (survivors of a batch of thirty-two optimistically registered between JX470 and JX501) and in the event ultimately taken over by an equally

Above: Catalina JX215 sitting on the compass at Beaumaris, looking like any well bred submarine killer. The aircraft would also take part in the RATOG (rocket assisted take-off) and Airborne Lifeboat trials.

Above: Catalina JX216 and a Coronado on the ramp and a Catalina on the compass circle. [Reg Chambers Jones]

Above: Coronado JX470 lying at anchor off Saro. In the foreground is Kingfisher FN660 and a Catalina off to the right.

Left: Coronado JX496, a frequent visitor to Beaumaris, awaiting beaching just off the slipway at Saro.

Left: Consolidated (Model 29) PB2Y-3B, Coronado, RAF serial number JX470, seen here with Nº 231 Squadron, being one of the first ten delivered to Beaumaris on Lend-Lease from the USA. She was given the name **Beaumaris**. *On her last visit to Anglesey, she spent ten weeks at anchor before leaving for Wig Bay on 17 September 1944..*

Right: Mariner JX103 standing on the concrete at Saro Beaumaris.

Consolidated Coronados at Beaumaris

Nº	In	Ashore	Away	To
JX470 (1)	27.04.43	28.04.43	09.05.43	Helensburgh
JX496 (1)	18.09.43	18.09.43	24.09.43	Greenock
JX496 (2)	11.02.44	14.02.44	29.03.44	BOAC
JX496 (3)	31.03.44	06.04.44	30.09.44	Wig Bay
JX471	31.05.44	07.07.44	17.08.44	Wig Bay
JX470 (2)	07.06.44	25.08.44	17.09.44	Wig Bay

Martin Mariners at Beaumaris

Nº	In	Ashore	Away	To
JX103*	23.08.43	23.08.43	04.09.43	Helensburgh
JX105*	06.10.43	07.10.43	01.11.43	Oban
JX100*	09.10.43	10.10.43	17.11.43	Oban
JX106*	24.10.43	25.10.43	26.11.43	Oban
JX110*	03.11.43	04.11.43	25.11.43	Oban
JX107#	06.11.43	09.11.43	04.05.44	Wig Bay
JX113#	09.11.43	12.11.43	16.12.43	Wig Bay
JX116	11.11.43	20.11.43	03.07.44	Wig Bay
JX111*	18.11.43		02.12.43	Wig Bay
JX117*	19.11.43	26.11.43		
		25.10.44	31.10.44	Wig Bay
JX102#	20.11.43	09.12.43		Wig Bay

* = with Nº 524 Squadron   # = returned to USA

Right: Four Mariners at Saro Beaumaris.

*Below: Coronado JX496 flew with BOAC and N°
231 Squadron on freight services. seen here on the
Llangoed road, stripped of its armaments.*

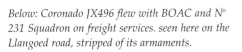

*Below: Martin Mariner JX117 at
anchor off Beaumaris.*

*Below:Mariner JX103 standing on the grass by
Friars mansion.*

Right: A Coronado on the ramp on the Llangoed road at Saro. [Mr John Morris]

reluctant Nº 231 Squadron, Transport Command, for their freight and passenger services on the Montreal–Iceland, Largs–Newfoundland, and West Indies–Africa routes.

Immediately after the war five were scrapped and four scuttled off Largs. JX472 had earlier (26 September 1944) been chewed up beyond economic repair by Mariner JX111 whilst moored at Wig Bay — perhaps not unfitting endings for unwanted, unloved 'ugly ducklings'. The clip-winged Coronado, powered by four 1,200hp Pratt & Whitney Twin Wasp engines, was the largest aircraft hitherto handled by Saro, Beaumaris. According to Ash's records JX470 was the first to touch down on Friars Roads on 27 April 1943, followed by JX496 on 18 September and JX471 on 31 May the following year. These are the only Coronados recorded at Beaumaris, the remainder presumably going to MAEE and/or Scottish Aviation for assessment and modifications. JX470 is pictured here whilst with Nº 231 Squadron, its on-off Friars association commemorated by the name 'Beaumaris' painted on its nose.

In passing it is interesting to note that the name 'Bangor' was given to a larger BOAC flying boat (NC18619/G-AGCB), one of three Boeing 314A Clippers bought second-hand from Pan American Airways in April 1941 and operated (June 1941–April 44) on the vital UK–Lagos route and thereafter on North Atlantic routes until returned to the USA in April 1948. Also prominent on the Poole–Lagos run (March 1941–December 1943) was Guba ('squall'), which

Ash notes as arriving at Beaumaris on 14 January 1944, flown by F/Lt Swaffin. Statistically this was Catalina AM258 (erroneous)/civil registration G-AGBJ, reverting to RAF serial SM706 in September 1944 when taken on charge by MAP. At Beaumaris it was beached the same day, inspected but found wanting, The Register shows it re-launched 10 May 1944 and remarks 'Towed to Pwllheli for mooring trials'. Here, after capsizing and sinking in a gale, it was salvaged, stripped of equipment and scuttled on 10 August 1945 — an inglorious end for such a veteran.

Equally a waste of space, especially after the expense of tooling up to meet the new contract, was the Martin Mariner, also a reconnaissance amphibian bomber and in the eyes of British historians another ill conceived Lend-Lease fiasco, although in the USA the Mariner and its derivations went on to be one of the most successful sea planes of all times right up to and including the Korean War. Twenty-eight (of a batch of thirty-three, JX100-JX132) were delivered between August–December 1943. Five of the batch were never delivered and between 23 February 1944–11 January 1945 some 16 were ferried back to the USA! Five were vested for a short period in Nº 45 Group, Dorval Airport, Canada. This Group was the rump of Ferry Command (disbanded and redesignated 25 March 1943) and was now the Atlantic Transport

Saro A37, RAF serial TK580 Shrimp (right). This was a scaled research aircraft tested at Beaumaris. This started life as G-AFZS (above). Note the different tail configuration.

Spitfire floatplane MJ892 on the Llangoed road, having just been hauled out of the water.

Group in Transport Command. Two of these were duly returned to the USA, but three were not struck off charge until February/March 1944. One assumes these were used for trans-Atlantic ferry work although details are uncertain. However, ten were taken on the books of N° 524 Squadron, then based at Oban, a unit formed 20 October 1944 specifically for the purpose of obtaining operational experience on the Mariner flying boats. To this end, as the above table shows, seven Mariners were flown into Friars for minor modifications.

S/Ldr Ash notes the first, JX103, as touching down from Largs on 24 August 1943. The Register and day book have 1530hrs on 23 August. Piloted by S/Ldr Lowery; almost immediately it took off again to show off its paces to the Saro's curious test pilots. It had been beached by 1845hrs the same evening, ready for inspection work to begin the following morning. JX103 was relaunched at 1455hrs on 3 September and test flown at 1515hrs with S/Ldrs Ash, Swaffin and Lowery on board, before the latter took it back to MAEE, Helensburgh the next day. On 29 November 1943 Ash's diary contains the laconic 'Work stopped on Mariners'. No reasons were given by MAP. Beyond some reservations as to handling, possibly a major design drawback in this model was the location of the fuel tanks immediately below the flight deck, a good a reason as any perhaps for rejection for front line operations, one would have thought! A retrospective marginal note in the Register records JX117 as 'Burnt out and sank at Wig Bay'. This was on 4 November 1944 and may point to MAP's reservations as being well grounded. The knee-jerk repercussions were swift — on 7 December 1943 No 254 Squadron was disbanded, to reform in April 1944 at Davidstow Moor, Cornwall, still in Coastal Command, but equipped with Wellingtons and tasked with anti-E-boat and anti-submarine patrols off the northern coast of France. Over the next few months the Mariners in hand at Friars were flown out to storage at N° 57 MU, Wig Bay.

Another blow to Saunders Roe occurred early in 1944. Ash's diary notes on 3 February: 'Shetland contract stopped(?)', the question mark reflecting uncertainties arising from currently ambivalent attitudes at the Air Ministry to flying boats. The axe had been hovering since June; now it had fallen. The development of the Shetland as a larger long range version of the Sunderland was a joint private venture with Short Bros and had been on the boil since 1940, Saro

Taylorcraft Auster V float plane TJ207, fitted with floats taken from a DH82 Queen Bee.

Vought-Sikorsky 052U-3 Kingfisher MkI, FN660, on the compass at Beaumaris. This Lend-Lease aircraft was used to evaluate potential use with the Royal Navy as a two-seater reconnaissance aircraft.

Following the collapse of the Coronado, Mariner, 'Shrimps' and Shetland projects Leslie Ash's diary zooms in on more esoteric triallings — notably efforts to put floats on the Spitfire and Taylorcraft Auster — only the latter meeting with limited success. Additionally the Vought Sikorsky OSU2 Kingfisher and Curtiss Seamew, were occasional American visitors, the first certainly for MAP trials, but the latter (FN451) only as part of the static dry-land display put on by Friars for Bangor's 'Wings for Victory Week' (24–31 May 1943) — a forlorn attempt to impress the public with another Lend-Lease design failure. It was conveyed to Friars from RAF Mona by road on the back of a Hunting Aviation 'Queen Mary' and left again the same way, en route for its eventual destination, that 'great scrapyard in the sky' at RAF Hawarden.

taking special responsibility for the design of wings and engines, to which end a wind tunnel had been built at Beaumaris. Two prototypes only were completed. DX171, given the civil registration G-AGVD in November 1945, was scrapped in 1951 without actually entering service. DX166 was destroyed by fire whilst at moorings at Felixstowe on 28 January 1946. The Friars 'Visitors' Book' shows DX166 having made an overnight stop on 13/14 January 1945 whilst in transit from Rochester to Windermere. It was flown on that occasion by test pilot Geoffrey Tyson, OBE, RAFO.

The diary notes for 13 June 1944: 'Spitfire on floats first

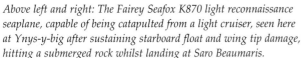

Above left and right: The Fairey Seafox K870 light reconnaissance seaplane, capable of being catapulted from a light cruiser, seen here at Ynys-y-big after sustaining starboard float and wing tip damage, hitting a submerged rock whilst landing at Saro Beaumaris.

Lower right: Winifred Brown and Mr Adams, the Marine Superintendent at Saro Beaumaris, standing in front of the Fairey Seafox. Both were members of the Lancashire Aero Club pre-war. Winifred won the King's Cup in an Avro 504 'Avian III' G-EBVZ.

launched and flown by Geoffrey Quill' (a MkIX, MJ892). But if the incidence of logged Sea Otter visits, qualified by the single word 'Spitfire', is anything to go by, bringing test pilots from MAEE to fly Spitfires, tests also occurred on 18 and 25 June 1944 (JM831/Quill), 11 July (JM831/ L/Cdr Furlong) and 18 July (JM738/Furlong, see diary for that date — obviously not the first Sea Otter to visit). At the longest both test pilots were at Friars for 3–6 hours only, which makes one wonder at the thoroughness of the tests. Strangely, Ron Adams's otherwise immaculately kept register of aircraft movements, makes no reference to the arrival of earlier Spitfire float-plane prototypes, EP751 and EP754, all the more puzzling when extant photographs shows the former still on winch cable at the head of the Friars slipway some time in 1943. The idea of a fighter on floats was not new, being mooted as a possibility for areas of rough terrain where airfields and landing strips were absent e.g. Norway and the Greek islands. A resurgence of interest in 1944 perhaps anticipated a protracted island-hopping campaign in the Pacific, where the Japanese air force operated float planes with some success. The earliest prototype Spitfire VB earmarked for conversion to a float fighter was W3760, a DTD aircraft since 15 August 1941, but otherwise the 'Wrexham Spitfire', bought by the inhabitants of East Denbighshire (see Chapter 14 below) and is logged by Ron Adams as making a three-hour stop-over at Beaumaris for refuelling on 1 September 1943 in transit from Helensburgh to Hamble. The pilot was F/Lt Ripley. None of these Spitfire float planes would see operational service.

The Vought Sikorsky 'Kingfisher' was a low wing amphibian intended for use by the Fleet Air Arm as a reconnaissance aircraft. FN660 was provided by MAP as a DTD aircraft. It underwent modifications at Friars in May 1942, before trialling passed in its entirety, because of the imminence of the Catalina programme, to Scottish Aviation, Greenock. Other Kingfishers are logged at Beaumaris — FN675 (18 and 29 August 1942), FN691 (29 August 1942), and FN670 (26 September 1942) and FN684 (28 April 1943) — either in transit or staying a few hours for minor jobs such as the 'fitting of slings'.

The Taylorcraft Auster experiments take up the closing entries of Leslie Ash's diary between 11 November–15 December 1944. Ash was the pilot on each of seven test flights, examining particularly the aero-dynamics of the 'Queen Bee' floats with which the aircraft was fitted, and on its return flight to the MAEE at Helensburgh.

Throughout 1942 Ash's diary picks up on the visits of the Fairey 'Seafox', a catapult seaplane, replacing the 'Osprey' and capable of being launched from light cruisers. Issue to ship was slow, and most Seafoxes had spent long periods in storage at either N° 3 ASU (Sealand) or N° 27 MU (Shawbury). Visits to Friars of K5892 (14.3.42) and K8606 (20.3.42) were convenient refuelling stops in transit from Dundee to Lee-on-Solent and vice-versa. L4823 remained at Beaumaris for three days 11/14.3.42, obviously for some minor technical modifications. The last Seafox logged was K8615 on 2 April 1942, which remained at Friars all of 1hr 25 minutes. Why they prompted excited comments 'More Seafox' each time when Ash did not even fly them is a matter

of some minor mystery! No mention is made of K8570 (ex-DTD at Fairey), pictured here after a forced landing at Ynys-y-Big, an island in the Menai Strait, between Menai Bridge and Craig-y-don. The starboard float and wing tip were damaged and the aircraft was towed into Beaumaris harbour.

Finally, in our brief commentary on Leslie Ash's diary the entry for 30 September 1942, which records the arrival of a Catalina of N° 210 Squadron from Sullom Voe, ostensibly to collect Catalina W8416 which duly let for Pembroke Dock (the squadron's new posting as from 4 October), on 1 October. The intriguing reference: 'They had 28 bodies on board!' has given rise to some controversy. The use of 'bodies' as distinct from 'people, crew, personnel etc.' implies cadavers or corpses. It is difficult to pin point gross carelessness on part of the RAF to produce such a total, but one incident does spring to mind about this period, and that is the controversial loss of Sunderland W4026, which crashed into a hillside in Caithness, killing most of those on board including Air Commodore HRH the Duke of Kent. Did these 'bodies' flown into Friars include those from this tragic accident. With the 'convenient' loss, withdrawal or destruction of all papers and records relating to the loss of W4026, we may never know the answer. It must remain in the realms of tantalising speculation, otherwise unrecorded save for the chance pen of S/Ldr. Leslie Ash.

Journal Extracts, 2 August 1940–24 July 1945
[...] = *editorial interpolations*

1940

Friars [Friars] was 'discovered' on Friday, 2 August, 1940, in conjunction with W. Owen of Bangor, after several other unsuitable sites had been viewed in Caernarfonshire and Anglesey.

Notice issued to D.O. [? Drawing Office] re transfer on Wednesday, 18 September 1940.

Most of D.O. at Beaumaris by 3 October 1940, when I paid my first visit.

No knowledge of anything at Friars between 6 October 1940–7 January 1941.

1941

13 January Wooden Walrus arrived for inspection and recording by D.O.

13 January–18 January. Constant trouble with *Cornubia* (Saro II launch), on which I worked myself to put it reasonable condition.

16 January Saro 37 [Saro A.37, half-scale experimental seaplane TK582/G-AFZS] first flown by myself at Beaumaris (Note — date of its delivery to us from MAEE is not known as I was not then at Friars).

Right: Saro staff. [John Morris via Reg Chambers Jones]

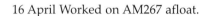

Below: Female staff with Meirona Hopkins. [Mrs Meirona Hopkins, Bangor]

18 January *Cornubia* dragged moorings off Beaumaris Pier and only rescued after a struggle by Leavett and Williams and moved to Menai Bridge.

6 February Argument with Mrs Adams re charter of *Perula.*

13 February Mr Westbrooke put Catalinas on our shoulders at Beaumaris.

1 March Messrs. Knowley, Brewer, Bridges and Adams left for Scottish Aviation Ltd. at Greenock.

2 March Messrs. Farrow, Ball, Cooper and Graham to Greenock.

4 March Self, with Mr Taylor and Mr Smith to Greenock.

15 April First Catalina, AM267, arrived at Beaumaris, G/Cpt Cahill, pilot.

Above right: Laird (Anglesey) staff outside the main door at Friars, c.1960. [John Morris via Reg Chambers Jones]

Right: Laird (Anglesey) staff, Friars, Beaumaris, 1940s.

16 April Worked on AM267 afloat.

28 April Second Catalina arrived from Pembroke Dock. F/Lt Fleming, DFC, pilot — Nº AM266.

2 May Colonel Outram visited us.
Catalina AM267 hauled ashore — first one on land at Friars.

6 May Botha aircraft crashed in Bay and crew rescued. [L6265 of 3SGR, Squires Gate; engine failure, ditched and overturned off Puffin Island].

7 May Aircraft salvaged in 10 hours.

8 May Bridges returned from Greenock (last man).

Member of the Saro staff with a Martin Mariner outside Friars.

16 May AM267 collected by F/Lt Jones and F/O Neugebar. [Cleared to Nº 4 (Coastal Command) OTU, Stranraer].

4 June F/Lt Hunter ('Tiny') arrived with crew to collect AM266. [Cleared to No 210 Squadron, Oban/Sullom Voe/Stranraer] F/Lt Baraclough and F/Lt Fitzpatrick delivered Catalina W8419 to us.

8 June Catalina AH 564 arrived from MAEE. (Our first CRD [Controller of Research and Development] aircraft).

22 June AH565 arrived from Greenock with original Trans-At crew (F/Lt McKinley, pilot). Note: this is the McKinley who had just been flying over the North Pole.

23 June Catalina W8419 cleared [back to MAEE]. (As operations are now established no further entries of normal movements will be made).

3 July Catalina Z2146 arrived from Greenock piloted by S.A.L's [Scottish Aviation, Ltd.] own test pilot, Mr R. Holland ('Dutch').

21 July First Catalina Brochure conference with S/Ldr Lundy, Mr Mason, and Mr Foulkes from MAP.

25 July W/Cdr (then Major) Arthur visited us re Trans-At arrivals.

27 July G/Cpt Pearce DPCA [Directorate of Production, Canadian and American, a special Department of MAP] paid his first visit.

13 August Mr P. Cooper arrived at Friars (also J. Arnell and R. Bungey).

10 September S/Ldr Moreton, test pilot of Short Bros. arrived and flew Saro 37.

29 September Works employees made recording for BBC to transmit to America.

6 October Leigh Light first mooted. Major Savage and Mr Goudy visited us.

24 October Air raid on Bangor approx. 2200hrs.

12 November First wooden Walrus X1046 [ex- L2309, 765 Sqn.] flown at Beaumaris.

23 November (Sunday) First direct arrivals AJ154 (Capt Kleaver, RAF Ferry Command) and AJ 157 (Capt Broadbent, RAF Ferry Command).

25 November Two more direct arrivals AJ158 — Capt Phillips and AJ 159 — Capt Grey. Both of Ferry Command. Capt Grey was a wild Texas-born Yank and insisted on drinking his own Whisky in the Bulkeley Lounge at tea time.

6 December Large W/T and R/T motor vans arrive to set up a station for Trans-At work.

11 December Conference called by Air Ministry held at Friars to decide the Trans-At set-up.

Present: Major Arthur   F/Lt Stone
         S/Ldr Bamford   F/Lt Lloyd Jones
         F/Lt Douglas   F/Lt Lusk
         F/Lt Marler.

21 December G/Cpt Pearce and S/Ldr Lundy arrived for 2nd Brochure Conference.

1942

22 January Lady Kathleen Stanley [Beaumaris] visited us re W.V.S. help in feeding our small night shift until Canteen was built.

28 January W/Cdr Leigh, Mr Goudy (Savage & Parsons), Mr Angell, RDS2 and F/Lt Ackermann visited us on first conference on Leigh Light.

11 February The first of several Sea Fox aircraft [L4523] called for fuel, en route South Coast to Scotland. Pilot — P/O Davies.

12 February Direct arrival V 9725 — Capt Lloyd & F/Lt Godsby.

16 February First official RAF crews posted here for special trials.
F/Lt (Junior) Bradley (now W/Cdr & DFC)
F/Lt Lawson Smith
F/O Smallman (now W/Cdr & DSO, DFC).

21 February First crew recalled and replaced by:
F/Lt Stacey F/Lt Edgar F/O Smith, average age 21–3 years. F/O Bracken who did some long flights on ASV [Air-to-Surface Vessel] radar trials.

23 February G/Capt Williamson (CO Pembroke Dock) and other officers visited us.

8 March Admiral Sir Frederick Cryer and his PA (Lt A. Sinclair) disembarked (Sunday) from Sunderland en route for naval Base at Holyhead.

18 March Direct arrival — V9718 — Capt Hearsum & 7 others.
S/Ldr Randall of N° 413 Squadron force-landed [en route to Pembroke Dock] due to bad weather (Cat Z2149). This was our first diversion arranged by N° 15 Group RAF.

20 March F/Sgt Pilot Monaghan and crew replaced previous stand-by crew who left about 10 March.

21 March More Sea Fox (about the 4th pair) [this K8606; L4523 called 1.2.42, and K8592 on 14.3.42].

22 March Direct arrivals:
V9714 — S/Ldr King, RAF
        1st Officer Sanderman, ATA
        F/Lt Dodson, RAF
V9716 — S/Ldr Gething, RAF
        W/Cdr Dunwood, RAF
        P/O Drewery, RCAF.

29 March First arrivals of RAF fitting party for ASV.
F/O Baggs plus 2 corporals and 1 AC2.

31 March F/Sgt Monoghan and crew replaced by:
F/Lt Furseman
P/O Fielding (the 'Hon' Hugh)
P/O Vivian and P/O Tomlin
with Sgts Maycock, Kelly, Edgar, Robertson and McGuire. This was indeed our first crew throughout.

2 April More Sea Fox [K8616] (and 'Shark'). ASV gear commenced arriving in quantities with special Police Guards etc. etc.

13 April First amphibian arrived [FP529] — F/Lt Furseman collected it from Prestwick.

21 April Our first contact with the Norwegians:
Commander Lambrechts

L/Cdr Johganson
Lt Roenegan 2/Lt Stennieng
re Catalina amphibians [W8424] (from Leuchars).

12 May Visit from HRH Duke of Kent.

21 May Our 'Permanent' crew — 'Fursy & Co' — replaced by:
F/Sgt Monaghan
Sgt Flowers — Canadian
Sgt Guy
Sgt Moore
Sgt Mainwood — Canadian.

22 June F/Lt Major of SMV arranged for commencement of a course of instruction for Flight Engineers on Catalinas.

15 July Direct arrival — FP101 — F/O Denike.
First Kingfisher arrived.

18 July Direct arrival — Capt. Lorber — FP103.

23 July Collected a Liverpool barrage balloon from Llandonna beach.

1 August FP107 arrived — Pilot, Andre Chatel. (I think this must have been Direct Arrival, but cannot confirm.

14–17 September More Sea Fox.

30 September Catalina [FP115] from N° 210 Squadron, Sullom Voe arrived to collect W8416 — They had 28 bodies on board!

21 October Our first contact with an afterwards constant visitor — S/Ldr (now W/Cdr) Lyewood. Came on FP105 to collect FP238 and FP245 together with:
        W/Cdr Wallace
        W/Cdr Dodd
        S/Ldr Johnson White (Australia)
        F/Lt Edwards
        F/Lt Elms.

13 November Vice Admiral Somerville visited us with Cmdr Weblin re moorings.

19 November First visit to Beaumaris of G/Cpt Castor (an old visitor to Saunders Roe at Cowes) now OC at Lough Erne.

8 December Sunderland W4004 ('Z' of N° 10 Squadron) force-landed due to weather and rode out a 48 hours gale off Friars.

20 December Direct arrival — FP287—
        André Chatel, F/Lt Leitch, P/O Barr.

First trial of the Saro Beaumaris-built sea rescue hydroplane 'Bras Dor' (Golden Arm), 7 January 1943.
[Reg Chambers Jones]

20/21 December — Night of, FP 127 slipped its moorings without asking. Located off Blackpool at 10am 21st. Taken in tow by Royal Navy at 11.20am and sunk by them at 1830hrs (through sheer negligence) at 53°46'N, 3°30'W.

1943

1 January Mr Metcalf of DPCA visited us re 3rd Brochure.

7 January In passing — first trials of our amphibious Sea Rescue Hydroplane.

24 February W/O Monaghan replaced by F/Lt Swaffin as Pilot and Officer i/c of Ferry crew.
Our first contact with Mr L. Drayner of Consolidated Aircraft Corporation.

27 March First Coronado JX470 arrived — Pilot Capt Gentry.

29 May–5 June — Our display for 'Wings for Victory' Week.

26 June Visit by Vice-President of Consolidated [Aircraft] Corporation.

13 August Ferrying of aircraft taken over by ATA.

24 August First Mariner, JX103, arrived from Largs — Pilot S/Ldr Lowery.

23 September G/Cpt Pearce bought G/Capt Wincotte to see Friars.

13 October S/Ldr Ottignon joined us as MAP overseer.

10 November W/Cdr Morris arrived to swing the Fluxgate compasses on Mariners. (This is noted because W/Cdr Morris now lives at Lower Helliots(?) Farm, near Godshill (on the Whitwell Road out).
Francis Francis forced landed on Sunderland ML739 with engine trouble [en route Shorts to Wig Bay].

29 November Work stopped on Mariners [JX102, JX107, JX111, JX113, JX116, JX117 beached, all eventually cleared for Wig Bay.

November Some of our hardest work in engine running afloat (including Sunderland).

1944

5/6 January G/Cpt Pearce and Mr Metcalfe on Brochure. (West Bangor stores) Star lighting and telephones.

14 January 'Guba' [Catalina SM706 ex AM258] arrived from BOAC [ex G-AGBJ] (F/Lt Swaffin). SM706 as used for mooring trials both on Menai Strait and post 10 May 1944, at Pwllheli, where it was eventually scuttled and sunk].

15 January Direct arrival — JX313 — Capt Spiller & F/O Russel.

23 January Direct arrival — JX290 — Capt Baird.

25 January Direct arrivals — JX292 — Capt Bach
JX294 — F/O Green.

2 February Marquis of Anglesey and party visited us.

3 February Shetland contract stopped(?). [Refers to wider context of Saro at large. Only Shetland

S/Ldr. L. S. Ash (white overalls) test-flew the Taylorcraft Auster V float plane TJ207 for the first time at Beaumaris on 24 November 1944.

recorded at Beaumaris is DX166 which stopped off 13/14.1.45 in transit Rochester–Windermere.]

8 February Direct arrival — JX315 — Capt Lorber.

10 February Tar barrel fire on West Hangar apron. (Our first blaze). No damage.

22 February W/Cdr Monk, plus 10 BOAC and RAF Transport Command officers visited us re moorings for use during 'D'-Day preparations. BOAC sent Captains Bailey and Wynne.

9 March New Mk VIII radar (in nacelle) introduced by Conference.

20 March Direct arrival (unexpected) JX234 — Capt Baird.

23 March Bridges expected to go to the USA.

7 April–10 April — Our busiest Easter with arrivals and departures both to and from ourselves and en route South Coast to Scotland. All ATA crews.

9 June BOAC party (11 strong) to carry out tests on Coronado. Left on the 12th due to leaking tanks on Coronado.

18 June Spitfire on floats first launched and flown by Geoffrey Quill [MJ892, left Friars by road 15.9.44 for Air Service Training, Hamble and conversion to land plane].

18 July Our first Sea Otter [JM738] visited us (Lt/Cmdr Furlong brought it when coming to fly

the Spitfire) [Sea Otter JM831 visited 13.6.44 and again 25.6.44, both in connection with Spitfire floatplane trials].

16 September Coronado JX470 (Capt MacDonald) ran aground when taking off due to retracting floats too early.

26 September G/Cpt Isherwood left Valley after three years in command there, during which time he proved a very good friend to us.

29 September Direct arrival — JX593 — Capt Bach.

13 November Visited Taylorcraft at Leicester re flight tests on Seaplane. [Auster TJ207 would arrive Friars 19.11.44].

16 November TLC arrived and unloaded radar van on slipway en route for Naval Base, Holyhead.

24 November Flight tests on Taylorcraft seaplane [Further tests on TJ207 would take place 5–15.12.44].

15 December Final tests on Taylorcraft seaplane [cleared May 1945 to Helensburgh].

1945

16 February TLC arrived at slipway to take off radar van from Royal Navy, Holyhead.

18 May Sir Stafford Cripps visit.

5 July Saro37 — final test flight.

23/24 July Final test flight on our two CRD aircraft i.e. RATOG [Rocket Assisted Take Off Gear], Catalina JX215, cleared for Felixtowe 8.8.45] and Airborne Lifeboat.

We have today, 27 July, finished all Catalina with the exception of one which I will test fly immediately on my return after the holidays,

Two types to leave the Saro works:
Above: Motor Anti-Submarine Boat (MASB) T201.
[Reg Chambers Jones]

Right: Motor Torpedo Boat (MTB) P1103. [John Morris]

Below: Diversification under way — Saro Beaumaris, late 1940s. Leyland buses at the Friars works.
[National Assembly for Wales]

Saro Beaumaris, 2004

Right: At the entrance to the Second World War Saro works, recently vacated by Faun Municipal VEI.

Above: B1 type aircraft shed at the entrance to the old Saro works.

Right: Looking back towards the B1 hangar. The add-on buildings on the right hand side are post war.

Left: Friars mansion, Beaumaris.

Left: A well photographed scene of Friars looking over the Menai Strait towards Snowdonia.

Right: The old radar workshop and small B1 type hangar on the right.

Left: A T2 type aircraft shed.

Above: Inside the T2 aircraft shed. These buildings were known as 'transportables'.

Left: A B1 type recently used as a workshop.

*Right: Second World War workshops
facing demolition.*

*Left: The Second World War canteen
and mess room.*

*Below: Boat building at the Friars works in the late 1940s. The new slipway is visible in the centre of the photograph.
A number of buses are still on the yard. [Reg Chambers Jones]*

Catalinas modified or tested at SARO, Beaunmaris, 1943-5

Part batch of 226 Catalina IBs supplied July1942–February 1943

No	In	Ashore	Out	To
FP100	16.11.42	16.11.42	14.12.42	Stranraer
FP101	15.07.42	15.07.42	09.08.42	Greenock
FP102	18.07.42	18.07.42	12.08.42	Greenock
FP103*	18.07.42	19.07.42	30.07.42	Greenock
FP107	01.08.42	01.08.42	28.08.42	Greenock
FP108	06.10.42	16.10.42	06.12.42	Greenock
FP113	07.08.42	09.08.42	26.08.42	Greenock
FP114	28.08.42	29.08.42	17.09.42	Greenock
FP115	17.08.42	18.08.42	11.09.42	Greenock
FP117	27.08.42	28.08.42	15.09.42	Greenock
FP123	19.08.42	19.08.42	17.11.42	Greenock
FP124	17.08.42	18.08.42	28.08.42	Greenock
FP125	22.08.42	24.08.42	12.09.42	Greenock
FP127	20.12.42	(Lost, broke mooring, located, lost on tow)		
FP131	08.04.43	08.04.43	02.07.43	Poole
FP154	29.08.42	02.09.42	23.09.42	Greenock
FP155	01.09.42	15.09.42	09.1042	Felixstowe
FP159	06.07.49	06.07.43	24.09.43	MAEE
FP162	04.09.42	06.09.42	08.10.42	Greenock
FP165	01.09.42	09.09.42	13.10.42	Battery Park
FP172	13.09.42	17.09.42	23.10.42	Greenock
FP181*	08.09.42	21.09.42	21.10.42	Greenock
FP183*	08.09.42	23.09.42	28.10.42	Greenock
FP185*	08.09.42	5.10.42	07.11.42	Felixtowe
FP191*	08.09.42	10.09.42	16.10.42	Greenock
FP194*	08.09.42	10.09.42	06.10.42	Greenock
FP201	17.09.42	07.10.42	04.11.42	Greenock
FP212	29.09.42	30.09.42	04.11.42	Greenock
FP214	23.09.42	30.09.42	30.11.42	Greenock (damaged by fishing boat)
FP215	19.09.42	11.10.42	10.11.42	Stranraer
FP232*	09.11.42	10.1142	29.11.42	Felixstowe
FP233	13.10.42	21.10.42	13.11.42	Greenock
FP234	13.10.42	18.10.42	11.11.42	Greenock
FP237	19.10.42	22.10.42	19.11.42	Felixstowe
FP238	24,20.42	26.10.42	01.11.42	Lough Erne
FP243	22.10.42	23.10.42	01.11.42	Lough Erne
FP248	01.11.42	02.11.42	21.11.42	Greenock
FP249*	09.11.42	09.11.42	09.01.43	Felixstowe
FP250*	09.11.42	09.11.42	18.01.43	Greenock (gun tests)
FP251	18.11.42	19.11.42	21.01.43	Stranraer
FP252	26.01.43	02.02.43	26.03.43	Felixstowe
FP253	20.11.42	21.11.42	21.01.43	Stranraer
FP254	20.11.42	22.11.42	10.03.43	Felixstowe
FP255	12.11.42	13.11.42	03.12.42	MAEE
FP258	08.01.43	19.01.43	11.02.43	MAEE
FP259	08.01.43	09.01.43	15.02.43	Felixstowe
FP260	30.01.43	13.02.43	30.04.43	Helensburgh (DTD)
FP260 (2)	17.05.43	25.06.43	23.1043	Greenock
FP262	22.02.43	23.02.43	08.04.43	Felixstowe
FP263	26.01.43	26.01.43	08.03.43	Greenock
FP264	30.01.43	09.02.43	31.03.43	Felixstowe
FP265	08.01.43	09.01.43	18.02.43	Stranraer
FP267	09.02.43	18.02.43	19.03.43	Greenock
FP268	13.02.43	21.02.43	26.03.43	Greenock (S.I. trouble in test)
FP269	16.02.43	21.02.43	23.03.43	Greenock

FP270	20.12.42	20.12.42	29.01.43	Stranraer
FP271	12.12.42	12.12.42	01.03.43	Felixstowe
FP273	26.11.42	26.11.42	16.02.43	Stranraer
FP274	30.12.42	01.01.43	03.02.43	Stranraer
FP277	14.01.43	23.02.43	08.03.43	Felixstowe
FP278	12.12.42	12.12.42	26.01.43	Stranraer
FP280	11.03.43	12.03.43	05.05.43	Greenock
FP282	17.01.43	18.02.43	04.03.43	Stranraer
FP285	26.01.43	26.01.43	21.02.43	Greenock (hull damage)
FP286*	20.12.42	22.12.42	26.01.43	Felixstowe
FP287*	20.12.42	22.12.42	20.01.43	Felixstowe
FP300	26.01.43	26.01.43	06.03.43	Greenock
FP303	19.03.43	20.03.43	18.09.43	Oban ('George' u.s.)
FP305	08.01.43	03.02.43	12.03.43	Stranraer
FP308	23.03.43	25.03.43	15.05.43	Greenock
FP316	18.03.43	19.03.43	14.04.43	Felixstowe
FP317	23.03.43	23.03.43	05.05.43	Greenock
FP318	06.03.43	07.03.43	30.04.43	Greenock
FP322	07.03.43	08.03.43	30.04.43	Greenock

* = D.A. (Direct Arrival)

Part batch 12 Catalina IIIAs supplied April–May 1942

FP525	17.04.42	20.04.42	22.05.42	Leuchars
FP529	13.04.42	13.04.42	27.05.42	Nº 119 Sqn
FP533	17.04.42	21.04.42	07.06.42	Nº 119 Sqn
FP534	21.05.42	21.05.42	17.08.42	MAEE
FP536	07.05.43	08.05.43	12.09.43	Killadeas

Part batch of 11 Catalina IVAs supplied September-November 1943

JV925	06.10.43	?	19.12.43	Killadeas
JV926	27.09.43	29.09.43	09.02.44	Felixstowe
JV928	02. 10.43	06.10.43	12.06.44	Felixstowe
JV929	07.10.43	01.03.44	17.06.44	Felixstowe
JV930	08.10.43	01.03.44	18.05.44	Wig Bay
JV933	09.10.43	29.04.44	28.05.44	Woodhaven

Part batch 70 Catalina IVAs supplied may–September 1943

JX200	27.05.43	06.07.43	07.09.43	Greenock (for Nº 202 Sqn)
JX201	4.06.43	07.06.43	15.09.43	Greenock (1st test on 'George')
JX202	25.06.43	12.08.43	24.10.43	Felixstowe
JX203	21.09.43	22.09.43	25.10.43	Felixstowe
JX205	31.08.43	07.09.43	11.02.44	Felixstowe
JX208	25.08.43	26.08.43	05.02.44	Felixstowe
JX210	16.06.43	10.07.43	07.10.43	Felixstowe
JX214	02.06.43	14.07.43	18.09.43	Greenock (for Nº 202 Sqn. beached for fuel)
JX215	4.05.43	5.05.43	08.08.45	Felixstowe
JX216	06.05.43	06.05.43	05.07.43	Alness
JX218	10.05.43	11.05.43	05.07.43	Alness
JX221	02.06.43	24.06.43	21.08.43	Greenock (1st test on 'George')
JX222	13.07.43	12.08.43	02.10.43	Felixstowe
JX224	20.05.43	20.05.43	13.07.43	Helensburgh
JX226	19.05.43	24.06.43	25.08.43	Greenock
JX227	24.05.43	24.05.43	25.08.43	Greenock
JX229	5.06.43	16.07.43	16.09.43	Greenock (for Nº 202 Sqn)
JX242	14.09.43	15.09.43	12.10.43	Helensburgh
JX243	16.09.43	17.09.43	29.10.43	Felixstowe

JX244	02.10.43	13.10.43	22.04.44	Felixstowe
JX246	26.09.43	27.09.43	17.11.43	Felixstowe
JX247	28.09.43	04.10.43	06.03.44	Felixstowe
JX248	08.10.43	?	19.12.43	Killadeas
JX252	22.10.43	?	22.12.43	Killadeas
JX254	02.10.43	22.10.43	06.11.44	Wig Bay
JX255	24.09.43	25.09.55	22.11.43	Felixstowe
JX258	26.09.43	17.09.43	28.01.44	Felixstowe
JX259	12.10.43	06.03.44	12.05.44	Wig Bay
JX266	27.09.43	02.10.43	16.03.44	Wig Bay
JX267	11.10.43	19.10.43	20.12.43	Felixstowe
JX268	07.10.43	26.02.44	27.06.44	Battery Park

Part batch 168 Catalina IVBs supplied November 1943–September 1944

JX271	25.11.43	26.11.43	20.01.44	Oban
JX272	26.11.43	27.1143	05.02.44	Oban
JX274	4.11.43	04.11.43	13.04.44	MAEE
JX276	4.12.43	04.12.43	21.02.44	Oban
JX279	17.02.44	18.02.44	05.04.44	Felixstowe
JX281	10.01.44	14.01.44	16.02.44	Oban
JX282	16.12.43	11.01.44	10.02.44	Oban
JX283	4.04.45	17.04.45	Broken up for scrap	
JX285	08.03.44	09.03.44	12.04.44	Oban
JX286	11.03.44	11.03.44	20.04.44	Pembroke Dock
JX286 (2)	27.06.44	19.06.44	21.09.44	Oban
JX286 (3)	19.12.44	01.01.45	18.07.45	Wig Bay
JX288	16.0244	16.02.44	10.04.44	Oban
IX290*	23.01.44	26.01.44	08.03.44	Oban
JX291	10.12.43	14.12.43	08.02.44	Oban
JX292*	25.01.44	31.01.44	09.03.44	Oban
JX294*	25.01.44	31.01.44	19.03.44	Felixstowe
JX295	12.05.44	09.06.44	18.07.44	Wig Bay
JX295 (2)	20.02.45	17.03.45	18.06.45	Wig Bay
JX300	31.03.44	24.04.44	29.05.44	Oban
JX302	17.05.44	17.06.44	08.07.44	Wig Bay
JX304	15.02.45	06.03.45	23.04.45	Wig Bay
JX305	09.05.44	12.06.44	08.07.44	Wig Bay
JX306	24.04.44	24.05.44	21.06.44	Battery Park
JX309	08.05.44	06.06.44	06.07.44	Wig Bay
JX311	11.02.44	11.02.44	06.04.44	Felixstowe
JX312	15.03.44	27.03.44	25.04.44	Oban
JX313*	15.01.44	19.01.44	24.02.44	Oban
JX315*	08.02.44	08.02.44	07.03.44	Oban
JX316	08.02.44	09.02.44	28.03.44	Felixstowe
JX318	09.03.44	13.03.44	20.04.44	Felixstowe
JX321	21.03.44	31.03.44	06.05.44	Oban
JX322	06.03.44	07.03.44	08.04.44	Oban
JX323	19.05.44	14.06.44	05.07.44	Wig Bay
JX323 (2)	05.03.45	11.04.45	10.07.45	Wig Bay
JX324*	20.03.44	21.03.44	25.04.44	Oban
JX326	27.03.44	11.04.44	27.05.44	Oban
JX327	26.04.44	30.05.44	20.06.44	Battery Park
JX329	18.04.44	06.06.44	05.07.44	Wig Bay
JX329 (2)	28.02.45	09.04.45	31.05.45	Wig Bay
JX330	15.03.44	29.03.44	18.05.44	Oban
JX333	15.04.44	02.05.44	10.06.44	Greenock
JX336	30.03.44	18.04.44	12.06.44	Greenock
JX337	25.04.44	09.05.44	29.06.44	Battery Park
JX340	22.04.44	04.05.44	28.07.44	Wig Bay
JX341	28.04.44	02.06.44	29.06.44	Battery Park
JX342	24.03.44	05.04.44	18.05.44	Oban

JX343	16.04.44	03.05.44	24.06.44	Oban
JX344	16.04.44	25.04.44	02.06.44	Oban
JX345	08.05.44	08.06.44	05.07.44	Battery Park
JX349	23.03.44	04.04.44	06.05.44	Oban
JX350	25.04.44	24.05.44	22.06.44	Battery Park
JX352	24.04.44	15.05.44	19.06.44	Battery Park
JX355	24.04.44	20.05.44	22.06.44	Battery Park
JX356	14.06.44	20.06.44	16.07.44	Wig Bay
JX356 (2)	26.03.45	10.05.45	27.07.45	Wig Bay
JX357	22.04.44	19.05.44	14.06.44	Battery Park
JX361	09.05.44	13.06.44	11.07.44	Wig Bay
JX363	17.06.44	22.06.44	15.07.44	Wig Bay
JX364	16.09.44	06.10.44	07.04.45	Wig Bay
JX365	27.04.44	05.05.44	16.06.44	Battery Park
JX366	24.05.44	02.06.44	25.06.44	Battery Park
JX368	16.03.45	11.05.45	10.08.45	Wig Bay
JX370	01.02.45	05.02.45	04.04.45	Wig Bay
JX371	06.07.44	08.07.44	19.08.44	Wig Bay
JX371 (2)	27.02.45	28.03.45	13.06.45	Wig Bay
JX372	12.03.45	25.04.45	10.07.45	Wig Bay
JX373	11.07.44	12.07.44	21.09.44	Oban
JX373 (2)	15.02.45	12.03.45	06.05.45	Wig Bay
JX376	29.12.44	05.01.45	03.03.45	Wig Bay
JX377	29.06.44	30.06.44	05.08.44	Wig Bay
JX378	05.07.44	06.07.44	19.08.44	Wig Bay
JX378 (2)	26.03.45	02.05.45	24.07.45	Wig Bay
JX380	29.06.44	01.07.44	31.07.44	Wig Bay
JX382	01.10.44	15.12.44	09.03.45	Wig Bay
JX386	25.06.44	25.06.44	18.07.44	MAEE
JX386 (2)	20.02.45	22.03.45	28.05.45	Wig Bay
JX387	05.02.45	24.02.45	04.05.45	Luce Bay
JX389	06.07.44	10.07.44	02.09.44	Killadeas
JX390	11.07.44	17.07.44	25.08.44	Wig Bay
JX390 (2)	05.03.45	13.03.45	24.05.45	Wig Bay
JX391	05.07.44	07.07.44	12.08.44	Wig Bay
JX391 (2)	09.03.45	24.04.45	20.06.45	Wig Bay
JX392	18.07.44	19.07.44	08.11.44	Helensburgh
JX392 (2)	22.01.45	31.01.45	09.08.45	Felixstowe
JX393	11.07.44	12.07.44	25.08.44	Wig Bay
JX394	28.07.44	28.07.44	07.09.44	Oban
JX394 (2)	15.01.45	01.02.45	20.03.45	Wig Bay
JX395	20.07.44	24.07.44	08.09.44	Oban
JX395 (2)	15.02.45	28.02.45	23.04.45	Wig Bay
JX396	09.08.44	09.08.44	30.09.44	Oban
JX397	09.08.44	09.08.44	13.09.44	Oban
JX397 (2)	05.02.45	13.02.45	06.05.45	Wig Bay
JX398	20.02.45	14.03.45	11.05.45	Wig Bay
JX399	11.01.45	16.01.45	24.03.45	Wig Bay
JX400	08.09.44	22.09.44	21.11.44	Wig Bay
JX400 (2)	02.01.45	15.01.45	03.03.45	Wig Bay
JX401	14.08.44	24.08.44	28.09.44	Wig Bay
JX402	19.09.44	07.10.44	05.12.44	Wig Bay
JX402(2)	19.12.44	30.12.44	05.03.45	Wig Bay
JX403	19.08.44	24.08.44	02.10.44	Oban
JX404	08.02.45	27.02.45	11.05.45	Wig Bay
JX405	25.08.44	30.08.44	19.10.44	Wig Bay
JX405 (2)	23.02.45	27.03.45	20.06.45	Wig Bay
JX406	08.09.44	28.09.44	06.11.44	Wig Bay
JX407	20.08.44	28.08.44	02.10.44	Oban
JX408	25.08.44	31.08.44	19.10,44	Wig Bay
JX408 (2)	01.02.45	09.02.45	10.04.45	Wig Bay
JX409	26.08.44	04.09.44	23.10.44	Wig Bay

JX410	20.08.44	24.08.44	21.09.44	Oban
JX410 (2)	15.01.45	26.01.45	20.03.45	Wig Bay
JX411	26.08.44	01.09.44	21.10.44	Wig Bay
JX412	29.08.44	14.09.44	24.10.44	Wig Bay
JX412 (2)	28.02.45	11.04.45	18.06.45	Wig Bay
JX413	29.08.44	18.09.44	03.02.45	Wig Bay
JX414	21.08.44	28.08.44	06.10.44	Wig Bay
JX414 (2)	26.03.45	18.05.45	17.08.45	Wig Bay
JX415	31.08.44	19.09.44	01.11.44	Wig Bay
JX416	31.08.44	26.09.44	06.11.44	Wig Bay
JX417	08.09.44	26.09.44	06.11.44	Wig Bay
JX418	13.09.44	03.10.44	15.11.44	Wig Bay
JX418 (2)	15.01.45	17.01.45	04.04.45	Wig Bay
JX419	02.01.45	15.01.45	16.03.45	Wig Bay
JX420	30.09.44	13.12.44	12.07.45	Wig Bay
JX421	11.08.44	15.08.44	27.10.44	Wig Bay
JX423	09.10.44	17.10.44	13.12.44	Wig bay
JX433	09.11.44	09.11.44	15.02.45	Wig Bay
JX436	09.10.44	30.10.44	12.12.44	Wig Bay
JX437	12.10.44	28.10.44	19.12.44	Wig Bay

* = D.A. (Direct Arrival)

Part batch 16 Catalina IVas supplied May 1943

JX573	18.05.43	18.05.43	26.07.43	Alness
JX574	15.06.43	20.07.43	26.09.43	Felixstowe
JX576	05.05.43	06.05.43	26.07.43	Sullom Voe
JX578	15.05.43	17.05.43	05.07.43	Alness
JX584	20.05.43	20.05.43	17.07.43	Alness
JX586	19.09.44	19.09.44	21.12.44	Wig Bay

Part batch 25 Catalina IVbs supplied September–October 1944

JX593*	29.09.44	12.10.44	11.12.44	Wig Bay
JX594	21.10.44	31.10.44	09.01.45	Wig Bay
JX595	09.10.44	21.10.44	11.12.44	Wig Bay
JX598	23.10.44	01.11.44	22.01.45	Wig Bay
JX601	06.11.44	13.11.44	02.02.45	Wig Bay
JX602	24.11.44	29.11.44	27.02.45	Wig Bay
JX604	23.10.44	07.11.44	04.05.45	Wig Bay
JX605	16.11.44	21.11.44	02.02.45	Wig Bay
JX606	06.11.44	14.11.44	08.02.45	Wig Bay
JX607	19.10.44	19.10.44	05.02.45	Wig Bay
JX609	24.10.44	08.11.44	11.01.45	Wig Bay
JX610	24.11.44	06.12.44	05.02.45	Wig Bay

* = D.A. (Direct Arrival)

Part batch 6 Catalina VIs supplied December 1944–January 1945

JX629	21.12.44	21.12.44	21.02.45	Largs
JX632	21.12.44	21.12.44	02.02.45	Helensburgh
JX632 (2)	01.03.45	01.03.45	07.04.45	Wig Bay

Catalina I (G-AGBJ) purchased from BOAC January 1944 (renumbered from AM 258)

SM701	14.01.44	15.01.44	Towed to Pwllheli for mooring trials

9. Wrecks and wreckage

In the so-called back areas, until the German invasion of the Low Countries on 10 May 1940, pushing the British Expeditionary Force the first faltering steps along the road to Dunkirk, the general awareness of the work of the RAF was coloured largely by the activities of Training Command, if for no other reason than the work of N° 23 Group was largely localised and carried on in daylight under the full scrutiny (censorship permitting) of the public eye. As hinted in earlier pages, this consciousness was shaped largely by incidents involving N° 5 SFTS at Sealand with a significant input on the part of the flying training training units at Shawbury and Tern Hill. Strangely, for the first seven weeks of the war nothing fell from the skies locally, almost as if trainee pilots were holding their breath, taking stock of the situation. Then on 18 October the spell was broken, with Hawker Hind K5161 of N° 5 SFTS ploughing in on its final approach to Sealand. N° 10 SFTS at Tern Hill joined in on 30 October, losing Hind L7193 at Waverton, near Chester whilst attempting a forced landing after becoming lost in poor visibility. It hit a hedge and flipped over on to its back. Not to be outdone, on 7 November 1939 Airspeed Oxford II P1845 of N° 11 SFTS Shawbury crashed in low thick cloud onto the summit of the Wrekin, killing Acting P/O G. H. H. Coates. His instructor escaped with slight injuries. This was the first war-time fatality at the base.

From the outbreak of war to December 1940, when it migrated to Tern Hill, N° 5 SFTS totted up some 54 aircraft damaged or written off — Audax, Hind, Oxford and Master — with the loss of at least twenty-eight instructors or trainee pilots. From its inception in June 1940 — as part of N° 81 Group, Fighter Command's training arm — to the end of the year, N° (5)7 OTU wrote off one Hurricane, 16 Spitfires, 6 Masters, one Battle, and two 'unknown', with a further 32 aircraft (including 6 Hurricanes and 23 Spitfires) badly damaged, for a total of 37 pilots injured and 15 killed.

These are dire statistics. They would be even more bleak and discouraging in 1941, when, for example, N° 57 OTU lost or damaged some 100 planes, 16 of them whilst flying from their newly appropriated temporary RLG at Wrexham. Pilots were a scarce commodity, and the further 27 killed and 50 injured in that year, had the raw statistics been published, they would hardly have boosted public morale. This is but one of the reasons behind the strict censorship crack-down, RAF-related incidents earning but the briefest mention even in official Civil Defence logs, and certainly finding no place in local newspapers — a far cry from the detailed and often gruesome accident and coroner's reports of peace time.

Most of the incidents referred to occurred spasmodically over time and place so that for the layman it was difficult to gain an overall picture of events as they were occurring in the air. However, isolated episodes still loom large in a community's collective memory, and no doubt, back in 1940, would have provided many a talking point in school, pub, living room and air-raid shelter. The present-day researcher has to look long and hard through the yellowing files of local newspapers in wartime to find something that has escaped the censor's blue-pencil. When found such a bonus item literally screams from the dreary, intensely parochial pages, as, for example, those of the *Whitchurch Herald* in September 1941. No other local paper in Flintshire and Denbighshire covers this particular event. By some strange oversight it was left to a Shropshire journal to carry the story, buried deep in its permitted four scanty pages.

The write-up involves the demise of Spitfire I X4653 of N° 57 OTU, Hawarden, on 20 September 1941, before a thrilled yet horrified crowd of holiday-makers thronging the promenade at Rhyl. Seven soldiers from the camps at Kinmel and Prestatyn, along with a Southport clergyman, scambled through the anti-invasion defences to attempt a rescue from the stricken aircraft half-submerged off-shore. Unfortunately the tide was just beginning to turn. X4653 had been flying point in a 'Vic' formation of three off the Talacre ranges when it developed engine trouble. It came down in the sea 'about a mile opposite the Coliseum', burying its nose in the sandy sea bottom, fuselage awash. From the shore it first seemed that the pilot might have scrambled out of his aircraft before it was engulfed by the steadily rising waters.

The rescuers, including recently graduated Rev. Frederick Arthur Gadd, in his first curacy (1940–3) at St Emmanuel's, Southport, ran across the wet sands, waded the treacherous gutters, and then swam to the pilot, who was still trapped in his cockpit. First to arrive was Signalman George Munday who exhausted himself trying to keep the pilot's head above water. Other rescuers arrived and after a concerted struggle, fighting against waves that were beginning to bury the nose of the Spitfire even further in the shifting sands, managed to extricate the pilot and to tow him none too gently to the shore. Before resuscitation could be attempted ambulances arrived and rescued and rescuers were whipped off to the Alexandra Hospital, Rhyl. Signalman Munday was detained overnight for observation. The pilot never regained consciousness, dying later from injuries, shock, and exposure.

Yet while the *Whitchurch Herald* carried this particular story — after all Rhyl was a popular resort for north Shropshire folk and a cub reporter from the town may have even filed a 'scoop' story — its pages carry not the slightest vestige of other happenings such as the machine-gunning of the town's (Royal) Observer Corps post (A.3, N° 27 Shrewsbury Group) and a petrol storage depot shortly before mid-day on Saturday, 9 November 1940. It was one of several opportunist 'beatings-up' of Midland towns by single armed reconnaissance aircraft that morning. Presumably this was the sort of information categorised as being directly helpful to enemy ntelligence.

Censors had a difficult task. A report on the machine-gunning of a goods train on the Shrewsbury–Welshpool line was published only because details were 'leaked' by 'Lord

Haw Haw' in one of his propoganda bulletins the following evening. Early on Wednesday, 16 October 1940, the 'Down' goods casually shunting out Yockleton station, received two bursts of machine-gun fire. There was no damage except for a tail lamp being knocked off the guard's van! Seconds earlier, down the line towards Plas-y-Court Halt, a gang of plate layers working in the Wollaston cutting had been sprayed by machine-gun fire. They dived for cover beneath the road bridge and the wooden steps that gave access to the Woolaston lane above. No one was hurt, but the experience gave a new sense of purpose to one Bill Meredith, a sergeant in the local Home Guard. The local press were predictably dismissive of 'the typically extravagant claim on the German radio', which alleged that a squadron of Ju88s were returning from a raid when one of the pilots spotted a troop train and immediately dive-bombed and machine-gunned it. They claimed the engine was blown up, carriages derailed and as the Ju88 turned for home the train was burning fiercely. No incident remotely matching the German story filtered its way through to the Ministry of Home Security Daily Appreciation Reports. Scoring propaganda points in its turn the BBC 'felt justified in expressing the view that the Germans were giving a garbled version of the incident on the Welsh border'.

To the aircraft of flying training schools and fighter OTUs that seemed intent on modifying the Welsh border landscape must be added those of bomber Group Pools and bomber OTUs at Abingdon, Harwell and Pershore. The latter were even more effective agents of change, and their demise whilst in transit up the Welsh border inevitably made a greater impact on the sensibilities of the local populace. In this back area the nearest bomber airfields would be those eventually built at Tilstock (Prees Heath), and Sleap in Shropshire, and Seighford and Hixon in Staffordshire, all of 1942–3 vintage.

Thereafter the number of bomber 'drop-outs' increased markedly. On occasion, perhaps because people were becoming rather blasé, they fell to earth with the slightest of fuss, their demise barely earning a confused foot-note in local folk lore and memory. Such was the fate of ArmstrongWhitworth Whitley LA766 from N° 81 OTU, RAF Tilstock, which crashed almost unnoticed in the hills west of Wrexham at 2040hrs on 11 January 1943. No details were entered in the Denbighshire CD log, although the latter carefully records the loss of Wellington R1491 (N° 15 OTU, Harwell) which crashed on Bwlch-y-rhiw farmhouse, Llansilin, on 26 January, killing the five crew and two residents, and the crash of Wellington X3608 (N° 23 OTU, Pershore) on 12 February at Llanrhaeadr-ym-Mochnant.

The destruction of Whitley LA766 was so complete that the Aber Carriers salvage team that attended most of the high ground crashes in Welsh-speaking areas on behalf of N° 34 MU Monkmoor were under the impression that they were scraping up the remains of a Wellington. This is strange in view of the fact the team was burying two shattered Rolls-Royce Merlin X engines. But this fact may have been lost on non-technical laymen, the confusion more likely stemming from the Nash and Thompson rear gun turret which remained near enough intact, complete with dead air-

Plas-y-Court Halt (1934–60) looking 'Up' (east) from the accommodation crossing. Plate layers were machine-gunned in the cutting round the bend top of picture. [Sally Anne Richards]

gunner, after being catapulted almost a quarter of a mile from the initial point of impact. It took almost six days to clear the site and bury the debris. A week or so later an immediate identification of the aircraft as a Whitley V would have been possible from the dozen or so aluminium sheds that suddenly sprouted in smallholders' yards and crofts, each nicely camouflaged, and one carrying part of the Whitley's serial number in red and green at its base. The crash site was investigated by Mike Grant and the WARG in October 1982 and it was only during the necessary preliminary paper work that the possible true identity of the crashed bomber was established.

Whitley LA766, with a crew of eight, had been on a cross-country NAVEX and bombing practice flight and was on the home leg. The weather was poor, with only moderate visibility and gradually worsening. The pilot acknowledged QDMs, but did not use. He overshot Tilstock airfield and was not heard again. 'Standard procedures were followed and neighbouring police forces, ROC Centres, and aerodromes alerted. At 2115 hrs a message was received by Tilstock ATC fromDenbighshire Police to the effect that 'the missing plane had probably come down in the Welsh hills 3 miles NNW of the town of Wrexham'. More exactly the Whitley had hit the 1,158ft hill at Gwernto-bâch midway between Bwlchgwyn and Rhydtalog, strictly in Llanfynydd parish, Flintshire. In 1982 two surviving eye-witnesses spoke for the first time of their experiences that Monday night forty years previously,

Mr G. Williams was checking on livestock before supper: 'I heard an aircraft approach from the Wrexham direction, very low and engines thumping. It passed over the farm, heading out towards Rhydtalog. A minute later it came back down the valley towards Wrexham. This time the engine noise did not fade away. It seemed to turn again, very low, but on the Gwernto side of the hill. The next moment the sky and the whole hillside lit up and we heard a loud explosion. Minutes passed and I was still staring at the flames leaping high into the sky. I made my way up the road to Gwernto (Hall). It was only afterwards that I realised I must have passed the rear gunner still in his turret hidden in the line of trees alongside the road. He was found at day-break. The Hall had already phoned the police at Wrexham when I got there.'

Mist enshrouded hill at Gwern, west of Bwlchgwyn, where Whitley LA766 made its last landing.

Mr George Edwards, local bus and taxi proprietor, takes up the story:

> I was sitting at home around 10pm, taking my shoes off, when we heard an aeroplane fly very low over the house. Five minutes later the phone rang. It was Wrexham Police Station wanting to speak to PC William Henry Jones who was staying with us at the time. He was quickly off the phone and said that someone had rung HQ to say that an aircraft had crashed on the hillside at Gwernto. We all rushed to the front door and opened it. Sure enough, there in front of us was the mountain all lit up in flames a hundred feet high. I dashed back into the house, put on by boots and made my way to the Armstrong Siddley 25hp taxi … then like a bat out of hell to pick up my mates, Arthur Kelly Jones and Emlyn Morris. Lucky they were dressed and ready to help.
>
> When we arrived at the scene of the accident PC Jones took charge. We started to look for airmen. God! What a sight. The whole ground was alight, flames leaping high into the air. Driven by the strong wind, the flames had scorched a wide area and aircraft wreckage could be seen strewn for over 300 yards down the hill. It had hit the lower slopes and skidded up to the top of the hill, disintegrating as it did so. For a moment we just stared, all of us, at this towering wall of flame. I must mention at this point something we have never told anyone before in case they thought us a bit 'queer'. In the light of the flames we all saw white birds flying in and out of the darkness … !
>
> But there was no time to stand around. We quickly turned back to the airmen. We found two lying near a large piece of the fuselage, one dead and one still alive. A quick discussion and it was decided to carry him to the car and get him to a hospital. We started back down the hill, carrying him on a piece of wing. After staring at the bright flames for so long we found it difficult to find our way in the darkness. At last we arrived back at the car, put the airman in the back and made our way back to Bwlchgwyn and down to Wrexham. But the lad died on the Ruthin road before we got to town. All our efforts had been in vain. The next day we all had to make statements to the police and later we received a good rollicking from an RAF officer for moving the airman! As you can imagine, we were all very much put out by this … !

The mysterious 'white birds' seen by the rescuers have been interpreted as burning fragments of the Whitley's aluminium skin, whirled upwards by the intense heat, or possibly even 'window', the foil strips used to confuse radar. But probably they were just that — birds, some of the thousands of wood pigeons that nested in the woods that clothed Nant-y-ffrith, flying around panic-stricken by the explosion. Tragically for the crew of LA766 the searchlight battery which for two years had been positioned at Pen-y-bont on the southern side of the hill, had been redeployed a month previously, so there had been no friendly beacon or homing beam to indicate the nearest emergency airfield.

The crew were W/O D. R. Roberts (pilot), P/O R. J. Binham (navigator), F/Sgt R. Smeaton (WO/AG) and Sgt W. H. Stewart (AG), with four pupils under instruction, Sgts D. B. Lister, H. T. Strachan, M. J. Buckle and C. E. Aaron. The bodies were taken to Wrexham Cemetery mortuary and the four crew lie buried in Wrexham Cemetery (the Commonwealth War Graves Cemetery at Blacon would not be opened until later in the year). But with the perversity of officialdom obsessed with keeping unpleasant facets of war

The graves of the crew of Whitley LA766 in Wrexham Cemetery.

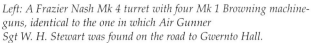

Left: A Frazier Nash Mk 4 turret with four Mk 1 Browning machine-guns, identical to the one in which Air Gunner Sgt W. H. Stewart was found on the road to Gwernto Hall.

Right: A nice study of a Whitley and its crew, similar to LA766 which crashed at Bwlchgwyn.

Left: Burnt aluminium dross from LA766. Note the shallow depth of the excavation trench opened in October 1982.

Below: Excavators from the W.A.R.G., Neil Pennington, Don Morris and Mike Grant looking for LA766, October 1982.

Recovered artefacts from LA766, after renovation now on display at Sleap aerodrome.
Left: Control quadrant
Below left: Control panel instrument.
Below right: Various items ranging from a body harness to a vacuum diaphragm.

from the public at large, the crew that flew — and died — together, are not buried side by side but dispersed so that an immediate association with a tragic incident in the hills above Wrexham could not, and cannot, readily be made.

On the operational side, in the early months of the war, Bomber Command maintained a relatively low profile, not helped by the politically ill-advised moratorium limiting the RAF to attacks on well-defined military targets where civilian lives would not be placed at risk. Leaflet raids ('Nickels'), mine-laying ('Gardening'), reconnaissance, targets at sea, for the moment cut little ice with the public at large. The scourge of the German night-fighter was some months away.

Spring 1940 saw the end of the 'Phoney War'. Despite clinging tenaciously to their neutrality, Denmark and Norway were occupied in a four-week campaign, 9 April–9 May. For both Fighter and Bomber Commands this was a frustrating 'interlude', not helped by the War Cabinet refusing to sanction the bombing of north German ports. This allowed German convoys to sail the Baltic unmolested. A slight breather and then, on 10–15 May it was the turn of the three hapless Benelux countries. Headlines such as 'ALLIES ANSWER CALL FOR AID. RAF PLANES IN ACTION! (*Evening Standard*, 10 May) gloss over a situation in which the German *Wehrmacht* and *Luftwaffe* seized the initiative they were never to lose, and the squadrons of the AASF found themselves totally outclassed and quite unable to meet the demands thrust upon them.

On 15 May, Churchill, barely five days into highest office, gave the green light for Bomber Command operations east of the Rhine. Escalation of the night bombing campaigns was covered by both national and local press, literally grasping after some good news to print. Any report of Bomber Command striking at targets across the length and breadth of Germany — and Italy after Mussolini took that country into the war on 11 June — was good for public consumption and morale. There was a vague comforting feeling that something practical and positive was being done, and momentarily switched the spotlight from the rapidly deteriorating situation in France where both the AASF and the Air Component BEF were in turmoil as they constantly relocated as bases were bombed and over-run.

After the miraculous shambles of Dunkirk, and the fall of France on 22 June 1940 the man-in-the-street, guided by the outpourings of his daily news-sheet, would show an even greater appreciation of the worth of RAF Bomber Command. TEN GERMAN TOWNS RAIDED FOR 3 HOURS: RAF HAVOC IN RHINELAND: RAILWAY LINES DEMOLISHED: RUHR OIL CENTRES ABLAZE (*Daily Telegraph*, 19 June 1940) and RAF BOMB BERLIN, SINK SHIPS AND SET OIL STORE ON FIRE: DIRECT HITS ON KRUPPS & PLANE FACTORY (*Daily Express*, 13 August 1940) — such were the headlines that gave comfort in a nation's hour of need, Bomber Command continuing to carry the war into the enemy camp, doing their bit to convince the German High Command that 'Operation Sealion' (the planned invasion of England) was fraught with peril.

The bomber offensive was launched from airfields located largely in Yorkshire, Lincolnshire and East Anglia, not the best placed for mounting sorties against targets in Brittany and south-west France. Such large scale operations inevitably had repercussions in western back areas, not in the least the periodic stripping of bomber OTUs and Air Gunnery Schools of ageing Whitleys to make up numbers for the controversial '1,000 Bomber' raids. But it is perhaps not generally realised that a bomber's homeward journey was often fraught with more hazards than encountered in an attack on a target in the centre of Germany. Bad weather closing in after take-off impaired navigation and made home airfields difficult to locate. Diversions were the order of the day, with little room for error as fuel gauges registered zero. To trespass upon Gun Defended Areas was asking for trouble from trigger-happy gunners and blinding searchlights. Thick cloud hid lurking mountains and barrage balloon cables. Congested circuits or localised red alerts meant further delays in putting wheels down, rendering lumbering bombers at unguarded moments easy prey to enemy intruders,

Thus at 0142hrs on the evening of 12/13 November 1940 a Whitley V, T4232 ('ZAW') of N° 10 Squadron outward bound from RAF Leeming (Yorkshire) to Lorient hit the hills around Rhymney (Glamorgan). It had taken off $2^{1}/_{2}$ hrs earlier and was well adrift of its intended course, obviously lost. Similarly straying off track was Wellington T2520 ('KO-A') of N° 115 Squadron (Marham, Norfolk), which ploughed into a hillside at Tredegar (Glamorgan) on 8/9 December 1940 as it returned from a raid on Bordeaux. The six crew were killed. Again, on 2/3 March 1941 a Whitley V, Z6465 ('GE-U'), of N° 58 Squadron, Linton-upon-Ouse, was an incredible six hours into a bombing mission to Brest (only some 450 miles distant) when it was aborted. Two hours later, at 0156hrs, Z6465 crashed three miles north-west of Tern Hill and burst into flames. All five crew were killed. The Whitley would seem to have been airborne an inordinate length of time without achieving anything and would appear to have been well and truly 'lost'.

A series of unfortunate incidents contributed to the demise of Wellington R3288 ('JNB') of N° 150 Squadron on the evening of Friday 21/22 March 1941. Just before midnight it broke cloud at 2,000ft hoping to fix its position. It promptly crashed onto the rocky slopes of Moel Farlwyd on the Merioneth/Caernarfonshire border at the 'Crimea Pass' north of Blaenau Ffestiniog. It had taken off at 1810hrs from RAF Newton, near Nottingham, to attack Lorient naval base in Brittany. The mission was aborted because of thick cloud over target. Just after bombs had been jettisoned in the Channel R3288 was attacked by a Messerschmitt Bf 110, which may have been shot down or seriously damaged by Sgt Peter Martlew, tail gunner. During the violent evasive action the navigator, Sgt H. Beddall became disorientated, and was only able to set an estimated course for home, with fatal results …. Five of the crew were killed Sgt Martlew was found with a broken leg and severe bruising, still in his turret which had broken off and been hurled some 50ft on impact.

The Welsh mountains and Irish Sea were equally as indiscriminate in their reception of lost and ailing aircraft from operations over Central Europe and northern Italy. The remarkable story surrounding the forced landing in the hills above Llanasa (Flintshire), of Whitley IV, K9038, of N° 50 Squadron, Dishforth (Yorkshire), well adrift in low cloud and blanket fog on 21/22 May 1940 after raiding the marshalling yards at Krefeld, has been related in greater detail in Chapter 4. Suffice it to say the story had a happy ending with K9038 being flown off the Clwydian Range under its own power. Equally fortunate were the crew of a N° 50 Squadron WhitleyV, P5095, which, in attempting to return to RAF Wattisham (Suffolk) from a raid on Milan on 20/21 October 1940, overflew the whole country in cloud, to ditch with empty tanks on a sandbank at the mouth of the River Mersey. The plotting of this aircraft was a tour de force on the part of the (Royal) Observer Corps and is dealt with more fully in the chapters outlining the history of N° 26 (Wrexham) Group, ROC (see *Wings Across the Border*, Vol. 2).

Obviously lost or straying aircraft cluttered up ROC and Fighter Command plotting tables until positively identified, which at night was not always possible in the early days of the war, at least not until the errant plane had come to earth somewhere! On 11/12 February 1941 Hampden AD734 ('OL-K') of N° 83 Squadron was responsible for one of the periodic 'flaps' at the ROC Centre, Wrexham. At 0200hrs it had taken over an 'X' or unidentified plot from N° 27 (Shrewsbury) Group, where on sound only it had been tentatively 'told' by H.1 Ludlow and H.3 Knighton posts. Its approximate course was taken up by N° 26 Group posts R.1 Llananno and S.2 Llanidloes but the track was lost by N° 28/1 Carmarthen Group. AD734, as it later turned out, had taken off at 1820hrs from RAF Scampton (Lincolnshire), along with the Wellingtons of N° 3 Group and N° 4 Group's Whitleys, to raid Bremen. Mission accomplished, the Hampden was slightly off course on the return flight and got itself entangled in the Birmingham balloon barrage. AD734 was abandoned by its crew and, on automatic pilot, trundled its way across southern Shropshire and mid-Wales, eventually, it was thought, to crash into Cardigan Bay — certainly it did not come down anywhere on *terra firma*!

If not on bombing missions, operational aircrews trained hard, honing further their navigational and gunnery skills. Prudence demanded that such training should take place in less hostile skies. But natural and mechanical hazards were not diminished and, despite being manned by veteran crews, the steady loss of operational squadron aircraft in a training role helps swell the melancholy catalogue of RAF losses over the north-west.

So it was that at 1240hrs on 23 July 1940 a Blenheim IV, L9204 of N° 114 Squadron crash landed on the outskirts of Nantwich, Cheshire. It was on a routine NAVEX from Horsham St Faith, Norfolk, to RAF Sealand when the escape hatch flew off in flight. Despite smashing through a line of trees whilst attempting to land, the crew survived virtually unscathed — which is more than can be said for the crew of Blenheim IV, R3813 ('RT-S'). 'S for Sugar' was N° 114 Squadron's final loss before leaving Bomber Command on 15 November 1942 for Blida, Algeria, where it would give tactical support to the North African invasion. On 3 August 1942, as part of 'Exercise Dryshod', R3813 had taken off from West Raynham, Norfolk, en route to Wigtown in Scotland. It

was also carrying two fitters as supernumerary crew. Following a fire in its starboard engine the Blenheim crashed at Lache House, Lache Lane, south-west of Chester, trying to make an emergency landing at RAF Hawarden. All on board were killed.

N° 106 Squadron, based at Finningley, Yorkshire, spent the early months of the war working up on Hampdens, and began its minelaying activities in the Elbe and Baltic early in September 1940, sustaining its first operational loss on the 19 September. By December its was back in a training role, preparing for bombing raids on Germany. Night cross-country navigational exercises loomed large in the training programme. At 1930hrs on 23 December 1940 Hampden I P2071 crashed at Adderley, three miles NNW of Market Drayton after turning onto a new leg at Tern Hill where night-flying was in full swing. None of the crew were seriously injured. N° 106 Squadron had lost two Hampdens and one crew only two days previously during night exercises in bad weather over Rotheram and Derbyshire.

Similarly the night lights of RAF Sealand were the last fix for Blenheim IV, L8758 ('YH-B') of N° 21 Squadron as it headed up the Dee estuary and out over Liverpool Bay en route to the Isle of Man. This was on the evening of 5 May 1941. The Blenheim was never seen or heard from again. At the time N° 21 Squadron, based at Finningley (Yorkshire), was engaged in North Sea anti-shipping and reconnaissance sorties, and it is thought that L8758 hit the sea whilst simulating low level, mast height attacks. The body of F/Sgt G. A. Cole (WO/AG) was washed ashore a week later and lies buried in St Andrew's Churchyard, Andreas (Isle of Man). By official reckoning the period 10 July–31 October 1940 constitutes the 'Battle of Britain'. The *Sunday Dispatch* on 23 June prophetically comments: 'RAIDS START. The first large scale raids were launched the nights of Tuesday and Wednesday. We can have no doubt that they herald even fiercer raids to come'. One tends to overlook the bizarre situation whereby each evening, as the squadrons of Bomber Command flew east and south across the North Sea and English Channel, so German bombers flew west and north in even greater numbers, passing each other unseen or ignored and again in the early hours of the morning as opponents wearily flew reciprocal courses home. But for the ordinary person the air war now took on a new dimension.They themselves were at the receiving end as the *Luftwaffe* hordes streamed up the Welsh border making for Merseyside and the Manchester conurbation. Liverpool's war became Wrexham's war, and Shropshire's war. To British debris raining from the border skies were now added German bits and pieces. Back area training airfields suddenly took on some strategic importance, real or imagined and in the early months were bombed and strafed with apparent impunity. The task of meeting this new threat fell fairly and squarely upon the shoulders of Fighter Command, and new heroes, the young Spitfire and Hurricane pilots, momentarily hogged centre stage in public affection. But on the ground purpose designed Fighter Command airfields at High Ercall, Wrexham and Atcham would not become operational until 1941. Until then 'improvisation' was the key word.

The remarkable achievements of N° 7 OTU's so-called 'Battle Flight' in downing three enemy bombers and seriously damaging a fourth during August and September 1940 have been touched upon elsewhere in this narrative. Such successes not only bolstered public morale but reinforced and sustained Fighter Command's desperate defensive measures focussing on Tern Hill. From here, and also using RAF Penrhos as a forward base, the Spitfires of 'A' Flight N° 611 Squadron, on detachment from RAF Digby in N° 12 Group, patrolled the north-west approaches during hours of daylight, while two (later four) Blenheims of N° 29 Squadron — all that could be spared — flew into Tern Hill each evening to take over the night shift.

This was a daunting task for the two units. With such a large area to cover it would be a matter of luck to encounter the enemy. N° 29 Squadron were first off the mark when, on the night of Sunday, 18 August 1940, P/O R. A. Rhodes and Sgt Gregory (WO/AG) occasioned upon a Heinkel He 111 between Chester and Mold and painstakingly stalked it for over two hours before shooting it down off Spurn Head. It was probably the lone raider responsible for bombing, or trying to bomb, Sandycroft factories at 2330hrs.

Then it was N° 611 Squadron's turn. At 1635 on Saturday, 21 September, newly promoted F/O D. Adams, investigating an unidentified aircraft over Liverpool, picked up a lone Dornier Do215 of 2(F)/121 (N° 2 Long-distance PR Squadron/121 Wing) returning from a photo-reconnaissance sortie over Merseyside. The port had been visited by the *Luftwaffe* on the previous Thursday, and from 2000hrs that same Saturday a steady stream of aircraft would again head that way via the Bristol Channel and 'Adolf's Railway' up the Welsh border — without any reported loss! It is therefore interesting to speculate what might have happened had not this opportunist Spitfire thrown a spanner in the works.

Somewhere over the Clwydian Range between Mold and Ruthin, Adams launched his attack, trying to divert the Dornier back to Hooton Park but the Germans had other thoughts. After a stern chase covering some 60 miles, during which both engines were damaged and three of the crew were wounded and one killed, Adams finally shot the plane down over Dolgellau. The Do215 (coded **VB+KK**) glided to earth at 1655hrs between Berth-ddu and Tyddyn Sais farms alongside the A470 just south of Trawsfynydd reservoir, and was quickly surrounded by soldiers from the nearby Royal Artillery training camp, who rendered first aid and mounted a guard on the wreckage. Three of the crew, *Lt* W. Book, *Fw.* K. Jensen and *Fw.* H. Kohl, eventually ended up in a Canadian POW camp. Two days later, 26-year old *Uffz.* Gustav Pelzer, a native of Isselburg, was buried with full military honours at Pwllheli.

F/O Dennis Arthur Adams first makes himself known to the local historian as the pilot (and just a humble P/O) of a Spitfire I, N3062 of N° 611 Squadron, which, whilst on patrol out of Tern Hill on 22 July 1940, made a forced landing on the beach at Colwyn Bay. Fortunately the aircraft was towed to above the High Water Mark with heavy tackle from the Royal Artillery camp at Kinmel. The Spitfire was repaired and ended up at N° 57 OTU Hawarden. Sadly it would turn out to be the mount in which 23-year old Sgt George Murray,

a native of Southern Rhodesia, was killed when, almost exactly a year later on 27 July 1941, he nose-dived into the sea two miles south-west of Caernarfon. Sgt Murray lies buried in Pwllheli Cemetery.

F/O Adams already had a couple of 'kills' beneath his belt from the period when N° 611 Squadron was called upon to assist the hard-pressed squadrons covering the Dunkirk evacuation, a welcome change from the monotony of east coast patrols and the occasional scramble. On 2 June 1940 he destroyed a Junkers Ju87 dive-bomber over the beaches and claimed a 'probable' Messerschmitt Bf 109. But his successful sojourn on the Welsh border was short-lived. On 29 September 1940 Adams was transferred to N° 41 Squadron at Hornchurch. At 1430hrs on Tuesday, 1 October 1940, he would claim a half-share with his new CO in the destruction of a Messerschmitt Bf 109 of 4/JG26 in combat over Sussex. The German aircraft dived vertically from 28,000ft and exploded. Its pilot *Uffz.* H. Bluder was vaporised and has no known grave. But F/O Adams was not permitted to linger too long in a euphoric state. In an early morning encounter with a Do17 over Folkstone on 7 October, his plane, Spitfire N3267, was badly damaged by the enemy's accurate return fire and was abandoned by its pilot who managed to bale out safely over Postling, Kent. Adams was promoted Flight Lieutenant in September 1941 and Squadron Leader in July 1944.

The loss of the Do215 (*W.Nr.0023*, **VB+KK**) had some remarkable repercussions forty-eight years later. On Thursday, 8 September 1988, North Wales Police were a week into a month-long fire-arms amnesty and had already collected some 119 guns and over 3,800 rounds of ammunition! The duty constable at Chirk's tiny police station was startled to find dumped on the desk, by a former member of the Home Guard, one live hand grenade (destroyed in a controlled explosion by a bomb disposal squad) and a Rheinmetall 7.9mm MG 15 machine gun in perfect working order, complete with saddle magazine, allegedly 'from the rear turret of a Heinkel bomber which came down over Penycae Mountain and crashed near Llangollen whilst on a bombing mission to Liverpool'. Apparently the Home Guard soldier was one of the first on the scene of the crash and quietly 'liberated' the gun as a souvenir. Pricked by an uneasy conscience ever since, he now wanted to get rid of it to the proper authorities. This was the story spun to the police constable at Chirk and embroidered as the machine-gun was successively and reverently moved to Ruabon (Sub-Divisional), Wrexham (Divisional) and Colwyn Bay (HQ) police stations, the star item in the arms amnesty. At that distance in time they had no cause to disbelieve it! But as far as the aviation historian is concerned, a little white lie has been told. No German aircraft ever came to grief on the Ruabon or Llantysilio Mountains.

As always, the truth is stranger than the fiction and begins with one Norman Horspool, in 1940 a Llangollen café and cinema owner, greengrocer and nurseryman, and a member of 'D' Coy 7th Den/Flint Batt. Home Guard. Just before mid-day on Thursday, 24 September 1940, Mr Horspool's platoon was warned for 'special duties' that night. A 'top secret' convoy was moving slowly down the A5 from the Corwen direction and would park after dark behind the protective walls of the Llangollen Smithfield, where sheep pens had been hastily removed to accommodate the lorries. These included a 'Queen Mary', the RAF specialist low-loader used for transporting the fuselage and wings of aircraft.

To Norman Horspool had been delegated the task of finding lodgings for the RAF drivers. Friendly 'gossip' quickly elicited the fact that the load comprised the remains of a German aircraft brought down three or four days earlier 'in the Welsh mountains'. The Home Guard cautiously lifted a corner of the tarpaulin to inspect the fuselage of what turned out to be the Trawsfynydd Dornier on its¨ way to be examined by AI1(g) or Air Intelligence (Technical). They were foolishly given permission by a lowly 'erk' to help themselves to 'just a small piece' of the aircraft as a souvenir, to any serving soldier an invitation tantamount to *carte blanche*!

Come the dawn, and before the guard was relieved, the tarpaulin was eased back and the men scrambled into the wrecked fuselage, inspecting what was left of the 'conservatory' or cockpit, and fingering instruments and dials. Suddenly attention was drawn to a machine-gun still hanging on its mounting amidst the shattered glazing of the Dornier's nose. This would make a grand souvenir! It was quickly removed, covered in a great-coat and carried through the deserted streets of Llangollen on a stretcher. It was later surreptitiously transferred to the Horspool greenhouses along Abbey Road. Here, as the enormity of their offence rapidly dawned on the conspirators, the gun would remain for almost fifty years, wrapped in oily rags and seeing the light of day only to impress family and trusted friends.

The Trawsfynydd Dornier was of particular interest to Air Intelligence because it was a development of the earlier Do17, an export version pressed into use with the *Luftwaffe* in bomber and reconnaissance roles, with modifications mainly affecting the forward fuselage — completely 'glazed' nose, and deep cockpit with a domed glazed top — and slightly more powerful Daimler Benz 601 engines.

Over the next ten days, following persistent strafing of RAF Penrhos on an opportunist basis, the Tern Hill Spitfires would push their patrol lines even further into north Wales. Around 1830hrs on Friday, 11 October they hit the jackpot, meeting a stream of Dornier Do17s of 1/KüFlGr606 and 2/KüFlGr606 based at Brest and Cherbourg, making for Liverpool, with RAF Speke as one of the *Zielpunkte* or primary targets. The squadron ORB tersely reports:

'A' Flight took off from Tern Hill at 17.30hrs to patrol Anglesey. At about 1820hrs at 17,000ft, three enemy aircraft (B/A), Do17s, were sighted about twelve miles away approaching from the south-west. Yellow section attacked out of sun, meeting fire from the enemy leader. The E/A broke formation and were attacked by both sections. Yellow leader opened fire at 15° deflection and hit E/A's starboard engine and return fire ceased. Yellow 3 followed with N° 3 and then N° 1 attack, and Yellow 1 from above attacked causing E/A to lose height, but return fire had recommenced.

Yellow 1 saw E/A jettison five bombs into the sea and then crash into the water. Yellow 3 received an explosive bullet or shell in the bottom of his cockpit, making his airspeed indicator unserviceable.

Red section carried out two N° 1 attacks on another E/A whose starboard engine stopped, and he finally crashed in the hills south of Caernarvon. They then attacked E/A leader and on the third attack saw two crew bale out and both engines on fire. Aircraft glided down and crashed in flames near Capel Curig.

This report is as the combatants saw it in the rough and tumble of an aerial battle fought at a great height and at speed. In the colder light of impersonal documents Red Section's first victim was Dornier Do 17Z-3 (*W.Nr 2772* coded **7T+EH**) of 1/606 which actually crashed into the sea (according to the authority used) 'in Caernarvon Bay 16 miles off Bardsey Island' or 'off Abersoch'! Three of the crew were picked up by trawler; the fourth, *Fw.* J. Vetterl drowned when his parachute harness snagged the sinking aircraft. The second Do17 (*W.Nr.2787* coded **7T+HH**), also of 1/606, although on fire and in an apparently fatal dive, did not crash at Capel Curig. Two of the crew baled out, one being killed through parachute malfunction or being hit by the tailplane. No one was more surprised than the pilot, *Lt zur See* Kipfmuller, when the fires in the starboard engine and bomb bay blew themselves out. Despite 45% structural damage he was able to regain control and fly on one engine and minus cockpit canopy back to Brest-Lanvéoc.

Yellow Section's victim was Do17 (*W.Nr.3475 23* coded **7T+EK**) of 2/KüFlGr606. This was bought down (again varying according to authority consulted) 'in the sea between Carmel head and the Skerries' or 'in the Irish Sea 50 miles west of Holyhead'. All four members of the crew were killed. Two bodies were washed up in the Irish Republic two weeks later, and a third near Amlwch on 7 November. Yellow 3 was 27-year old Sgt K. C. Pattison in Spitfire IIA, P7323. He was badly wounded by the Dornier's return fire as he pressed home his two attacks. With radio and instruments smashed, and possibly losing consciousness, he drifted across mid-Wales, and with one last supreme effort brought his aircraft down in a field at Cooksey Green, east of Hartlebury, Worcestershire. Sgt Pattison died of his injuries two days later at Barnsley Hall Hospital, Bromsgrove. On 12 October, following all this enemy activity over Caernarfonshire and off the Welsh coast, 'A' Flight, N° 611 Squadron, was transferred in its entirety from Tern Hill to RAF Penrhos, there, as Fate would have it, just to kick their heels — and curse — when, on Wednesday, 16 October, their base at Tern Hill was strafed and bombed by an opportunist German raider!

There were no further losses for KüFlGr606 that Friday night. At this stage of the game N° 29 Squadron's two Blenheims working out of Tern Hill and the six Hurricanes of 'A' Flight, N° 264 Squadron, based as a stop-gap at Ringway, were flying in the cats eyes' mode, unassisted by any experimental form of AI radar. Seventeen other Do17s reached their target unseen and unmolested, with Liverpool under a continuous 'Red Alert' from 1900–2330hrs. If the apparent haphazard jettisoning of HE and IBs over Flint-shire and Denbighshire that night is plotted cartograph-ically, the route followed by some of the attackers would appear to have been Cardigan Bay coast — Betws-y-coed — Cerrig-y-drudion — Eriviat — Ruthin — Leeswood, a popular access route for *Luftwaffe* units based in Brittany and the lower Loire.

From October onwards, while Nº 611 Squadron guarded the front door as it were, the back door approaches to Merseyside were entrusted during daylight hours to Nº 312 (Czech) Squadron at Speke, newly operational as from Wednesday, 2 October. The same afternoon as Nº 611 Squadron scored its hat-trick, six Hurricanes from Nº 312 Squadron pounced on a Do215 on an armed photo-reconnaissance sortie at 18,000ft over the Dee estuary. Remarkably, despite the odds, they failed to nail it; indeed, Hurricane L1807 was damaged by enemy return fire, but managed to land safely at Speke. The Do215 dived steeply to the south into thick cloud over Halkyn Mountain, obviously making for the Welsh coast and home to Normandy.

It was possibly a case of trying too hard, but one should not forget that the squadron's close-knit world was in some turmoil. Only the previous day, 10 October, they had lost founder member Sgt Otto Hanzlicek, whose Hurricane L1547 caught fire during a training flight and dived into a Mersey sandbank. The pilot baled out too low and was drowned, his chute-entangled body being recovered three weeks later at Widnes, whence the tidal currents had carried it. Like so many others of his compatriots in Nº 312 Squadron Sgt Hanzlicek had fled the Nazi occupation of his country and had fought with a French fighter squadron, destroying a He 111, a Bf 109 (half-share), and a Do17 'probable'. Until this incident the squadron had been on cloud nine, lapping up the adulation of the Liverpool populace and basking in strangely uncensored media coverage, having downed their first enemy aircraft on 8 October. Self-confidence would be further shaken when, on 13 October, as noted more fully elsewhere, a section of Hurricanes attacked Nº 29 Squadron's two Blenheims from Tern Hill and shot one down down into the sea off Point of Ayr, leaving the other to limp home, badly damaged.

At 1610hrs on Tuesday afternoon, 8 October Yellow Section, Nº 312 Squadron, was scrambled at Speke to intercept a single enemy aircraft heading for Liverpool. Over Ellesmere Port the three Hurricanes pounced on a Junkers Ju88 of 2/KGr806 (perhaps more correctly 2/KüFlGr806). This unit, based at Nantes and Cherbourg/Carpiquet, was originally a specialist long-range photo-reconnaissance wing, but as the change in nomenclature suggests, was now in the process of being integrated into the main stream long-range bomber force used in the *Blitz*. While the change to a *Kampfgruppe* status occurs in some official documents from September 1940 onwards, crews still considered themselves as part of a *Kustenfliegergruppe* (coastal reconnaissance wing) as late as March 1941.

The population of Merseyside was desperately in need of a morale booster, Since the first major *Blitz* of 29 August–1 September there had been no fewer than seventeen raids, some of them heavy. This may explain why on 9 October the *Liverpool Daily Post* was able to print a blow-by-blow account of the three-minute air battle over the Mersey, complete with photographs. TheJu88 (*W.Nr.4068* coded **M7+DK**), intent on assessing the damage from the previous evening's raids, didn't stand much of a chance.

Both engines were quickly damaged and set on fire and the pilot, 23-year old *Lt zur See* Hergert Schlegel, killed. The stricken Junkers went into a long shallow glide, engines smoking, but three of its 7.9mm machine guns still putting up a withering and accurate return fire.

The brief encounter was watched in fascinated

The victim of Czech revenge. Ju88 W.Nr.4068, coded M71+4DK, comes to the end of its war in Bromborough Dock on 8 October 1940.

The grave at the Soldatenfriedhof, Cannock Chase, of Herbert Schlegel, pilot of the Ju88 brought down in three minutes by Nº 312 (Czech) Squadron at Bromborough Dock.

silence by the ground crews at Hooton Park working on the Ansons of N° 48 Squadron. They saw the second pilot, *Oberlt* H. Bruckmann, work the undercarriage up and down as a sign of surrender, but the Czechs were having none of it! Yellow Section went into line astern and took turns at firing at the stubborn enemy, hammering away at the port side, blowing off the port engine cowling and almost severing the engine from the port wing. They paid the price for this little vanity. All three Hurricanes were damaged and F/Lt D. E. Gillam, one of the squadron's British liaison officers in Spitfire P2575 ('DU-P'), had his windscreen smashed in a hail of bullets. By an extraordinary feat of airmanship *Oberlt* Bruckmann brought the Ju88 down for an almost perfect belly landing in a field at Bromborough, the port engine finally breaking away on impact. *Uffz*. H. Weth suffered cuts and bruises, but poor *Sonderflgr* H. Lehmann of *Lw.Kr.Ber.Komp.2* (a special war correspondent of the *Luftwaffe's* N° 2 Propaganda Company) was possibly more distraught at losing the scoop of a lifetime than stopping a .303 bullet in his arm

The whole incident, witnessed by cheering crowds in Ellesmere Port, Bromborough and Garston,was over in a few minutes, the demise of **M7+DK** a welcome sign to the beleaguered populace of Merseyside that the RAF was at last getting its act together. At Speke aerodrome the gates were shut to keep excited townsfolk at bay. On landing the victorious pilots were carried shoulder high by colleagues from dispersals to debriefing. Congratulations poured in, not in the least from Dr Eduard Benes, Czech President-in-Exile, and the AOC-in-C N° 9 Group, Fighter Command. For the latter the destruction of this particular Junkers was a milestone. N° 9 Group had been formed on 9 August 1940 but did not become operational until late September. **M7+DK** was therefore the first enemy aircraft to be brought down by a N° 9 Group squadron. It would be seven weeks before N° 9 Group could claim another — a Ju88 of 3(F)/123 destroyed by the Hurricanesof N° 308 (Polish) Squadron, Baginton, on 24 November 1940.

When in 1943 N° 9 Group relinquished its front-line defensive role within Fighter Command and assumed overall responsibility for the Command's OTUs it published an official valedictory list of enemy aircraft losses directly attributable to N° 9 Group squadrons and anti-aircraft units within N° 9 Group boundaries. Up to the end of July 1943 N° 9 Group fighters had destroyed 36 German aircraft (including twelve Ju88s and fifteen He 111s), with 10 'probables' and 27 'possibles' damaged. Between 13 March 1941 and 31 July 1942 the 'back area' AA guns claimed 20 destroyed, 5 'probables' and 12 'possibles'. Such a list, compiled from official sources as events unrolled, would seem to solve the problem as to who, or what, caused the crash of a Dornier Do 17Z at Nantglyn, near Denbigh, on the evening of 16 October 1940 with the loss of all four crew.

Some reports suggest that it was struck by AA fire, others that it was shot down by a Spitfire of either N° 610 Squadron (although what an aircraft from RAF Acklington Northumberland, would be doing over the Vale of Clwyd is never made clear!) or of N° 611 Squadron's 'A' Flight operating out of Tern Hill. The only problem with the latter

explanation is that from 12–21 October, as already noted, 'A' Flight was on temporary detachment to RAF Penrhos to cover emergencies there. Despite the fact that 'a witness reportedly saw a Spitfire attacking the Dornier before it crashed in flames', the exclusion of Do17 (*W.Nr.2682* coded **7T+LL**) of 3/KüFlGr606 from N° 9 Group's official lists of enemy 'casualties' would seem to rule out all of these suggestions. Additionally there is the noticeable reluctance on the part of any unit ORB to report such an encounter with an enemy aircraft or for some over-zealous pilot to claim even his statutory 'possible'. Adverse weather would seem to have been the most likely cause, the Dornier crashing at 1925hrs in thick fog and low cloud (in which no self-respecting Spitfire would be found!) on the 1,300ft ridge between Hafodwen Farm and Rhiwiau, 1½ miles south-west of Nantglyn. A large crater and two smaller ones marked where cockpit section and engines had buried themselves in the ground. Wreckage was strewn over a large area.

Then what followed was like something from Fred Karno's Circus. The wreckage was left to burn out, as the auxiliary fire appliance (otherwise a Denbighshire County Council lorry with a collapsible canvas water tank at the back), turned up without any water! With unbeatable logic, the lorry had been summoned, and arrived with all possible haste. But someone had omitted to tell its driver to fill the tank with water before leaving Denbigh! A guard was eventually mounted by the Nantglyn platoon of the Home Guard, but not before an unedifying argument with the CO of the Llansannan platoon as to who should have the privilege. The four crew were buried three days later at Hawarden Cemetery. *Lt zur See* Heinz Havemann, *Uffz.* Gerhard Locknitz, *Uffz.* Karl Holscher and *Gefr.* Rudolf Faehrmann now lie buried in the *Soldatenfriedhof*, Cannock Chase.

Families living in nearby farms were temporarily evacuated, but were allowed to return when the assumption was made, erroneously as it turned out, that its bombs were jettisoned before the crash. The next day sight-seers were allowed to view the wreckage. It took recovery crews from RAF Sealand, working under NCOs from N° 34 MU, Monkmoor (Shrewsbury), along with its civilian sub-contractor Aber Carriers, Welshpool, nearly two weeks to clear the site and fill in the craters. It was a straightforward superficial tidying-up with no obvious reason to probe further looking for bombs. It was assumed that **7T+LL** was returning from a raid on Liverpool and had already got rid of its bombs. Some weight was also given to the possibility that the four HE bombs and 38 IBs that fell at Rhydybedd, five miles due west on the Aled river, may have come from the crashed Dornier.

In neither the 1940 clearance of the wreckage or the 1983 excavation of the wreck by the WARG (Wartime Aircraft Recovery Group) was any evidence for photo-reconnaissance equipment found. As hinted previously, in late 1940 the aircraft of KüFlGr606 were working in a largely bombing role. The Do17 variants had a bomb load of 1,000kg, carried internally as either 20 x 50kg or 4 x 250kg, a fact driven forcibly home to 'warbird archaeologists' when,

Above left: Part of the Nantglyn Dornier's deadly load of 50kg bombs.

Above right: The starboard engine, a Bramo Fafnir 323 9-cylinder radial, a rare prize in recovery circles.

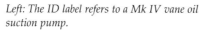

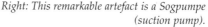

Above: The renovated Bramo Fafnir 323 on display at Sleap aerodrome msueum.

Right: This remarkable artefact is a Sogpumpe (suction pump).

Left: The ID label refers to a Mk IV vane oil suction pump.

on 25 September 1983, they moved on site to begin a recovery 'dig'. The site potential had been recognised way back in the 1950s by WARG founder-member Ken Hadleton, of Warley, West Midlands, who had sifted through the Civil Defence logs and Air Intelligence (AI1(g)) records. But at that time Second World War aircraft investigation and recovery was in its infancy, and it took another two decades of delicate, persistent negotiations with the Air Ministry before site excavation was sanctioned.

A mechanical digger was used, driven by one William Pierce of Bryn Amel, who was an eight-year old when the Dornier came down near his home at Rhiwiau. Excavation started with the starboard engine crater, the intention being to work through to the central cockpit area and on to the port engine. The JCB quickly revealed airframe fragments, corroded light alloy and exploded 7.9mm ammunition. Beneath these were larger bits of airframe, armour plating, electric cables and a cylinder head valve rocker. At some 5ft, with Ron Heath and Mike Grant in the muddy hole guiding the jib bucket, several pistons, an oxygen cylinder, oil filter and control rod linkages came to light, leading to a section of

engine mounting and one of the Bramo Fafnir 323 radial engines with three of its nine cylinders still attached.

The hole was gradually widened and deepened. At seven feet both men were commenting on how the smell of aviation fuel had lingered in the ground despite the passage of time, when suddenly they froze, looked at each other, and whispered 'Bombs?' The last scoop of the bucket had revealed the ends of three cylindrical objects. Some more oxygen cylinders — but devoid of any attachments. Using spades and hands they gently removed some of the clogging earth and found two more. Dawning suspicions were confirmed by the discovery of a crushed sheet-metal object resembling a bomb tail fin assembly. These were held to a bomb body only by screws or rivets, but often small incendiaries would be clipped onto the tail vanes … . That was it. Mike and Ron were out of the hole like rabbits and the site cleared faster than fast. The Denbigh police were informed and at Chattenden, Kent, a bomb disposal squad under Lt A. Miller, RE, was scrambled.

On Tuesday, 27 September the bomb disposal team, after digging out the whole impact site, discovered a further five

50kg bombs, making ten SC50s in all. Fuses were taken out and, the weather remaining fine, the bombs were detonated one by one in the disued quarry on Gorsedd Bran. Vibrations were felt up to six miles away. It took just 1^1/$_2$ hours. Farms within half a mile of the detonation site were evacuated as a precaution and people within a mile radius advised to leave their windows open — just in case!

10. Picking up the pieces

As the war progressed the number of flying accidents increased, especially over the Berwyns and the Shropshire hills. This was inevitable under the relentless pressure of training — mountains and inexperienced fliers did not mix. Increased flying hours in marginal weather, congested air space and circuits, technical failure and human error, all played their part. Few communities did not receive one or more unexpected callers, with inhabitants risking life and limb to rescue aircrew, to collect broken bodies or to assist in salvage in remote and dangerous places. These were experiences foreign to normal routine. Hardened Penycae hill farmers, accustomed to death amongst their flocks, blanched and wretched as they toiled to recover the body of Sgt Cyril Cocks from his Spitfire I, X4713, high on Eglwyseg Mountain. For seventeen days, 16 November–3 December 1941 the aircraft had lain undiscovered. The body had been badly mutilated by the force of the crash, but even further mangled and dismembered by carrion and preying animals, to whom a human corpse was but an extension to a daily diet of ewe or lamb. Intestines had been pulled out, exposed flesh eaten to the bone, and parts of the body were missing.

What happened to the wreckage of crashed aircraft? There was a compromise. Near towns and in comfortably populated rural areas all traces of an aircraft were removed as quickly as possible. Not only would wreckage interfere with essential farming, but smoking funeral pyres and giant cairns of scrap would not do much for public morale. On inaccessible mountain slopes and in rocky gullies serviceable items were salvaged for re-cycling. The rest was burnt or buried. But much wreckage had perforce to remain in situ. With the current interest in wartime 'wreckology' and the proliferation of aviation museums such relics — shattered engines, twisted propellers, a crumpled wing section or tail gun-turret — are gradually disappearing, taken legitimately for official displays or plundered by souvenir hunters with considerable climbing skills!

In the more leisurely pre-war period crash recovery was a simple matter, starting with the local constable and sub-divisional police-station. Immediately RAF Sealand was notified as the sole RAF presence in north Wales. Injured aircrew were dealt with at local hospitals, and fatalities removed to the station mortuary. Ground crews assessed damage category and the Chief Flying Instructor the possibilities of the aircraft, if airworthy, being flown off either by pupil or more experienced pilot. Generally it was easier to dismantle a Tutor, Hart, Hind or Moth and cart it away. To men of the RAF Packing Depôt (at Sealand since May 1929 and becoming N° 36 MU in October 1939) this was all in a days work. Additionally hill farmers, forestry workers and quarrymen were only too willing to loan horses, sleds and other tackle to move wreckage off a mountainside to the nearest track or road.

Come the war, with the rising incidence of crashes and increasing size and sophistication of aircraft, something more than an *ad hoc* station-based salvage operation was needed. Accordingly, in September 1939, the RAF established six Salvage Centres or Sections to recover crashed aircraft nationwide (including the Isle of Man). These were at Cambridge (later N° 54 MU), Carluke (N° 63 MU), Horsham/Faygate (N° 49 MU), Newark (N° 58 MU), Oxford/Cowley (N° 50 MU) and Shipton (N° 60 MU). Not surprisingly, considering the station's long involvement with aircraft recovery in North Wales and adjacent areas N° 6 Salvage Section, under S/Ldr W. N. Ash, was established at RAF Sealand. The administrative chaos of the early weeks of the war saw the Section set up on a shoe-string, personnel, transport and equipment having to come from N° 30 MU, Sealand's specialist engine, instrument, armament and wireless repair unit which itself had only been formed the previous July and which was still in the throes of settling in and formulating operational policy.

N° 6 Salvage Section had dealt with only a couple of crashes — Hawker Audax K5161 which crashed on 18 October 1939 on approach to Sealand aerodrome and one of 5 FTS's new Masters, N7415, which spun in over Burton Meadows, Rossett, on 14 October — when the section was posted (on 27 October) to a ground station at Carluke, Lanarkshire, which would remain its base as N° 63 MU until May 1946, when it moved to RAF Woolsington, Northumberland. The Section travelled north by road via an unsuspecting N° 14 MU at Kingstown, Cumberland, from which further transport and equipment were scrounged.

On 21 September 1939, within Maintenance Command, N° 43 Group, Andover (later Oxford), was established to administer these six salvage depots and four associated repair depots, one of the latter being N° 30 MU, Sealand. For reasons of security — and possibly public morale — salvage units were quickly re-designated 'Maintenance Units'. By May 1941, N° 43 Group would have thirteen salvage and seven repair MUs under its wing. Amongst the new ones was N° 34 MU, Monkmoor, Shrewsbury, commissioned on 1 March 1940 with 4 officers and 148 other ranks, under the command of S/Ldr Eidler. In addition to collecting crashed aircraft within its allotted area N° 34 MU's task was also to supply spares. Its two great hangars housed many working sections which were manned by experts in the various trades to deal with airframes, engines, armament, electrics and instruments. Monkmoor was a ground station on the site of Shrewsbury's First World War aerodrome, where two of the original Belfast hangars and some domestic site buildings yet remained. These were duly re-requisitioned.

As already noticed the First World War flying ground itself had been used by the barn-storming Berkshire Aviation Tours throughout the 1920s and even as recently as September 1937 was the site for an unscheduled forced-landing by a Vickers Wellesley bomber. It would now become Nº 34 MU's main scrap dump.

The two surviving hangars were brick-built, 170 x 80ft, with annexes — stores and offices along the side walls. By 1939 the asbestos/cement sheeting of the roofs was very much dilapidated. It took three weeks to clear the concrete aprons and surrounds, a not very pleasant task as the last major user had been a battery chicken farm! For the moment officers and men were billeted out in the Shrewsbury suburbs and KSLI barracks. It would be July before the first group of 118 personnel moved onto the Monkmoor domestic site where two new barrack blocks and dining room cum-NAAFI had just been completed. The MT office, orderly room and officers' mess never graduated beyond their original giant aircraft packing cases!

Domestic problems notwithstanding the first three crash inspections were carried out on 21 March 1940, with ten more by the end of the month. By the end of April Nº 34 MU was in full swing. Twenty-nine crash sites had been inspected with twenty-four aircraft recovered. Twelve aircraft, damaged beyond repair had been broken up for scrap. Nº 34 MU's territory included Worcestershire, Shropshire, Staffordshire, Derbyshire and the six north Wales counties. Cheshire and the Isle of Man were covered by Nº 75 MU, who maintained depôts and scrap yards at Wilmslow and Jurby (IoM). Yorkshire came under Nº 60 MU at Shipton-by-Beningbrough. As will be seen later, the latter had a chequered and highly mobile post-war career, somewhere along the line swapping salvage functions for an exclusively engineering role. Recovery and salvage in south Wales fell to Nº 78 MU at Pencoed Tinplate Works, Bynea, Carmarthenshire, a ground station on the then A484 (now B4297) three miles south-east of Llanelli.

By July 1940 Nº 34 MU had some twelve salvage teams working out of Monkmoor, each under its own NCO. Initially there was a shortage of small tools and transport so that the teams worked on or close to existing RAF stations where equipment could be borrowed. This pattern was to persist, with Nº 34 MU personnel concentrating on the lowland crashes and the high ground recoveries contracted out, almost exclusively to Aber Carriers of Welshpool, whose fleet of HGVs and vans were a familiar sight in the nooks and crannies of north Wales and whose employees were well-acquainted with the hostile terrain, the Welsh weather in all its moods, and, most importantly in the light of latent Welsh nationalism smouldering below the surface, were Welsh speaking. Operational boundaries were not sacrosanct. RAF Sealand and Hawarden, with MUs on site often chipped in to help out in salvage operations e.g. Sealand recovered the 'Bradley' Spitfire (P8267, Nº 61 OTU Rednal, crashed 15 May 1944) and Hawarden Nº 60 OTU's Mosquitos that came to grief whilst using the Burton Marsh bombing range (HX984 on 30 May 1944, LR263 on 30 August 1944). In fact RAF Hawarden would appear to have been a permanent out-station to one of Nº 34 MU's salvage teams!

Then between December 1942 and August 1944 Nº 3 Radio School (later Nº 11 RS) at Hooton Park, initially equipped with Bothas and latterly with Ansons, supervised the clearance of their own crashed aircraft down to the last fragment. Most of Nº 11 Radio School's crashes were aerodrome generated — overshoots, tyre bursts, engine stalling on landing etc. They suffered several losses at sea, but when their Blackburn Bothas came to grief over high ground in thick cloud, they provided some of the most spectacular crashes in the Snowdonia catalogue and, of course, some of the most difficult recoveries, e.g. Botha L6202 which flew into the west face of Llwydmor south of Bethesda on 28 August 1944. With aircraft crammed full of sensitive radio equipment secrecy during a meticulous recovery was paramount. Nº 11 RS worked with 'top secret' electronic equipment such as AI radar and calibrating the eighteen CH and CHL radar installations along the north Wales coast as well as the experimental artillery and searchlight radar units run by the Army. Again, when Beaufighter X7845 of Nº 256 Squadron, Woodvale, collided over Bangor (Caernarfonshire) with Wellington BK234 of Nº 25 OTU Finningley, on 31 October 1942, killing both crews, a special team from Nº 77 Signals Wing, Liverpool, was mustered to clear the Beaufighter wreckage because of the AI and RDF equipment it was carrying. Nothing was left on site, everything being carted away by L.E.P. Transport, Liverpool, the secret scouse equivalent of Aber Carriers.

Like so many others of its ilk, Nº 34 MU's Operational Record Book is a disappointing document, albeit an invaluable roll-call of all crashes in ten counties. It is a largely statistical account date, aircraft type and number, damage category and location and marginal notes when the recovery was sub-contracted out. So much depended upon the interest, flair and imagination shown by a unit's duly appointed 'diary keeper' but clearly that of Nº 34 MU was in the keeping of a lowly clerk and its updating little more than a routine chore. But occasionally, perhaps impressed by the enormity of the task facing a recovery team, the unit scribe is moved, with not a little sweat and pen chewing, to expand an entry to three or four lines!

Thus: 'May 1944. Two difficult salvage tasks. Two Spitfires collided, diving into the ground to a depth of twenty feet. A considerable amount of work was entailed in digging and pumping during recovery. The task took two days. Mosquito aircraft dived into the grounds of an American hospital, burying itself to a depth of twenty feet in a filled-in pit. Recovery of wreckage was completed after considerable digging and pumping'. The two Spitfires mentioned were P7608 and P8079 of Nº 61 OTU Rednal. On 27 April 1944 they were practising dog-fighting over the Long Mynd when they collided and spun in at Marshbrook, a small hamlet on the A49, three miles south of Church Stretton. The Mosquito was DZ747 of Nº 60 OTU High Ercall. On the night of 6 May 1944 it was on the final leg of a NAVEX to Northern Ireland and back when it ran into bad weather. The pilot, F/Lt J. R. Milne lost control. The navigator, P/O Rice, was ordered to bale out, which he accomplished safely — no mean feat in a Mosquito landing in a field at Park Lane, Penley, where he was promptly

Site of RAF Monkmoor, Shrewsbury, looking south April 2004, home to Nº 34 MU during the Second World War. Centre, the triple Belfast hangar (two have been re-roofed) and a double Belfast hangar in the distance. The housing on the left has been built on the Second World War airfield. Bottom right, converted RAF domestic site buildings. [W Alister Williams Collection]

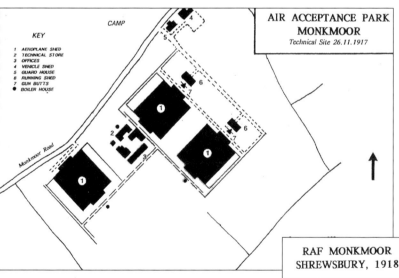

RAF Monkmoor started life as an Air Acceptance Park with multiple Belfast hangars.

A flying field was attached along with a domestic site, home to the Observers School of Reconnaissance and Aerial Photography. The third hangar was later moved and partly survives at the former dairy site in Frankwell, Shrewsbury.

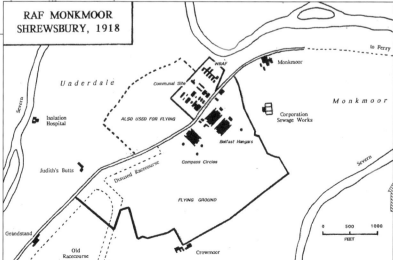

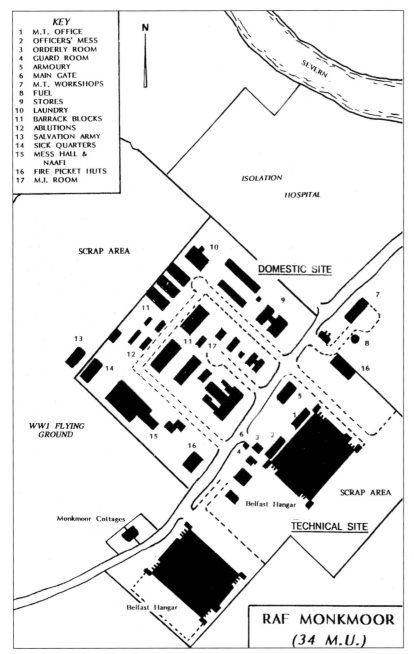

KEY
1   M.T. OFFICE
2   OFFICERS' MESS
3   ORDERLY ROOM
4   GUARD ROOM
5   ARMOURY
6   MAIN GATE
7   M.T. WORKSHOPS
8   FUEL
9   STORES
10 LAUNDRY
11 BARRACK BLOCKS
12 ABLUTIONS
13 SALVATION ARMY
14 SICK QUARTERS
15 MESS HALL & NAAFI
16 FIRE PICKET HUTS
17 M.I. ROOM

N

SEVERN

ISOLATION
HOSPITAL

SCRAP AREA

DOMESTIC SITE

WW1 FLYING
GROUND

Monkmoor Cottages

Belfast Hangar

SCRAP AREA

Belfast Hangar

TECHNICAL SITE

RAF MONKMOOR
(34 M.U.)

*N° 34 MU Salvage/Stores and domestic site
in the northern suburbs of Shrewsbury.*

mistaken for a German parachutist! The pilot stayed with the aircraft which crashed almost unnoticed during the thunderstorm, into the grounds of N° 129 American Military Hospital, Penley. It clipped a tree in front of Penley Hall, bounced off, and buried itself in the made-up ground of what was once the 'outer moat'.

But recovery was not as complete as the ORB entry suggests. In view of the unstable nature of the ground and the water problem, much wreckage, including a virtually complete Merlin 21 engine, was left behind by the Monkmoor salvage team. Thirty years later, contravening accepted guidelines in such matters, the Mosquito crash site at Penley Hall was the scene of a well-planned unlicensed 'dig', carried out with military precision by a 'warbird' enthusiasts splinter group, desperate to enhance their museum display. The 'dig' lasted barely an hour, during which the engine, dinghy and other bits and pieces, including the pilot's flying helmet, were recovered. Objective attained the 'dig' was immediately closed down. Incidents like this did little to further the cause of aviation archaeology at either official or land-owner level. The Penley Hall site was the last excavation in a succession of frustrated illegitimate 'digs' at potential Merlin engine sites across north Shropshire.

The salvaging of Spitfires P7608 and P8079 was but the latest in a series of N° 34 MU recoveries made in the Marshbrook area, and would not be the last. On 14 May 1943 another N° 61 OTU Spitfire, P8268, piloted by 20-year old F/Sgt A. J. Webb, RAAF, was on an affiliation exercise — practice interceptions — with a Wellington III (BK186) trundling up the Welsh border from N° 23 OTU, Pershore (Worcestershire). F/Sgt Webb completely misjudged one of his attacks, collided with the bomber in a climbing turn and fell away into an almost vertical dive to crash into the hillside at Marshbrook. N° 34 MU did the recovery, 'another deep one', which received no more than the statutory one-liner in the unit's ORB. This may point to the fact that salvage teams were by now immune to the horrors of their task. No recovery was too difficult or impossible, the impossible perhaps taking a little longer and meriting a grudging write-up in the log! BK186 was badly damaged but managed to land safely back at Pershore, demonstrating in a training rôle what operational crews often found — that

*The recovery of a Merlin engine from Mosquito DZ747
in the grounds of the Polish hospital, Penley Hall.*

Wellingtons, by virtue of their geodetic structure, could absorb tremendous punishment yet remain flying. After repair BK186 went to N° 22 OTU at Wellesbourne Mountford (Warwickshire). It was finally written off on 11 June 1944 after it suffered another accident — a collapsed under-carriage — on landing at N° 22 OTU's satellite at Stratford.

One assumes that it was purely coincidence when on 23 October 1944 a Halifax II, BB284, of N° 1656 Heavy Conversion Unit (HCU) crashed at Upper Whittingslow Farm, Marshbrook, after the outer starboard engine caught fire whilst on a shake-down NAVEX from Lindholme (Yorkshire). The main wreckage burnt out on site, badly damaging the winter wheat that was just appearing above ground. Recovery work, which took the best part of five days, finished off the crop. To rub salt into the wounds the farmer had to lend the N° 34 MU salvage team most of the heavy tackle to complete the job! At least two of the engines falling some distance away; fortunately for everyone's health and temper these fields were down to pasture. Subsequent investigation by the WARG produced small fragments at a depth of no more than a foot over a seventy-yard square area, pointing to BB284 crashing and burning out on the surface, without deep penetration. One of the crew, 28-year old P/O T. A. Ellison lies buried at Blacon CWGC Cemetery. Throughout 1941 Lindholme, although a Bomber Command station, had served as a RLG (especially for night-flying) to the Oxfords of N° 11 SFTS, Shawbury, whilst the latter's all-grass airfield was untenable and when concrete runway construction began in the September. Now its Halifaxes were working under great pressure preparing air-crews for the final part of a 'heavy conversion' course, the 'Lancaster Finishing School', the ultimate experience in four-engined flying, were it not for the fact that flying hours logged were woefully inadequate before crews were posted to operational squadrons.

To the layman it seems almost incredible that, with thousands of feet of air space at a pilot's disposal, the relatively subdued relief of the Shropshire/Montgomery-shire hill country, rarely exceeding 1,700ft, should have claimed so many RAF and Allied aircraft. But the evidence points to the valleys of the Onny and Cound Brook, followed by the A49(T) Shrewsbury–Hereford road, being used by aircraft almost as if they were cars or buses. The latter were not troubled by the narrowing of the valley as the walls of The Long Mynd and Caer Caradoc Hills encroached on either side. To aircraft this quirk of relief often proved fatal, especially in poor visibility and with low cloud base. The three-mile strip between Church Stretton and Leebotwood would far exceed Marshbrook to the south when it came to crashed aircraft and aircrew fatalities. These hills also gave some of N° 34 MU's salvage teams their first taste of 'hell on high ground'.

On 20 January 1943 two Spitfires, P9329 and X4852, both from N° 61 OTU, Rednal, ploughed into the hills between Church Stretton and Hope Bowdier whilst flying, in formation in very bad visibility. 'Ear'-witnesses had heard them flying southwards, hidden by cloud - then a rending crash followed by an explosion. Both pilots — Sgt H. K. Adams, RCAF, and Sgt D. L. Moulds, RCAF — were killed

A WAAF member of N° 34 MU, posing for a photograph whilst airmen load parachutes destined for Whitehall.
[Mary Corfield, Shrewsbury]

and lie buried in the military plot of Oswestry cemetery. N° 34 MU's resources were so stretched at this time that recovery work was entrusted to an Army detachment from Church Stretton. Soldiers had been first on the scene of the accident, had recovered the burnt and broken bodies, and mounted a guard over the wreckage. As was the way with all squaddies they knew exactly what had happened! The pilots had been ordered to abort their mission because of deteriorating weather, turned to port still in formation, not knowing that they were now on course for 1,067ft Helmuth Hill. X4852 ploughed into the wooded crest and completely disintegrated. P9329 hurdled the trees only to explode at Gaer Stone farm on the higher (1,178ft) Hope Bowdler Hill, some 300 yards further east. The impact area can still be identified by the gap ripped in the high wind-break hedge. The/official Court of Inquiry recorded a mid-air collision as the probable cause of the double accident, although evidence for this could not be deduced from the wreckage, so complete had been the destruction!

If a pilot was unfamiliar with the area, the dangers were even more real. Thus on 11 June 1943 22-year old P/O J. W. Grant, RCAF, of N° 52 OTU, Aston Down (Gloucestershire) was killed instantly when his Spitfire (AR221) crashed west of Church Stretton onto the slopes of the Long Mynd in thick cloud. The wreck gave N° 34 MU its most difficult recovery to-date. The burial of the pilot was handled by RAF Shawbury and P/O Grant lies buried in St Mary's Churchyard nearby, his stone one of fifty silently confirming the hazards of flying too close to the often invisible hills of the Welsh border country. This was one of N° 52 OTU's last accidents before the unit was disbanded in August 1943

Still extant — the First World War Belfast hangars used to store parts and equipment at Nº 34 MU Monkmoor.

During the Second World War, the area in front of these Belfast hangars was covered with aircraft wreckage awaiting re-cycling.

when, for the first time, the supply of fighter pilots began to exceed demand.

Equally lost, a long way from home, was Mosquito KB224, belonging to Nº 1655 MCU (Mosquito Conversion Unit) from Warboys, Hunts. This was a training unit within Nº 8 (PFF) Group, Bomber Command, producing specialist air crews for the Pathfinder Force or target markers that flew in Lancasters and Mosquitoes from airfields around the Cambridgeshire Fenlands. KB224 smashed into the hills at Leebotwood on 24 August 1944. It was closely followed, on 28 August by a Miles Master (AZ841) of Nº 5 (P)AFU, Tern Hill, which ploughed in whilst practising solo aerobatics over Leebotwood. Sgt N. E. Saulde, Free French Air Force, was killed and lay buried in the CWGC cemetery at Blacon until exhumation to France on (according to cemetery records) 14 November 1944. This date is probably erroneous — at this particular time the Allies had yet to breach the defensive line of the Meuse–Sigfried Line–Moselle and Vosges. The other Free French remaining at Blacon were exhumed together on 16 November 1948.

In Nº 34 MU's ORB the entry for 28 November 1944 reads: 'Spitfire crashed in the bottom of a ravine in Wynnstay Park, Ruabon. Wreckage was discovered in a swiftly flowing stream. This was approximately ninety feet in vertical depth, the only approach being via the sixty

degree bank by means of a rope. The engine was eventually discovered under rocks, completely submerged and dislodged by the crash impact, and was winched to the bank. Other wreckage was then reached. Although salvage operations were retarded for a period of three days due to a substantial increase in the volume of water, 95 per cent of the aircraft was recovered and the engine salvaged by winching to the top of the ravine by stages. The salvage party spent nine days on this particular operation'. This was Spitfire AA933 ('YB') of Nº 61 OTU Rednal, logged as crashing on 18 November, killing the pilot, F/O John Robert Dunne. The latter lies buried in the CWGC Cemetery, Blacon, near Chester.

The recovery was done by Nº 34 MU's 'direct labour force' and well merited the extra lineage devoted to it in the ORB. The Afon Eitha rises on the moorland collecting grounds of Ruabon Mountain and is indeed subject to temperamental surges in level. It has incised a narrow densely wooded gorge, 175ft deep at its confluence with the Dee. A hundred feet further south and the Spitfire would have landed in the middle of the Dee. The official Court of Enquiry adjudged that P/O Dunne had suffered a blackout due to oxygen deprivation at high altitude. This would explain how AA933 must have gone in almost vertically as there was little, if any, damage to the surrounding woodland. Ropes were slung from tree to tree as a sort of 'handrail' down the slope. To avoid being washed into the Dee salvage crews worked lashed to trees and to each other by ropes. Nights were drawing in and working hours short — at least with sufficient daylight to work safely. Unfortunately since D-Day Army units had withdrawn from nearby Wynnstay Park so there was no over-night hospitality and drying out. It was a damp and bedraggled crew that made the 40-minute journey in the back of a 3-tonner to Monkmoor each night. Another four or five months would elapse before someone had the bright idea to provide a

How it was done. Re-cycling Vickers Wellington parts at Nº 34 MU Monkmoor.

mobile caravan for teams working in such isolated areas. Having thus reduced valuable time lost by commuting to and from a crash site, the problem of morale sapping boredom was then addressed, whether successfully, one shall never know.

The last recovery to receive red-letter treatment in N° 34 MU's ORB was the recovery of an USAAF Liberator (42-51361) which in March 1945 had crashed on the bank of the Severn near Shrawardine, killing five of the six crew and leaving part of the tail unit overhanging the river with a large piece of the fuselage submerged. 'The site of the crash was approximately one mile from the nearest point of access by a lorry, a long low-loader. This point was situated at the top of a fairly steep gradient leading down across marshland to the site of the crash. Salvage was accomplished by means of a Cletrac and sledge. This was the first time the units had cause to use this tractor and the operation was successfully completed with the minimum of manpower and time, proving to be ideal for this type of salvage work. A mobile caravan was used by the salvage party on site, thus further reducing the total time spent in travelling. For practical use, it was decided that the occupants of the caravan required some form of relaxation after working hours, being denied the usual daily newspapers'. Allowing for grammar and syntax this passage could only have been written at the dictation of an officer! One wonders where top-brass had been for five years, the fuss that was being made about the use of a tracked vehicle and sledge! N° 34 MU would appear to have been very slow to learn from its civilian high-ground contractors.

Liberator 42-51361, piloted by Lt Mitchell Copthorne, was attached to N° 453BG (Bomb Group), USAAF at Old Buckenham, Norfolk, and according to eye-witnesses had been trying to land at RAF Montford Bridge, a satellite to N° 61 OTU, Rednal. Dennis Diggory takes up the story:

The aircraft came into view from the east at an altitude of about 750ft, lowered its undercarriage, and made three or four very low right-handed circuits of RAF Montford Bridge. At the time, around 1500hrs, there was considerable Spitfire activity in the area, and the Liberator took up a holding pattern about half a mile from the aerodrome, flew

tight right-handed circuits for some five minutes and then headed west in preparation for its final approach. On turning into line with runway 19, the aircraft lost height. I lost sight of it behind high ground and trees, but could hear its engines very clearly. Suddenly the engines were opened up to what sounded to be full power and the Liberator struck the top of a large tree at the summit of a wooded slope overlooking the River Severn. After falling some 200ft into the valley, the aircraft crashed on the river bank, scattering pieces of wreckage over a wide area. Prior to the recovery operations, the crash site was guarded USAAF servicemen who were billeted in the outbuildings of a nearby farm.

N° 34 MU must have done their job well. Although it was believed that some sections of the aircraft remain in the river, a WARG examination in August 1981, assisted by sub-aqua divers, produced only small fragments of alloy.

The teams from Aber Carriers could tap civilian resources. They knew key people in each locality. These in turn fingered individuals — shepherds, farmers, bailiffs, foresters and quarrymen — who had a detailed knowledge of a mountain and its wiles and could act as guides or provide resources such as horses, tractors, sleds, carts, half-tracks, chains, block and tackle, winches etc. With the goodwill of Grade 5 stationmasters, tiny goods-yards at remote railway stations could be pressed into use as temporary scrap dumps. Some authorities will hint at the establishment of a N° 34 MU sub-centre at Capel Curig, following the rapid increase in Snowdonia crashes. This is not reflected in the parent unit's ORB, which is not surprising. The 'sub-centre' was set up by Aber Carriers on their own initiative. In practice it was simply the yard or open space behind the Mountain Rescue Centre then at Bethesda — but it obviated the need for too many long hauls back to the Distiller's Yard in Welshpool.

Aber Carriers did not keep an Operational Record Book. Team members were 'getting on' fifty years ago and most, unfortunately, are no longer with us, while younger men were with the teams only for short periods before being called up for military service. But the recollections of the late David ('Dai') Davies and Charlie Jones — the latter formerly Aber Carriers' transport manager — more than compensate

N° 34 MU's 'high ground' contractors, Aberystwyth Carriers, known locally as Aber Carriers. They worked out from Henfaes Lane, Welshpool and delivered into RAF Shawbury for investigation and RAF Monkmoor for re-cycling.

for the barrenness of the official ORB. Charlie Jones cleared most of the wreck sites in Snowdonia and Cader Idris areas and whilst working at Tywyn on 22 October 1942, witnessed the demise of three Spitfires BL518, BM573 and R7296 of 'A' Flight, N° 41 Squadron, RAF Llanbedr. Officially the three planes and their pilots were lost 'whilst practising formation flying in cloud'. Six miles ENE of Tywyn they flew into the 2,076ft ridge of Tarrenhendre. According to Charlie Jones the three Spitfires collided before hitting the mountain top. Whatever, all three pilots were killed instantly. Their bodies were not recovered until two days later. In Charlie's words: 'There was very little surface wreckage as the three Spitfires went in vertically'.

In recalling an 'Avro Lancaster' which came to grief on the shores of Lake Vyrnwy failing memory was at fault. The story persists, with local inhabitants convinced that it was a Lancaster of N° 617 Squadron in training for the famous 'Dam-buster' raid of 16/17 May 1943. In reality the stricken aircraft was a Wellington III (X3785) of N° 27 OTU Lichfield on a night NAVEX. It caught fire in the air and crashed above Moel y Bryn on the northern shores of the lake, killing all six crew. The date — 15 May, the evening before N° 617 Squadron blew the Ruhr dams! The idea of 'a 617 Lanc. out on a final training jaunt' is a marvellous one; little wonder locals refused to be shaken in their beliefs! Aber Carriers were alerted by the Welshpool fire brigade that 'a bomber had crashed and was on fire at Lake Vyrnwy'. Charlie's salvage team brought most of the wreckage down to the track that ran round the lake, now hardly recognisable as the upgraded B4393. Charlie's assertion that 'some of the wreckage still (1981) lies along the shore' possibly yet holds good, since the Wellington started to break up before piling in, scattering debris over the lake and foreshore. Periodic drops in water-level in drought years are bound to reveal to the curious onlooker scraps of twisted metal completely unrelated to the footings of the drowned village of Llanwyddyn and the long vanished hamlets of Eunant and Rhiwargor.

Some of the confusion in peoples' minds may stem from the fact that an Avro Lancaster did crash in the neighbourhood, but on 16/17 November 1942. Again Aber Carriers salvaged what was left, but it was more of a token clearance so inaccessible was the spot and so completely had

the aircraft disintegrated. However, over the last fifty years the crash site, isolated as it is, has been picked clean by aviation buffs. In September 1942 N° 101 Squadron had transferred with their Wellington Ills from Stradishall, Suffolk, to Holme-on-Spalding Moor, Yorkshire. The following month they began to convert to Lancasters. On the date in question Lancaster W4236 crashed on a night training flight into the 1,407ft ridge at Nant Craigyfran, the aptly named 'valley of the crag of the crow' some four miles south-west of Llangadfan, Montgomeryshire. At 0400hrs as the Lancaster was flying over the Llanerfyl area a dull explosion was heard and the bomber spiralled out of the sky, scattering debris over a wide area before impacting on the desolate moor above Dolwen. There was little the police, Home Guard and rescue services could do until first light. Six bodies were found in and around the wrecked fuselage. A seventh, that of Sgt J. R. Gould, RCAF, was found some distance away. He and the pilot, Sgt J. W. Spinney, RCAF, and the navigator, Sgt H. W. A. Collett, RNZAF, lie buried in Tywyn Cemetery, possibly because rescue and salvage operations were co-ordinated from Tywyn aerodrome. The subsequent inquest found it difficult to pin-point the exact cause of the crash but it is believed that a photo-flash flare exploded inside the aircraft followed by structural failure of the rear fuselage.

Charlie Jones' final recollection involved a salvage job on a bomber, 'possibly a Halifax' that came down in the Dyfnant Forest near the mill at Parc Llwydiarth, some three miles south of the Lake Vyrnwy dam. Forty years on the exact year, never mind date, was uncertain, but place and event were crystal clear and may be confirmed by a new generation of custodians of oral tradition. People today hint darkly at 'the supplies' and 'large quantities of kröne paper money scattered about the woods' around the impact point. The Aber Carriers team deduced that the bomber had been 'a supply mission to Norway', that the mission had been aborted, and still lost had overflown the breadth of England to possibly run out of fuel and crash at Parc Llwydiarth. It had been abandoned by its Polish crew in good order and their landing places are known — Pontrobert, Meifod, Llanfihangel-yng-Ngwynfa straggling out in a line eastwards of the impact point. When Charlie Jones and his team finally arrived at the crash site they left the depth charges well alone but assumed that, as was the practice, the N° 34 MU armourer had already defused the bombs. This was not the case. But it was not until they arrived back in Welshpool with the bombs carefully stowed on the back of a lorry that they received a message from the CO of N° 34 MU that the armourer had been delayed and would not be on site until later in the day! It was a sweating driver who had to take his load to an isolated spot outside town and off load them.

So runs Charlie's story. It is the stuff of which legends are

The W.A.R.G. digging through water-sodden peat and mud to retrieve parts from Avro Lancaster W4236. The excavation took place in August 1980 on the Dolwyn hill.

Two views of a badly damaged glycol thermostat housing from the cooling system on one of Lancaster W4236's Merlin engines.

made. Given so much detail, albeit embroidered over the years, but with so many eye-witnesses, it is puzzling how aviation historians and 'wreckologists' have hitherto not been able to supply details of aircraft type, serial number, date, crew. squadron and mission in connection with this incident.

Fifty-four years later some intensive painstaking detective work has finally paid off. The first clue came from Charlie's testimony regarding Polish air-crew having baled out. This immediately narrowed the search down, figuratively speaking, to three possible squadrons, N⁰ˢ 301, 304 and 305. Bomber Command Accident Cards and Loss Cards, given that they are complete (and perhaps more easily consultable in W. R. Chorley's ongoing volumes in the *RAF Bomber Command Losses* series), threw up no likely candidate for a substantiated loss in the Dyfnant Forest. Attention therefore focussed on N⁰ 304 'Slaski' Squadron which had only thirteen months as an operational unit with Bomber Command before being transferred to Coastal Command on 10 May 1942. In July 1945 it transferred to Transport Command.

First under the microscope came Wellington IA, N2899, an aircraft of N⁰ 304 Squadron the records of which are endorsed NFD ('No Further detail') apart from a crash/loss date, 7 May 1942. The latter might explain why the aircraft's history has for so long lain in limbo-land.

It was on that date that the advance party of N⁰ 304 Squadron, stationed at RAF Lindholme, and newly transferred as a General Reconnaissance unit in Coastal Command flew from Yorkshire on the first leg of a circuitous route to Pembrokeshire. For a month the squadron would operate from Tiree, an island in the Inner Hebrides, opened in March as an anti-submarine/maritime patrol base and where N⁰ 224 Squadron with its Hudsons and Liberators had been in residence since 12 April. This was a move possibly forced by plans for a general facelift to Lindholme aerodrome, including the construction of concrete runways. N⁰ 304 Squadron became operational at its new base on 10 May. It would appear, therefore, that N2899 was lost without trace as it was flying to its new base in Scotland. Charlie Jones' story would seem to hold more than a grain of truth. The fact that the unit was in the throes of moving house almost certainly accounts for why nothing appears in the squadron ORB or either of the two station ORBs. That for Tiree is of the skimpiest, because hardly was it up and

running when its squadrons were withdrawn (N⁰ 224 Squadron leaving for Hampshire in September) and the station went on 'Care and Maintenance' as from 9 September, remaining so until the advent of N⁰ 518 Sqn, a specialist meteorological unit, in September 1943. But in the cold light of reason N2899 must be discarded as the Dyfnant Forest casualty, if for no other reason all five crew survived and the local Home Guard, Police and MU subcontractors were involved after the crash, hardly warranting the all-embracing NFD of the records. Additionally, Montgomery-shire does not lie on a course Lindholme–Tiree, and one is reluctant to assume that an experienced operational crew would be so far off course within such a short distance and space of time.

On 15 June 1942 the Polish unit at last was able to move into to RAF Dale, Pembrokeshire, commissioned two weeks earlier, to carry out anti-submarine sweeps and shipping raids over the Bay of Biscay and along the French coast. On 25 August a N⁰ 304 Squadron Wellington IC, Z1172, suffered engine failure whilst on patrol and crashed into the sea off the South Stack lighthouse, Anglesey. But it was the Loss Card for a Broughton-built Wellington IC, HE103, that next caught the eye: 'Ran out of fuel and abandoned at Llanafyllan, Salop [sic], 4.2.43'. This must be the other side of the equation. There was already the incontrovertible record of a bomber crashing in the Dyfnant Forest. Now there is a Wellington whose crash site has not been investigated further because it should actually read 'Llanfyllin, Montgomeryshire', a small market town with a ROC post and Home Guard Company HQ some six miles from the crash site at Parc Llwydiarth. This was much more likely than a non-existent Welsh place-name in the wrong county! The important point is the note on the Loss Card that HE103 was abandoned, i.e. the crew managed to bale out successfully. All this ties in nicely with what is known of the Dyfnant Forest crash.

Piecing together the accounts of eye-witnesses, relying heavily on the testimony of Mrs Mary Evans (née Jones), of Plasgwyn, Llangadfan, the first indication that an aircraft

*Wellington HE103 flew into the hills above Lake Vyrnwy,
seen in the background of this photograph*

*A Wellington of Nº 304 (Slaski) Polish Squadron,
RAF Dale, south Wales.*

had come to grief was its sudden loss to the plotting table at ROC HQ, Wrexham. It was a dark dirty night, with thick low cloud masking the hills tops, and driving rain and strong winds making for poor visibility. A sound plot had been accepted from Nº 27 Group (Shrewsbury) Group, then lost before being picked up by T.3 Llanfyllin post and plotted by T.4 Llanwddyn, which suddenly lost it again. Time 2200hrs.

Then occurred one of those break-downs in communication; Pte. Watkin Jones, of the Llwydiarth platoon, Home Guard, was returning home along the track through Parc Llwydiarth to his home at 'Tynfedw', a small holding the other side of the forest. He had been attending a MOI film on 'Air Raid Security' at the village hall. Suddenly he stumbled over a large cylinder lying across the track. By the dimmed light of his torch he could make out the words 'Oxygen' stencilled on the side. Swinging the beam of his torch about, carelessly contravening ARP regulations, he picked out other twisted metal fragments scattered over the road and larger pieces hanging from the trees clothing the slopes above the track. Against the grey skyline he could see that many of the trees had been neatly topped as if by a giant scythe. He got home, but in response to his questioning no one had heard anything out of the ordinary, only the howling of the wind in the chimney. This notwithstanding, he decided to report the matter and made his tortuous way back to the village call box.

The ROC was one of the war's super intelligence~gathering agencies, adding aircraft in distress, aircraft crashes, explosions, parachute landings, suspicious persons or events to their spotting functions. From its 'T'-cluster posts Wrexham centre was beginning to get garbled versions of possible aircraft crash and enemy parachutists. The Llanwddyn post shared its position with a Home Guard observation post and just below was one of the LAA batteries guarding the Lake Vyrnwy dam. The latter reported 'German' parachutists on the hairpin bend below the dam at Boncyn Celyn. It turned out to be the Polish pilot

of HE103, the last person to leave the Wellington before its engines cut and it nose-dived into the forested hill at Y Parc. He sustained a broken leg and in his agony forgot the few words of English he had learnt. The rest of the crew had landed in a ragged line straggling out eastwards some eight miles as far as Meifod, intensifying the 'invasion scare' as village constables and isolated Home Guard members made their 'captures' and reported in to their different HQs.

It did not help that Watkin Jones in the urgency of the situation, reported straight to Lt Col Mead, Meifod, OC north Montgomeryshire Home Guard, by-passing his company commander on the ground, Major Howard, of the Liverpool Corporation Waterworks, Llanwddyn, who was desperately trying to sort out fact from rumour, get his Polish 'prisoner' hospitalised, and find the remains of the wrecked Wellington to ascertain whether there were any other survivors. ROC Liason Officers had passed the information on to Fighter Command Filter Room, Bentley Priory, and they in turn were burning wire to try and establish who had lost what aircraft and where. It would appear that the crew of HE103 had aborted their Biscay patrol but on returning to base had found the country blanketed in thick cloud. They had unwittingly overflown south Wales and somewhere over Church Stretton, well and truly lost and not daring to break cloud base for a possible fix, had taken the decision to abandon ship — arrived at quite easily when fuel gauges register zero! The pilot may have set an autocourse on a westerly heading, hoping that the Wellington would eventually fall in either the Irish Sea or some unpopulated hill area.

By first light Police and Home Guard had managed to get things sorted out and a rescue party set out from the Hendre to the crash site. Today the latter lies completely under coniferous trees in the middle of the Dyfnant Forest. In 1943 the Wellington crashed on the forest's northern edge, cutting a giant swathe uphill through the trees, shedding wreckage over a wide area before impacting relatively lightly — at least its bombs and depth charges did not detonate — but making a large hole and clearing some sixty-yards in diameter. A guard was mounted until the Aber Carriers salvage team could arrive. This is where Charlie Jones story merges with eye-witness accounts — apart from the unresolved mystery of the paper money found in the clearing. Bombs and depth-charges were indeed the first items to be recovered, taken away — and brought back again!

The six depth-charges were detonated in a controlled explosion in another forest clearing. The whole district was alerted as to the exact time and warned to leave doors and windows open and for people to lie flat on the ground, preferably in the open! Nevertheless the odd ceiling did fall and many others were cracked or lifted by the force of the blast. Nothing, however, could be done about the leaded windows of St Mary's Parish Church, Llwydiarth even today many of them still show traces of bowing, severe in places, as they withstood the blast. Charlie Jones made light of this particular recovery. In practice it took his team over five weeks in difficult wooded terrain to clear the wreckage. For the whole of that period there was a tight Army guard, billeted locally and using the old saw-mill as their HQ and mess room. It was not certain then, and is even less so now, whether all ordnance had been removed from the wrecked aircraft.

Such was the increase in 'business' that N° 34 MU had quickly outgrown its main site at Monkmoor. In the peak month, November 1942, it had inspected 124 crashes — all RAF — of which 64 were repairable on site, 30 repairable in factories and 12 fit for scrap only. Some 18 aircraft had been reduced 'to produce', and five others collected and delivered for ground-frame instructional purposes. At this period the MU's strength was 20 officers and 781 other ranks. On 16 June 1945 N° 61 OTU moved from Rednal to Keevil in Wiltshire. Rednal was put on a care and maintenance basis, but on 30 July its satellite at Montford Bridge was transferred from 12 Group, Fighter Command to 43 Group Maintenance Command and allotted by the latter as a sub-site to N° 34 MU. As things turned out, Montford Bridge would become the main site and Monkmoor relegated to scrap dump status. The N° 34 MU advanced party moved to Montford Bridge on 8 August 1945, and the main party between 10–17 August. A rear party remained at Monkmoor to safeguard equipment etc. until such time as it could be moved.

The move was well timed. On 1 July N° 34 MU had taken over the salvage area of N° 75 MU (Cheshire and the Isle of Man) and N° 78 MU (South Wales). This was inevitable with the run down in training and a massive drop in the number of crashes. This is reflected in N° 34 MU's strength: officers (RAF and WAAF), 29; senior NCOs (RAF and WAAF), 73; other ranks RAF 471, WAAF 67. The MU was still working at pressure, breaking up surplus aircraft from other units. One of its final tasks was to reduce 23 Master/Hotspur combinations flown in during November from N° 5 Gliding Training School at Shobdon, Herefordshire. This task was completed by the end of December and one notes the

melancholy but matter-of-fact entry in the ORB: '149 tons of scrap metal were moved to N° 2 Metal and Produce Recovery Unit, Eaglescliffe, during the month'.

In October 1945, according to its ORB, N° 34 MU also took over N° 60 MU (Shipton) on a 'Care and Maintenance' basis.. This was a strange arrangement. Considering the logistics involved time, distance, transport — it is unlikely that N° 34 MU was adding salvage operations east of the Pennines to its already extensive commitments in Wales and the north-west. One must note that N° 60 MU was not disbanded. It vacated Shipton for Church Fenton. But did it retain its salvage function? In December 1961 it was at Dishforth and moved again in January 1966, briefly to Leconfield but later in the same year to Abingdon, where in 1976 it merged with N° 71 MU (Bicester) to form the Engineering Wing of RAF Support Command, specialising initially in the overhaul and repair of Jaguars.

Shipton-by-Beningbrough (to give it its full name) was no more than a large grass field with minimal facilities. In practice, therefore, did N° 34 MU just have the task of clearing the site of the last scrap prior to final closure in 1946 and reversion to agricultural land?

It was perhaps only fitting that N° 34 MU should have been the last service occupant of RAF Montford Bridge for it was in tackling crashes in and around that airfield that the salvage teams cut their teeth, learning as they went along the essential military craft of making-do, scrounging and living off the land. The tendency for the large fields between Montford village and Shrawardine to attract aircraft lost, out of fuel or in difficulty has been touched upon earlier. The beginning of runway construction on Forton Heath (the local name for the RAF station) on the other side of the A5 heralded a significant shift in crash impact points, as if semi-finished runways cluttered up with cranes, steam-rollers and barbergreens offered greater chances of survival to panic stricken aircrews in distress.

Thus on Friday, 24 October 1941 Bristol Blenheim IV, V6004, of N° 17 OTU, Upwood and Warboys, put the fear of God both into construction workers on the aerodrome and farm workers and children busy lifting potatoes over the half-term holiday. It was another loss that N° 17 OTU could add to its tally of 38 Blenheims and two Ansons destroyed that year (a slight increase on the 25 Blenheims, 2 Anson and one Battle that came to grief on training flights during 1940). The official Loss Card states simply 'Crashed on overshoot at Grafton, Shropshire' (some records will actually have Grafton Underwood airfield in Northamptonshire!). This is the area immediately north of the aerodrome, defined by Grafton and Grafton Lodge farms. The card does not make clear that it was an unfinished airfield about which the pilot had second thoughts on trying to land. There was a vast difference between viewing an airfield vertically from above and obliquely as when making an approach — only then would the potential hazards reveal themselves to a desperate pilot who had already committed his aircraft. Dennis Diggory again takes up the story:

> I was gathering potatoes during the school holidays
> when my attention was drawn to an unusual aircraft noise,

much heavier than the familiar sound of Miles Masters and other trainers from Tern Hill and Shawbury. In the distance an aircraft could be seen approaching from the south. I recognised it as a Blenheim, flying at an altitude of some 2,000ft but gradually losing height with port propeller feathered. As it passed overhead we could clearly see damage to the starboard wing-tip. We followed it as it made a shallow turn to starboard as if the pilot was going to attempt to put down on the as yet unfinished airfield. Suddenly at this point the starboard engine also cut out. For an agonising moment the Blenheim hung motionless in the air and then spun vertically into the ground.

Putting the roof on a hutment was Mr T. H. Butler, now of Welshpool, but then of Marton, a small village on the B4836 Shrewsbury–Montgomery road. He was a carpenter by trade and the building of RAF Montford Bridge was his first job in a war reserved occupation. He recalls: 'This particular runway was laid in the direction from which the aircraft was coming, Shrewsbury. I think the pilot was going to make a landing, but he was too high, and passed right over us. We were holding our breath thinking that our last hour had come. He zoomed over us. At that moment the engine stopped and he dived into the field just beyond where we were working. A fire broke out on the one side and the plane started to break up. We sprinted across to see if we could help, but it was no use. Both airmen had been killed, although during the day there was talk of one baling out.' Was there a third member of the crew?

The coroner's inquest was held at Oswestry, a mere formality as both bodies were thoroughly cremated. Sgt Peter Desmond Thompson, aged 19, is remembered only on the Runnymede Memorial. The token ashes of Sgt A. I. W. Fairbairn were interred without a headstone at Streatham Park Cemetery, adjacent to South London Crematorium, and his name inscribed on a tablet on the screen wall of the memorial to British, Commonwealth and Allied airmen of both World Wars. But the local Home Guard platoon had to guard the wreckage for ten days before N⁰ 34 MU finally turned up to clear the site, deficient in tools as usual — which may account for the fact that for days afterwards local lads could pick up all sorts of 'mementoes', ranging from a complete seat to bomb safety pins with metal tags attached. From the latter it would appear that V6004 had a bombing exercise written into its NAVEX briefing, possibly on the Fenn's Moss Bombing Range. The practice bombs would have also acted as on-board incendiaries, precipitating the Blenheim's destruction by fire.

Long memories agree on an even earlier visitor to Montford Bridge, but unfortunately the aircraft cannot be positively identified, although the general consensus is that it probably came from N⁰ 57 OTU, Hawarden, or more precisely, from the detachment working out of RAF Wrexham at the time. At about 1900hrs one evening a Spitfire suddenly appeared out of the gathering gloom on a north-westerly heading, flying at tree top level. It climbed steeply to clear a coppice on the airfield boundary. made a tight turn to starboard to attempt a landing approach. A quick change of mind, throttle opened, and the Spitfire climbed away over the trees for a second attempt. Then a

sudden silence, broken by the sound of tearing and scraping metal. The Spitfire had touched down in approved fashion with under-carriage retracted, sliding along 200 yards of incomplete runway, ploughing through hard-core and timber shuttering, before tipping onto its nose in the mud. Willing hands from around the airfield, carrying hurricane lamps and breaking all black-out regulations, converged on the Spitfire's last resting place. The shaken pilot, still in the cockpit, flashed the navigation lights to show that he was unhurt and to warn would-be rescuers to keep well away in case of fire and an explosion. He was taken to a nearby farmhouse and remained there for several days, guarding his aircraft at night until it was removed by N⁰ 34 MU. It seems that at the time of this incident both the Home Guard and N⁰ 34 MU had yet to get themselves properly organised, which would put the Spitfire's recovery very early on in the latter's history.

N⁰ 34 MU continued to break up aircraft at Montford Bridge until July 1947, but whether it still filled a salvage/recovery rôle is uncertain, this function seemingly reverting to local aerodromes, at least those that for the moment remained operational. For some reason the station's four Blister hangars were dismantled in December 1945 and the MU had to make do with a canvas Bessonneau hangar. The aircraft were mainly redundant Masters from the many defunct flying training establishments, but N⁰ 34 MU also handled the rag-bag of assorted aircraft that had been at the disposal of the TFU (Telecommunications Flying Unit) at Defford (Worcestershire). Some of the Masters were overhauled, air tested and ferried off to makers for conversion into target tugs. In July 1947 N⁰ 34 MU moved to RAF Sleap which had been on 'Care and Maintenance' since the departure of N⁰ 1380 TSCU (Transport Support Conversion Unit) in December 1945. In 1949 N⁰ 34 MU would move yet again, this time to RAF Tern Hill.

11. Trespassers

Early in the morning of Saturday, 28 September 1940, three Wrexham schoolboys, Hewitt Hughes, Douglas Parrot and Geoffrey Williams, met, as was their custom, at the latter's home, Borras Lodge farm. Here they made a great show of quartering the large field above the house, looking for mushrooms in the grass still wet from a heavy dew. Rather too early for mushrooms, it was a ruse they had hit upon to get as close as possible to the Miles Masters of N° 5 SFTS. On this particular morning flying had not yet started; instructors and pupils had yet to be bussed in. Ground crews were warming up aircraft outside the Bellman hangar tucked away in the NE corner of the field whilst a lame Master was being checked out in the Bessoneau hangar in front of the 'New Buildings'. Colourful banter was exchanged with the corporal of the guard collecting his outlying pickets ready for dismounting.

Little did any of them suspect that it was going to be 'one of those days'. A 'Purple' alert had been flashed through from Sealand at 0540hrs and the 'All Clear' half an hour later. Before midnight in the Wrexham Police Division there had been six alerts, with sirens sounding three times. 'What was keeping them?', the boys asked each other as they scanned the skies out towards Llay and Gresford. The answer came from the opposite direction. Thoughts of mushrooms were immediately forgotten as an aircraft approaching from the Marchwiel direction took their attention.

It was a sound with which they had become increasingly familiar over the past few weeks, the distinctive pulse of twin Junkers Jumo 211 12-cylinder liquid cooled engines. As every schoolboy knew, at least those who read Colston Shepherds's articles on aircraft identification published by *The Aeroplane*, these were attached to a Heinkel He111. Sure enough, there it was, a large beast looming black and green, a ridiculously small black swastika picked out in white on its tail! The RAF personnel watched apprehensively. There was not much they could do. The corporal had the clip of five rounds; the pickets had empty rifles.

The He111 circled the Borras area, and came down low over the boys' heads, before turning to follow the road to Holt. Almost immediately it re-appeared from the direction of Common Wood, banking slowly over Borras Head to get on to a southerly heading. The pilot waved to the boys. In the extensively glazed cockpit/nose section they could clearly see a second crew member with 'something that looked like a large light, but did not shine'. He did not move, so the three boys waved heartily, thinking it was a camera and not wishing to be excluded from the action. The Heinkel flew round once more in a circle and then made off in the direction of Marchwiel again.

They were not to realise that an evening raid almost inevitably followed early morning reconnaissance and that, even before a sod was cut, the putative RAF Wrexham would be on *Luftwaffe* intelligence maps. So too, almost certainly would be the half-finished Royal Ordnance Factory, sprawling over a green-field site less than a mile from where the schoolboys were standing. Later that night Merseyside did indeed receive visits from detachments of *Luftflotte 3* between 2040–2117hrs and 2255–2318hrs. In Flintshire, Mold Junction and the railway marshalling yards at Saltney were the evening's alternative targets. In the Wrexham area, twelve incendiary bombs fell between Trefalun and Parkside, the latter not far from the Borras RLG. A coincidence, or a direct result of that morning's visitation? Somewhere in the *Luftwaffe* archives may yet lie crucial pictures of a hitherto unrecorded landing ground, with three gesticulating schoolboys adding local colour!

As a result of this incident a searchlight battery was sited on the Holt side of Common Wood, and the flattened grass, wheel marks, spent shell casings etc., in gateways to adjacent fields provided evidence for the nocturnal visitations of a peripatetic Bofors gun and crew. They arrived after dusk and disappeared by first light, rather defeating the purpose of the exercise!

At that time Doug Parrot's father, Stan, ran a hairdressing salon at 13 Yorke Street, Wrexham. He was also a retail tobacconist, an official supplier to HM Forces, employing girls to make up the requisite packets of tens, twenties etc. His shop was therefore frequented by airmen trying to supplement their 'fag ration' via a haircut! In October 1941, into the shop walked Sgts A.E. Scott and 'Little Willie' Streeter, N° 96 Squadron, which had just moved from Cranage to its new home at RAF Wrexham. The two airmen were immediately recognised and introduced to all and sundry as the destroyers of 'the 'Wrexham Heinkel' five months earlier, in the early hours of Thursday, 8 May 1941. Later that same Thursday pilot and air-gunner had flown into Wrexham to view their 'kill' at first hand. Somehow they had found their way to Stan's shop, and, before returning to Cranage, had managed to obtain a supply of cigarettes 'on the house' and a promise of free haircuts 'for the duration'. For one small schoolboy this was more than adequate compensation for the mortification of witnessing a German aircraft fly over Wrexham unmolested!

A loose cannon of the *Luftwaffe* careering thus unopposed along the Welsh border was not an isolated incident. At 1300hrs on Saturday, 9 November 1940, a single Junkers Ju88 flew up the Ironbridge Gorge, swooping low over Jackfield to drop three SC250 bombs in Benthall Edge Wood — possible target the coal-fired power station at Buildwas. Nevertheless the explosions slightly injured one Joe Finch, timber haulier, and two of his horses, fractured a storm-water drain, demolished a quarry explosives store and scattered lumps of limestone over a large area. Over a hundred houses across the river in Ironbridge were damaged by flying debris and the blast. Police quickly sealed off the B4373 at Ladywood around the station end of the famous iron bridge when it was suspected that a fourth bomb might have fallen into the Severn.

Right: Luftwaffe *target reconnaissance photograph (Hauptkraftwerk)*
of Ironbridge and the power station at Buildwas, taken 4 September
1940 [Imperial War Museum]

Below: Possible target for the 9 November 1940 — Buildwas power
station. Photograph taken from the Leighton road.

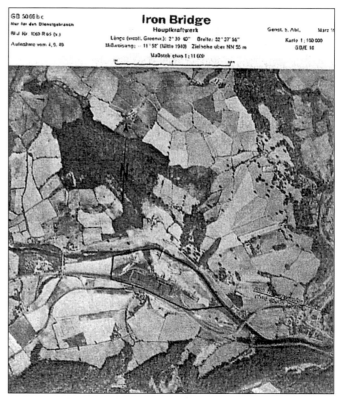

It must have been a huge lump of flying limestone or clay. The lone Junkers flew on, over Leighton, where it survived an attempt to bring it down with a double-barrelled shot-gun, and over Shrewsbury. Shoppers stood transfixed. No sirens had sounded and no one sought cover — not that there were any public shelters at this stage of the war! Three off-duty Observer Corps members snatching 'a quick fag' outside County Hall, could scarce believe their eyes as the Ju88 loomed overhead. Throwing down their cigarettes they made a wild dash for the cellar steps — N° 27 Group (Shrewsbury) had its HQ in the bowels of the building and tried to stammer out a coherent report to the Centre Controller, only to find that the 'hostile' was already out on the plotting table. Even as they watched a report from L.2 Hadnall observer post confirmed the passage of the German aircraft towards Whitchurch. It is too much of a coincidence to have two maverick Ju88s swanning about Shropshire on the same day. This is almost certainly the same aircraft noted previously as machine-gunning A.3 Whitchurch observer post and a nearby petrol storage facility. Each observer post had on charge two .303 rifles and bayonets, a practice clip of five dummy rounds, and 100 rounds of live ammunition held 'in reserve'. Such weaponry was intended to defend the post against invaders, giving duty crews sufficient time to destroy their equipment rather than let it fall into the hands of the enemy. Rifles would also come in useful in rounding up stray and/or stroppy parachutists or German air-crew who had been forced to bale out. They were not for taking on a Ju88. For their temerity the Whitchurch observers received a burst of 7.8mm machine gun fire from the rear cockpit starboard gun! After making two circuits of Whitchurch railway station, trying to spray the 1.35pm Shrewsbury train, which had arrived five minutes earlier from Crewe, the Junkers turned back on a southerly course, and bombed a pond at Coton on the northern outskirts of Shrewsbury — either a

botched attempt at getting the GWR marshalling yard or a 'hang up' (i.e. a bomb stuck in its release mechanism) after the Ironbridge attack.

Lone raiders did not achieve much from point of view of destruction, but in dislocation of everyday life and industry they had an impact out of all proportion to the number of aircraft involved. Thus on Tuesday, 17 September 1940 — the day when Hitler decided to postpone 'Operation Sealion' until further notice — there were 'Red Alerts' on Deeside at 1029–1120hrs, 1124–1135hrs, and 1510–1542hrs as reconnaissance planes overflew the Wirral and Merseyside in advance of the evenings attacks on the Speke aircraft factories by the Junkers of II/LG1 from Orléans/Bricy (N° 2 Wing *Lehrgeschwäder* I, the equivalent of an RAF Operational Training Unit). By this time the *Lehrgeschwäder* had been absorbed into the *Luftwaffe* command and flew largely conventional attack missions — just as Bomber Command OTUs would be stripped of aircraft and crews to make up numbers on the 'Thousand Bomber Raids' over Germany. Although ostensibly on reconnaissance targets of opportunity were too good to miss, with Courtaulds factories at Greenfield and the Chester–Holyhead railway line at Holywell Junction being bombed and strafed. The morning incursions would seem to have been by the same aircraft, a Do17 of 3(F)/121, with someone a little too eager to sound the 'All Clear'! Strangely these nuisance raiders got away scot free. The next day, as noted elsewhere, N° 57 OTU's 'Battle Flight' from Hawarden was waiting … the result, one Do17 shot down into the sea off Rhyl and another damaged.

Daylight incursions deep into back areas in *Kette* (section) or *Staffel* (squadron) strength were rare, but according to eye-witnesses did happen. Almost certainly they were the early waves of enemy aircraft moving on to targets in the Liverpool, Manchester and Crewe areas just before dusk. Such raids involved a 5–6 hour round trip and bombing runs over target areas were staggered to provide maximum dislocation and discomfiture. Thus on Wednesday, 4 September 1940 the historian must correlate three widely disparate reports which can relate only to the same event — that of fifteen Heinkel He111s maintaining perfect formation, seen at about 1945–2000hrs first over Oswestry, Shropshire, then Overton-on-Dee and a little later over Malpas as harvesters prepared to pack up for the day. They were a Manchester-bound detachment, although Liverpool is known to have been visited that same evening. It was not a major raid. In Greater Manchester these would begin with Salford on 2/3 October. It begins to dawn on the inhabitants of Shocklach that for some reason, almost as if signposted, Manchester 'traffic' diverged from the Merseyside-bound raiders right over their heads! (It is perhaps no coincidence that at the present time one of the main approach corridors into Manchester International Airport lies only a couple of miles west and north of the wartime flightpath preferred by the *Luftwaffe*.) But in 1940 the 'dog-leg' course was probably adopted either through the exigencies of *Knickebein* radio-beam navigation or the real need to miss the balloon barrages in the West Midlands and Crewe.

On this particular night comparatively little damage was inflicted and official appraisals suggest that there might have been a considerable number of enemy crews under training or being gently 'broken-in' for night bombing and attacks — not too dark to start with, please! But there was a sinister rider to the daily intelligence synopsis: 'Attacks may be expected against places where parachute flares have been dropped. That night flares were seen over the partially built Royal Ordnance Factory, Isycoed and Llay Main Colliery — the latter would be bombed on 30 September. The parachute flares gave rise to panic-stricken reports of parachutists seen along the Dee north of Worthenbury. A cold, wet and miserable night was spent by 'A' Company (Maelor) and 'F' and 'G' Companies (ROF) of the 7th Denbighshire/ Flintshire Home Guard combing the water meadows either side of the Dee, perhaps the only instance when this particular Home Guard unit operated in anything approaching battalion strength!

Even more damaging to morale was when these opportunist 'lone rangers' bombed military targets, especially RAF airfields which a deluded public fondly thought were there to protect them! One immediately thinks of the Lysanders of N° 13 Squadron, essentially Army co-operation aircraft, who moved to Speke from Hooton Park on 17 June 1940 and were forced to take off and fly out to sea as photographic reconnaissance missions triggered off alerts on Merseyside. The first bombs did not fall in the Liverpool area until 28 July 1940, but the region had experienced so many false 'Red Alerts' that morale was at a low ebb. On Friday, 17 November 1939 sirens had sounded over a wide area — Liverpool–Chester–Deeside–Colwyn Bay — all because of a single overflying marauder. It was the first real

test and the Civil Defence organisation was found wanting, mainly because congested telephone lines meant a delay in transmitting air raid warning messages from the Post Office to the Police sirens (and whistles!). After all the kerfuffle, sirens sounded at about 1122hrs and the 'Raiders Passed' ten minutes later! Time and time again it was a case of 'Cry Wolf!' One never knew when it was going to be the real thing. So why were N° 13 Squadron's Lysanders standing neatly parked at Speke when the 'Red Alert' had been given? At least they could look as if they were going to tackle the enemy! Just to take off and fly in formation down the estuary and across the Wirral was a great boost to the morale of city dwellers to whom there was little point in explaining that the Westland 'Lizzie', despite being armed with two fixed .303 machine guns forward and one manually operated in the the rear cockpit, as not exactly a front-line fighter! Small wonder the squadron was glad to return to Hooton Park on 13 July.

RAF Sealand was bombed twice (28 June and 14 August 1940) and RAF Hawarden once (14 November 1940). Just for two days, 11/12 July 1940, Sealand boasted its own squadron of Hurricane Is, but N° 79 Squadron did not fly in with the intention of providing defensive aircover for this part of the north-west. The unit had been heavily involved in the Battle of Britain, flying from Biggin Hill and Hawkinge. It was now being rested at a relatively quieter 'back-area' station — Acklington in Northumberland. Either the move north was being made in two stages with Sealand as a staging post, or there was some delay in N° 152 Squadron's Spitfires vacating Acklington for Warmwell, Dorset. RAF Hooton Park was splattered by 'stray' bombs during any major raid on Merseyside. RAF Shawbury 'copped it' on the nights of 25 June and 5/25 September. Out on the Llyn peninsula RAF Penrhos had been bombed on 9 July and would be again on 2–4 and 9–10 October. The visitation of 4 October cratered the landing ground, demolished flight offices, and badly damaged the main hangar and workshops. That between 1810–1850hrs on Wednesday, 9 October, peppered the airfield with over 30 HE and IBs, again damaging hangars (and the station CO's office!).

The surprise is that these airfields did not receive more attention, since the written briefs for raids on Liverpool invariably included the following information:

Alternative Targets (*Sonstiges*):
    4km to the south lies Liverpool seaplane anchorage (*Seeflughafen*)
    9.8km SE lies Liverpool-Speke airbase (*Fliegerhorst*)
    11km SSE lies Liverpool-Hooton Park airbase
    19km to the south lies Sealand airbase.

Although regularly photographed by *Luftwaffe* reconnaissance from 18 September 1940 onwards, RAF Hawarden had yet to to be included in *Luftwaffe* Intelligence operational directives — but they soon made up for this omission. These particular raids were carried out under cover of darkness, not in the least German aircrews being helped by the aerodromes lit up like Christmas trees for night flying.

On the other hand the sneak-bombing of RAF Tern Hill was carried out by a solitary Junkers Ju88 in broad daylight, at 0721hrs on Wednesday, 16 October 1940 — the correct date, although some histories give a Sunday. There would also appear to be some conflicting evidence as to the exact type of German raider. The valedictory history of Tern Hill aerodrome, written in 1976 when the RAF relinquished control of the airfield to the Army, has the following eye-witness account of the incident:

We had N° 29 Squadron, Blenheim night-fighters, operating here at the time. On returning after a long night sortie it was usual for them to 'beat-up' the Station before landing. On this particular morning I heard what I thought was a Blenheim returning and, being very keen on aircraft recognition, rushed out to see it land. As the aircraft flew overhead, I realised that it was a Junkers Ju88. It came in low at about 250ft from the south-east and flew over the airfield. I was standing outside a hut on the south-west side of the Station at the time, and realising what was about to happen, rushed into the hut and yelled that there was a raid on. Very few people believed me at the time and stared at me as if I was joking!

By this time the Ju88 had turned and was beginning its bombing run. It released a stick of high-explosive and incendiary bombs on the south-west side of the Station in line with the three main hangars. The first bomb fell between the two most easterly hangars, destroying the old wooden tower that had been intended as a bombing trainer. The remaining bombs were far more destructive, smashing through the roof of the most easterly main hangar. They hit the concrete floor and then bounced back into the roof again before exploding. The

subsequent fire and blast damage was disastrous. The roof and the upper part of the walls of the hangar were completely demolished, leaving only the flight offices around the base intact.

At least eight Ansons and two Blenheims aircraft which were in the hangar at the time were also totally destroyed. Still watching in a dazed fashion, I saw the Ju88 climb slightly and after a tight turn begin a strafing run across the messes and domestic quarters. By this time everyone had realised what was happening and were frantically taking cover. Luckily the strafing was quickly cut short so that only superficial structural damage was done. Making another tight turn, the Ju88 flew off low and fast towards Newport. Only a pall of black smoke and silence remained'.

Servicemen were on early morning parade and N° 24 MU's civilian workforce were reporting for the day shift. It took several long moments for the penny to drop — and then the wild surge to take cover. It was a miracle that that there were no casualties apart from a store-keeper knocked unconscious by flying debris. The aerodrome's defences were unmanned — lessons had obviously not been learnt from the Shawbury and Sealand debacles of the previous June or from earlier attempts to bomb Tern Hill itself. On

This aerial photograph of RAF Tern Hill, taken in October 1942, shows the burnt out hangar (A) and its temporary replacement, a Bellman hangar (B).

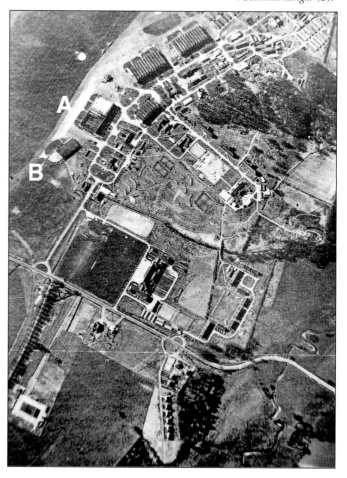

The remains of the hangar wrecked by enemy bombs on 15 October 1940 were removed post-war and the damaged office and stores area which ran alongside the hangar can be seen in the centre of this photograph. Note the 'temporary' Bellman still in situ in 2000. In his biography, Reg Miles recalls working at No 34 MU Monkmoor and being called to RAF Tern Hill to remove some twenty Avro Ansons from a hangar. He thought they were being transferred to another airfield but, when he got there, he found them all burnt out. It looked like an elephants graveyard, with just the steel tubing frames connected to melted engines and propellors standing neatly in two long rows'.

23/24 July a stick of ten HE bombs had straddled the A41 alongside the aerodrome and on 29 August some 70 HE and IBs landed in a wide arc outside the perimeter fence! This last raid was incidental to the sustained four-day *Blitz* on Merseyside, during which Shropshire towns — Bridgnorth, Shrewsbury, Bishop's Castle, Craven Arms — and Wrexham and its tributary villages were given their first taste of aerial warfare.

Conflictingly, some eye-witnesses suggest that the intruder was not a Ju88 but a Dormer Do17, the 'Flying Pencil' with twin fin and rudder assembly, an unmistakable silhouette. It may well have been, for some twenty plus Do17s of *KüFlGr* 606, operating that night out of Brest/Lanvéoc naval base, did in fact attack Birmingham. Tern Hill would have offered an easy alternative target for an opportunist German crew. Ostensibly a coastal reconnaissance and minelaying unit, KüFlGr 606 was increasingly integrated into the normal bombing operations of IV *Fliegerkorps*, but not without loss. The previous Friday, by some strange coincidence, the unit had lost three Do17s to the guns of Nᵒ 611 Squadron's Spitfires on a 9-week detachment to RAF Penrhos as a forward base to Tern Hill, where a flight was on loan from RAF Digby (Nᵒ 12 Group) to provide the only daylight cover for Nᵒ 9 Group's as yet non-operational Tern Hill sector. On the same Wednesday evening *KüFlGr* 606 would lose two more aircraft as they sortied to attack Liverpool, one of them coming to grief in poor visibility on a hillside at Nantglyn, near Denbigh. The latter is frequently held responsible for the Tern Hill bombing, but the times, assuming that they are accurate, do not support such an attribution. There is a much better candidate for the honour the lone-ranger that, the very same morning (as noted above), had machine-gunned the goods train standing in the passing loop at Yockleton station.

All this notwithstanding, forty years on, a serving RAF officer could at last legitimately beg the question why the dawn intruder was never intercepted, and permitted to return safely to base. A partial answer immediately suggests itself. Not only was Tern Hill sector (Nᵒ 9 Group, Fighter Command) not yet operational, but the 'borrowed' daylight rapid response force nominally stationed at Tern Hill, namely a flight of Nᵒ 611 Squadron's Spitfires, had been moved in its entirety on 12 October to patrol RAF Penrhos, Caernarfonshire. As noted above the latter station had suffered no less than five hit-and-run raids in the first ten days of October. It was a matter of quickly re-assessing priorities. But on 21 October, following the bombing of Tern Hill, a section of three Spitfires had perforce return thence — a real case of trying to spread too few defensive resources too far. With hindsight, these precautions were unnecessary as the *Luftwaffe* never attacked Penrhos again. On 21 December Nᵒ 611 Squadron finally withdrew from Penrhos and Tern Hill to make ready for the unit move from Digby to Rochford, Essex.

Nᵒ 611 Squadron had been preceded at Tern Hill by a detachment of Nᵒ 46 Squadron's Hurricanes. This unit, too, was stationed at Digby from 13 June–31 August with a sortie south to Duxford on Sunday, 18 August to meet the massed formations of the *Luftwaffe* on what was their final attempt to destroy Fighter Command within Goering's promised seven days! But it was a shadow of the squadron that had left Digby for the Narvik battle zone on 9 May 1940. Four weeks later, on 8 July, Nᵒ 46 Squadron's ten surviving Hurricanes and eight of its pilots, lay at the bottom of the North Sea after the aircraft-carrier HMS *Glorious*, upon which they had earlier embarked, had been intercepted and sunk by the German surface raider *Scharnhorst*. Survivors re-grouped at Digby where it worked up to full strength and was operational again by 25 June, flying mainly night patrols with the occasional daylight scramble. It was one of Tern Hill flight's Hurricanes that on 5 August 1940 mistakenly attacked a Whitley V, N1411, of Nᵒ 10 OTU Abingdon on a night NAVEX up the Welsh border and on to the Isle of Man. The Whitley was not seriously damaged and none of the crew were hit. But discretion was better than valour and N1411 made a forced landing at Squire's Gate to effect running repairs and await the dawn!

One commentator would claim that 'a bomb or mine' demolished the Tern Hill hangar. Others are more precise — 'four 250kg bombs and heavy incendiaries' or 'four 250kg bombs and several containers of incendiaries' or, as quoted above, 'a stick of HE and IBs'. The German *Luftminen* or 'land mines' as they were known to the British, were of 500kg or 1,000kg. They would be beyond the carrying capacity of both Ju88 and Do17 in the context of the varying reports of the Tern Hill raid, although some parachute mines carried up to thirty-six 1kg incendiaries in the tail, to be thrown out on impact to start fires over a large area. But this fits neither the description of 'heavy incendiaries' (presumably the 2kg *Brandbomben*) or 'containers of IBs', that is, missile containers carrying anything from 10–70 IBs which would be released at any predetermined height by a small burster charge. The internal bomb load of a Dornier Do17 was 1,000kg, so possibly, despite its distinctive shape and the conviction of several eye-witnesses, this type of aircraft may not have been able to deliver the mixed bomb load noted in the various narratives. On the other hand the pay-load of a Junkers Ju88 was 1,500kg. It was therefore capable of dropping any of the various combinations of HE and IBs noted above. But there is still a nagging doubt as to whether several dependent eye-witnesses could all have been mistaken in the grey light of an autumn about something as distinctive as the shape and outline of a 'Flying Pencil'.

The aircraft lost or damaged in the Tern Hill bombing belonged either to Nᵒ 10 SFTS, the home flying training establishment, or Nᵒ 6 SFTS, then based at Little Rissington (Gloucestershire), with Ansons N5305 and N9723 possibly having flown in on exercise or were temporarily at Nᵒ 24 MU. Hitherto Nᵒ 10 SFTS training aircraft had been largely hangared as protection from the elements, but following the raid of 16 October most of the serviceable aircraft were dispersed around the airfield perimeter — nothing like shutting the stable door after the horse had bolted! Even in front-line 'back areas', with airfields 'in season' on an opportunity basis, the decision possibly should have been taken earlier, certainly in the wake of the most spectacular onslaught on any British aerodrome, the 30-second attack by two Ju88s on Brize Norton airfield on 16 August, when two similar 'C' Type hangars were destroyed and a staggering 36 aircraft of N° 6 MU, 2 SFTS, 15 SFTS wasted. Final write-offs would boost the total to forty-six!

It would appear that twelve months into the war some lessons were only slowly, if ever, learnt. As already noted it was RAF Hawarden's turn on the night of Thursday, 14 November and on 27 April 1941 RAF Shawbury would be bombed yet again (but for the last time as it turned out). The Hawarden raid was overshadowed by the great raid that same night which tore the heart out of the city of Coventry. As part of Operation *Mondschein Serenade Korn* ('Moonlight Seranade Corn' — *Korn* being the German code-word for Coventry), while the city was attacked by some 449 aircraft of *Luftflotten* 2 and 3, nineteen aircraft of *Luftflotte* 3 made diversionary raids elsewhere. Hawarden and the Royal Ordnance Factory Wrexham lay across the path of one of these. A nicely lit up airfield and a partly built ROF under contractor's floodlighting was a fair exchange for the guns and balloons of the Merseyside GDA! To rub salt into wounds there was not even a 'Yellow Alert' in the Deeside and Wrexham Police Divisions. Not that this mattered much. The events of the last three months had shown that Fighter Command the guns of AA Command were next to useless at night.

The Flintshire Police records time the Hawarden raid at 2200hrs but this is 'message received' time. Bombs actually fell on the aerodrome at 2005hrs, about the same time as the first wave of Pathfinder Heinkels of KGr100 and KG55 were leaving Coventry. Nineteen HE and some 300–350 IBs fell on the airfield and N° 48 MU's hangars and dispersals. Another five HE fell at Well House Farm, just beyond the MU's N° 3 Site. Both hangars on the main MU site the other side of the railway from Cop Farm received direct hits, seriously damaging eight aircraft inside and two more parked outside. Eighteen further aircraft received varying degrees

Blenheim V5495	Magister L8074, P6397,
Botha L6125, L6164	T9965, V1012, V1013
Henley L3306	Master L5941, T9966, T9967
Hereford N9062	Roc L3098
Magister P6397	Wellington N2988, R1037,
Hurricane P2919	R1140, R1333
Lysander L4808, R2629,	
R2639, R9073, R9114	

of repairable damage:

This listing provides a random cross-section of N° 48 MU's activities as an aircraft storage facility and acceptance test centre. Here, too, specialist RAF equipment such as radio, long-range tanks, was installed. The Blackburn Rocs were destined for the Royal Navy, the Lysanders for India and Near East, the Hereford for conversion to a Hampden, and the Wellingtons for operational squadrons and OTUs at Benson and Finningley. R1333 was a 'named' bomber, the *Broughton Wellington*, having been subscribed for by the work-force at the Vickers-Armstrong factory, the other occupier of Hawarden aerodrome. It had only been accepted and 'launched' on 7 November. As seen elsewhere, it would come to an inglorious end with N° 99 Squadron at

Newmarket on 18 December 1940 whilst taking off on a raid on Ludwigshafen.

The building of Wrexham's ROF had commenced on 8 October 1939. The late Mr Tom Percival, Gwersyllt, was working on the excavation, embanking and camouflaging the great 'nitro-glycerine hills' on what was Cacca Dutton Farm, when the stick of 10 HE bombs fell just outside the perimeter fence, causing some slight damage to the windows of the pub and cottages at Ridley Wood. The last HE came quite close, and in Tom's words: 'I took cover in a shallow manhole and my mate dived under an upturned skip …' News of both bombings was suppressed, or perhaps stood little chance against the yardage given over to the flattening of Coventry. But somehow William Joyce, better known as Lord Haw Haw, and drawing upon his obviously detailed personal knowledge of the Wrexham–Llangollen region, could not resist bragging the following night on the radio about the destruction of Wrexham ROF.

Whilst the Tern Hill incident did not find its way into the national or local papers, or even into the Prime Minister's Daily Appreciation Report, it would not be just to spare the blushes of 'top brass' caught napping. Churchill himself was so worried about the effect on morale of the land mine as a weapon that he personally ordered the Air Ministry, War Office, and Ministries of Home Security and Information: 'No disclosure should be made of the severity of effect, in public estimation, of these mines …' The faintest suspicion that a parachute mine might have been dropped at Tern Hill was sufficient for the strictest news black-out to be imposed, although the bombing, inevitably, was all the talk in pubs and the High Street. Hence the conflicting reports that yet circulate - an essential part of the region's oral history. For the record the N° 10 SFTS Ansons destroyed or badly damaged included:

K6294	K6295	K8728	L7061
L7068	N5040	N5280	N5328
N5329	N9570	N9684	N9769
N9544	R3412	R3449	

A N° 10 SFTS North American Harvard, N7075, often cited as as a victim of the bomb blast, had actually been damaged in an earlier flying accident in August, and was undergoing repair by N° 24 MU, later to be shipped out to Southern Rhodesia, ending its training days with N° 20 SFTS at Grandbourne.

Two Blenheims belonging to N° 29 Squadron, Digby, on nightly detachment to Tern Hill as the sole night-fighter defence of the north-west, were also badly damaged or destroyed. Only three days earlier, on 13 October, Blenheim K7135 had been one a pair set upon by three Hurricanes of N° 312 (Czech) Squadron, Speke, whilst patrolling off the Point of Ayr, Flintshire. Blenheim L6637 was shot down into the sea and its crew killed. K7135, damaged almost beyond repair, limped back to Tern Hill — with a very subdued and contrite fighter escort — only to be given the *coup de grace* by a German bomb a couple of days later! The second Blenheim, L6741, although damaged by the blast, was repaired on site and eventually relegated to N° 54 OTU at Church Fenton.

After these incidents N° 29 Squadron crews must have viewed with some trepidation their nocturnal forays to hold the fort in the Tern Hill sector. The detachment, varying from 2–4 Blenheims, moved to RAF Cranage for night-fighter duties under N° 9 Group control on 1 December 1940, remaining there until relieved on 18 December by the Hurricanes of N° 96 Squadron which, apart from N° 307 (Polish) Squadron forming at Jurby, was the first purpose-raised night-fighter squadron in the north-west. But even at Cranage N° 29 Squadron aircraft seemed fated. On 3 December 1940 Blenheim K7172 came to grief at Woolley Bridge, near Mottram, Cheshire, whilst providing homing practice for local R/T and D/F stations.

12. Empathy — the pilots

Historic ties between border people and the Army would remain firm throughout the war. Wrexham people related to the Royal Welch Fusiliers (now four battalions strong) and the various units such as the Royal Marine Commandos that flitted in and out of the Hermitage Camp. Stemming from First World War service with Lord Kenyon's regiment, the Welsh Horse, peacetime Maelor had forged strong links with the Cheshire and Shropshire Yeomanries, strengthened upon mobilisation. Across the border the King's Shropshire Light Infantry and the Cheshire Regiment claimed the loyalties of their respective county towns and their satellites. It was only as new events took centre stage that these garrison towns forsook some of their traditional insularity and in a common war effort began to identify with other branches of the armed forces.

But it was a slow process. Despite the increasing frequency with which Allied aircraft fell out of border skies, the high-profile work of N° 34 MU in picking up the pieces, and the seeming impunity with which German raiders trundled up 'Adolf's Railway' en route to Crewe, Manchester and Merseyside, strict censorship and precautions on the ground made it difficult for most people to relate to, and gain a clear understanding of, events in the civil and military aviation world. This would change dramatically when, in August/September 1940, Liverpool's war touched them personally and, as an apparent direct consequence, a N° 9 Group fighter station began to take shape on the outskirts of Wrexham, closely followed by N° 92 Group airfields at Tilstock and Sleap and N° 81 Group aerodromes at Rednal, Montford Bridge and Poulton.

Apart from military service and essential and voluntary war work the public's increasing involvement in the war effort may be accurately gauged by their response to the various National Savings appeals, raising funds for specific purposes — from the creaking fumbling beginnings of the Spitfire Appeal in August/September 1940, through to the more efficiently organised 'Lend to Win' or War Weapons Week (October/November 1940), Battleship Weeks (1941/2), Wings for Victory Week (July 1943), and Salute the Soldier Campaign in April/May 1944.

There may have been a more effective spur to patriotic endeavour, and a much needed boost given to morale in the darkest months of the war, if the censor had permitted the inhabitants of Wrexham to know that, flying dangerously and defying the *Luftwaffe* on almost clandestine operations, was an RAF Whitley bomber-cum-civil passenger/cargo plane that to all intents and purposes was named *Wrexham* after the custom of the civil airlines of the period. Until superseded by more powerful aircraft the *Wrexham* did stirling work on the perilous and exposed Whitchurch (Bristol)–Gibraltar–Malta and Leuchars (Scotland)–Stockholm routes across enemy controlled territory and skies.

The Armstrong Whitworth Whitley was essentially a military aircraft, but a number also saw service in a civil rôle. With the Vickers Wellington and Handley Page Hampden the Whitley was one of the mainstays of Bomber Command in the early years of the war. It was used mainly as a night bomber. Many will recall its leaflet dropping raids (Nickelling) over the Ruhr, Hamburg and Bremen on the first night of the war. (Lingering even more vividly in ageing memories is the picture of a group of excited teenagers waving frantically at an anonymous Whitley lumbering slowly over the Eagles Meadow, Wrexham — to be rewarded by some unusual 'Nickel' from the tail-gunner's turret, a shower of used toilet paper that came fluttering down over the Smithfield area of Wrexham!). On 19/20 March 1940 Whitleys dropped the first bombs to fall on German soil during the Second World War in an attack on the mine-laying seaplane base at Hörnum on the Island of Sylt. This was in direct retaliation for the inadvertant bombing of some Orkney crofts during a *Luftwaffe* raid on Scapa Flow on 16 March when 27-year old Jim Isbister became the first civilian casualty from enemy action over Great Britain. Great was the satisfaction over the Hörnum raid expressed not only in Parliament but also in the national press and local papers everywhere.

Whitleys were the first British bombers to visit Berlin (on a leaflet raid) on 1/2 October 1939, and also the first to attack targets in Italy (Genoa and Turin) in June 1940. They were retired from Bomber Command front-line early in 1942, yet were still in production for OTUs and were trialled to fill a gap in the civil air service. The British Overseas Airways Corporation (BOAC) had few aircraft that could carry worthwhile payloads over considerable distances, especially on the Bristol–Gibraltar–Malta–Egypt route. The Consolidated Liberator could not be spared from the Trans-Atlantic Return Ferry Service (flying ferry pilots to Canada to collect and fly back American aircraft for the RAF) and Coastal Command patrols. Hence the fall-back in April 1942 on twelve brand-new Whitleys straight off the production line at Baginton, Coventry.

It was still the custom to give BOAC aircraft individual names. The twelve new Whitleys were to be named after British towns beginning with the letter 'W' and having two syllables. (The 'W' and three syllables were being reserved

One of the named BOAC Whitleys which ran the gauntlet of the Luftwaffe *out over the Bay of Biscay.* [Flight]

for the Vickers Armstrong Wellingtons that BOAC were hoping to operate later in 1942). The names chosen for the Whitleys were *Warwick, Wakefield, Wareham, Watford, Weymouth, Whitley, Wigan, Windsor, Witney, Woolwich* and *Wrexham*. The *Wrexham*-to-be was registered as G-AGEC and delivered to Bristol in May 1942 where it was converted for civilian use by the removal of all gun-turrets, fitting extra-long-range fuel tanks in the bomb bay, and adapting the interior as a cargo hold. However, the name *Wrexham* was never painted on the fuselage; no doubt such trivial things were low on the list of priorities.

The UK–Gibraltar–Malta service began in May 1942, but by July it was obvious that the use of Whitleys was self-defeating since they were only carrying a 1,000lbs payload and using up Malta's precious fuel supplies for the return journey. BOAC's Lockheed Hudsons on the Leuchars–Stockholm run were transferred to the Gibraltar route, being replaced in August 1942 by four Whitleys including G-AGEC (*Wrexham*). The Stockholm run was important for diplomatic mail and ball bearings! But again the Whitleys were found unsuitable due to a tendency to ice up and for their Merlin engines to overheat. On October 1942 Whitley G-AGEC was transferred to the Bristol–Shannon run. But between January and May 1943 most of them were recalled to OTUs, a relative failure in civilian operations, but *Wrexham* remained on BOAC's books until struck off charge on 15 December 1944.

In common with the rest of the country Wrexham people were moved by the heroic efforts of 'the Few' in the Battle of Britain. As 'the Battle' increased in intensity and ferocity the border rode the ground swell of popular reaction. *Ad hoc* fundraising machinery creaked into action to raise money for replacement aircraft, but little could be done about the more serious pilot wastage save sorrow in due course as attenuated funeral or 'missing in action' reports filtered into the columns of the local press. The 'Initial Skirmishes' period (10 July–12 August 1940) saw 127 British aircraft lost; the 'Assault on the Airfields' (13 August–6 September) 385 aircraft; the 'Attack on London' (7 September–1 October) 241 aircraft, and in the final period as recognized by British historians, the 'Night Blitz and Tip-and-Run Raids' (1 October–1 November), another 152 aircraft were lost. Inevitably local airmen were to be numbered amongst those who lost their lives during these four crucial months. Many had established lasting friendships and relationships during

their months of training at Sealand, Shawbury or Tern Hill. Nothing served more to outrage local sensibilities and to steel resolve than the news of 'atrocities' committed against these men, friends and relatives.

The funeral of 25-year old Sqn/Ldr Harold Morley Starr was widely reported in the Wrexham papers. He had been a frequent visitor to the area and had turned out for local cricket teams. In January 1940 he had married the daughter of Mr H. R. Rees, Gardden Hall, Ruabon. H. M. Starr had joined the RAF in March 1934 on a short service commission and trained at RAF Sealand between April 1934 and March 1935. Posted to N° 13 Squadron at Old Sarum he survived a serious crash in Hawker Audax K2028 on 5 June 1936. In July 1940, after a short stint as a flying instructor on Hurricanes at N° 6 OTU, Sutton Bridge, he went to N° 245 Squadron at Aldergrove as supernumerary Squadron Leader, flying mainly convoy patrols. On 8 August he was given command of N° 253 Squadron then at Turnhouse, Midlothian, working-up in the relative calm of N° 13 Group after their ill-conceived incursion into France in the May. On Thursday, 29 August 1940, Sqn/Ldr Starr brought his command south to Kenley to join battle. On the Friday, one of the most savage days fighting to-date as the *Luftwaffe* turned its attention to N° 11 Group sector airfields, his Hurricane was badly damaged in combat over Redhill. He returned to base unhurt. On Saturday, 31 August, Sqn/Ldr Starr was dead. Whilst on an interception patrol his Hurricane (L1830) was shot down by a Me Bf109. Starr managed to bale out, but was machine-gunned by another Bf109 on the way down. His lifeless body fell to earth at Hammill Brickworks, Eastry (near Sandwich), while L1830 piled in at Grove Ferry.

A lot of propaganda points were scored as incidents such as this became public knowledge. Yet in the cold dispassionate world of air combat such deeds made sense — a dead pilot would not fly again the next day! Self-appointed 'avengers' were also found in the RAF, especially in Allied squadrons whose fliers had experienced at first hand the German occupation of their homeland. The neat but messy dissection of a German parachutist by the propellor of a Polish Spitfire was not unknown in N° 11 Group skies!

In September 1940 Mold went into mourning as news was received of the death of P/O Paul John Davies-Cooke, scion of the ancient family of Gwysaney. His Spitfire I, N3068 of N° 72 Squadron, Biggin Hill, had been shot down by a Me Bf109 in combat over Sevenoaks at 0940hrs on

Friday, 27 September 1940. He managed to bale out but fell dead near Hayes station. The Spitfire crashed onto two houses in West Wickham (east of Croydon). F/O Davies-Cooke lies buried in the family plot in St John's Churchyard, Rhydymwyn. A product of Shrewsbury School and Trinity College, Cambridge, P. J. Davies-Cooke, like so many sons of north Wales gentry, had joined Nº 610 ('County of Chester') Squadron, AAF, based at Hooton Park, when it was still a designated day bomber squadron flying Harts and Hinds. He was commissioned P/O (AuxAF) on 1 July 1937, and on 18 December 1937 joined the RAF on a direct entry Permanent Commission. He was moved cross country to Nº 613 ('City of Manchester') Squadron, an Army co-operation unit based at Ringway and then Odiham, Hampshire.

On 26 May 1940 Nº 613 Squadron's ancient Hawker Hectors actually dive-bombed German gun emplacements encircling Calais! This was the last time RAF (as distinct from Fleet Air Arm) bi-planes ever dropped bombs on mainland Europe. The experience may have triggered off some latent schoolboyish ambition, for Davies-Cooke promptly volunteered for Fighter Command. He went on a Spitfire conversion course at Nº 7 OTU Hawarden in August 1940. On 3 September he was posted to his old squadron, Nº 610, now a fighter unit resting and re-equipping at Acklington, and thence to Nº 72 Squadron at Biggin Hill on 20 September. A week later he was dead, killed in repelling the day's first wave of London-bound enemy aircraft (some 80 bombers with 100 fighters) as they crossed the coast between Dover and Folkstone. Nº 72 Squadron lost another Spitfire and had one seriously damaged in a forced landing during the same encounter.

Because of the strict censorship incidents such as these were rarely reported in detail, if at all. How? when? where? the type of aircraft flown etc. was classified information. Yet, possibly because of local pride engendered by the great number of 'named' Spitfires *Wrexham, Colwyn Bay, Denbighshire, Flintshire I, II, III, Merionethshire* etc. — spawned by the first halting National Savings Campaigns of the war, the average person still believes that only the Spitfire and Hurricane of Fighter Command saved the day during the Battle of Britain. True, these familiar but perhaps over glamourised aircraft, were to the forefront in defending British skies, but one should not forget the Defiant, Beaufighter, Gladiator and even the humble Westland Lysander in their fighter rôles! At the same time Coastal Command Blenheims, Ansons, Bothas, Beauforts, Hudsons, Whitleys and sundry makes of flying-boats patrolled the seas and attacked the French and Belgian ports from whence would come the invasion. The latter duty, especially in September 1940, when invasion seemed imminent, was shared by a Bomber Command not yet the 'medium/heavy' attack force it was to become.

For obvious reasons the population of Wrexham could not appreciate such subtle differences or apportion credit where credit was due. The name of F/O Charles Robert Delauney Thomas, Nº 236 Squadron, appears in the list of aircrew who fought under the operational control of Fighter Command, only because for short periods his squadron did belong to that Command — on reforming from 31 October 1939 to 27 February 1940, and again between 23 April–4 July 1940. The rest of the time the squadron was part of Coastal Command until disbanded on 25 May 1945. Thomas had joined the RAF on a short service commission in June 1937 completing his training at Nº 10 FTS in September 1938. After 28 months with the FAA pool at Gosport he joined Nº 236 Squadron in January 1940.

In Coastal Command Nº 236 Squadron carried out escort, anti-shipping and reconnaissance missions. On 4 July the squadron quit Middle Wallop in Nº 10 Group for Thorney Island in Nº 16 Group. On 18 July three Blenheim 1(f)s of Nº 236 Squadron — rather ancient beasts with two-man crews — undertook to escort a photo-reconnaissance mission to Le Havre, an almost daily routine 'Traffic' sortie, observing shipping and road and rail movements in and around the port. The mission was hampered by deteriorating weather. Two of the Blenheims, L6639 and L6779, the latter piloted by F/O Thomas, were not seen again after they broke formation and entered low cloud and blanketing rain amidst heavy AA fire at Cap de la Hague, the northwestern extremity of the Cotentin Peninsula near Cherbourg. It would appear, too, that German naval surface vessels were more in evidence that day. However, *Luftwaffe* records credit *Hptm* W. Schnellmann of II/JG2 with shooting down L6779. F/O Thomas lies buried in Quiberville Churchyard. His WO/AG, Sgt H. D. B. Elsdon is remembered on the Runnymede memorial.

F/O Thomas was the elder son of Mr Charles Thomas, 'Cherry Hill', Borras, who ran a gentleman's outfitters in Regent Street, Wrexham. The local papers carried successive 'Missing' and 'Presumed Killed' reports, but failed to make any association with the great air battle currently raging. The family suffered a second bereavement when their younger son, P/O Anthony Delauney Thomas, was killed in action on 7 March 1941, flying Wellingtons with the detachment of Nº 37 Squadron, Middle East Air Force, that had just arrived at Menidi, Greece, for operations over Albania. P/O Thomas lies buried in Pheleron Cemetery near Athens. Such a loss was partly assuaged by Mr and Mrs Thomas throwing open 'Cherry Hill', a delightful suburban house built in 1936 in the Edwardian Arts and Crafts idiom of Baillie Scott, to the officers of RAF Wrexham, just up the road, as a quiet retreat or club. This was a much appreciated facility especially for those squashed into the requisitioned farmhouse and out-buildings at Borras Lodge! Officer accommodation and messing on the airfield was not finally completed until May 1942 when billeting out ceased — except for the Station Commander who still had his comfortable little farmhouse in Cefn Road, Wrexham!

The gung-ho attitude that newspaper editors looked for in RAF pilots was perhaps best personified by two Shropshire men. The courteous apology for unavoidable absence by Sir Richard Tihel Leighton, Loton Park, Alberbury, to the South Shropshire Hunt meeting at Shawbury on Saturday, 29 June 1940, seems to have been syndicated to almost every local and provincial newspaper! Sir Richard was a First World War veteran, having joined the RFC in 1916. He had been wounded over Courtrai on 17 August 1917, with Nº 56 Sqn, further injured as his SE5a

One of 'The Few', a Shropshire lad in the Battle of Britain.
Eric Lock (left) with W. G. G. Duncan Smith and M. Gilmour.
The fourth pilot is unidentified.

(B514) crashed, and he was made a POW. In peace-time he had risen to become (1932–7) Commanding Officer of the Shropshire Yeomanry, with the rank of Brevet Colonel. Now he had again answered his country's call and, at 47 years of age, had been commissioned as a P/O in the RAFVR! He ended the war as Squadron-Leader.

But the nation needed heroes and all eyes were on 'Sawn-off Lockie', from Bomere, near Shrewsbury, otherwise F/Lt Eric Stanley Lock, DSO, DFC and bar, dubbed by *Life* magazine as 'Britain's greatest air ace of the War'. He was with Nº 611 Squadron, Hornchurch, when he lost his life on 3 August 1941 whilst on a fighter sweep over northern France. He was last seen in a diving attack on a column of German troops on the march. He was just 22 years old.

During his earlier attachment to Nº 41 Squadron P/O Lock claimed 22 enemy aircraft destroyed with eight 'probables'. After three weeks 'rest and recuperation' at Catterick the squadron moved south again to Hornchurch on 3 September 1940. They were soon in the thick of it. At the end of the month P/O Lock was awarded the DFC after shooting down nine enemy machines (three in one day, eight in one week). By the end of October, when he was awarded a bar to the DFC, he had raised his tally to fifteen 'certain' and several 'probables'. On 9 December he was awarded the DSO '… in recognition of the gallantry displayed in flying operations against the enemy. P/O Lock showed exceptional keenness and courage in his attacks when engaged last month with his squadron in attacking a superior number of enemy forces. He destroyed two Messerschmitt Bf109s, bringing his total to at least 22. His magnificent fighting spirit and personal example have been in the highest traditions of the service'. Thus runs the official citation. Small wonder that, as 'local boy made good', his few precious leaves were taken up with PR and morale-boosting lectures, factory tours etc. in Shrewsbury and the surrounding villages, and with the launching of the county's Spitfire Appeal.

The records of the concentrated air fighting in the summer of 1940 are not a little confused and contemporary claims and casualty figures have since been drastically revised as official documents on both sides have come under scrutiny. For the period 8–23 August 1940 the RAF claimed 755 German aircraft 'definitely destroyed'; actual figure (taken from the *Luftwaffe* Quartermaster General's returns) should read 403 aircraft destroyed, 127 damaged. For the bitterest period of fighting (24 August–6 September) the RAF claimed 643 destroyed; as against an actual 378 destroyed, 115 damaged. Similarly, for the period 7–27 September German losses of 435 destroyed, 161 damaged must be set against the RAF's claim of 846. Five times during the Battle of Britain the Air Ministry claimed over 100 German aircraft destroyed in one day. On no occasion did the *Luftwaffe* lose more than 100 aircraft in one day; only on four occasions did they lose more than 50 (15 and 18 August, 15 and 27 September). Now celebrated annually as Battle of Britain Day, Sunday, 15 September 1940 was remarkable for the total of German aircraft claimed. A nation was given a much need shot in the arm as it tuned in to the BBC's evening news bulletin and heard '185 enemy aircraft were shot down'. P/O Lock was concerned in the destruction of six of them. As he himself said afterwards, 'It was the best party I can remember'. Fifty years on, the actual German losses on that day — 61 machines — makes poor reading for aviation historian and layman alike.

The fact that there were far more claims submitted by RAF pilots than aircraft destroyed is not surprising. Isolated one-to-one engagements generally offered no problems, but with several pilots attacking an enemy formation one might see an aircraft fall away and each assume it to be their victim. At night flashes from return gunfire, exhaust flames as throttles were opened in evasive action, or even jettisoned bombs exploding on the ground were often misconstrued as an aircraft fatally hit as an attack was pressed home. Of Lock's two Heinkel 111s, both from 7/KG53 at Lille, shot down on 5 September whilst on sortie to the Thameshaven oil storage depôt, the first, He111 (W.Nr.2632) **A1+GR**, was also claimed by three Hurricanes of Nº 17 Squadron (Debden) and Nº 73 Squadron straying over from Castle Camps (Cambridgeshire). The second He111, (W.Nr.3338) **A1+CR**, was additionally claimed by both Nºs 17 and 73 Squadrons (the latter's CO no less) and a couple of AA batteries. Similarly, in retrospect, Lock has to share an Me Bf 109 of 6/LG2, downed on 14 September whilst on an escort sortie to London, with two Spitfires from Nº 72 Squadron which had just moved into Biggin Hill from Croydon.

The Lock Achievement

(a) with N° 41 Squadron at Catterick (> 2 September 1940)

Thursday, 15 August 1940 (flying Spitfire I R6885)
Over Bishop Auckland: Messerschmitt Bf110D **(M8+EK)** of 2/ZG76, long range fighter escort to KG26 in attacks on east coast airfields; in dog fight also claimed by pilots of N°ˢ 72 and 79 Sqns. Such was the damage inflicted on *Luftflotte* 5 (crossing the north Sea from Scandinavian bases) that this day was referred to as *Schwarzer Donnerstag* — 'Black Thursday'.

(b) with N° 41 Squadron at Hornchurch (3 September 1940>22 February 1941)

Thursday, 5 September 1940 (flying Spitfire I N3162)
Over West Malling–Ashford: Messerschmitt Bf 109E-4 of JG3
Over Kent: Messerschmitt Bf 109E-4 JG3 - probable
Over Isle of Sheppey: Messerschmitte Bf 109E-4 of JG53 & two He111 or Ju88
A busy day for N° 11 Group, Fighter Command, with three main waves of 70 (0935hrs), 50 1500hrs) and 50 (1530hrs). The Bf 109s provided a fighter escort for bombers making for Isle of Sheppey, east Kent and Thames estuary. At 1530hrs Lock was slightly wounded in the left leg by fire from an escort 'during the destruction of an He111. N3162 was also damaged and after repair by Heston Aircraft Ltd. would find its way to N° 57 OTU, Hawarden.
In the event the two bombers claimed were Heinkel He111s of 7/KG53:
Heinkel He111H-3 (*Wrk. Nr. 3338*) **A1+CR** was hit by AA fire before being attacked by Lock and F/O Count M. B. Czerin (N° 17 Sqn) and Sgt J. J. Brember (N° 73 Sqn). Ditched in the sea off the Nore. Two crew picked up by RN patrol boat; three presumed drowned.
Heinkel He 111H-2 (*Wrk.Nr. 2632*) **A1+GR** was attacked by many pilots including Lock. and Sgt C. A. Chew and F/O Czerin (N° 17 Sqn) and S/Ldr M. W. S. Robinson (N° 73 Sqn)

Friday, 6 September 1940
Behind Calais: Junkers Ju88A-5
Identified as Ju88 (*Wrk.Nr. 8078*) **F1+DP** of 6/KG76. Force-landed at Evreux, following bombing sortie over Thames estuary aerodromes and refineries. No crew casualties. Damage state not recorded.

Monday, 9 September 1940 (flying Spitfire I X4325)
Over Maidstone and south London: Two Messerschmitt Bf109E & Messerschmitt Bf 109E
One main attack during daylight — from 1430hrs 400+ aircraft crossed Kent coast making for London and Thames estuary. Bf 109s of JG27 and JG53 escort bombers of KG1, KG30 and KG53. The *Luftwaffe* lost some 43 aircraft this day, compared with RAF claims for 52 destroyed, 11 probables and 13 damaged.

Wednesday, 11 September 1940 (flying Spitfire I R6610)
Over Maidstone: Messerschmitt Bf 110 & Junkers Ju88
The *Luftwaffe* did not lose a Ju88 in combat this day and Lock's claim for a Ju88 resolves itself into that for a He111, namely Heinkel He111H-4 (*Wrk.Nr.6962*) **1H+AH** of 1/KG26 lost on a sortie to bomb Woolwich Arsenal. It crashed at Cripps Corner, Sedlesdombe and its bomb load exploded. Three crew captured unhurt. This was part of a force of 250+ aircraft which crossed into Kent between 1545-1645hrs. The escorting Bf 110 may have been Messerschmitt Bf 110C-3 (*Wrk.Nr.1372*) **U8+HL** of 2/ZG26 which suffered failure of one engine and lost formation. It was attacked by several British fighters, the remaining engine being put out of action. It was again attacked and seriously damaged, eventually force-landing at Cobham Farm, Charing, *c.*1700hrs.

Saturday, 14 September 1940 (flying Spitfire R6610)
Over Hornchurch: Messerschmitt Bf 109Es
RAF figures give 16 E/A destroyed, 3 probables 12 damaged. The Luftwaffe sctually lost some 21 aircraft from all causes; only 6 from combat, 5 of which were Bf 109s. Two of these struggled back to France and crash-landed, and the remaining three are attributed to N°ˢ 72, 222, 253 and 603 Sqns. Lock is provisionally give a third share in Bf 109E-7 (*Wrk.Nr.2014*) **+I** of 6/LG2, which crashed at Tennant Wood, New Street Farm, Great Chart.

Sunday, 15 September 1940 (flying Spitfire I X4409)
Over London: Messerschmitt Bf 109E
Over France: Dornier Do17
Traditionally the climax to the Battle of Britain. RAF claim 188 E/A destroyed, 45 probables, 78 damaged. The *Luftwaffe* admits the loss of 79 inccluding 30 Do17s from KG2 (12), KG3 (10) and KG 76 (8) all of which were lost by either AA fire and/or multi-engagements by fighters from N°ˢ 1 (RCAF), 19, 41, 46, 66, 92, 110, 229, 242, 249, 253, 257, 310, 504, 602, 605, 607, 609, and 611 Sqns. N° 41 Squadron's Dornier, Do 17Z-3 (*Wrk.Nr.2881*) **5K+CM** of 4/KG3 is attributed to F/Lt E. N. Ryder and F/O J. G. Boyle as well as pilots from N°ˢ 310 and 603 Sqns. It was first damaged by AA fire as it bombed railway targets along the Thames.

Wednesday, 18 September 1940 (flying Spitfire I X4338)
Over east Kent: Messerschmitt Bf 109E probable
Over Gravesend: Messerschmitt Bf 109E & Messerschmitt Bf 109E probable
RAF claimed E/A: 46 destroyed, 15 probable, 19 damaged. *Luftwaffe* — 22 aircraft lost through combat or AA fire.

Friday, 20 September 1940 (flying Spitfire I X4338)
NW of Boulogne: Heinkel 'H113'? claim against Bf 109 & Henschel Hs126
Both these rather esoteric 'warbirds'. The Heinkel He113 was an 'in line' Daimler Benz-engined prototype closely matching the Bf 109f specification. Its existence was rarely acknowledged by the *Luftwaffe*. (Royal) Observer Corps identification silhouettes may indicate that one or two actually flew and that RAF air crew were expected to be familiar with it. There is no *Luftwaffe* record of a He113 being destroyed during the Battle of Britain. A likely candidate for Lock's Bf 109 is that flown by *Uffz*. E. Clauser — Wrk.Nr.2789, of 9/JG27, pulverised by every British fighter aloft. Crashed at Ospringe, disintegrated and burnt out. Pilot buried locally as 'Unknown German Airman'. Similarly of the parasol-winged short-range reconnaissance Hs126 some 24 were lost over the same period, but only two from combat or eneny action, and none on this date.

Tuesday, 1 October 1940
P/O E. S. Lock awarded the DFC for nine victories, eight of them in one week (5–11 September)

Saturday, 5 October 1940 (flying Spitfire I X4338)
Over Maidstone: Messerschmitt Bf 109E & Messerschmitt Bf 109E probable
Over Dungeness: Messerschmitt Bf 109E probable
　Luftwaffe mount four daylight sweeps of up to 150 aircraft across Straits of Dover. Raf claim 23 destroyed, 5 probables, 16 damaged. *Luftwaffe* register 25 losses from all causes, including eleven Bf 109s, only eight of which were from combat.

Wednesday, 9 October 1940 (flying Spitfire X4017)
Over SE Kent: Messerschmitt Bf 109E & Messerschmitt Bf 109 E probable & Messerschmitt Bf 109E probable
　RAF claim 4 E/A destroyed, 4 probable, 5 damaged. *Luftwaffe* lost 22 aircraft from all causes but only seven Bf 109s from combat. One of Lock's victims was Messerschmitt Bf 109E-4 (*Wrk.Nr. 1573*) of 9/JG54 which crashed in the sea some 10 miles off Dover. Shared with F/O J. R. Walker, DFC of the same squadron

Friday, 11 October 1940 (flying Spitfire I X4589)
Off Dungeness: Messerschmitt Bf 109E
　RAF claim 8 E/A destroyed, 4 probable, 11 damaged. *Luftwaffe* lost ten aircraft on operational sorties. Four Bf 109s were lost but only two in combat. Lock's Bf 109 can only be Bf 109E-1 of 5/JG27 (*Wrk.Nr.6267*) attacked by several fighters before crashing into the Channel.

Sunday, 20 October 1940 (flying Spitfire I X4589)
Over Biggin Hill: Messerschmitt Bf 109E
　RAF claim 9 E/A destroyed, 7 probable, 6 damaged. Luftwaffe lost 15 on operational sorties including five Bf 109Es, all with direct attribution as to probable destroyer F/O MP Brown of Nº 41 Squadron is credited with Bf 109E-7 (*Wrk.Nr.5930*) **4+** of 5/JG52. Possibly Lock shared in this.

Tuesday, 22 October 1940
P/O E. S. Lock awarded bar to DFC for fifteen E/A in sixteen days (14 September >)

Friday 25 October 1940 (flying Spitfire II P7314)
SE of Biggin Hill: Messerschmitt Bf. 109E probable
　Four enemy fighter sweeps over Kent towards London. RAF claim 14 E/A destroyed, 12 probable, 16 damaged. Lufwaffe admit loss 16 Bf 109s to fighters and 2 to AA fire..

Thursday, 31 October 1940
'End' of Battle of Britain

Sunday 17 November 1940 (flying Spitfire II P7554)
Over Thames estuary: Two Messerschmitt Bf 109Es
　Lock in turn was jumped by a Bf 109 of JG54 and was wounded in the right arm and both legs. He crash-landed at Martlesham Heath and was trapped for two hours before being rescued by two soldiers who carried him for two miles on a makeshift stretcher. This particular Spitfire, P7554, is something of an enigma. Nothing is known of its history between arriving at Nº 39 MU, Llandow (Glamorgan) on 29 October 1940 and appearing on Nº 234 Squadron's books (Predannack, Cornwall) w.e.f. 8 March 1941. Spitfires did not linger long at an ASU. Clearly it was with Nº 41 Sqn in November 1940 and was repaired after its forced landing. It would end its days with Nº 61 OTU Rednal.

Tuesday, 17 December 1940
Lock awarded the DSO. He remained in hospital until May 1941 undergoing some fifteen operations to remove cannon shell fragments.

Wednesday, 18 June 1941
Promoted Flying Officer and sent on a refresher flying course before being posted to N° 611 Squadron as a Flight Commander.

(c) with N° 611 (West Lancashire) Squadron, Hornchurch

Sunday, 6 July 1941 (flying Spitfire V, W3247)
Over St Omer: Messerschmitt Bf 109f

Tuesday, 8 July 1941 (flying Spitfire V, W3309)
Over St Omer: Messerschmitt: Bf 109f

Monday, 14 July 1941
Over NE France: Messerschmitt Bf 109f

Sunday 3 August 1941 (flying Spitfire V, W3257)
Duty — *Rhubarb* — freelance fighter sortie against targets of opportunity. Dived to strafe some German soldiers on a road near Calais and was not seen again. Remembered 'with honour' on the Runnymede Memorial, Panel 29.

Eric Lock poses for a publicity photograph with 26 'kills' marked up on his Spitfire.

13. Empathy — the raids

As hinted in the previous chapter, since the war there has been a steady reassessment of almost every aspect of the Battle of Britain. Such an overhaul, sorting out actual fact from carefully manipulated propaganda, was perhaps inevitable but it is just as well that the process has been retrospective otherwise there would have been very few props to bolster public morale — and the inhabitants of the Wrexham area certainly needed something to cling to when the air war threatened to swamp them! With hindsight their experience of the *Blitz* was short and sharp, focussing on a few violent days between 29 August and 5 September 1940. Thereafter, attacks from the air were sporadic and niggling. But the short-term nature of events was not to be suspected and the local historian can only present a picture of little unity on the 'Home Front' at least not in the three local authorities of Wrexham Borough Council, Wrexham Rural District Council and Overton Rural District Council — the latter an essentially rural authority that somehow managed to bungle its way through the war by sheer inertia and an ostrich-like mentality on the part of officers and councillors, and at little cost to the tax payer, a most satisfactory situation! The cosy image of Wrexhamites wholly united against the Nazis is a myth carefully fostered by Government propaganda on the one hand and Wrexham RDC's own glossy post-war publication briefing a surprised and disbelieving populace on that authority's achievements during the war years! All this is at variance with the picture painted by the local press, one of sheer incompetence, of unpreparedness, of escalating social conflicts and divisions, of enhanced nepotism in the corridors of power, of the most vulnerable sections of the population being forced to face the *Blitz* (had it developed further) with inadequate shelters. It was a desperate situation rescued, as always by the intiative of voluntary organisations and far-seeing individuals who saw clearly what was needed and did it!

June and July 1940 saw preparations to meet the expected invasion slowly get underway in the Wrexham area. Anti-tank obstacles, most of them inadequate and easily by-passed, mushroomed at road junctions, river crossings and at places of apparently little strategic significance. Apart from those that sprouted around the permiter fence of N° 35 ROF and RAF Wrexham, pillboxes did not feature in local defence plans, with one half-way up the Horshoe Pass, one defending the 'Crown' Bridge crossing of the River Alun at Llandegla, and one downhill of Llanbedr D.C.

It was not lost on officialdom that the Wrexham area straddled an obvious *Luftwaffe* route to and from Merseyside and Manchester. In July 1940 *First Aid in Brief* pamphlets dropped through every householder's letter-box describing the action to be taken 'in the event of householders, their families, friends and neighbours becoming casualties in an air raid'. Dr T. P. Edwards, joint Medical Officer of Health for Wrexham Borough and Rural District, urged that

Above left: Pillbox defending the river Alun crossing on the A525 Wrexham– Ruthin road at Llandegla.

Above right: Defensive position at the Crown bridge crossing of the river Alun at Llandegla.

Below left: A strategically useless pillbox defending the Horseshoe Pass at Oernant on the side of Maesyrychen Mountain.

Below right: This pillbox was part of the intricate defence system at the Royal Ordnance Factory, Marchwiel. It is situated on the bank of the river Clywedog on the southern perimeter of the ROF.

'consultaion with medical practitioners should be done now and not when an air-raid actually takes place'.

On 7 June appeals to Wrexham's cyclists appeared in the local press for 'parachute patrols', an extension of a scheme already operated by the National Union of Cyclists and the Cyclists Touring Club whereby members 'patrolled the highways and byways watching for possible parachute landings and other suspicious incidents'. Wheelers were still meeting at weekends for spins out into the country, but now they also sought to put their 'speed and mobility' to some use in the emergency, especially to patrol areas between the relatively static armed posts set up by the LDV. Cheshire went one better. On 23 June the Chief Constable called a rally of all motorcyclists interested in 'war work'. Sufficient petrol was promised and an appeal made for bikes laid-up for the duration to be got back on the road. Over 1,000 bikers attended and 600 were enrolled for duties involving linking up police stations and ARP depots should an invasion materialise. Riders were divided into three groups: 'A' Group star riders would report to HQ for 'long distance riding', 'B' Group riders for conveying nessages to all parts of the county, and 'C' Group would operate locally. Petrol coupons would be made available only for dispatch duties;

as well as cheaper tyres, 1d. a mile was payable for wear and tear and repair. Bikers were to report to their respective police stations as soon as the sirens sounded.

On 11 June the Town Clerk of Wrexham was arranging for Incendiary Bomb control groups at the borough's eleven ARP posts, 'leaving the Fire brigade to deal with larger fires'. For the guidance of the LDV and CD volunteers the *Wrexham Leader*, the *Shrewsbury Chronicle*, the *Whitchurch Herald* and other local newspapers in their editions of 21/28 June carried official silhouettes of German troop-carrying transports, a Junkers Ju52 — 'the most important troop carrier and used in parachute dropping', a Ju86, a Ju90 and the Focke-Wulf 200 'Condor'. Everyone was urged to cut the pictures out, paste on cardboard and hang them somewhere for easy reference.

On 5 July the Mayor of Wrexham appealed for volunteers to assist hard-pressed Council workmen to dig trenches in grounds adjacent to schools, but 'bring your own picks and shovels'! It was impossible to provide air-raid shelters for every schoolchild. Classrooms had large windows with the increased chance of injury from blast and flying glass, but proposals to convert cloakrooms and strengthen corridors with pit-props, although inexpensive, found little favour. It

THESE ARE THE TYPES OF GERMAN AIRCRAFT YOU ARE MOST LIKELY TO SEE

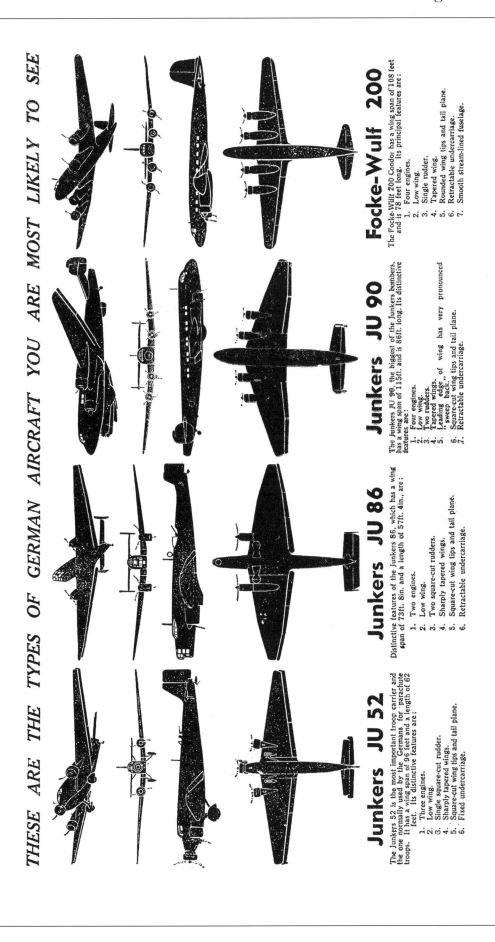

Junkers JU 52

The Junkers 52 is the most important troop carrier and the one normally used by the Germans for parachute troops. It has a wing span of 96 feet and a length of 62 feet. Its distinctive features are:

1. Three engines.
2. Low wing.
3. Single square-cut rudder.
4. Sharply tapered wings.
5. Square-cut wing tips and tail plane.
6. Fixed undercarriage.

Junkers JU 86

Distinctive features of the Junkers 86, which has a wing span of 73ft. 8in. and a length of 57ft. 4in., are:

1. Two engines.
2. Low wing.
3. Two square-cut rudders.
4. Sharply tapered wings.
5. Square-cut wing tips and tail plane.
6. Retractable undercarriage.

Junkers JU 90

The Junkers JU 90, the biggest of the Junkers bombers, has a wing span of 115ft. and is 86ft. long. Its distinctive features are:

1. Four engines.
2. Low wing.
3. Two rudders.
4. Tapered wings.
5. Leading edge, of wing has very pronounced "sweep back."
6. Square-cut wing tips and tail plane.
7. Retractable undercarriage.

Focke-Wulf 200

The Focke-Wulf 200 Condor has a wing span of 108 feet and is 78 feet long. Its principal features are:

1. Four engines.
2. Low wing.
3. Single rudder.
4. Tapered wing.
5. Rounded wing tips and tail plane.
6. Retractable undercarriage.
7. Smooth stream-lined fuselage.

was estimated that some 1,519 elementary children in the Borough could reach home (at walking pace) within five minutes of the sirens sounding; 1,738 could not! Victoria Junior School did manage to find six people who were willing to take in children stranded outside in the streets. Rhosnesni and Rhosddu Schools complained that Wrexham's two sirens could not be heard. No problem. These would be supplemented by works' hooters! In Flintshire junior children were to be given priority in public shelters and would not be released from school unless guaranteed some sort of house protection; otherwise they would be dispersed — with their teachers — into suitable fields, along embankments and sunken roadways, etc.

In May 1940, Wrexham's public provision of air-raid shelters had extended no further than a cursory examination of the deep cellars beneath the Island Green Brewery (holding 189), the Butchers' Market (93) and the Church House or St Mary's Institute (109 seated), and earmarking open spaces such as car parks and bus stations for the erection of surface shelters — alongside the Fire Station, in St George's Crescent (2), King Street (2), off Yorke Street (2), the Wynnstay Yard (2) and Chester Street. Working on the assumption that they would not be occupied for any considerable length of time, these shelters would have no 'mechanised ventilation', lights or toilets — but sand would be provided just in case someone was sick!

The problem was one of materials. The Borough Surveyor had just used 1,500 bricks in building two blast walls at the Fire Station; he only had 6,000 bricks left to meet a guideline target of blast walls to 75% of town properties! Then brainwave! Use the bricks from recently demolished cottages in Market Street and Pentre'r-felin and sell the slates and timbers to defray expenses. In the middle of the interminable discussion — which passed for immediate action — came the bombs! Overnight another seven cellars and railway arches were quickly made available in the town centre. But even then there was only sheltered accommodation for 1,300 instead of the suggested 10% of the the town's 36,000 population. On 20 September, accusing the

Borough Council of 'being sadly behind the times', Alderman William Aston himself initiated a communal shelter-building scheme on the Maesydre and Spring Lodge housing estates, using bricks supplied by Border Breweries and with tenants supplying their own labour. In November he would propose the formation of yet another Committee, but this time 'for the erection, supervision and control of air-raid shelters', removing the obligation from the hands of the town's hapless War Emergency Committee. Out in the Rural District long abandoned railway tunnels on the former Wheatsheaf branch line at Summerhill were inspected and approved as air raid shelters.

Wrexham's shelter provision programme was never completed. Such as were built were subject to abuse — as emergency urinals, places of assignation and so on, so much so that they became health hazards despite being disinfected every day. An attempt to keep public toilets open longer to alleviate the problem failed. The shelter on the Beast Market lost beds almost as soon as they were put in. This was not surprising as many working-class families in the vicinity were still sleeping on mattresses on the floor. As a result, shelters were locked. Initially keys were kept in a glass case — 'In Case of Emergency Break Glass' — but tended to vanish on Saturday nights! Latterly, as sirens sounded, one had to wait for the local ARP warden to open up. To crown everything there were loud complaints from small bus operators that the King Street shelter had effectively cut the bus station in two and that they were isolated from the stands used by Crosville Motor Services.

The clandestine use of shelters by 'groping' couples highlighted some of the problems associated with any garrison town bursting at the seams with a larger than normal complement of military. Indignant borough councillors found time to get all steamed up about 'the practice of young girls, 14 or 15 years of age, walking the streets of Wrexham late at night, painted up like the women on the streets of London or Paris'. They pressed for women police constables to be posted to Wrexham to counteract this 'new social menace'. The only snag was that Denbighshire's Standing Joint Committee 'had not yet seen its way to employ women constables'. All this would change under the pressures of war, and Wrexham's assiduously cultivated Puritan image would be buried for ever. In September's meeting of the Flintshire County Council the Home Office circular on the subject of women police officers was only debated at the insistence of Ruth, Lady Lewis, Caerwys. She was on a certain loser in that she 'knew the views of the Chief

To break the deadlock in the provision of air raid shelters, Sir Alfred McAlpine stepped in to provide Gresford school children with their own walk-in 'Super Shelter'. [NLW Geoff Charles Collection]

Wrexham Civil Defence. Photograph taken alongside Trinity Church schoolroom, King Street.

Constable and that he didn't want any women police in Flintshire'. Lady Lewis argued 'it is desirable to have some women police to protect soldiers from women'! But the Chief Constable was not to be swayed. He 'did not think anything was likely to happen in this war to justify the appointment of women just yet!'. Perhaps later, 'but not for outside work'.

In June and July every village in the Wrexham area began holding joint ARP/AFS exercises covering first aid, dealing with IBs, mustard gas decontamination, etc. as well as training the nuclei of crews to man the trailer pumps. Denbighshire was a large county rarely unified on any local government issue. As usual the Wrexham authorities were pressing hard for their own Civil Defence Controller. There were inadequate ARP ambulances in the Wrexham area, those allocated by Denbighshire being considered 'clapped out and near the end of their useful life'. The Borough War Eemergency Committee was empowered to spend £2,000 on equipping Wrexham, with adequate ambulances. But as usual women took command in a crisis and under the Mayoress, Mrs John Davies, the WVS decided to raise an Ambulance Fund. They were irresistible. The first ambulance from this source was dedicated and in service on 20 September 1940! Not to be outdone, Mrs Higgins, The Beeches, Llangollen, presented a motor ambulance to that town

In Wrexham itself CD exercises in various parts of the town during the last two weeks in July were less successful. They involved wardens, police, specials, auxiliary firemen and their pumps, ambulance and first aid crews, decontamination workers and repair and rescue squads. All had their frustrating moments. Possibly officials were asking for trouble when they set up temporary hospitals and field dressing stations in the outbuildings of 'well known

hostelries'. Inevitably a wet evening was chosen, so that there were many instances of 'road rage' as frustrated drivers ignored road diversion signs and got hopelessly tangled up with sewer, water main, and electricty supply cable repair parties.

The first large-scale 'Black Out', as the simplest response to air attacks at night, had taken place on 13/14 July 1939, covering eighteen counties from Norfolk to Flintshire. The regions involved were selected according to the readiness of Observer Corps Groups. Denbighshire was omitted because most of the county's observer posts in N° 26 Observer Group (Wrexham) would not be functioning until August or September. Deeside lay within N° 7 Observer Group (Manchester), operational since 1937 while N° 27 Observer Group (Shrewsbury) had come on stream in 1938. The whole point of the exercise was to have no lights visible from the air between 0001 and 0400hrs on Friday, 14 July. While much of the country was monitored by the RAF on night exercise, in the border region Tern Hill, Shawbury and Sealand training aircraft carried 'referees' aloft to adjudge the effectiveness of the exercise locally. In Shropshire and Deeside street lights were extinguished. Householders, if they were up and about were asked to darken their windows and screen external lights so that they were not visible from the air. Motorists were to drive on sidelights only. Factories, marshalling yards, and docks were to either screen lights or stop work altogether for the four-hour test period. Police, specials, a few wardens, and the whole of the Observer Corps acted as observers on the ground.

These were calm, unhurried days compared with the hysteria and paranoia, stemming from doing too little too late, that gripped Wrexham in the middle of 1940. Petty officialdom ran wild. Lighting a cigarette in the black-out was treated as an offence by some police constables and wardens. A councillor felt personally affronted when threatened by a policeman with prosecution for failing to lock his car and remove the rotor arm whilst on the Guildhall car park. In rural Maelor, after years of tolerance, gypsies and totters were suddenly and persistently harassed and fined 'for illegal camping on the grass verges' along the main roads and down country lanes.

From early May onwards large numbers of offenders against air-raid precautions were regularly wheeled before Wrexham magistrates in batches of 10–25 'for exposing of lights from buildings'. From being widely scattered throughout the Borough, offences and offenders seem to have been 'zoned' as if each ARP area received the undivided attention of wardens in turn — there couldn't have been all that many bellicose and belligerent wardens. Or could there? One week offenders were almost all from the Spring Lodge council estate (with its hard core of second offenders), the next from Garden Village and adjacent parts of Rhosddu, the next Westminster Drive, Park Avenue and Camberley Drive — no section of the community was immune from these purges. The Chairman of the Wrexham magistrates was asked (indeed, ordered) by prosecuting counsel, who just happened to be the Chief ARP Controller for Denbighshire, to issue a stern warning to all Wrexham householders: 'The residents of Wrexham did not seem to realise the importance of preventing lights showing, and would not provide the necessary material to ensure the necessary black-out'. As the gravity of the situation increased so did the fines, anything between 10s. and £2 'according to the position and resources of the person' — substantial sums for those days. Not even the wife of Wrexham's Chief Air Raid Warden was exempt. Outraged, she elected to go for trial. Although witnesses for the defence seemingly perjured their immortal souls, the magistrates sensibly refused to believe that ARP wardens had confused lights from an unprotected doorway with signal lamps on the GWR railway!

Caergwrle magistrates, too, were not to be trifled with and would seem to have had a grudge against motor-cyclists of any species, whether riding with or without diffusers! The black-out claimed its first victim on 13 June 1940 when a passenger in a car travelling from Mold to Wrexham was shot and killed at a LDV check-point at Gwersyllt. It gave local and national newspapers and lawyers a field day. The

case certainly prompted ambivalent fence-sitters to sharply refocus their priorities, underscored by repeated headlines and warnings: 'If a sentry challenges, obey at once!', especially during the hours of darkness when roads were increasingly obstructed. Ripples were felt nationwide and in laying down a precedent for his own Home Guard units in the light of the Gwersyllt incident and attempting to clarify that grey area whereby a primarily civilian force faces an enemy in uniform, the Lord Lieutenant of Hampshire argued thus: (a) every male citizen is duty bound 'to use all necessary force to prevent a felonious act being committed' (legal jargon for *inter alia* the invasion); (b) no court would circumscribe or deny such rights, and (c) when on duty a LDV man would not be considered a civilian but a member of the armed forces of the Crown.

On 21 August 1940, Wrexham Borough, Rhos, Rhostyllen and Gresford held simultaneous ARP/AFS exercises, testing the joint responses of widely disparate groups to the utmost. The post-mortem revealed alarming weaknesses in control and communications. But there was little time for buck-passing or mutual recrimination — a week later it was for real! On Wednesday, 28 Agust 1940 Merseyside experienced the first of four successive nights of bombing, described officially as 'the first major night attack on the United Kingdom'. London had been bombed mainly by daylight, but here was a change of tactics. The *Luftwaffe* flew over 600 sorties against Liverpool and its satellites for the loss of only seven aircraft. According to German records a total of 446 tons of high explosive (HE) and 37,044 incendiary (IB) bombs were dropped on Merseyside during these four nights. But, as many in the Wrexham area still recall, a substantial portion fell on Esclusham and Ruabon Mountains, the moorland areas to the east of the town. Whether accidentally or deliberately is still a matter for some debate. The summer of 1940 was as glorious as the straddling winters were atrocious, and after three months without any measurable rainfall, the bracken, heather, peat and mountain grass were tinder dry.

Apart from three 'Red Alerts' the first night was an uneventful one for the Wrexham area, the lull before the storm. The only air action was 35 miles away, possibly a botched attempt to bomb the Royal Artillery depôt at Kinmel Park, resulting in two sheep killed and some blast damage to Lowther College. On the night of Thursday/Friday, 29/30 August the mountains went up in flames, an incident which has become an indelible part of local folklore, much of it apocryphal. Clusters of of IBs probably started the fires which lit up the whole of the surrounding countryside, but, as seen in earlier chapters, the bombs themselves were almost certainly attracted by a makeshift 'Q'-site or decoy. But grizzled RWF veterans will talk darkly of the tempting targets offered by the great *Cae llwyd* and *Tŷ mawr* reservoirs above Legacy and their puzzlement in rounding up on the smouldering moors numerous 'Nazi sympathisers' and suspect 'fifth columnists'. Whether these were the real thing or merely innocent, but stupid, sight-seers or souvenir hunters after bomb fragments, will never be known as records of their incarceration and interrogation at the Wrexham Barracks

One of Wrexham's Home Guard units at a local rifle range.

and Police Station have not survived. This is not as far-fetched as it may seem. In many parts of Wales attitudes to the war were coloured by Welsh nationalistic feelings, and as seen elsewhere in relation to the CHL radar station at Gwaunysgor, deliberate acts of sabotage were not unknown. But whatever the reason, falling flares started other fires and all hell broke loose, the constant distinctive drone of Daimler-Benz and Junkers Jumo engines interspersed with the 'crump' of HE bombs and the dropping of further incendiaries until the early hours of Friday morning.

Cheshire and Shropshire LDV patrols as far afield as Beeston Castle had ring-side seats for the great pyrotechnic display and their eye-witness accounts lend substance to the belief that the fires were started deliberately *before* the *Luftwaffe* bombers came along to fan the blaze. The *A, C, N* and *P Series* decoys, *Starfish* and *Strategic Starfish*, and the airfield *Q* and *QF* decoys have been discussed at some length elswhere in this narrative. 'Col (John) Turner's Department', the hush-hush unit that had oversight of decoy deception, had been up and running since January 1940, but whether it arranged the contraptions on Ruabon Mountain is uncertain. Certainly they did not match the sophistication of any of the four different decoys which covered the mountain top in 1941.

The potential use of mountain or lowland wastes as ready-made decoys would not have been lost on Army Area Commanders. On the night of Thursday, 18 January 1940 a line of gorse and bracken fires on Moel Fammau, mostly on the Denbighshire side, had been visible in several counties. Despite the efforts of police and volunteer beaters it was two days before the fires burnt themselves out. In February at Afonwen, near Caerwys, another bracken fire, caused by someone lighting a pipe and throwing the match away, was seen for miles around in the black-out. Lacking documentation, it may be just coincidence that during the Friday night raid, 30/31 August, Ercall Heath, Shropshire, was also set ablaze by 400–500 IBs with many others landing in open fields. Was this the result of the fortuitous jettisoning of a bomb load, or was there something on the ground which prompted a speculative release of IBs?

On the morning the gentle anti-cyclonic south-easterly breezes veered round and the mountain fires took on fresh heart in a strengthening westerly wind. Over 30 square miles of moorland was consumed, the barren hills tops burning for days. On Saturday, 31 August, although Liverpool and Bootle had over 100 major fires, including Dingle oil jetty, and Wallasey Town Hall and its valuable organ were destroyed, and casualties totalled 23 killed and 86 seriously injured, matters could have been much worse had not the blazing mountains to the west of Wrexham diverted a high proportion of the bombs meant for Liverpool. By Saturday smoke and ash had eclipsed the sun and was causing acute discomfort all over the Wrexham area, seriously hampering efforts to get in the corn harvest. By the following Wednesday the side effects of the smoke and finer ash were being felt as far afield as Manchester, which city had troubles enough of its own!

On the Thursday night (29 August) HE bombs also damaged a row of houses in Gresford. Windows were blown

out, slates removed, and bedroom ceilings raised. Bomb fragments passed clean through some walls. The blast stove in shop and hotel windows, people fled their homes and took refuge in the hedges. There were several injuries attended to in the village first-aid room. The Village Hall afforded temporary shelter, blankets, food and tea for those from the wrecked houses. Several CD workers had to be treated for shock after their cars collided in the black-out whilst racing to the scene. One of the bombs was a delayed-action bomb and blew up at 0930hrs on the Friday morning, killing six over-curious sight-seers inspecting the damage from the previous night, along with two elderly ladies who had refused to leave their homes and were buried in the rubble.

The same night rural Maelor got its first bombs. These may have been due to errors in 'dead-reckoning' navigation, or malfunctioning *Knickebein*, radio navigational beam and probably represent an attempt to plaster Nº 35 ROF that sprawled over farmland east of Wrexham just three months from completion. IBs were scattered over a wide area between Bangor and Penley. The pattern of HE was such that, when plotted, the NW–SE course (or vice versa) being followed by the plane can be recovered — four HE on Bangor Racecourse, and one each at Althrey Woodhouse, Corner Farm, Cloy, Adra felin, Rhydycyffin, Little Green Farm and Lane Farm, Penley. At the Buck Farm three heifers in a field were killed — a far cry from Hugo Sperrle's vaunted aim of flattening Liverpool.

South Shropshire had suffered from sporadic night bombing since late July, usually from single aircraft utilising prevailing cloud cover to attack industrial targets in the West Midlands. Bombs fell harmlessly near Much Wenlock on 25 July and around Great Bolas on 29 July, and spattered the southern part of the Longmynd the following day. Here 'Adolf's Railway', the *Luftwaffe* route up the Welsh border, was being established. French based squadrons crossed the English coast at Lyme Bay, picked up the Bristol Channel and Severn and then the Dee, on moonlit nights silvery strips of water leading enemy bombers unerringly to their target. For Liverpool carry straight on, for Birmingham and Black Country towns follow the Stour or turn right at Bridgnorth. Craven Arms had a few bombs on the night of 19 August. Ten HE were counted in the Lydbury North on Friday, 23 August when there were five minor sorties to Birmingham but with low cloud and persistent rain hindering target finding. On Sunday, 25 August, industrial targets in the west Midlands were again attacked, which may account for bomb damage at Newcastle, Clun, and a field of barley on the lower slopes of the Wrekin set on fire by IBs from a lone raider way off its original target at Walsall.

The first Shropshire casualties occurred in the early morning of Thursday, 29 August, but by a quirk of censorship the full story was not released to the press until 13 December 1940! Whilst the *Luftwaffe's* major thrusts were aimed at Liverpool and Manchester, a number of enemy aircraft, working singly and in twos or threes on an opportunist basis, were swanning about the west Midlands. A single raider, possibly a Junkers Ju88, transected

Bridgnorth with its load of 'screamers', at least nine SC5O general-purpose bombs and two clusters of IBs, doing much damage, killing two people and injuring seven. Fortunately a couple of C5OA 'oil bombs', the *Phosphorbrandbomben* or Phosphorous Incendiary Bombs did not explode. They carried a highly inflammable viscous mixture of phosphrous, oil and a rubber solution and could have done even greater damage to the Old Town. The tail units of the HE were fitted with a device called the 'Trumpets of Jericho'. These were black cardboard tubes, some l4" long, 1¹/2" in diameter, shaped like an organ pipe; as they dropped the air rushing through the tubes caused them to 'shriek', a din calculated to weaken the morale of a civilian population.

This it certainly did on the night Bridgnorth met its destiny! A HE bomb near St Leonard's Church killed two elderly spinsters, Misses Jospehine and Alice Maynard. By a quirk of fate the condemned cottages in Church Street remained intact, with not a window broken. In contrast, the blast rebounding off the stone buttresses of the town wall in Pound Street blew in every door and window of 'The Squirrel' inn and sent masonry flying into the air, exposing Mr and Mrs Rich, evacuees from Cardiff who had only arrived that night, to the elements. Incendiary bombs consumed a photographic studio and the local AFS struggled manfully, but vainly, to contain the flames as Bridgnorth 'sucked the mop up'. Five months later, in reviewing the year's events, the *Shrewsbury Chronicle* could comment: 'Bridgnorth learnt to appreciate and rely on the emergency services, the ARP, the AFS and the demolition squads, who restored everything to order in a few hours … and to observe simple precautions such as gluing netting to windows and using the shelters …'

Lessons were learnt the hard way but one is impressed with the courage shown by the AFS as practice drills were suddenly for real. On the night of Thursday, 5 September, when raids were mounted against targets on Merseyside, Manchester and the west Midlands, HE bombs fell within 150 yards of where the Bishop's Castle AFS was tackling a fire at Church Stoke caused by an earlier marauder. They stuck to their task as other HE and IBs fell in the fields round the village, and were warmly praised for their heroism. Elsewhere, in areas free from barrage balloons, enemy aircraft would fly just a few hundred feet above the flames to observe the effectiveness of their bombing. Then Fire Brigade personnel and machines frequently found themselves targets of opportunity for German air-gunners — one recalls the consternation amongst Cannock firemen as they were fighting a fire started by IBs at Little Wyrley (Staffordshire) when they were machine-gunned by a He111, possibly from KG55, that had been hovering around the edge of Wolverhampton, one of the targets for that night. Logically flames attracted further bombs.

Speaking in 1974, Mr D. Wheway Davies, former Chief Fire Officer of the Denbighshire and Montgomeryshire Joint Fire Service, recalled the 'finest hour' of Denbighshire's ten local authority brigades, when crews and appliances from Wrexham, Denbigh, Colwyn Bay, Abergele and Ruthin were mobilised as required to help and relieve the hard pressed fire-fighters of Liverpool, Manchester and the west Midland

towns. On occasion even the village AFS units were roped in to fight Birkenhead's *Blitz*. Surviving members of Gresford AFS are persuaded only with difficulty to speak of the horrors of fire-fighting in a milieu light-years removed from their tiny rural community in which they had enrolled to serve. Shoulders rounded with age are (not too seriously) blamed on being forced to hunch those same shoulders to reduce the target area offered by their bodies. The thump of falling IBs is still vividly heard in the mind's ear. The penetrating power of a 1kg S.N.I.B. (Steel Nose Incendiary Bomb) into tarmac or concret is furiously debated and eventually acknowledged as unavailing efforts are made to wipe out memories of colleagues and emergency workers writhing screaming on the ground with an IB embedded in their backs.

But even on home ground these AFS units (integrated into the NFS with effect from 18 August 1941) never knew when interminable drills and practices would give way to the real thing. On 6 September 1942, long after night raids had dwindled away, members of Holt NFS detachment, as was their Sunday morning custom, were busy trying to empty a duck pond on Common Wood, when on the airfield above them a Bristol Beaufighter II, T3046, of 'A' Flight, Nº 96 Squadron, taking off for RAF Honiley stalled at 300' and crashed onto a parked Blenheim, L8671. Both aircraft burst into flames and the crew of T3046 killed. It was Holt NFS trailer pump hitched to Henry Jones's lorry that smashed through the security barrier at Borras Head, scuttled round through the west gate and beat the station foam tender and the Wrexham appliances to the scene of the accident.

Yet it is difficult to credit that at Holywell, Flintshire, on 20 March 1942, there had taken place a 'Local Authority Conference on 'Extravagant NFS Expenditure', with the object of protesting officially on NFS costs to the rate-payer. From the conference report one gathers (a) that the NFS as currently deployed was considered an extravagant waste of public funds; (b) that fewer paid personnel should be retained, with a reversion to a system of voluntary and unpaid auxiliary firemen; and (c) that all Local Authorities should have control of NFS expenditure in depôts and stations. Only three or four of the latter were envisaged in each authority, with services 'radiating outwards'. What possibly upset councillors most was 'all the hanging about waiting for something to happen' and the fact that it took at least six girls to crew even the smallest station control room! This was not quite true as the HQ of Holt NFS was in the wooden shed at Deeside Farm shared with the ARP Wardens! Sadly all this local government fractiousness surfaced barely two months after the last German bomb had fallen in north-east Wales.

A correlation of Civil Defence and Police records will show the night of Saturday, 31 August / 1 September 1940 as perhaps being the worst night of the war for the Wrexham area as yet more HE and IBs were dropped on the still burning mountains and the villages and farms peripheral to them — from Pentre Saeson, Glascoed, Cefnybedd, Caer Estyn, Brymbo and Brynteg to Coedpoeth, Bronwylfa, Rhostyllen, Rhos, Ruabon, Acrefair, Garth and Llandegla, with a parallel line of damage east of Wrexham, from

Plas Ucha, destroyed by a high explosive bomb on the night of 31 August/1 September 1940. Since rebuilt.

Burton, Common Wood and the ROF to Eyton. With the exception of UXBs in a field near Moorland Avenue, Spring Lodge and at the back of the ARP post in Union Road (dangerously close to the Lager Brewery!), bombs seem to have missed the town of Wrexham altogether.

Plas Ucha, a splendid hillside farm above Penycae, was wrecked. The farmer, Peter Morris, had a miraculous escape, but his two sisters and a farm labourer were killed. The ruined farm-house was finally destroyed by fire on 2 April 1941, but has since been rebuilt. Fortunately this was in the middle of a 25-day lull in the desultory raids into which Wrexham's air war had now degenerated, otherwise the burning timbers may have served as an unwitting decoy, attracting more bombs to the mountain on which *inter alia* RAF Wrexham now had its official Q-site.

On the Sunday two houses in Osborne Street, Rhos, were flattened and seven people killed and five injured when a delayed action bomb exploded. These were the unfortun-

ates. UXBs frequently went off before bomb-disposal squads could tackle them, such was the pressure on the latters' finite resources. Over 40 UXBs dropped in the Wrexham area that night. Some would explode within the hour, that at Cefnybedd actually self-destructing fifteen minutes after being dropped, damaging several houses. Others were more tricky. Four UXBs closed Aberderfyn Road, Ponciau for 19 days until cleared on the 23 September. Similarly the Bronygarth–Glynceiriog road was closed for two weeks until 20 September. UXBs at Coedpoeth and Minera lay undiscovered until 8 September, but it was another fortnight before they were dug up, carefully transported onto Minera Mountain, and destroyed by a controlled detonation.

A stick of HE fell on Brymbo, one in the steelwork's scrapyard, causing considerable damage to buildings and railway track; a second exploded on The Green, blowing the walls off Harry Grainger's Cinema ('Brymbo Pictures'), fracturing a gas main and causing a serious fire. But a third landed in Grainger's garden just across the road from the Queen's Head pub… and did not explode. The area was evacuated, but it was four weeks before the arrival of a bomb disposal squad. The bomb was considered too dangerous to move or defuse, and so was blown up *in situ*, the ensuing blast causing the gable end of the Queen's Head to collapse, burying the licensee's husband under the rubble! He had returned to the pub for some purpose, but after treatment in hospital for severe shock he was allowed home.

Shortly after midnight on the Saturday night, Shrewsbury also sustained its only fatal casualties of the war. Wave after wave of enemy aircraft had been heard overhead en route to Liverpool and the Wirral ports. A couple of speculative bombs were dropped in the Ellesmere Road miraculously leaving Hencote Villa intact but demolishing Ivy Cottage, killing Mrs Jessie Mary Broxton and her two grandchildren, Margaret Eileen Meredith (aged

A near miss for Brymbo Steel Works. The Queen's Head public house below the works was severely damaged by a UXB.
[Geoffrey Charles Collection, NLW]

6) and John Terence Meredith (aged 4). The latter lived in Llangollen but had been sent to stay with their mother's parents in Shrewsbury whilst Ruabon Mountain was the focus of *Luftwaffe* attention. By a quirk of fate old William Broxton had stayed in the kitchen for a final pipe before going to bed. His dog lay at his feet. The lives of both were saved by heavy ceiling joists falling across the fireplace and protecting them as the cottage collapsed. Less than a mile away in Ditherington there was the giant Sentinel works on night shift and the 'Spitfire' factory churning out aircraft parts. The maltings, requisitioned by the Army, was packed with soldiers and on the LMS Crewe line sidings an ammunition train was being marshalled. But these were not a target, even if German Intelligence knew of their existence. It may have been the considerable area of glass in the Greenfield Nursery, reflecting in the moonlight, or simply the probing, irritating searchlight beams from a battery only two fields away, which may have prompted the release of the HE that did all the damage.

Thus the air war along the Welsh border got under way. In September, October and November, Merseyside received some 44 visitations from the *Luftwaffe*, averaging one every other night. The year ended rather unseasonably with the 'Christmas *Blitz*', which left Wrexham relatively undisturbed except for incessant 'Red Alerts', bomb damage on the 21/22 December 1940 being confined largely to the coastal strip between Gwrych Castle, Abergele, and Trelogan.

14. Empathy — the aeroplanes

The six week campaign for France, culminating in Dunkirk, cost the RAF some 931 aircraft of all types. Of these 386 were Hurricanes and 67 Spitfires. Also lost were some 320 British pilots killed or reported missing, with a further 115 ending up as POWs. These could not be replaced so easily. In June Dowding began to rebuild and reorganise Fighter Command, hoping desperately for some momentary respite. He got a month.

In May 1940, even before the full extent of the wastage in France became apparent, the Government was encouraging towns, counties and individuals to donate fighters to the RAF at a cost of £5,000 each. Strangely the campaign focussed on the Supermarine Spitfire which in public regard still hogs all the glory, glamour and commendation to the relative disadvantage of the Hawker Hurricane which was the most numerous operational aircraft in both the battles for France and Britain. The Hurricane destroyed more enemy aircraft than any other RAF type and to it must be largely attributed the ultimate victory in the Battle of Britain. But it was a 'Spitfire' Fund that was set up all over the country with the obligatory 'barometer' outside the Town Hall to indicate progress being made. It took two or three months for the idea of sponsoring a an RAF fighter to gain momentum, not until the *Blitz* was in full swing, the 'Battle' joined, and the obvious empathy with 'the Few' teetered on he brink of adulation.

In the border region of north-east Wales the *Whitchurch Herald* was first off the mark. On 19 July 1940 a correspondent, possibly with tongue firmly in cheek and taking his cue from the patriotic leader columns of the national press and stirrings in some major provincial cities, suggested 'A Spitfire for Whitchurch?' with the *Herald* as clearing house and organiser! It seemed an ambitious project, but would involve less than £1 per head of the town's population, with perhaps the affluent giving more than the less well placed! By the next week two 'substantial' contributions had been received. But the *Herald's* editor poured cold water on the whole thing, not in the least because his own depleted office staff could not administer the scheme, but possibly also because he was putting the whole weight of his newspaper behind the request of 'the state' for several thousand motor-bikes and some 500 motor-cycle combinations, between 350–500cc, in good condition. and not older than 1936!

He suggested that the town should lower its sights and go for a Red Cross ambulance costing £700. Indeed '1,400 Shillings!' became the paper's monotonous slogan. It would take 18 months to raise the necessary sum. There was no organised infrastructure for collecting monies and the local effort would be overtaken by the early National Savings Campaigns. On 21 November 1941 the *Herald* solemnly announced that an ambulance, registration number GGW542, carrying the inscription 'Subscribed for by the people of Whitchurch & District', was even then operational somewhere in Scotland!

As the 'Battle of Britain' intensified, moving on from the 'Initial Skirmishes' phase, so suddenly 'Spitfire Funds' started to proliferate. By later standards, when in 'Wings for Victory Week' east Denbighshire alone could set, and surpass within a week, a target of £570,000 for one bomber, three fighters, and two ambulance aircraft squadrons, these early efforts at fund-raising seem almost derisory — but the idea was new, everyone green and untried in organisation and method, and until now rather luke-warm and somewhat detached as far as a civilian war effort was concerned. Again the period of collecting was inordinately long, overlapping with the 'Lend to Win Weeks' of November–December 1940, but this was due more to intense intercounty/area rivalries — between Flintshire and Denbighshire, and within the latter county between Colwyn Bay and Wrexham. Once on the campaign trail local pride meant no giving in until targets were met.

The first moves were made 7–9 August 1940 by the Lord Lieutenant of Flintshire, Rear-admiral R. Rowley-Conwy, Bodrhyddan, an initiative typical of a man who had entered the Royal Navy in 1888, commanded a destroyer in the First World War, retired in 1922, but in 1941–2 would re-emerge in the limelight as commodore North Atlantic convoys. Indeed he brought a convoy of over 60 ships into the Mersey on his 67th birthday! The timing was appropriate and the old sea-dog might have been moved by the attack on Channel convoy C.W.9, code-named *Peewit*, which had sailed from the Thames estuary on the evening of 7 August, and sustained three major attacks from German E-boats and Stukas, the greatest effort made against shipping during the Battle of Britain and met by up to seven squadrons from N[os] 10 and 11 Groups, Fighter Command. The RAF claimed 24 enemy bombers and 36 fighters destroyed (actual *Luftwaffe* losses were 31) and the *Luftwaffe* reported 49 British fighters shot down (actual RAF losses were 19). These were currently the highest losses on both sides since the commencement of the 'Battle'. Thus a nautical background against which to launch a Flintshire campaign for a replacement aircraft was not inappropriate. A county Spitfire would cost about £5,000, a seemingly colossal sum in those untried early days, but was achievable if every adult aimed at buying a bolt (cost 2s. 6d.) and every child a nut (cost 6d.). The WVS and the British Legion were lumbered with organizing the collection.

Not to be outdone the Lord Lieutenant of Denbighshire, Robert Williams Wynn, launched a similar appeal nine days later. Wrexham decided they would co-operate, but at a special meeting on 27 August decided to go after a Spitfire 'to be known as the Wrexham Spitfire … if the appropriate sum was raised'. Nothing like hedging one's bets! The 'sponsoring' of fighter aircraft had suddenly become a very high profile matter with a lot of 'Brownie points' to be gained. On the 15 August the nation was flabbergasted by the seemingly' casual donation of £100,000 by Canadian Willard Garfield Weston, MP for Macclesfield and Chairman of Weston Biscuit Companies, to the Ministry of Aircraft Production to replace 12 Hurricanes and/or Spitfires lost in that day's air battles over the Channel. N[os] 234, 236 and 501 Squadrons in particular had received a mauling. As already noted this was that euphoric day when the RAF claimed 182 German aircraft shot down.

As a matter of civic pride Wrexham had always been out on a limb ever since it had become a separate Parliamentary constituency in 1885 and 1918, the latter re-organisation prompting a vigorous but frustrated campaign for County Borough status in the 1930s. Theoretically the area had also got its National Savings fund-raising well organised with, in August 1940, some 76 savings groups on a street, factory, society, canteen and CD post basis. Where these were lacking there was always the WVS! It was calculated that 3s. 6d. per head would see the target achieved. However, Borough and Rural District councillors balked at the suggestion that they individually should give 1d. for every enemy plane brought down! This did not deter a cheque for £16 12s. from an anonymous donor being received by the county fund on the basis of 3,995 pennies for every German aircraft lost (according to a local newspaper audit) since the invasion of the Netherlands on 10 May 1940: '… at a penny each, a good bargain!' With hindsight actual German losses in the Battle of France were 1,065 aircraft destroyed. Add to this a further 495 *Luftwaffe* losses for the period 10 July–23 August and the anonymous donation appears somewhat over-generous! By 13 September 1940 the Wrexham area had raised £1,578 but 'with a bit of a struggle', and the Mayor

was rather put out by the fact that Oldham had raised over £4,000 in just two weeks. By 20 September the Flintshire Spitfire Fund had sent Lord Beaverbrook, Minister of Aircraft Production, the first £5,000 and 'were well on their way to providing a second'. This was like a red rag to a bull!

By 11 October Wrexham had raised £3,411, helped not a little by the myriad of individual 'efforts' such as the donation by the Duke of Westminster, for auction at Wrexham Smithfield, of a pedigree ram and a children's riding pony. Flagging enthusiasm was revived by the fact that negotiations were underway to bring a German bomber to Wrexham to form the basis of a temporary 'War Trophies Exhibition'. A Heinkel He111 did materialise on the back of an RAF 'Queen Mary' low-loader aircraft transporter. Failing to get onto Frank Lloyd's Horse repository behind the Wynnstay Arms Hotel, it was displayed 28 October–2 November in the field at the back of the WVS Canteen, Bodhyfryd, and raised £157 from admissions and the sale of emblems. The provenance of this Heinkel remains a mystery. It was not one of the few shot down locally.

Wrexham's fund-raising officially closed on 4 November, three days after the end of the Battle of Britain, although sporadic donations continued to be received for a couple of months afterwards. On 8 November Flintshire sent a final gift of £1,000 to Lord Beaverbrook on top of the £12,000 already raised for two Spitfires. Not being enough for a third aeroplane this last sum was to be used in aircraft construction generally. On 15 November the Denbighshire Spitfire Fund stood at £6,671, not including Wrexham's £5,800 or 'the £4,000–5,000 at Colwyn Bay'. Perverse to the end, Wrexham sent their cheque to Lord Beaverbrook and in return received the following acknowledgement:

Dear Mr Mayor,

The citizens of Wrexham stand forth as generous champions of the cause of freedom. By their gift of the purchase of a Spitfire they give warning to Hitler of his impending defeat, even as they pay noble tribute to the gallantry of our airmen who are making that defeat certain.

I am deeply grateful to them and I derive encouragement and inspiration in my work from the proof they give me of their determination to do and give their all for victory.

Wrexham's plane will bear the borough's name and in the triumph it wins in the skies your people will know they have their share.

Beaverbrook.

But there was to be no derring-do in the skies by brave pilots flying the *Wrexham* Spitfire. Along with other local authorities eager to claim a Spitfire as their own, the borough of Wrexham had to queue, waiting some nine months for a Spitfire to roll off the assembly line before the town was allocated the one destined to bear its name — the 1,947th Spitfire, an Eastleigh (Southampton)-built Mk V, serial W3760. Regretfully, historic images of this aircraft, as

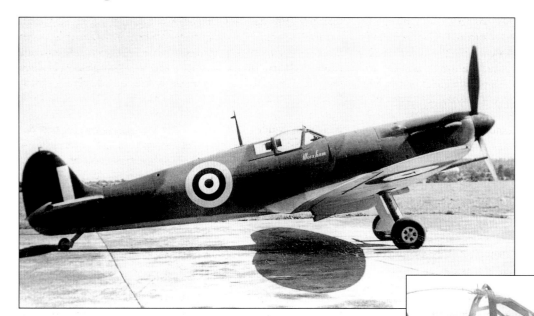

Above and right: The 'Wrexham Spitfire' A Mk V (W3760) pictured at Eastleigh, Southampton before delivery but already bearing the name 'Wrexham' on the fuselage, below the cockpit.

Right: The 'Wrexham' Spitfire, the first floatplane Spitfire to fly, seen here on taxying trials with an enlarged tail fin, a lower fin (replacing the tail-wheel), a tropical air filter and floats fitted (in place of undercarriage).

Left: The 'Wrexham' Spitfire floatplane after the new tail unit and air intake have been added.

befits a 'forward-looking' County Borough, no longer grace the walls of the Guildhall. Construction of W3760 had started in July 1941 and it was first flown on 11 August 1941. Thereafter it suffered something of an identity crisis. On 15 August it was allocated to the Director(ate) of Technical Development, beginning a long period of trials as 'a Spitfire with floats' before finally being struck off charge at Nº 108 MU, El Firdan, Sudan, on 28 December 1944 without a shot being fired in anger. The Air Ministry had begun its quest for a seaplane fighter way back in April 1940 when a German invasion of Norway was perceived as imminent. Basically, something was needed that could operate beyond the range of the shore based fighters and to defend fleet anchorages where there was no aerodrome. After several botched experiements and cancellations of projects, pure chance determined that W3760 was to become the latest production model guinea pig. From the DTD it was sent to Vickers and from there to Folland Aircraft, Hamble, for the installation of floats, a process necessitating, *inter alia*, the removal of undercarriage and retracting gear and strengthening wing spars to suit, the removal of the tail wheel and the addition of a Rotol 11' 3" diameter propeller. A tropical filter, added for operations in the Middle East, marred the smooth lines of the engine cowling. In November 1942 the Spitfire was delivered to the MAEE, Helensburgh for a further series of tests — maintenance and performance. Along with EP951 and EP754, two other floatplane conversions (already noted as regular visitors to Saro Beaumaris) W3760 arrived at Nº 52 MU, Lichfield on 27 September 1943 for packing and dispatch to the Middle East on board the SS *Penrith Castle*. The latter left the UK on 6 October 1943 arriving safely at Alexandria on 30 October. Service trials were begun immediately on the Great Bitter Lakes under the auspices of Nº 107 MU, Kasfareet. If things had gone well, it was intended that this flight of three float planes would operate against the Junkers Ju52 tri-motor transports flying between the Greek islands. On trials W3760, persistently buried one

float beneath the water on its take-off run and submerged its tail unit towards the end of the landing run. Corrosion was therefore rampant, and it had to have a new tail unit sent out from England. In the event, someone had also seriously miscalculated the logistical problems of supplying these float fighters by submarine and none of the three would see operational service. At the end of November all further tests were suspended. This particular shambles notwithstanding, the idea of a Spitfire on floats refused to die. Interest now focussed on converting a Mk IX. The single prototype MJ892 was weighed at Beaumaris on 14 June 1944 and test-flown by L/Cmdr F. C. Furlong between 6 and 11 July.

At least the western part of Denbighshire has the satisfaction of knowing that photographs of their Spitfire are in good hands, with the words *Borough of Colwyn Bay* boldly stencilled on the fuselage. For security reasons its registration number is not immediately visible. Fortunately its identity is known — a Castle Bromwich-built Supermarine Spitfire Mk II, registration number P8529. With this information the aircraft's history is immediately traceable. It served with Nº 118 Squadron at Ibsley (Hampshire), providing bomber escorts and making fighter sweeps over northern France, and then on defensive patrols with Nº 132 Squadron at Peterhead before being honourably retired in 1942 to Nº 58 OTU at Grangemouth and Balado Bridge (Kinross).

The *County of Montgomery*, a Spitfire VB, W3844, delivered new from Nº 8 MU Little Rissington, flew in 1941 with Nº 234 Squadron at Warmwell (Dorset) and Ibsley on defensive patrols and fighter sweeps, before transferring to Nº 302 (Polish) Squadron at Harrowbeer (Devon) as that unit converted from Hurricanes. The 'Poznanski' Squadron carried out aggressive fighter sweeps over Normandy and Brittany. On 27 January 1942 W3844 was shot down.

The Mk I Spitfire *Ceredigion* (P8691) was converted to a FIIB, before delivery to Nº 12 MU (Aircraft Storage) Kirkbride on 23 May 1941. It was delivered to Nº 72

Left and below: The "Colwyn Bay' Spitfire. Two photographs of a fitter putting the finishing touches to Spitfire Mk II (P8529) at Castle Bromwich prior to delivery. [Below: W. Alister Williams Collection; Left: Denbighshire Record Office 23/267]

Squadron at Gravesend on 9 July then to N° 416 Squadron (RCAF) at Peterhead on 14 January 1942. The aircraft was involved in a flying accident on 9 March but was repaired then delivered to N° 58 OTU on 31 December 1942. Three months later, on 22 March, it was transferred to No 1 Coastal Artillery Co-operation Unit, Gosport. Its final home was with N° 61 OTU, Rednal, where it was damgaed beyond repair on 26 January 1945.

Caernarvonshire, a Spitfire FIIB (P8690) was delivered to N° 12 MU (Aircraft Storage), Kirkbride, on 25 May 1941 from where it was delivered to N° 610 (County of Chester) Squadron at RAF Westhampnett on 3 June. It was transferred to N° 616 (South Yorkshire) Squadron at Westhampnett on 19 July. Both of these squadrons, along with N° 145, were part of a three squadron protective blanket which had been given the task of both escorting day bombers on their raids over occupied Europe and providing with 'Rhubarb' sorties. The aircraft failed to return on 21 July 1941, presumed shot down whilst escorting Stirling bombers.

The registration of *Flint I* is known — P8654. It was delivered from N° 33MU (Lyneham) to N° 609 ('West Riding') Squadron then based at Biggin Hill on 24 May 1941. On 11 June 1941 it was shot down by a Messerschmitt Bf109 whilst on a fighter sweep over the Channel. Its pilot, Sgt G. A. Chestnut, was killed. The reconstituted county of Flintshire

still treasures a plaque on a wooden shield, preserved in the FRO and inscribed:

IN THE HOUR OF PERIL
THE PEOPLE OF THE COUNTY OF FLINT EARNED THE
GRATITUDE OF THE BRITISH NATION SUSTAINING
THE VALOUR OF THE ROYAL AIR FORCE AND
FORTIFYING THE CAUSE OF FREEDOM BY THE GIFT
OF SPITFIRE AIRCRAFT.
'THEY SHALL MOUNT UP WITH WINGS AS EAGLES'
ISSUED BY THE MINISTRY OF AIRCRAFT
PRODUCTION 1941

After the wear and tear of operational units, squadron Spitfires were relegated to no less essential duties with the OTUs. *Spirit of Crewe I*, a Mk IIA Spitfire P8425, completed tours with N°s 611, 308, 403, 54 and 457 Squadrons before joing N° 61 OTU at Rednal. On the other hand *Spirit of Crewe II*, P8395, was delivered from N° 33 MU to N° 234 Squadron at Warmwell and on 17 July 1941, failed to return from operations. *Cheshire County I*, AD248 began life as a Spitfire Mk V, was converted during a six squadron pilgrimage to a Mk IX to meet the challenge of the *Luftwaffe's* new Focke Wulf Fw109, before it, too, ended up at Rednal. *Cheshire*, R7158 a Spitfire I/V, was on the books of eight operational squadrons (including Polish, Free French and Czech units) before it was finally taken on the strength of N° 57 OTU, now at Eshott. Spitfire I, R7136, *Merioneth*, spent most of its life in a training or working-up rôle. In 1941 it was delivered from N° 12 MU, Kirkbride, to N° 124 Squadron which had reformed at Castletown (Caithness) in the May, becoming operational in the defence of Scapa Flow on 29 June. As the squadron converted to Spitfire IIBs, R7136 passed for a brief period to N° 340 Squadron, the first Free French fighter unit, working up at Turnhouse and Drem, before passing on to N°

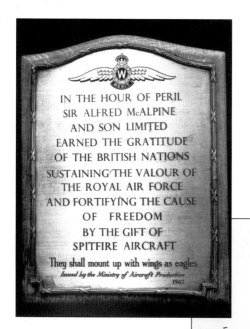

IN THE HOUR OF PERIL
SIR ALFRED McALPINE
AND SON LIMITED
EARNED THE GRATITUDE
OF THE BRITISH NATIONS
SUSTAINING THE VALOUR OF
THE ROYAL AIR FORCE
AND FORTIFYING THE CAUSE
OF   FREEDOM
BY THE GIFT OF
SPITFIRE   AIRCRAFT
They shall mount up with wings as eagles
Issued by the Ministry of Aircraft Production
1942

Spitfire VB (W3774) 'Samson', at Eastleigh in August 1941, one of the aircraft donated by Sir Alfred McAlpine & Co., before delivery to N° 9 MU, Cosford, at the start of its RAF service with N° 485 Squadron.

52 OTU at Aston Down. It was then transferred to the Admiralty and taken on the strength of RNAS Yeovilton, which station, carrying in 1943 a mixed bag of Sea Hurricanes, Spitfires, Masters, Fulmars and Martlets, was largely devoted to training FAA fighter pilots. R7136 was finally struck off charge on 23 November 1943.

A Spitfire VB, W3774, was named *Samson*, short for Sir Alfred McAlpine & Son, the civil engineering firm with quarries in the Wrexham area and the contractor responsible for the building of many local airfields, including RAF Wrexham, Sleap and Tilstock. *Samson* served with Nº 485 Squadron (RNZAF) at Redhill from July 1941 on fighter sweeps over France, then flying escort missions with Nº 124 Squadron Gravesend in July 1942. It ended its career in Nº 12 Group Fighter Command with Nºˢ 306 and 308 Polish Squadrons. On 14 May 1943 whilst with the latter unit at Church Fenton, W3774 collided in mid-air with Spitfire P8746 over a Stockwell potato farm, Yorkshire. P/O A. T. Habela and Sgt J. Osoba were killed instantly.

With hindsight these were remarkable fund raising efforts, especially since the campaign covered the period when most north Wales airfields were still on the drawing board. The 'Spitfire Weeks' of 1940 were a spontaneous response to the Battle of Britain, with people everywhere beginning to empathise with the achievements of the RAF. But although Flintshire and Shropshire each had two pre-war training airfields within their boundaries this was not a speedy process. As hinted earlier, in the provincial outback it took some time to come to terms with the full scope and dimensions of modern aerial warfare, not in the least because the RAF itself, compared with the other Services, embodied certain apparent illogicalities which even Churchill, never mind the inhabitants of bucolic garrison towns, was slow to assimilate and comprehend.

In the war at sea officers and ratings fought together in the same ship. On land, platoon, company and battalion commanders led their men into battle. This the inhabitants of Wrexham, Shrewsbury and Chester, the vast majority of whose menfolk served in these two Services, had long appreciated and responded to wholeheartedly in the appropriate fund raising campaigns. On the other hand, in the RAF fighting was done by officers or senior NCO aircrew, a wings wearing élite group, some 17% of an air force of over one million men, with basically no other function than combat. They were launched into battle, but rarely accompanied, by the remaining 83%, but had few responsibilities in matters of administration, discipline and welfare. The RAF ground establishment differed, too. The RAF was essentially a technical service demanding the recruitment of men with above the average skills and a higher level of education — implicit in the terms 'trade' (of which there were some 190 by 1944) and 'tradesman' — than normally associated with the mass of wartime soldiers and sailors. So that, when RAF Wrexham and Poulton were opened in 1941–3, their complements were drawn largely from outside the Wrexham area, to vanish with equal precipitancy in 1945 when the airfields were closed, except, that is, for the relatively few who chose to put down new roots in Wrexham and the surrounding villages.

All this became easier to relate to as the Wrexham area, no less than the north-west generally, became increasingly air conscious as aerodromes were built, aircraft crashed, the pieces picked up, airmen buried, and air raids got underway. In 1941 Wrexham people witnessed the mushrooming of an operational airfield less than three miles from the town centre and, barely recovered from the trauma of earlier evacuation exercises, experienced the enforced billeting in Acton, Rhosnesni and Maesydre of officers and airmen whose own dispersed living quarters would not be ready for twelve months or more. But above all local people had to resign themselves to increased aerial activity in Wrexham skies, with the incessant rasping din of aero-engines at all hours. Inevitably there was a rise in the number of incidents — crashes, forced landings and fatalities of the most horrible sort, both on and off the aerodrome. On the other hand, 2,000 airmen tried desperately to

Advert for Wings for Victory Week

involve themselves in the social, recreational, sporting, civic and military life of the community — from Armistice Day parades, concert parties and dance bands, to soccer, rugby and athletics fixtures and even the McAlpine Cup cricket competition — but always playing away from home.

By 'Warship Week' (19 November–6 December 1941) fund raising in the Wrexham area was in top gear. Their target of £210,000 to adopt a destroyer (HMS *Veteran*) was the largest in Denbighshire and was easily surpassed during the week. But there was only a finite sum available for 'Savings'. 'Tank for Attack Week', held ten months later, fell relatively flat. But the all-pervading presence and impact of the RAF in the area, focussed primarily on RAF Wrexham and Poulton, no doubt influenced the setting and exceeding of the most ambitious targets todate (to equip six RAF squadrons) in 'Wings for Victory Week', 15–22 May 1943. Each district set a target representing a selected number of aircraft. Those

East Denbighshire 'Wings for Victory' Appeal

	Target	Bombers (£20,000)	Fighters (£5,000)	Ambulance Aircraft (£5,000)	Totals Raised
West Wrexham Rural	£ 60,000	-	6	8	£ 85,128
Tanat/Cynllaith Valleys	£ 25,000	-	3	2	£ 32,763
Wrexham	£275,000	12	6	1	£360,151
Ruabon/Cefn	£ 45,000	-	9	-	£ 76,852
Ceiriog Valley	£ 25,000	-	3	2	£ 31,821
Rhos/Minera	£ 60,000	-	6	6	£ 82,057
Chirk	£ 25,000	-	3	2	£ 29,231
Llangollen	£ 55,000	-	6	5	£ 80,736
Total	**£570,000**	**12** (1 squadron)	**42** (3 squadrons, 1 Flight)	**24** (2 squadrons)	**£778,738**

Maelor, Flintshire 'Wings for Victory' Appeal

	Target	Totals Raised
Worthenbury	£ 2,250	£ 5,175
Bangor	£ 2,500	£ 6,295
Willington	£ 2,000	£ 4,884
Overton	£ 5,600	£14,236
Penley	£ 1,500	£ 3,221
Hanmer	£ 2,000	£ 2,223
Bronington	£ 2,500	£ 2,609
Iscoyd	£ 2,250	£ 4,503
Tybroughton	£ 1,000	£ 1,567
Halghton	£ 1,000	£ 8,187
Bettisfield	£ 1,500	£ 1,676
Totals	**£24,100**	**£54,576 (actually £52,900 but figures as given in the local press)**

attaining their targets were said to have gained their 'Victory Wings'. Details of targets and actual results for east Denbighshire are shown above.

The surplus of some £208,000 meant another 41 fighters or 10 bombers. Across the Dee, Maelor's 'Wings for Victory Week' was staggered, 26 June–6 July 1943. This detached part of Flintshire set itself a modest target of £25,000 for one Wellington bomber and a Spitfire. But for a thinly peopled rural area it did not stint on the opening ceremonies. Headed by an RAF band, 433 'military' personnel paraded at Overton, drawn from ATS and RAOC, Lightwood Green Depôt, RAF pilots ('some fifty different nationalties') and WAAFs from RAF Wrexham, 7th Den/Flint Home Guard, ACF, N° 1193 Squadron (Ellesmere) ATC, ROC Overton post, ARP, and WLA Queensbridge Hostel. Sqn/Ldr J. D. McEwan took the salute. No sooner had the various units been reviewed when they were whipped away to Hanmer for a second march past — but with 531 on parade! There are some apparent anomalies about Maelor's final collection figures. The local press quoted the remarkable overall total of £72,109 9s. 9d. but a breakdown by parishes nowhere approaches this amount. Nevertheless, even the more

realistic figure of over £54,000 is still an amazing result.

In 1943 most of the civil parishes in Maelor had a population of under 400. Indeed, Tybroughton had less than 200 and was steadily declining. As the largest village, Overton, a decayed medieval borough, could perhaps have beeen expected to fund three Spitfires on its own, but the Penley and Iscoyd figures could have been managed only with considerable financial input from the newly established American military hospitals at those places. But, with a population of 350 and falling, the Halghton achievement still intrigues. Fifty years on it has been impossible to discover whether the £8,000 (representing an 810% increase on target) included a large individual donation, as frequently happened, or was reached with the help of some 1,800 American troops stationed or hospitalised in Penley.

Other areas were just as successful in their fund raising. Mold and District aimed for £120,000, sufficient for six Wellingtons. They exceeded that sum by some £66,000. Caergwrle, another of Flintshire's slumbering medieval boroughs, took on the challenge of raising £20,000 for four fighters and actually made £43,000, with its tiny hamlets of Ffrith and Llanfynydd, lost in the folds of the Welsh hills,

Right: The MU band, RAF Hawarden, leads the Home Guard and Girls Brigade through the streets of Mold at the launch of the town's 'Wings for Victory' campaign, 1943. [Mosaic courtesy of Wrexham Archives]

Below: Maelor's 'Wings for Victory' campaign started off with a parade through Overton. Girl Guides, led by Margaret Owen, pass the Parish Church, watched by local members of the Auxilliary Fire Service.

exceeding their modest £500 target by £2,763 15s. 6d. Buckley, as ever, tried to beat everyone else, and instead of two Wellingtons managed to fund three bombers and a fighter. Those districts lying nearer the Vickers Armstrong aircraft factory at Broughton went for the Wellington bombers rather than fighters. Not unsurprisingly, Hawarden and District opted to buy twelve Wellingtons at £240,000 and raised £301,607. Similarly Holywell and District bought nine Wellingtons, two more than targeted, while the Flint area spread the load, going for '4 two-engined bombers and 8 fighters', a target exceed by some £31,000. Prestatyn went for the even larger stuff. The town set itself a target of two Lancaster bombers at £40,000 each, chucking in eight Spitfires on the side. The £105,000 target was exceeded by £25,5000.

Interestingly the smaller communities of Dyserth, Gronant and Newmarket out towards Point of Ayr chose to provide 'Air Sea Rescue Aircraft', not only because they were cheaper — at a nominal £2,500 — but also because their inhabitants were already heavily involved in ASR searches and picking up the pieces of literally dozens of aircraft that had come to grief on the Dee estuary mud flats and sandbanks and on and over the Talacre firing ranges. Was it a tongue-in-cheek gesture which prompted Dyserth also to provide a North American Mustang at £4,500? Those areas near RAF Hawarden were able to stage 'attractive Aeronautical Exhibitions' as centre-pieces to their Savings campaigns. These included 'train and tank buster' mock-

ups, hands-on bomb-aiming and R/T equipment, a Link Trainer, and static Spitfire displays. Besides these, all other events, such as horse shows, paled into insignificance!

In Shropshire, people were not unaware that since May 1942 Nº 60 OTU at High Ercall had been flying the de Havilland Mosquito and operational squadrons using the airfield were converting to the Hawker Typhoon. Not illogically, therefore, these aircraft begin to feature in local 'Wings for Victory' campaigns — Bishops Castle and Clun, 3 Mosquitos and 8 Spitfires; Oakengates, one Mosquito and 6 Typhoons. Bridgnorth went for '2 squadrons of Beaufighters', but at only £200,000 this seems remarkably cheap! Oswestry went shopping for 50 Spitfires, and bought 57; similarly Ellesmere ended up sponsoring 12 'single-engined fighters', two more than hoped for. Whitchurch, although with a bomber OTU on its doorstep at RAF Tilstock, opted to supply 25 Spitfires, but collected £182,928, sufficient for 36 fighters. It was left to Wem, which was the 'home town' for RAF Sleap, Tilstock's satellite, to try and provide five Wellingtons at £100,000. This latter campaign was almost a non-starter, for a misprint in the publicity had the little town going for *twenty-five* bombers. This would have set them back half-a-million pounds!

These bare statistics convey little of the tremendous amount of organisation that went on for some three months prior to an actual fund-raising campaign The RAF was spotlighted by every means possible — in the Wrexham area by RAF displays in the Church House, parish halls, shop windows, in schools by poster and modelling competitions, through special film shows in all local cinemas, by grand parades in every village of any size (with RAF 'not-so-top-brass' dashing from one saluting base to another), by patriotic addresses (preferably by 'local flying heroes') in factories and work place, through dances fronted by the RAF 'Ambassadors Dance band' and the band of the Lancashire Fusiliers, with a battle-weary, but nevertheless impressive, Hurricane displayed in Bodhyfryd Square, through sports fixtures (soccer, K.O. cricket, tug-of-war) between local teams and those from the RAF and ATC, while the Berwyn Squadron, ATC, took their dramatised version of the 'ATC on Parade' around Llangollen, Acrefair, Chirk and adjacent villages.

Wrexham schools early passed their target for an ambulance aircraft. Objections from rather pompous councillors and chapel elders on moral and religious grounds to involving schoolchildren in fund-raising for the war effort had been quickly swept aside by a ground swell of indignant patriotism. The emphasis placed on ambulance aircraft in the Wrexham area (two squadrons were the target) seemed something of an omen, presaging the area's real life involvement with them.

D-Day was less than a year away. In the summer of 1944 RAF Tilstock and RAF Rednal, although training airfields, would see an influx by air of the wounded from the Normandy beach-heads, destined for the five US Army hospital, specially set up at Penley Hall, Llannerch Panna (also in Penley), Iscoyd Park (all within Maelor) and at Halston Park (Whittington) and Otley Park (Ellesmere) just over the Flintshire/Shropshire border. Fortunately casualties were not as heavy as expected. Nevertheless over 600 casualties were landed at RAF Tilstock in July 1944. At Rednal mercy flights continued until the end of August, in which month 77 aircraft flew in over 1,770 Allied and German seriously wounded.

The presence of the latter was kept very low key but may partly account for the existence of a small German 'POW camp' to the rear of the Penley Hall Hospital, on a field now known as the *Prisoner of War Field* or *Cage Field*, usurping the pre-war *Carthouse Meadow* and even earlier *Cae Rhos* (='Moor Field'). The 'camp' was hutted and surrounded with barbed wire and watch-towers. Here, once they had recovered sufficiently, were kept the German 'patients', strictly segregated from the POW farmworkers, until such time as they were able to face interrogation and perhaps begin the long journey to a POW camp in Canada. This was the first occasion in the war when fighting men could expect to be cared for in proper hospitals within hours of being wounded. As Allied forces pushed further into Normandy, wounded arrived at the two Penley hospitals via a continuous stream of ambulance trains at Overton Station, working out from RAF Transport Command casevac airfields such as Down Ampney, Broadwell and Blakewell Farm in Oxfordshire and Gloucestershire. The only delay would occur in trying to fit Red Cross trains into the already complex operating schedule of the single-track Wrexham–Ellesmere railway, closed to civilian passenger traffic for the duration because, with only three passing loops, it could not otherwise handle the heavy munitions traffic emanating from N° 35 Royal Ordnance Factory on the outskirts of Wrexham.

15. Forgotten air force

This concluding chapter is something of a 'Cinderella' history, dealing with a subject too fleetingly covered in Chapter 7 of this present history — the Air Transport Auxiliary (ATA). While the ATA may have had fairy-tale beginnings, arriving central stage almost unnoticed, overcoming ingrained and latent prejudice in the RAF and Air Ministry, there would be no happy ending. At the very peak of its expansion and efficiency, no further use, apparently, could be made of the organisation. When the axe came it was blunt and swift. Within five months the ATA had been dismembered piecemeal; it disappeared unnoticed, unsung, and, with that remarkable propensity of British bureaucracy to knock success and achievement, unhonoured and unrewarded, save perhaps to be allocated a place amongst bus drivers and railwaymen in the Victory Parade, away from their erstwhile RAF colleagues in uniform. Although bare statistics show 199 'RAF attached' at the peak, the 551 male, and 110 female pilots and 127 flight engineers who flew with ATA (not forgetting some 2,600+ ground staff) were all civil aviators, volunteers who filled a desperate need in desperate times, without whose efforts the Battle of Britain would have been an even more closely run thing than it was, and the woeful attrition rate of early Bomber Command campaigns unsustainable over the two years it took the Command to get its act together. But former members of the ATA have their memories and the record of their work cannot be denied, if still largely unappreciated: 309,011 aircraft ferried; 414,984 hours flown in them; 179,325 hours flown and 18,250,000 miles travelled by the pool taxis, with only three passenger casualties.

Each of the inevitably dwindling band, former members of N° 3 Ferry Pilots Pool, Hawarden, who each year since 1945 have held their annual reunion on the first Saturday in November at the Blossoms Hotel, Chester, cherish the words of Lord Beaverbrook at the first — and last — air pageant held at White Waltham on 29 September 1945:

I am conscious that we are taking farewell of the ATA and the splendid chapter which it wrote in British history.

The ATA was formed at a time when pilots were in such demand that none could be spared except those who had attained to years of more than discretion. The ATA carried out the delivery of aircraft from the factories to the RAF thus relieving countless numbers of RAF pilots for duty in the battle. Just as the Battle of Britain is the accomplishment and achievement of the RAF, likewise it can be declared that the ATA sustained and supported them in the battle. They were soldiers fighting in the struggle just as completely as if they had been engaged on the battle front.

At least the Minister of Aircraft Production fully comprehended and valued the achievements of those men and women 'who were too old to fly and fight, but not too old to fall'. But sadly not all those who had ears were prepared to listen. Well could ex-First Officer Lettice Curtis entitle her very personal account of her days with the ATA, *Forgotten Pilots*. With considerable foresight First Officer E. C. Cheesman, called his history of the ATA, *Brief Glory*. This was published in 1946, less than six months after the Air Pageant at White Waltham to inform the general public about the ATA's work since its tentative beginnings in May 1938. With a similar aim this chapter focusses on the ATA as it functioned in the north-west of England and along the Welsh border with Hawarden and N° 3 FPP at the hub of events. On 30 November 1945 the ATA flag was lowered for the last time at Hawarden and Hatfield. But conraction had been going on for some time as the presssures of war eased and VE Day loomed, and threats of a protracted Pacific campaign against Japan receded. Hawarden was the largest aircraft movement pool in the country and, like so many ferry pools, was essentially male dominated. But in its last months it successfully coped with an influx of female pilots from N°ˢ 6 (Cosford) and 15 (Hamble) FPPs that had closed down in June and August respectively. ATA ferry pools at Aston Down and Cosford had stood down in June 1945, with Lossiemouth following in July. Hamble and Sydenham (Belfast) pools were disbanded in August, with massive redundancies at Whitchurch (Bristol), Ringway and Kirkbride in September. October saw Prestwick,

ATA ranks
Commodore
Senior-Commander
Commander
Captain
Flight-Captain
First-Officer
Second-Officer
Third-Officer
Cadet

Ratcliffe, and Sherburn-in-Elmet fold. N° 1 FPP at White Waltham would soldier on, tying up loose ends until 31 March 1946. In several instances, as the RAF tackled the problem of slimming down, demobilisation and the disposition of aircraft surplus to operational requirements, the ATA pools were replaced almost immediately by military (RAF) ferry pools — N° 1 FP at White Waltham, N° 2 FP at Aston Down, N° 3 at Lichfield, N° 5 at Silloth and, in our region, N° 4 Ferry Pool at Hawarden — all as in the past under the control of N° 41 Group, Maintenance Command. As Commander Sydney Watson Ogden ('Stan'), 'marched out', not even symbolically turning the key in the door of the ATA hut for the last time, simply exchanging signatures on innumerable forms, so the RAF 'marched in'. In the air the casual observer would perhaps have noted only an upgrading of veteran 'taxis' to Mks. XI and XIX Ansons — a luxury the RAF could now well afford — and the fact that the Hawarden ferry pool aircraft now sported the '3D' code of N° 48 MU next door. The latter, with the disbandment of N° 58 OTU in July 1945, had become the main occupier of

Above: The annual reunion held at the Blossoms Hotel, Chester. Known names are: Right-hand table — Lionel Davies, Jimmy Powell, Ken Day, George Foster, Jimmy Quaife, Steve Buckley. Standing at the back: Jimmy James, Harry Shepard. Top of left-hand table: Harry Ellis.   [K. Day]

Avro Anson VM312 from N° 4 Ferry Pool, Hawarden. The aircraft carries the code of N° 48 MU — '3D'.
[Arthur Percy via K. Day]

Approximate number of ATA pilots

Date	Female	Male	Total
February 1940	10	42	52
October 1940	25	175	200
December 1940	25	217	243
December 1941	48	377	425
June 1942	77	423	500
April 1943	95	471	569
April 1944	108	551	659
August 1944	125	550	675
February 1945	110	522	632
June 1945	148 (seconded or recalled RAF)		

Information: Lettice Curtis; Charles H. Moore, Buckley; Ken Day, Chester.

the aerodrome. Outlying dispersals were de-requisitioned. and Hooton Park had become a storage sub-site (N° 100 SLG) with an estimated capacity for 400 aircraft, but on occasion squeezing in 700+. To the mundane throughput of Halifaxes, Mosquitos, Wellingtons, Lancasters, were added rarer types — Lancastrians, Vikings, Dakotas and even Junkers Ju52s, the last two on their way to the small civilian air lines even then beginning to proliferate. But all this is to jump the gun. Let us start at the beginning.

Soon after the Vickers-Armstrong shadow aircraft factory at Hawarden came on stream in August 1939, an emergency conference was held to tackle the increasingly urgent logistical problem of moving aircraft out to Aircraft Storage Units, where they would await allocation and delivery to RAF squadrons and OTUs. The decision in September 1939 to also site an ASU (N° 48 MU) at Hawarden, did not help matters, leading to overcrowding of already crowded Flintshire skies. Along with 23 other MUs it came under the control of N° 41 Group, Maintenance Command Despite lack of equipment and dedicated hangarage the MU became operational on 6 March 1940 under the command of S/Ldr. G. Thornton. Additionally, since early January 1940 the as

yet incomplete all-grass aerodrome had been virtually unserviceable due to waterlogging. Only with difficulty had the first production Wellington been flown off by Maurice Hare, chief production test pilot, from a short stretch of dry land on the west side of the aerodrome. Subsequently all flight testing would be carried out at Weybridge. Hare had been transferred north specifically to set up the test flight programme at Hawarden. As the output of aircraft increased, more pilots arrived from Weybridge to join his team.

Their numbers were supplemented by pilots of RAF Reserve Command, more specifically of N°s 1 and 2 (Service) Ferry Pools (RAF), into whose ranks early members of the ATA would be posted — or was it the other way about? By September 1939 N° 2 (S) FPP Filton had ten ATA pilots on its books, increasing to thirteen by December. N° 1 (S)FPP, Hucknall, (Nottingham-shire), had a complement of some 18 ATA pilots, who cut their teeth on ferrying impressed aircraft out of Hooton Park, Hurricanes into Shawbury (the first of 29,401 deliveries on type) and by those qualified to fly twin-engined aircraft, Blenheims from Liverpool to Cosford. Ultimately 8,569 deliveries would be made on this type. A N° 4 (Continental) Ferry Pilots Pool, Cardiff, formed specifically to ferry replacement aircraft to France for the Air Component BEF reverted to N° 4 (S)FPP in September 1940 after that particular fiasco came to its inglorious end. Flights had already been detached to Kemble and Netheravon and on 11 October 1940 'B' Flight was detached to Hawarden where the ATA had

Ken Day joined the ATA after an accident. He had flown Blenheims with N° 57 Squadron and delivered many Blenheims into and out of Cosford. [K. Day]

Inset: Just over the perimeter fence of the MU and ATA sites lay Mold Junction, a designated **Luftwaffe** *target in its own right since 18 September 1940. The Chester–Holyhead mainline curves away in the left distance past the old timber Nº 4 signal box, re-built by LMS in 1939 'to withstand a bomb blast'. This tiny box controlled emergency distant signals protecting aerodrome runways and accommodation crossing to MU dispersals. [LMS/British Rail]*

Main picture: A corner at Hawarden aerodrome, January 1947.
A: Mold Junction   B: Site Nº 2
C: Site Nº 3   D: ATA Headquarters
[National Assembly for Wales]

Left: One of the Airspeed Couriers and the ground staff at Nº 3 Ferry Pilot Pool. L–R: Cyril Daniels, Jolly Hodgson, Bill Carrie and Hobbs. Note the motif of a vulture below the cockpit. [Charles H. Moore]

Below right: The other Airspeed Courier from Nº 3 FPP, complete with motif and fitter George (Yorky) Watson. [Charles H. Moore]

Below left: The first taxi aircraft allotted to Nº 3 FPP, Airspeed Courier G-ACLF, still with its civil registration but camouflaged and bearing an RAF roundel, which visited Hawarden on many occasions during the early months of C Section's existence. L–R: Bill Carrie, Cyril Daniles and George Watson. [Charles H. Moore]

already been in residence some six months. In October 'B' Flight Nº 4(S)FPP would become Nº 9(S) FPP in its own right, confirming the useful 'half-way house' nodality of Hawarden to both ferrying services. No 1 (S)FPP would disband on 10 May 1940, civilian pilots being re-absorbed into the ATA, by now established in its own right at White Waltham aerodrome, Berkshire, home since 1935 to the de Havilland School of Flying (later Nº 13 ERFTS/EFTS) which would quit the place in December 1940).

The first civilian Ferry Pool had been established at White Waltham on 15 February 1940 and numbered Nº 3 FPP to avoid confusion with existing RAF units. By now all civil ATA pilots had to undertake a 'conversion' course to service types at the Central Flying School at Upavon until such time as the CFS could not cope and the ATA had perforce set up their own flying schools.

This had not been achieved without some difficulty and inter-Ministry squabbling. In September 1940, Lord Beaverbrook, Minister of Aircraft Production, who, not unnaturally, took a very active interest in ATA matters, wrote to Sir Archibald Sinclair, Secretary of State for Air, as follows:

As you know, I have surrendered no less than 35 Service pilots from the RAF Ferry Pool for duty with operational units. Further, with our own increasing production and the arrival of American machines, taken in conjunction with the shorter hours of daylight, we shall have to increase greatly the size of our Ferry Pilots Pool if we are to maintain delivery of aircraft from factory to ASU and from ASU to operational units. At present the HQ of the Ferry Pilots Pool is at White Waltham and the training at Whitchurch. This is an inconvenient and uneconomical arrangement and I have definitely come to the conclusion that the training unit should move to White Waltham. The accommodation at White Waltham is totally inadequate as the Headquarters of a Ferry Pool; indeed, it is little short of disgraceful. However if I can take over all the buildings at White Waltham, it would be sufficient for the training units and will provide suitable accommodastion for the Headquarters of the Ferry Pool. I realise it will be difficult for you give up an Elementary Flying School at the present time, but I suggest that it should be moved to Hawarden, near Chester, which is a very suitable aerodrome for an EFTS and would not offer the same target to an enemy as does the OTU which is now at Hawarden and which I ask you to move therefrom. I should be most grateful if you could give this your favourable consideration at once so that I can start on a proper training establishment at White Waltham at the earliest possible date.

At the best of times a MAP factory presented a tempting target for the *Luftwaffe*. As noted earlier the aerodrome had adorned the German reconnaissance archive since 18

ATA Site Nº 3, Hawarden, 2004

Right: The best it got. The ATA's extended Bellman hangar and annexes, boiler house and engineering office.

Left:Site 3, the MU's Nº 1 L-type hangar, now home to Hawker Fuselage Assembly.

Left: The ATA garage, directly behind was the over-ground air raid shelter and rest room.

Right: L–R — in the deep grass are the taxi bay, parachute store, over-ground air raid shelter, cycle racks and transformer kiosk (updated version). The large building to the rear of these is the new offices and latrines.

Left: Rear view of the Bellman hangar. To its left is the ATA's Robin hangar. To the right, just around the corner, was the pilots' rest room.

Right: The new offices/latrines annex on the side of the Bellman hangar.

For over a year the ATA worked out of the semi-detached house on the left of this photograph. Wellingtons awaiting delivery in the background. [E. C. Cheesman]

September 1940, with hindsight justifying Beaverbrook's unease in this respect. The presence of an OTU on the same field added considerably to its drawing power as a legitimate military target. An internal memo would seem to indicate that Nº 10 Group Fighter Command would not be averse to moving its OTU from Hawarden:

> We imagine that since the Minister presses us to vacate Hawarden, you might agree that there is no real objection to our doing so when another [aerodrome] can be found. In practice it will perhaps mean that we shall never be able to do so … Would it be possible to carry out Hawarden's OTU night flying at a relief aerodrome, as we have stopped night flying at Hawarden some time ago at the urgent request of the Vickers works on the aerodrome, and owing to the fact that Hawarden has a lot of MU aircraft as well. Hawarden OTU are at present about to share night flying facilities at Cranage with the SFTS at Sealand. This was the best we could get after some scratching around for some suitable place …

Suggestions had been made as to perhaps utilising aerodromes at Sutton Bridge (Lincolnshire) and St Athan (Glamorganshire), but the former, well known pre-war as an Armament Training Camp (bombing and gunnery) had in March 1940 transmogrified into Nº 6 OTU within Nº 11 Group, training and supplying pilots, high accident rate notwithstanding, to seriously depleted Hurricane squadrons during the Battle of Britain. St Athan, too, could only offer restricted air and ground space. Nº 19 MU was well on its way to becoming the largest aircraft storage unit in the UK while Nº 32 MU was a specialist electronics (AI, IFF and ASV) installation unit. Not surprisingly, when faced with so many non-options, Sinclair's response to Beaverbrook's original letter, was brief and to the point:

> I'm afraid it is quite impossible for us to vacate Hawarden. It is one of the fighter OTUs and is absolutely essential at the present moment. There is no other place available for this purpose. It may be that in the future we may be able to provide another aerodrome but all the indications are that we shall have largely to increase the

number of OTUs next year. Consequently I am unable to see my way clear to give any undertaking to vacate. Incidentally we have spent many thousands of pounds in providing accommodation at Hawarden for an OTU. We cannot afford to see this standing empty at a time when we are so very short of winter accommodation. In order to meet the representations made by the MAP, we have stopped night flying. We are trying to find a relief landing ground in the district where night flying can be done. In the meantime we are sharing night flying facilities at Cranage with Nº 5 SFTS from September 1940.

On 1 May 1942 all ATA Ferry Pilots Pools were redesignated Ferry Pools, by which time the ATA was operating some fourteen such pools, in addition to its own Ferry Training Pool, an Air Movements Flight for ambulance, communications and spare-parts delivery duties, and Initial, Elementary and Advanced Flying Training Schools. Further regularisation of the situation had taken place on 1 April 1940, with the creation of BOAC as a successor body to Imperial Airways Ltd and British Airways Ltd, the latter the 'mother' civil aviation body under which the ATA initially had been placed for administration and finance purposes. Since the ferrying of all new aircraft from MAP factories had now become the responsibility of the ATA, 'operational control' of all civilian pilots became vested in Nº 41 Group, Maintenance Command. One immediate effect was that Nº 3 FPP was split into four more widely dispersed 'Sections', Section 'B' with twelve pilots and three Ansons posting out to Whitchurch, Bristol; Section 'D' (ex ATA Women's Section) to Hatfield; and Section 'C' with seventeen pilots and, on paper, four Ansons, to Hawarden. In practice 'C' Section had to manage with two clapped out Airspeed Couriers of 1933/5 vintage as air-taxis G-ACNZ, and G-ACVF, impressed in March 1940 as X9342,

The first CO of No 3 FPP, Hawarden was Walter Handley, seen here during his career as a TT rider. He won four TT races and held nine lap records. He was also a brilliant car racer before the war. He lost his life as a pilot with the ATA. [G. S. Davison, editor TT Special]

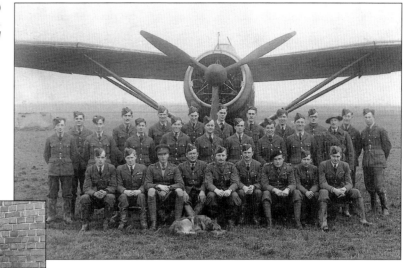

Right: Pilots and ground staff of Nº 13 (Army Co-operation) Squadron in France.
[Eric Illingworth, Nº 13 Squadron]

Below: Ground staff of Nº 13 Squadron at Mons-en-chaussee where they were stationed from 21 October 1939 until 11 May 1940.
[Eric Illingworth]

Below: A Westland Lysander Mk II (L6851) of Nº 13 (Army Co-operation) Squadron at RAF Hooton Park.
[K. Day]

X9346 and X9437 (not X9347 as given in some logs) respectively, noted as flying out of Hawarden 2–26 June 1940 in civil markings over military camouflage. A third impressed Courier (G-ADAY) later arrived at Hawarden from Nº 22 MU Silloth as a communications aircraft for Nº 48 MU and Nº 41 Group regional officers. As X9343 it was struck off charge on 13 May 1941 having failed a periodic check and declared 'beyond economic repair'. These were amongst what Cheesman feelingly described as 'an amazing assortment of light aircraft … put into service immediately and kept going until they practically fell to pieces'. As taxis the Couriers were a dead loss — old, often unserviceable, and carried only three passengers. They were quickly replaced by Avro Anson K8837 followed later by K6302, K6323-K6325, K8743 and K8760.

The opening up party arived at Hawarden on Tuesday,

16 April 1940 and was commanded by Captain Walter Leslie Handley, with Len Peters and Bert Jolly heading up ground crew and maintenance. Pre-war, Handley ran a motorcycle business at Birmingham and owned and flew Avro 625 Avian Monoplane G-AAYW. There is no record of this aircraft being impressed and Walter still owned it during his nineteen months at Hawarden. When Section 'C' opening-up party arrived at Hawarden they found 'organised chaos' with space and accommodation at a premium. The MU was still under construction and work had not yet started on the OTU. Tents were pegged out around the aerodrome perimeter, but, luckily for the moment, the good weather held.

Repercussions of a distant war were experienced at first hand in May 1940, when according to Bert Jolly several Lysanders flew into the ATA site 'looking more like a

ATA ground staff, officers, maintenance staff and Air Cadets. Known faces: second row, seated officers, L–R — Bert Jolly, F. Faraday, Jack Burrill, Commander Stan Ogden, Harry Miller, Reg Jones, Charles H. Moore. The man standing behind the lady seated fifth from the left is Thomas Jones, a foreman who came from Denbigh (he had served in the RFC/RAF in the First world War). [Brynmor Jones/Charles H. Moore]

Farmers' Union meeting than an RAF squadron. Never did get to the bottom of it. We patched up a few of the kites that were in bad condition. Kicked out of France in a hurry; left all their possessions behind. They stayed a few days and then flew out. Lots of interest shown by the MU lads'. With hindsight this tired, tattered remnant comprised the Lysander IIs of Nᵒ 13 (Army Co-operation) Squadron which had been badly mauled whilst carrying out 'tactical reconnaissance' with the Air Component of the BEF in France. The ground echelon had embarked for England on 29 May 1940, arriving at Hooton Park on 1 June. Aircraft had left Abbeville a day or two earlier, flying to Hawarden via an operational stop-over at Bekesbourne (Kent). Originally a First World War Home Defence airfield, until the outbreak of war the latter had been Canterbury Aerodrome, home to Kent Flying Club; in desperate times it had been reactivated as a *Back Violet* airfield at which aircraft would be based while operating from ALGs in France. Here the Lysanders of Nᵒ 2 (Army Co-operation) Squadron, also refugees from France, had been ensconced since 21 May. Now the two units carried out armed recces over France, largely without loss. But it must have been with some relief that Nᵒ 13 Squadron flew north to the relatively peaceful monotony of anti-submarine and convoy patrols along the north Wales coast!

It was intended that the ATA at Hawarden should have facilities on the MU's Nᵒ 3 Site, but in the early weeks the unit found itself squashed between the Vickers-Armstrong flight shed and the MU's Nᵒ 1 'L'-type hangar. Access was by a former farm track and an accommodation level crossing NE of Broughton & Bretton Station. For a maintenance workshop Handley managed to secure the temporary use of an ex-First World War Bessonneau canvas hangar which was being used by the aerodrome contractors for storing bags of cement; offices were set up nearby in a large timber hut constructed out of wooden aircraft packing cases. The rest of

'C' Section arrived from White Waltham on 6 May, three Ansons in the morning and one after lunch. Staff were billeted out in surrounding villages and even in Chester itself. Pressure was brought by ATA HQ, White Waltham for the provision of a 'proper' operations room and met. office. This particular problem was resolved by requisitioning the Warden's married quarters, a semi-detached house which had even earlier housed the level-crossing keeper's and a farm labourer's family. Handley's main office, dominated by a large wall map of the dispersal areas showing where individual aircraft were parked, was in the large ground floor room of one semi. Next door was ferry crew rest room

A pre-marked RAF chart emphasises Hawarden's crucial role as the hub of the ATA ferry activities.

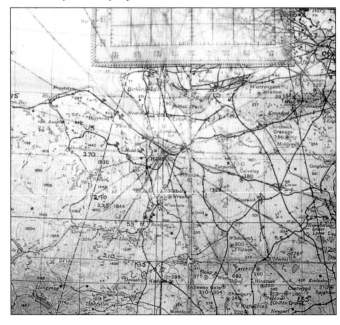

The long ride home. A poker session gets under way in a returning Anson. [J. A. Quaife]

and the RAF-run met office. The upper rooms were used for equipment stores, including a parachute issuing and checking-in counter. Food and drink were prepared by Mrs Jones in the tiny back kitchen of the 'Railway House' .

By 20 May the Pool could muster some twenty pilots including the CO. Walter ran a very tight ship and had the knack of applying gentle pressure in appropriate places. The ATA employed and trained local engineers, fitters and mechanics while the MAP factory oversaw building maintenance. Ground crews started work at 0700hrs, carrying out pre flight checks on aircraft due to be ferried that morning. Weather permitting ferrying commenced 0900hrs. Orders would be received daily from Nº 41 Group regarding aircraft to be ferried. The MT bus would do its round picking up pilots from billets. On arrival authorisations and aircraft delivery notes were picked up, locations checked from the wall map, met. forecasts perused and any necessary parachute collected. Taxi-cars awaited for transport round the MU site; on the field, a final check with engineering and the aircraft was able to take off, having 'showed intention' to the Aircraft Control Pilot and received the green light. There was no on-board radio in those early days, and constant visual checks had to be made for other aircraft, particulary after Nº 7 OTU received its aircraft and started flying in the July.

By July the MU had moved into Nº 1, 2 and 6 hangars and shared their facilities with the ATA, but in August as the whole MU site was nearing completion, the ATA were provided with a large dedicated Bellman hangar as their main workshop with engineering office and annexes, supplemented by a Robin hangar. A new parachute store and rest room were located alongside the Bellman. Later on the MT section had a garage and rest room, maintaining the ATA taxi rank. Refuellers had their own rest room. Incongruous and a potential danger to health was the siting of a cannon firing and testing range just 100 yards from the ATA complex. During the Battle of Britain and right through to March 1943 Nº 3 Site was also crawling with Army personnel in the shape of 'B' and 'C' Troops, Nº 188 Battery, Nº 63 Regiment, Royal Artillery. Billeted in a large hut along the perimeter fence, they manned the the machine gun and Bofors gun posts that also doubled up as the defences for the nearby Mold Junction marshalling yards. Addtional day and night security was provided by dog patrols from the MU Main Site.

On 18 June 1940 a Gloster Gauntlet II (K7811), on a ferry flight with Nº 3 FPP, from RAF St Athan ASU, collided with a heap of drainage pipes and contractor's rubble whilst landing at Hawarden. One of the last open cockpit fighter biplanes to serve with the RAF it had been on the books of Nºs 11 and 213 Squadrons, but was now destined for Nº 3 School of Technical Training, at Squires Gate, Blackpool, as a guinea pig for would-be flight mechanics and riggers; but after this accident it ended up at Marshalls of Cambridge instead and would be struck off charge as beyond economic

repair on 20 July 1940.

In July the transfer of the Ferry Pools to the Ministry of Aircraft Production (MAP) saw the ATA shouldering responsibility for ferrying aircraft from the factories to ASUs, with service pools moving them from ASUs to operational flying units. To this end, now that France had fallen, Nº 4 (Continental) FPP, RAF, based at Cardiff, was reorganised and split into separate flights based at Kemble, Hawarden and Silloth (Cumberland) to avoid overlaps and long uneconomical return rail journeys by ferry crews. In due course (11.10.40) 'B' Flight at Hawarden would become Nº 9 (Service) FPP. But this arrangement was obviously not sufficient to meet in-house service demands. In March–April 1941 Fighter Command groups, either singly or jointly, established their own fighter delivery service from the ASUs. At Hendon (for Nº 11 Group) Nº 1 Aircaft Delivery Flight (ADF) took the pressure off Nº 24 Squadron which hitherto had been saddled with the task. Nº 2 ADSF at Colerne served Nº 10 Group while Nº 4 Group at Grangemouth was responsible for the delivery of fighter aircraft to units in Nºs 13 and 14 Groups. An Aircraft Delivery Flight had been formed at Hawarden on 10 March 1941 and was redesignated Nº 3 ADF as from 7 April 1941. Initially with a couple of DH Dominies (R5992, X7331) as taxis this flight supplied the replacement needs of fighter units in Nºs 9 and 12 Groups.

Whatever the ferry unit, procedure was roughly the same. Pre-determined pick-up and delivery points were worked out daily, on the premise that nothing untowards would occur and pilots would reach their destination as planned. Failure to make the pick-up point meant a tiresome train journey back to base the next day. Flexibility was now the key word, with extended geographical distribution of pool bases reducing overlaps in ferry work and enabling pools to help each other when hard pressed as often happened following prolonged spells of adverse weather which led to back logs at the factories.

The summer of 1940 was a period when ATA taxi and ferried aircraft had several unforseen encounters with enemy aircraft. With as many as eight ferry pilots on board, an unarmed Anson was particularly vulnerable and it was decided to recruit air gunners for some protection, despite

*The result of a mid-air collision. Ju88 **9K+GN** lies in a crumpled heap at Lower Weir Farm, Oakridge, Lynch; the involuntary work of Sgt G. H. Bell from N° 5 FTS, Sealand.*

doubts as to the validity of the move under International Law, which considered civilian air gunners as no less than *franc tireurs* (lit. 'free shooters') or guerillas, members of an irregular fighting unit! After a two-week course the first ATA airgunners 'passed out'. One, complete with Lewis gun and ammunition was assigned to Hawarden. After being there a month or so he was sumoned to the Minstry of Labour Office at Chester, to establish whether or not he was engaged in an essential occupation. E. C. Cheesman records the interview something along these lines:

'Oh yes, we wanted to see you. You say you are employed by the ATA at Hawarden aerodrome. What do you do there?'

'Well, my job is to look after a Lewis gun.'

'Oh, you mean you work in the armoury?'

'No, I am an Air Gunner.'

'Oh, I see; you're in the RAF. We thought you were with the ATA, who are civilians and yet you are a gunner. What do you do?'

'I sit in the back of the Anson and fire the gun.'

At this point the Labour Exchange lost patience and rang up Walter Handley, commanding the ATA Ferry Pool:

'We've got a chap here who says he is with you and fires a machine gun. He must mean he is in the RAF at Hawarden.'

'No, he is not; he's with us and we're jolly glad to have him these days.'

'Well, what the heck do I put him down as? — licensed bandit?'

Single-seater fighters in the process of being ferried by RAF personnel were a different matter. Thus, on 25 July 1940 Hawker Hurricane P3271, ex-N° 242 Squadron, shot down a Junkers Ju88 into the Bristol Channel whilst on ferry by 'C' Flight, N° 4 (Service) FPP (Kemble). Unfortunately control was lost of the Hurricane and P3271 spun in at Ashton Down, (Gloucestershire). But no more haphazard a chance meeting with an enemy aircraft on the same date was that of Sgt G. H. Bell, N° 5 SFTS, Sealand, who 'involuntarily' downed a Junkers Ju88 whilst on a cross-country Navex to South Cerney. Earlier in the afternoon the latter aerodrome had been attacked by a couple of Heinkel 111s. A Ju88 of 5/KG51 trundled across the smoking airfield, en route to

bomb the Gloster factory at Huccelcote and collided with the Sealand Master making its final approach. Three crew members of the German bomber parachuted to safety — and a POW camp — and the crippled aircraft (**9K+GN**) crashed at 1425hrs at Lower Weir Farm, Oakridge Lynch. Despite it being wartime with invasion imminent, the niceties of armed civilians in the air occupied the finest legal brains. The possibility of ATA pilots being offered commissions in the RAFVR was re-examined (and discarded once more). MAP compared their status to that of skippers of armed Auxiliary Vessels. A suggestion was also made that ground staff should join the Home Guard and have their own platoon. The matter was finally solved or shelved, when air gunners were withdrawn in November 1940.

But aircraft especially bombers were still ferried with fully loaded guns and curious fingers could cause some embarrassment. First Officer Ken Day recalls a ferry flight he made as co-pilot from Belfast to the Midlands in a Mk III Stirling. There were two passengers, one female also aboard. The man asked if he could show the lady the upper turret of the aircraft, which said dorsal turret carried two .303 machine guns. They had been gone some time when the cockpit crew heard the rat a tat of guns being fired. Ken made his way aft and found a very shaken duo. The man out of ignorance had triggered the guns. As they returned forward the Stirling lurched violently to starboard. The pilot was looking ashen and gesticulating out of the window. 'What I saw put me back at the controls in seconds, awaiting the next violent manoeuvre as we tried to dodge the anti-aircraft bursts coming up from the guns on the coast of Anglesey. We dodged and weaved, but still they kept us under fire'. Unable to outwit the guns the pilot turned towards the mountain mass south of Caernarfon gaining height as they did. Snowdonia, normally out of bounds, was hidden in broken cloud. 'By this time we were flying by the seat of our pants as we passed peak after peak. After twenty minutes flying the ground beneath got deeper as the first landmarks came into view — the aqueduct and viaduct over the Dee south of Wrexham. A deep sigh of relief by all — and we went on to Shrewsbury … .' Ken recalls visiting Llangollen in the 1990s and standing on the tow path of Pontcysyllte Aqueduct. In his own words 'time stood still and I was 50 years younger'.

Ferry missions inevitably took their toll and the following accidents may be cited in the early months; sporadic mishaps at first, but by the end of 1940 seven of the fourteen ATA ferry pools had been established, 2,100 hours flown by ATA ferry pilots and 2,000+ ferry movements logged (on 81 different types). The accident rate was bound to increase; for convenience details (a representative

The graves of F/O Laursen, ATA and P/O Ensign, RAF in St Deiniol's churchyard, Hawarden. Ensign was an American, from Hollywood, California.

selection only) for 1942–45 are consigned to an Appendix to this chapter.

10.1.40. Oxford P1941. Overshot, landing at Sealand. Nº 2 FPP.

28.3.40. Walrus P5664. Collision landing at Sealand.

15.4.40. Hector K8129. Engine failure on flight to Cosford Nº 3 FPP.

11.5.40. Anson K8837. Take off accident, Wolverhampton. Nº 3 FPP.

20.5.40. Hurricane P2672. Forced landing, Westbury-on-Severn, Nº 4 FPP.

18.6.40. Gauntlet K7811. Hit contractor's debris, Hawarden, Nº 3 FPP.

1.7.40. Audax K5123. Tipped on to nose, landing at White Waltham, Nº 3 FPP.

13.7.40. Spitfire K9869. Engine failure on take-off; ditched Hamble, Nº 3 FPP.

15.7.40. Battle L5768. Engine failure, forced landing, Bewdley. Nº 3 FPP.

4.8.40. Master N7761. Flew into hill in fog, Burnhead Peebles, Nº 3 FPP.

14.8.40. Hurricane P 3768. Engine failure, spun in Sealand, Nº 4 FPP.

15.8.40. Caudron AX776. Collapsed undercarriage landing at Sealand.

17.8.40. Hampden P2086. Engine failure as landing, crashed Honeybourne, Nº 4 FPP.

23.8.40. Master N7500. Abandoned, when lost in cloud, Ayrshire, Nº 3 FPP.

26.8.40. Hurricane V6563. Crashed on approach, Kemble, Nº 4 FPP.

28.8.40. Defiant L7003. Forced landing, Busworth, Nuneaton Nº 1 FPP.

31.8.40. Anson R9771. Tail unit damaged by OTU Spitfire, Hawarden Nº 3 FPP.

5.10.40. Blenheim Z5975. Landed on decoy, Sarchet, Caithness Nº 4 FPP.

16.10.40. Harrow K7026. Tyre burst, undercarriage collapsed, Hawarden Nº 3 FPP.

25.10.40. Blenheim R 3840. Lost in Birmingham Balloon Battage Nº 3 FPP.

4.11.40. Oxford R6019. Flew into hill in bad visibility, Brynford, Flintshire, Nº 4 FPP.

29.11.40. Moth AW135. Overshot Hawarden onto Cop Farm Nº 9 FPP.

29.12.40. Spitfire L1045. Overshot, Squires Gate, ran into trench, overturned, Nº 9 FPP.

The loss of Master N7500 is illustrative of basic, even primitive, 'by the seat of their pants' flying arrangements ATA pilots had to contend withj in the early months. It was on a ferry flight to Nº 8 FTS, Montrose; the pilot was First Officer Roy Hallowell Carew, ATA. He had become lost in very bad weather and was low on fuel. Whilst flying over the Doon valley his engine failed and he decided to abandon his aircraft. This he did successfully, landing at Ben Beoch, north-east of Dalmellington, Ayrshire. The Master fell to earth near the mining village of Benquhat. Hazards at flying from an increasingly congested Hawarden airfield were driven home to FPP pilots when, on 31 August 1940, one of its Ansons, R9771 was badly damaged by Spitfire I, K9918, which took off its tail unit whilst both were landing. Again, on 26 March 1941 impressed Puss Moth BK846 (ex-G-ABEI) had an accident at Hawarden at the end of its landing run caused by the slip stream of a departing Wellington, which blew the lighter aircraft over, collapsing its undercarriage. The Moth had been ferried north by Nº 1 FPP, White Waltham, presumably as a communications hack for Nº 41 Group area office. But it was the loss of Airspeed Oxford R6019 that underscored the unforeseen dangers inherent in even the most routine ferry flight.

R6019 was scheduled to be ferried from Prestwick to Nº 15 FTS at Kidlington, Oxford. Pilot was First Officer Aaga

The crash site at Brynford cross-roads. Oxford R6019 came to ground on the hill at the back of the white house on the right of this photograph, flew on into the fields behind the house and slid down the drive, across the road, demolishing the wall in the foreground before coming to rest in the glebe field. The aircraft finally came to rest at point 'X'. The bungalow is a recent construction.

Valdemar Helstrop Laursen, age 24, a naturalised Canadian but a Dane by birth. As frequently occurred over a weekend, two RAF personnel had succeeded in hitching a lift southwards — P/O Richard Clyde Ensign, age 26, returning to the CFS, Upavon, Wiltshire, and LAC Carrick, based at RAF Hawarden. Weather at Prestwick was considered fit for flying. Their proposed route, as filed, would take them out over the Rinns of Kells and Solway Firth, hugging the coast, Silloth, Workington, Barrow, Blackpool before picking up the Mersey and Dee estuaries. But the morning of Monday, 4 November, 1940 had broken with most of north Wales covered in ten- tenths low cloud. Over the Clwydian Range visibility worsened as thick sea mists set in; by 1130hrs, the Wirral Peninsula, Halkyn Mountain and the hamlet of Brynford were invisible from the air. R6019 had entered the fog off Crosby. There was a momentary glimpse of the Flintshire coastline, above Holywell, and the Oxford began to make its turn eastwards making for Hawarden, possisbly too late, over rising ground. Eye witness statements hint at engine trouble.

Mrs Annie Tyler from the Llyn-y-Mawn ('Peat Lake') inn, Brynford, was walking down the road to Holywell with her daughter Dorothy, age 11, when they heard an aircraft coming towards them very low and very fast, from the direction of Bryn Farm. She noticed black smoke 'coming from behind and trailing'. She then saw a door open, and man's hand being waved and someone shouting. Mother and daughter both ducked below the roadside hedge just as the wheels tore through the same hedge. The Oxford passed over them, rose again and flew on towards Brynford. They then heard it crash a field's length away.

From the 'skid marks' it was deduced that the Oxford had hit a five-foot high bank in a field above Brynteg Farm, run on for a further 110 yards, colliding with a haystack and ploughing through a flock of sheep, killing thirteen and injuring six, taking out gateposts, crossing a lane, before demolishing a wall and hedge and coming to rest in the 'Glebe Field' at Brynford crossroads. This was borne out by the statements of of Sarah Williams, Bryn Cottages, and the rector of Ysgeifiog, driving a car from Lixwm. Visibility was less than 100 yards when a lady in an apparent state of shock

ran out in front of the latter's car and begged him to render assistance at the crash site. She ran off to the telephone the emergency services from St Michael's rectory just up the road. The Rev. D. J. Beavan found three bodies on the roadside amidst the wreck debris, two dead, one still alive but dying within a few minutes. Curious onlookers started arriving. The men had their work cut out preventing women and children getting too close to the plane. Aviation fuel was spilt everywhere. Police, doctor and ARP ambulance from Holywell were quickly on scene and the bodies of the airmen conveyed to Holywell mortuary. Men of the 25th LAA Regt, RA mounted guard over the wreckage. Later in the afternoon P/O Wiggins, engineer officer, P/O Williams, 'flying discipline officer' and F/Lt Polson, medical officer, all from N° 7 OTU visited the crash site, as did Walter Handley OC N° 3 FPP, Hawarden. The latter had been expecting R6019 at Hawarden for refuelling and to off-load LAC Carrick. P/O Richard Ensign, who hailed from Hollywood, California, and First Officer Valdemar Laursen lies buried in St Deiniol's Churchyard. Hawarden. LAC Carrick was taken home to Ayrshire for burial.

The north-west coast, with its firths and estuaries eventually beaded with military arifields, may seem to abound with landmarks essential to navigation. But this would hold true only in fine weather with good visibility. The dangers of this route as just illustrated may be further exemplified by the death of Captain Douglas Keith Fairweather, one of the ATA's 'ancient and tattered airmen' on a 'mercy' flight in April 1944, one of 25 fatalities incurred by the ATA that year. Poignancy is added in this particular case, in that five months later almost to the day his wife Flight-Captain the Hon. Mrs Margaret Fairweather sustained fatal injuries whilst on a ferrying mission — a faulty engine, a forced landing with fixed undercarriage, a hidden ditch and the ATA had lost both its Captains Fairweather!

Douglas Fairweather, a 50-year old Glasgow patent-agent who ran his own Puss Moth, was amongst the earliest batch of pilots to join the ATA in 1939. He knew all England visually and preferred to fly without a map. His in-built navigational skills, especially in bad weather, quickly became legendary. He took charge of the small pool of taxi pilots and in 1942 would be posted from Prestwick to take command of the re-organised Communications Flight (later Air Movements Flight) at White Waltham, which would use Ansons, Proctors and Dominies to ferry Service and Government VIPs about the country. The new flight rendered a valuable service in ferrying casualties to and from the Fifth Royal Canadian Hospital at Taplow, near Maidenhead. It was in connection with the latter that on 4 April 1944 Douglas Fairweather undertook what was to be his last flight, to Prestwick in the specially adapted ambulance Anson, N4875. Weather was bad over southern

Douglas Fairweather (second from the left), a man for all weather conditions. He volunteered to fly to Prestwick in appalling conditions to collect an ambulance case but ran out of airspace and was lost in the Irish Sea, along with Nursing Sister Kathleen Mary Henshaw. [K. Day]

The field at Lane End, Shocklach in which Percival Proctor LZ801 crash-landed and claimed the life of Margaret Fairweather. The tree line on the right of the photograph marks the river Dee.

England, considerably worse over the west Midlands, NW England and the west coast route. At 1345hrs as the trees at the edge of the aerodrome at White Waltham became visible, N4875, with Second Officer/Nursing Sister Kathleen Mary Hershaw, attached to White Waltham Sick Bay, in the passenger seat took off and disappeared into the low clound swirling over the Chilterns. Neither the Anson nor it occupants were ever seen again. At 1500hrs the Dee and Mersey estuaries were not visible at all. At Blackpool visibility was under a mile and at Stranraer there was steady rain and cloud base less than 100feet above the sea. Nineteen days later on 23 April Douglas Fairweather's body was washed up by the sea and he lies buried in Dunure cemetery in his native Scotland, ironically just nine miles short of his ultimate destination

His wife, the Hon. Margaret Fairweather, was the daughter of Lord Runciman, a private owner who had logged over 1,000 hours. The outbreak of hostilities saw her as an instructor in the Civil Air Guard at Renfrew, but on 1 January 1940 she joined the ATA, one of the oriiginal eight women pilots under the command of Pauline Gower upon formation of the ATA Women's Section at Hatfield ('D' Section, Nº 3 FPP as from June 1940 and Nº 5 FPP as from 5 November 1940). On 4 August 1944 Margaret Fairweather was rostered to fly Proctor III LZ801 from Heston to Scotland via Hawarden where a VIP, one L. H. Kendrick, was to be dropped off. Also on board was Margaret's sister, Mrs Farrer, Personnel Officer (Ground Staff) ATA, Prestwick bound. From the evidence given by survivors before an inquest held at Chester on 28 August 1944, the Proctor had barely picked up the River Dee at Bangor Isycoed ready to follow the river to Hawarden when the engine 'began to splutter'. Fuel tanks were quickly changed, whereupon it failed completely. Rapidly losing height the aircraft was put down in a large field on Shocklach Meadows. Unfortunately the field contained 'ridge and furrow' which tipped the Proctor onto its nose. Mrs Farrer was thrown clear but badly injured. Mr Kendrick was able to secure help from the nearest farm. Margaret Fairweather was transported to Chester Royal Informary where she later died from a fractured skull and fatal laceration of the brain.

As hinted in the above narrative, in the early years of the

ATA finding one's way about the UK without any electronic navigational aids whatsoever, proved something of a nightmare. Charts were available, RAF versions of the popular OS Aviation Map, produced at ¼-inch to one mile; but now overprinted with the War Office Cassini grid in brown and air information in red; but because these were now marked 'For official Use Only' they were adjudged secret documents. Every ferry pool HQ had one set of the twelve charts covering England and Wales, and necessary copies of the ten covering Scotland. Only these master sets were updated to show current situation as as regards danger areas — artillery ranges, gun-defended areas, balloon barrages, and prohibited flying areas etc. But with the best will in the world periodic map revision could not cope with the over-riding need for self-defeating secrecy nor keep up with the pace at which new aerodromes were being built and SLGs commissioned. As already noted, Hawarden aerodrome itself, home to the largest ferry pool in the UK, did not appear on air charts until 1942 although marked on *Luftwaffe* maps from September 1940. The master map was pinned to a wall and excluded from 'unofficial' gaze by a set of doors which were unlocked early morning as the ferry pilots received their chits, quickly worked out their routes, and the day's flying got underway. In keeping with the creeping, paralysing security paranoia of the time, ATA pilots were not permitted to mark their own maps with any information other than planned routes, but earnestly tried to memorise the potential hazards along the route(s) they would be flying that day. While air charts were issued to pilots it was but grudgingly, every copy marked by that pilot's service number, so that if mislaid the approriate careless person could be traced and reprimanded. Even as finger posts had disappeared from the nation's roads and station nameboards from its railways so aerodrome names had long disappeared from the centre of all-grass airfields, and code letters had yet to be introduced into signal squares or stuck on sides of watch offices, so there was always that exciting element of uncertainty on the part of ATA pilots, bereft ot any form of radio communication, as to whether they may have actually arrived at their destination or not. The destination of many Hawarden ferry flights was logically E and SE England, seat of the action, and it did not help, for example, that the 1942 (War Edition) of Sheet 9 (East Anglia) air chart showed less than 40 airfields, mainly those which had appeared on peace time maps, whilst the master chart in Walter Handley's office showed no fewer than 150, not including SLGs! Their location had to be committed to memory with a quick squint before the doors of the map cupboard were ceremoniously closed and locked.

Navigation was not eased by regulations which required ATA pilots to fly 'within sight of ground', for recognition purposes if nothing else, and to be able to fire specific very cartridges in 'the colours of the day' or flash recognition codes on an Aldis lamp — physical impossibilities for solo pilots struggling to maintain control of single engined aircraft, but deemed necessary in the light of poor aircraft recognition on the part of Army, and Navy (worst of the lot!), and even the RAF. There were some hairy moments when interrogation signals were ignored or there were fumbling delays before responding. Matters of aircraft recognition were only eased after the (Royal) Observer Corps got into its stride. The latter Corps also rendered valuable assistance in noting ATA aircraft in distress and directing searchers and rescuers to crash sites and forced landings. To avoid unnecessary 'clutter' on ROC plotting tables the ATA quickly moved to ferrying smaller aircraft in 'gaggles' of three or four. Captain Rosemary Theresa Rees recalls leading such a stick of four Tiger Moths from Hamble to Tern Hill taking the well worn 'western route' following the Severn between Kidderminster and the Cheshire Plain. They flew into a snow storm. All emerged safely above Market Drayton but on making a head-count she found there were now seven Moths. Somehow they had picked up three more Hawarden- and Ringway-bound Tigers in the middle of the snowstorm. Smog, balloons and the need to avoid high ground led to the emergence of preferred routes as firm as today's air corridors. Along the Welsh border the Severn naturally led on to the Dee which in turn gave direct access to Hawarden, Sealand and Hooton Park. The Nith valley was the main route between Dumfries and Prestwick. The Thames, via the Reading Gap, pointed the way to White Waltham when the Chilterns were shrounded in mist and fog; Roman roads such as the Fosse Way and Ermine Street, assuming one recognised the signs, provided an infallible guide to the airfield of Nos10 and 12 Groups respectively. The oft-told story of Douglas Fairweather flying his Anson taxi with the OS Map of Roman Britain perched aboved the instrument panel may not seem so apocryphal after all!

In the early days, as distinct from the RAF, no minimum criteria were laid down for flying by the ATA, but in April 1942 after a winter which had produced twenty-eight fatalities, fourteen of which directly attributable to bad weather, new rules were promulgated concerning minimum flying conditions for ferry flights. Railways obviously assisted navigation — 'Bradshawing' as it was known to the ATA. The problem in the UK is that complicated railway junctions e.g. Shrewsbury, Crewe, Chester, Oswestry, Wrexham ocurred every 15–20 miles or so; unless pilots were also railway buffs it was often a matter of counting the railway exits out of a station. Get it wrong and valuable time and fuel could be expended flying in the wrong direction. Matters were not helped by numerous branch lines that turned off every two or three miles. These often threw ATA pilots from the USA and Canada, accustomed to ribbons of shining steel running in dead straight lines for hundreds of miles. South of Shrewsbury four railway lines diverged. That to Wolverhampton and Birmingham was usually followed if making for Atcham or the MUs at Cosford or Shawbury. For part of its course it ran north of the Wrekin, a 1342ft volcanic plug with outliers standing proud on the Shropshire Plain. This was no great obstacle providing the weather held fine and the hill was unobscured. If shrouded in fog and mist, and especially after the RAF found it had to fly by night, the Wrekin became deeply ingrained in the psyche of every pilot, particularly those of N° 96 Squadron, as an ever lurking menace which, as the attached table indicates, would claim no fewer than nine aircraft between 1939-45, and still claims the odd careless civilian flier.

Wrekin Crashes

7.11.39. Airspeed Oxford, P1845. Hit summit of Wrekin in bad visibility. P/O G. H. H. Coates killed, first N° 11 SFTS casualty in war. One crew member thrown clear and survived.

25.9.40. Avro Anson, L7071 of N° 10 SFTS, Tern Hill. Flew into overhead wires at Eaton Constantine, Wrekin, whilst low flying.

First Officer Joan Naylor, ATA, about to deliver a Spitfire donated by Adele Astaire, sister of Fred Astaire. [K. Day]

26.10.4 Bristol Beaufighter, T3354, Nº 68 Sqn, High Ercall on training flight, flew into Wrekin, whilst in circuit in bad weather. F/O Morgan Ryan and AI operator Sgt Willis killed. This accident led to a red pundit light being erected on the Wrekin summit.

7.12.41. Supermarine Spitfire, P7746, Nº 131 Sqn, Atcham, crashed into Little Hill, Rushton, on the Wrekin ('Black Friday').

3.1.42. Hawker Hurricane, L1695, Nº 5 SFTS, Tern Hill. Unauthorised low flying, hit HT wires at Eaton Constantine. P/O RJ Tomlinson killed.

17.2.43. Airspeed Oxford, P8973, Nº 11 (P)AFU, Shawbury. Hit top of small hill at Eaton Constantine whilst low flying, momentum carried forward and belly-landed in field ahead.

5.1.44. Miles Masters, AZ726 and DM314, Nº 5 (P)AFU, Tern Hill. Formation flying exercise when buzzed by a Harvard, lost formation. DM 312 peeled off and chased Harvard. In regaining position AZ726 collided with DM314. Instructor in AZ726, F/Sgt M. Phillips, baled out; pupil F/O N. K. Srivastaua killed. Pilot of DM314, F/O J. King, also killed.

23.4.44. P47 Thunderbolt, 41-6585, 495th Training Squadron (USAAF), Atcham. Mid-air collision with Miles Master DL477, Nº 5 (P)AFU, Tern Hill. Thunderbolt pilot, Ed Lyons baled out and survived; Master pilot Sgt Arthur Goddard went in with a/c and was killed.

17.12.45. Airspeed Oxford, LX530, Nº 21 (P)AFU Atcham. 19 minutes into NAVEX, moonlight conditions; observed in shallow dive, at 100ft dived straight into ground on Wrekin Hill, completely destroyed. W/O Victor Servis and F/O William Cull killed.

12.9.52. Avro Anson, VV987, CN&CS, Shawbury. Pilot had completed a controlled descent through cloud, and was climbing away from Shawbury to make another attempt. Reported elevator problems, subsequently regained control. No further communication. Later discovered crashed on Wrekin. pilot F/Sgt Alexander Gee, 35, killed.

8.1.94. Mooney, M20J G-BSKJ. On return flight to Sleap aerodrome from White Waltham. At 1615hrs flew into 'Eye of the Needle' on summit of Wrekin in fog rain and semi-darkness. Pilot Melvyn Wroe, and passenger Harry Grocott killed.

In her book *Forgotten Pilots* First Officer Lettice Curtis recounts a near disastrous encounter with the Wrekin early in 1941 whilst with Nº 5 FPP, busily engaged in ferrying Lysanders from Elstree to MUs at Prestwick and Aldergrove:

... It was in a Lysander that I gave myself one of my worst frights ever. One day, in the vicinity of the Wrekin, looking for Cosford, I got into cloud. When this happens and you have no radio or navigational facilities you have two alternatives. One is to climb and commit yourself to an indefinite and exceedingly worrying period of instrument flying, in the hope that in due course you will find a suitable hole in the clouds through which to let down. The other is to descend immediately and try and sort oneself out whilst still knowing roughly one's position, and trusting to luck that in the meantime no high ground will intervene. Rather than postpone the moment of reckoning I took the latter course but, even so, when I caught sight once more of the cloud filled trees, I had lost all my reference points. I can remember as well as yesterday the feeling of utter despair at not knowing whether the Wrekin was ahead or behind — of experiencing a feeling of disembodiment, wondering

whether I was really still alive or whether I had, in fact, already flown into the hill and was no more than a temporary extrapolation of my previous existence. There was no fear of death as such, only a sickening frustration at having made a complete fool of oneself — an unforgivable error of judgement. 'Please God', I prayed, 'get me out of this and I promise never to let myself get caught like this again'.. In situations like this one become schizophrenic, half of the brain searching for some excuse to opt out of the whole situation whilst the other, driven by an instinct for survival, continues to battle for a way out. Then suddenly, as quickly as it all happened, a recognizable landmark came into view, bringing back the physical world in which there was a logical sequence of events to be followed, to whatever the end might be. In this case the end was a normal landing at Cosford only minutes later, but I was left with the feeling that in experience I had lived through many years.

An even more graphic account of dicing around the Wrekin is given by First Officer Edith Foltz Stearns (Oregon, USA) who had gained her licence in 1928 at the age of 25, and as one of America's first woman pilots barnstormed her way round the north-western States, before taking second place in the Women's Air Derby of 1929. She was a member of ther ATA 10.6.42–9.6.45. Described by her colleague Alison King erstwhile Operations Officer at Hamble, in her book *Golden Wings*, as 'Full of energy and enjoyment of life, She was vivid and colourful both in form and language...' but Edith would be trimmed down to size by the Wrekin:

... But my most unforgettable experience occurred in England, when I was with ATA. I was stationed at Hamble when orders came to deliver a Mosquito bomber to Hawarden, north Wales. It was one of those Nº 1 priority jobs. I volunteered to go but had little enthusiasm for the flight as the weather had been socko for days.. By mid-afternoon visibility was a little better and I prepared to take off. As I climbed the atmosphere became very muggy and visibility low. Luckily I hit a remarkably clear strip at about 1,000ft. It ran a straight horizontal course throught the clouds, like a white filling between two layers of chocolate cake. Flying this special express way I made good time until I approached what I thought was my destination. I dropped about 400ft to try and spot the landing field and fell into one of those pitch-black smogs for which the Midlands was so famous. Visibility was zero-zero, so I climbed again, but could not fight my way out of the darkness. I kept circling the area, climbing and dropping, praying for as miracle.

I couldn't keep this up indefinitely. Night was coming on and slim as my chances for a landing in the day time, they would be hopeless by night. I debated flying further north, but decided such a move would be even more risky. I've had some close calls in my time, but never felt so lost and alone, so utterly doomed. Then a voice rang out in my head: 'Edie, Look out!' and with no conscious reason for doing so, except to heed the warning I shot upwards, and at that moment a jagged moubntain peak loomed up on my left. Narrowly missing it I flew on and gained height. I must have been well off course by now. Glancing for a split second at my map there was a 700–1000ft peak called Wrekin', apparently the one I had just missed about 50 miles from Hawarden I calculated. I dropped down again not knowing why, except that I was being shown the way — then an eerie shaft of light descending down, cutting through the inky smog and spotlighting a highway immediately beneath me. I was a beautiful sight, a sort of 'Jacob's ladder' in reverse. I followed this highway for perhaps ten miles. Then I saw a runway so close to the highway the two seemed to converge. The 'Jacob's ladder only extended a little way onto the field. Beyond that the smog was as dense as ever. With that bit of visible corner as a reference point I tried to picture the rest of the airstrip. It would take some figuring to hit it but I had to make the attempt.

A Mosquito bomber is a tricky plane to land. You have to fly high and pounce down like a hawk. I set the giro at zero to show heading, then turned it left to 180° to parallel the runway. Then a left bank to 90⁻ and I should have been back where I started from but my timing must have been wrong. I tried four or five times, but each time I over shot the runway. Despair was bearing down on me again when I got a new idea. Why not go back and pick up the highway (if I could find it) and use it for a preliminary landing guide? I retraced my giro course following the highway for about five miles, but this time with flaps 15 degrees down. I turned at the runway, dropped flaps and undercarriage all the way. I maintained a speed of about 140mph until I saw a fence, then fishtailed down to a landing speed of 125mph. I landed squarely on what looked like a small fighter base without getting a scratch on the bomber. The plane had hardly come to a halt when great billowing clouds of smog rushed in to close my 'Jacob's ladder'. Now that I was safely down I felt myself going to pieces. I wanted to sit there and bawl like any normal American girl who had just had the daylights scared out of her. But I pulled myself together remembering that my mission had not been completed. I had been followed down the runway by the crash wagon and fire truck. They couldn't quite hide their astonishment at seeing a woman drop out of the sky into their all-male bastion. I taxied up to the control tower and identified myself. The officer in charge was irritated: 'This field is closed', he said. 'I told you to go away. Why did you land?' 'Sorry, sir', I said. 'My plane is not equipped with radio. It was an emergency landing.' I climbed down with wobbly legs, painfully aware of my dishevelled appearance. I squared my shoulders and said curtly to a couple of cadets hovering nearby 'Could you please hangar my plane. It looks as if I shall have to spend the night.

The next day the weather was still pretty dismal but I was able to proceed to Hawarden and deliver the bomber.. I returned to England in the late afternoon in a Spitfire that needed overhauling. On landing I learnt that the Germans

had strafed our Hamble base shortly after I had taken off the day before, heavily damaging our planes and killing a number of our force.

The reader with some knowledge of the geography about the Wrekin will, of course, have guessed that the aerodrome with the inconsiderate Flying Control Officer, was RAF Shawbury!

The Fairweathers, husband and wife, were amongst the 'characters', eccentrics even, that must spice up any ATA narrative. Douglas was a portly middle aged 'city type' who occasionally flew his Puss Moth in conventional black hat and rolled umbrella. He weighed in at over 16 stone which is why he found himself relegated to second-line communication work within the ATA, no less vital as things turned out and he will always be remembered in his capacity as organiser of the Air Movements Flight, and the ATA operated 'scheduled service' which daily carried urgently needed AOG (Aircraft on Ground) spares. Hawarden was a vital hub and onward ferrying point in this Fairweather network.

Not as extrovert as Douglas Fairweather, was Flight Captain Stewart Keith-Jopp, a First World War fighter pilot and influential contributor on matters aeronautical to the *Aeroplane*, and with the latter's editor C. Grey, an initial opponent of the involvement of women pilots in the ATA — or anywhere else for that matter. Over fifty, with but one arm and one eye, he had somehow managed to convince instructors at the Central Flying School of his 'airworthiness' on the North American Harvard, and went on to deliver without a scratch more than 1,300 operational aircraft. He flew replacement aircraft to Air Component squadrons in France in 1940 and in May 1944 was back in Normandy, clearing the MUs at Aston Down, Brize Norton and Filton of fighter aircraft — Typhoons and Tempests. He left the ATA on 30 November 1945. His last trip was with a Typhoon almost to the borders of Russia from whence as Cheesman logs it, 'he returned, satisfied, with a snapshot of himself in the centre of a group of our eastern allies'. First (Engineer) Officer Charles Moore, N° 3 FPP, recalls Keith-Jopp coming into Hawarden one afternoon in the summer of 1942. He was to return to White Waltham with a Hawker Tempest high-speed target towing tug 'a beast of an aircraft' even for a fully fit pilot.

Keith-Jopp had two disabilities; he had lost a hand and an eye and received serious internal injuries in action during his service, but in all my years in the ATA I never saw an accident report with his name on it. He was determined to fly this Tempest. It was the custom at Hawarden for engineering staff to accompany pilots to aircraft, if we had the time to go through some of the 'Do and Don'ts'. I accompanied Keith-Jopp out to the Tempest and he went thtough the pre-flight checks, but hit a snag. He could not manage to lock the tail wheel ready for take-off.

Two of N° 14 Ferry Pool pilots pose for a photograph on a Vultee Vengeance at Ringway.
[ATA newsletter via Charles H. Moore]

The renovated head of the control column of Spitfire IX MK616 in which Jane Winstone lost her life.

So I went out with him to the end of the runway. He brought it into the wind and I climbed up onto the wing, leant into the cockpit and locked the wheel for him. He powered the engine and was gone. I often wondered how he coped taxying at the other end of the flight.

Keith-Jopp certainly did not long persist in the anti-feminist opinions of his editor, C. G. Grey. One notes his daughter as also flying with the ATA. On 29 May 1945 Third Officer Miss Eleanor Betty Keith-Jopp, Nº 15 FPP Hamble, had a narrow dice with death whilst ferrying Fairey Barracuda II MX792 from RNAS, Crail (Fife) to HMS Urley, otherwise RNAS Ronaldsway (IoM). Both units held Barracudas for torpedo, dive bombing, reconnaissance and anti-submarine training of aircrews. It was a long single leg journey, requiring utmost concentration as there were not many landmarks. Eleanor managed to pick her way through the mountains and arrived over her departure point at Workington on the west coast. A heavy sea mist shrouded the coastal strip and it was with some trepidation that she decided to push on. As she made her way out to sea the weather began to close in and it began to rain very heavily. This in turn brought her lower until the grey cloud merged with the grey sea. It was only a matter of time before the aircraft stalled into the waves. Within seconds the cockpit was full of water and Eleanor and the Barracuda started to sink. She struggled to release herslf from her harness and the release of a great bubble of air brought her to the surface.. Luck was with her. A fishing boat had observed the aircraft in the gloom and had heard the loud smack as it hit the

Jane Winstone is buried in the ATA plot at Maidenhead Cemetery alongside F/O Rosamund Steenkamp, F/O D. R. Hayward, F/O Bee Acton, F/E Janice Harrington, F/O D. Lang, F/O S. R. Herringshaw, F/O A. B. Dorrell and Captain P. Randall. [R. D. Brown]

water. The skipper made for the area and found Eleanor floating on the surface. They brought her on board expressing surprise that their 'catch was a woman pilot, made her comfortable and duly brought her safely back to port — one very fortunate lady!

Other 'handicapped' ATA pilots flew in and out of Hawarden almost unnoticed, disabilities not allowed to impair performance. One such was First Officer W. R. Corrie, one handed pilot and film actor who flew Lockheed Hudsons unaided, regularly helping to clear out the Lockheed Co. subsidiary at Speke aerodrome, Liverpool. The latter port handled the early deliveries by sea of this anti-submarine and general reconnaissance aircraft, which was to supersede completely the shorter range Avro Anson (600+ cf. 2,100+ miles). But it is the antics of First Officer Richard Kemp that have stuck in the memory of onlookers who happened to be on the airfield at Hawarden on that particular day in March 1942. What his disabilities were, are not known exactly, but surely a failing memory must have been one of them. First Officer Ken Day again takes uo the story:

> However, an incident took place at Hawarden airfield where I was stationed in 1942. On 23 March First Officer Richard Kemp — an elderly and partly crippled pilot — was preparing to take off in Hurricane BN882. The hard standing was close to the take off runway and, as was customary, Richard 'ran up' with an airman on the tail to kcep it on the ground. Failure to follow this procedure on both the Hurricane and the Spitfire would often tip the aircraft on its nose. After run-up Richard was rather too precipitate in taxying the remaining few yards to the runway end, and in a matter of seconds he was belting along it with 12lbs boost on the clock — and AC2 Holmes on the tail!
>
> As the Hurricane climbed into the sky we expected Holmes to drop to his death at any moment — but he clung to the tail like a limpet. We soon realised of course that it was the slipstream that glued him to the tail, and he could not drop off even if he wished! Contemporary press cuttings state that another aircraft took off to warn Richard of what had happened. This is incorrect. Indeed to do so would have been futile in that Richard had no radio aboard. However, he soon diagnosed the tail-heavy attitude of the Hurricane when he glanced into the fighter reflector mirror above the cockpit and saw that he was not alone, with the hapless

Holmes 'bestriding his tail like a Colossus!' The press was again in error in stating that the Hurricane was doing 350mph. You, as an expert on the Hurricane, know full well that no Hurricane was ever built that could do 350mph — except downhill, down wind and with the throttle through the gate! Richard was probably doing about 120mph as he gingerly completed his circuit. He made his final approach at about 110mph, gently easing the flaps down, and finally made a 'daisy-cutter' at about 65mph — with the fire engine, doctor and ambulance thundering along beside him. He let the aircraft run slowly to a halt and Holmes dismounted with all the aplomb of Harvey Smith at Hixtead — his only worry being that his cap had blown off somewhere en route. This brilliant display of skilful and precision flying was rewarded only with a rocket for Richard for jumping the gun in the first place.

Ken Day added a post script to his notes which is worth an airing:

Not only did AC2 Holmes have a charmed life, but so did Richard Kemp — for shortly afterwards he made another hasty return to Mother Earth — beating the 'Reaper' with only seconds to spare. On 31 May 1944 a very senior American general — four stars, no less — wanted to fly to Bovington to attend a service consecrating the ground at what was to be a US Forces Cemetery. Always ready to oblige we sent him off in a Fairchild Argus I (HM177) with Richard at the helm. However, as they approached Leighton Buzzard, the Warner Super Scarab began to smoke and clatter in an alarming way. Fortunately they did not have much altitude, so Richard got his nose down sharpish and belted earthward as if he had all the hounds of hell after him — which he probably did! Before they even touched down the engine was well alight, and seconds after they landed Richard had the general's door open, through which he booted him with great disrespect for his rank! Richard jumped out after him, and moments later the aircraft exploded. Sabotage you may ask? No, I think not — although we were never told the general's name … . [PS] I often wonder if the American general mentioned above ever realised how close he was to becoming the first customer in the cemetery he was about to open?

The incidents related above just hint at their trials and tribulations of ATA ferry pilot as they daily accepted chits, collected their aircraft and took off in the sure knowledge that even on straight forward short hauls something untoward could, and did, happen. This was driven home with some force on 11 November 1941 when the ferry pool at Hawarden lost Walter Handley, its commanding officer of seventeen months. Under his leadership Hawarden had become the cross-roads of the UK. Here 'the south' ended and 'the north' began. Only a week previously (5.11.40) what had been 'C' Section, No 3 FPP, had been raised to full independent ferry pool status with a sub-pool established at smog-ridden, balloon embellished Ringway. This last move was perhaps inevitable — something had to be done to accelerate the dispatch of Ansons and Blenheims from Avro at Woodley, the Proctors from Trafford Park, and the Beaufighters, Fulmars and Swordfish made by Fairey Aviation at Ringway itself, not to mention Handley Page aircraft from Preston. Handley did not see Ringway come

into being, but on the day he was killed a small ferry pool was also established at Cosford, for the moment a sub-unit to No 6 FPP Ratcliffe, high up in the hills along the Fosse Way and peace-time home to Leicestershire Flying Club. Cosford was the base for No 9 MU and would later house the Vickers Armstrong shadow factory, forced out of Castle Bromwich after a devastating raid on 13 August 1940. This factory assembled Spitfires made from parts manufactured all over the Midland counties. Until it got its own Nissen hut, the ATA worked out of Cosford watch office. In July 1941 it became No 12 FPP and as from 30 March 1943 it reformed as the second all all-woman ferry pool (the other was No 15 FPP, Hamble) within the ATA, under the command of Commander Marion Katherine Wilberforce, who took over from Captain Gerald Stedall. This came about because No 5 FPP, Luton, which in turn had its roots in the ATA Women's Section at White Waltham was in the throes of becoming an ATA training unit, reforming at Thame (Haddenham) as No 5 (Training) Ferry Pool, taking the place of the in-house training pool also based at White Waltham which had disbanded. Like all self-contained women's pools No 12 FPP had its own female engineering staff, comprising fitters, electrical engineers and labourers, who during the winter months worked outside, wallowing in mud just like their male counterparts round the aerodrome perimeter.

It would not be long before the new pool lost its first woman pilot. On 22 May 1943 Second Officer Mary Webb Nicholson (USA) was ferrying Miles Master W9029 from No 10 MU, Hullavington to No 5 (P)AFU, Tern Hill, when the engine seized up and shed its propeller. The a/c forcelanded with no control over its speed, bounced and crashed into outbuildings at Cocksholme Farm, near Littleworth (Worcestershire). It caught fire. Mary was trapped and burnt to death. In 1929 she had become North Carolina's first licensed woman pilot and before being recruited into the ATA in 1939 she had made quite a name for herself as a member of a 'flying circus', starring as daredevil pilot, wing walker and parachutist.

There would be other recordable accidents with the Cosford ferry pool but none, perhaps, as tragic as Supermarine Spitfire IX, MK616, with Second Officer Jane Winstone, a New Zealander, at the helm. She had arrived at Cosford only two weeks previously, straight from ATA's No 5 (T)FPP at Tame, duly passed out on Class I ('single engined a/c') and Class II ('Fast single engined a/c') On the morning of 10 February 1944 Jane was rostered to fly MK616 from No 9 MU, Cosford to No 39 MU, Colerne. Flight checks completed she taxied out to the runway; the ground engineers heard the engine note rise as she took off, climbing at a sharp angle. MK616 did not level out but rolled over and went into a steep dive. Engine screaming it ploughed into the bank of a lake at Tong, just south of Cosford, killing its young pilot. AM Accident Form 1180 cites the cause as 'engine failure on take off'. In 1979 aviation archaeologists from the Wartime Aircraft Recovery Group, then based at Cosford, investigated the crash site, finding fragments of alloy at the water's edge. In 1984 an object recovered by an angler from the lake was brought into the WARG museum and identified as the head of a Spitfire's control column.

Later in that year a diving team recovered a large section of the Spitfire's 'skinning' in excellent condition with light blue paint still visible. Jane is not buried locally but in the small ATA plot set aside in Maidenhead cemetery, in days before the CWGC established their own dedicated cemeteries, for those who died such a long way from home.

On the day of his death Walter Handley had 'ambled' up to Kirkbride in an Anson. Here he found a chit to fly a Bell Airacobra back to N° 48 MU, Hawarden. EC Cheesman takes up the story (with comments from Ken Day:

> He smoked a cigarette with the adjutant of the ATA Ferry Pool (still a sub-pool to Prestwick, only becoming N° 16 FPP in July 1941), went out to the aircraft, started up, and taxied to the runway. After a short pause he turned into the wind and commenced his take off, but before he had passed over the end of the runway the engine was revving at an unnaturally high rate and black smoke poured from the exhaust. The motor continued to run imperfectly as the pilot climbed to about 700ft. When about three miles from the aerodrome there was a loud explosion, a sheet of flame enveloped the aft part of the machine and at the same time parts of the aircraft were seen to fly off. The Airacobra then turned about 45¯ to port, flew on a little on an even keel and went into a dive from which it never recovered. Trees hid the scene of the accident, but a rising pall of black smoke showed that a fire and explosion had followed the crash.

First Officer Ken Day is on record as stating that '... the Airacobra had boost and that the throttle gate was wired off to stop over-boost. It was found that this wire was not present in Walter's aircraft so he could have pushed through the gate causing the engine to explode'. The following year Ken himself experienced the scary result of botched maintenance. N° 3 FPP Hawarden was busily involved clearing out N° 7 Aircraft Assembly Unit at Hooton Park of its mixed bag of Ansons, Harvards, Hurricanes, Hampdens, Bostons, Mustangs, Argus etc. He had picked up an Anson for the five-minute trip back across the Wirral, but found that '... the flying controls had been wired up the wrong way round and it took me some time to suss the matter out. One lapse in concentration as I was heading up the Dee estuary and …! The flight lasted nearly an hour. It was the best flying lesson I had ever had … any pilot watching from the ground would have been spell-bound by my performance!' First Officer Diana Barnato-Walker, N° 5 FPP, Hamble, had a similar experience. On 27 June 1944 she had dropped off an aircraft at Hawarden, only to be given a taxi to RNAS Burscough, near Ormskirk, (Lancs.), from whence she was to ferry a Grumman Avenger (FN883) back to HMS *Kestrel*, Worthy Down. According to Navy records this a/c had experienced complete engine failure on delivery to Burscough, the ATA pilot force landing it on 14 October 1943. The aircraft must have been put in storage as Diana was warned by Sydney Ogden, OC Hawarden ferry pool, to make a thorough check with ground engineers before take off. She carried out all safety checks and ran up the engine; all seemed in order so she attempted take off. Having got into the air she climbed into the airfield circuit to test further the aircraft's performance. Flicking the switches to super-charger brought about failure of the engine. and a near stall.

So she flicked them back off and the engine burst back to life. It was now obvious that switches were wired up in the wrong direction. Only knowing this she was able to fly down to HMS *Kestrel* with switches in the wrong position. Diana would gain some fleeting fame as, strictly unofficially, the first woman to ferry a Spifire over to France after the D-Day landings.

The American Bell Airacobra was an unorthodox single-seater fighter, with a tricycle undercarriage, shaft driven by an Allison engine from behind the pilot's seat, and boasting a 20mm cannon firing through the propeller hub. Some 675 were ordered for the RAF by the British Purchasing Commission in 1940, before proper assessment by the AFDU. It was found wanting operationally in the anticipated ground-attack role. Its usefulness was further impaired by persistent unserviceability. It was withdrawn from service. Only one squadron (N° 610) was ever equipped with this type. Deliveries ceased the remaining aircraft going to the Soviet Air Force or reverting to the USAAF. Thus began the collection of unwanted Airacobras back to N° 47 MU Sealand, packing or crating for Russia. This is the background to Walter Handley's death. Ironically traffic movement orders show many ATA pilots left their Airacobras at Hawarden, not wishing to try putting down on 'Little Sealand'. The short hop was left to the local pool, 386 movements on this type being recorded during the period Febriary 1942–February 1943.

With the passing of Walter Handley so ended, according to most commentators, 'the first and colourful phase in the history of N° 3 FPP, Hawarden. Handley was replaced by Captain (newly promoted Commander) Sydney Watson Ogden, better known as 'Stan', who came down from Kirkbride, where, with five pilots he had run Prestwick's sub-pool since September 1940 — 'a fine pilot and disciplinarian who, in spite of his rather terrifying beetling eyebrows, proved a good friend to many of those under him'. With a wicked sense of humour he succeeeded in maintaining that essential sense of camaraderie at Hawarden as the pool continued to expand into the largest within the ATA — statistics for February 1944 will show that N° 3 FPP, Hawarden, then mustered 70 ground staff and three administrators whilst the flying side comprised 40 ferry pilots and 5 administrators/pilots. One suspects that Sydney Ogden was more than glad to exchange Kirkbride's lean-to shed for the comparative 'luxury' of Hawarden's new HQ, a large wooden hut, always warm, comprising seven rooms alongside the ATA's aircraft shed. Three days after Commander Ogden had taken over, the *Luftwaffe* found Hawarden or perhaps more accurately the Mold Junction marshalling yards, a more attractive alternative target. According to Ken Day the aerodrome received nearly a 1,000 IBs and 16 HE bombs. The MU's N° 3 Site and the ATA offices and hangars had miraculous escapes, with two direct hits on the railway at Mold Junction, just over the perimerter fence some 100 yards from N° 2 Hangar. A further five bombs exploded in the field beyond the railway on Well Farm, killing or injuring livestock. Like every other unit on site, the ferry pool 'was in chaos for weeks'.

But Stan's long term concern was the state of Hawarden's

Left: On 13 June 1945, ATA Avro Anson NK810 arrives at RAF Shawbury. L–R: Cadets Baldwin and Thomas, FirstOfficers Hastings and Steynor, Flt Capt Hon. Elizabeth May, First Officers Barnato, Walker, Guest and Leonard.
[Angus Brentwoods via K. Day]

Below: Avro Anson R9762 which was delivered to the ATA during the Battle of Britain and survived until November 1946.
[ATA Newsletter via Ken Day]

landing ground, water- and mud-logged for long periods during the bad winter of 1940/41. The ferry pool had six dispersals at its disposal and by November, with the inevitable backlog 'all were chokker'. The one hard runway, a short thing, strictly belonged to the Vickers Armstrong MAP factory but was of necessity pressed into use by ATA, MU and OTU. The runway was so angled that the approach to N° 3 (later 32) runway lay between two large MAP/MU hangars. Cheesman recalls: 'Ferry pilots landing fast fighters would pray that the aerodrome gates at the start of the runway might be open, so that they could come in even lower and thus gain another hundred yards in which to pull up'. Second (Engineer) Officer Richard Paget recalls: 'In the early days if an aircraft coming into 32 drifted south of track the old house used to shake as they went over the roof trying to correct the approach'. One notes this officer, along with Flight Captain C. A. Ellam, Operations Officer N° 3 FPP, as receiving Certicates of Commendation for acts of outstanding merit for rescuing a trapped OTU pilot from Miles Master T8331 which crashed on runway 32 and caught fire on 28 October 1941, a deed which in ATA logs roused more comment from the fact that the runway was out of action for two or three hours, delaying four ferry pilots that day!

Further disruption to ferrying work would come in the Spring of 1941 when Gerrards of Manchester finally began work on providing the aerodrome with runways, 'as a matter of priority', for in March/April 1941 the Hawarden pool undertook the ferrying work from Cranage, an arrangement that was to persist until the end of the war. The ATA's military counterpart at Hawarden since 1 November 1940, N° 9 (Service) FPP, had been disbanded on 10 February 1941, to be replaced two monrths later by N° 3 (Aircraft) Delivery Flight, under the command of F/Lt North,with responsibility for on-ferrying of fighter aircraft to operational units in N°s 9 and 12 Groups, Fighter Command. They would stay but nine months before moving on to High Ercall. When short handed N° 3 (A)DF called upon the services of 'spare' pilots from other units e.g. N° 9 Group

ACCF, Wrexham and N° 256 Squadron, Squires Gate. The last record of N° 3 (A)DF in our area is to the loss of Beaufighter X787 on 18 April 1943 whilst on a ferry flight from N° 153 Squadron detachment at Ballyhalbert (Co. Down) to 29 MU High Ercall. For some reason it ditched off the southern tip of the Isle of Man, its pilot F/O Stanislaw Sielinski sustaining what turned out to be fatal injuries. He was pick up by HMS *Mezerka*, but died later in Port Erin hospital.

The back half of 1941 also saw a few face changes at Hawarden Ferry Pool. Now that it was 'ticking over' nicely under Walter Handley's forceful leadership several of the original pilots were 'returned to unit' or promoted and moved to other pools. Thus in July Oliver Eric Armstrong ('Paddy') was promoted Commander and moved to take over the Ulster Pool (N° 8 FPP), which had commenced working out of Sydenham, ex-Belfast airport, ferrying Stirling four-engined bombers, built by Short and Harland, to the mainland. However, Armstrong is still noted as being at Hawarden in September 1941. 'Paddy' Armstrong had been well known civil pilot on the Railway Air Service between Liverpool and Belfast and would continue as CO until disbandment in August 1945. With him to Belfast went Thomas William Brooke-Smith ('Brookie'), N° 3 FPP's resident prankster, also newly promoted to First Officer. Flight-engineer Charlie Moore recalls an incident surrounding the guard of a goods train coming from Mold to Chester: 'Daily this pick-up goods was held by signals before entering Mold Junction marshalling yard. This usually left the guard's van straddling the level crossing near the ATA 'house' for five or six minutes. A routine developed whereby the guard would pop into the ATA

Above: Group photograph of Nº 3 FPP, Hawarden. Commander Stan Ogden centre, Charles H. Moore is in the second row, second from the right.
[Charles H. Moore]

Right: A 1944 photograph taken by Hangar Nº 1, Site Nº 3. The aircraft is DH Dominie NF875 from Nº 41 OTU. The ATA pilots and ground staff are, L–R: C. H. Moore, F. Faraday (inspection), J. T. Burill, Commander Stanley Ogden, Harry Miller (engineer), Reg Jones (engineer), Bert Jolly (inspection).

Left: The crash site (above World's End on Ruabon Mountain) of Bristol Beaufighter NE203 in which F/Sgt John Shepherd of Nº 2 FFP lost his life on 3 October 1943.

Right: This featureless landscape is where S/O Percival J. Collins lost his life in Hawker Hurricane V7001 on 29 January 1942. He was ferrying the aircraft from Rollasons Hanworth (Surrey) to Nº 18 MU Dunfries, calling at Hawarden to refuel. The crash site is on Ruabon Mountain on the Bryn Adda Flats. Sitting upright in the centre of the picture is the final drive sprocket connected to two big-end journals from the Merlin engine. The digger is Raymond Murphy from the WARG who excavated the site in 1984.

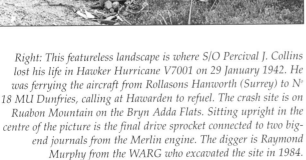

kitchen for a quick cup of tea off Mrs Jones the cook. On this occasion 'Brookie' was washing his car outside the house garage. Upon hearing an impatient whistle from the engine Brookie jumped into the guard's van put on the guard's hat and vigorously waved a green flag. The train moved off. Brookie hid behind the garage as the guard came running out of the house. Alas, too late. His train had gone too great a distance to be caught. There followed some furious telephone calls and a hot pursuit in the ATA taxi, an 'impressed' petrol-guzzling Rolls-Royce, before the guard was reunited with his train at Saltney Ferry station'.

It is hard to believe that 'Brookie' went on to become Chief Test Pilot for Short Brothers and Harland Ltd. flying the experimental Short SB 3 and SA 4 Sperrin bombers and the better known Delta-winged VTOL prototypes, the SC 1 (XG900 and XG905). 'Brookie' became the first pilot to conventionally fly a 'flat-riser' when on 2 April 1957 he took XG900 up at Boscombe Down. Brooke-Smith would be elected FRAeS in 1961.

Early in 1942 there were changes on the engineering side. Jack Kerswall was First (Engineer) Officer with Second (Engineer) Officer Richard Paget as his deputy. Charles Henry Moore was posted in from Marshalls of Cambridge who had the Anson repair contract at Bobbington, (Halfpenny Green), Staffordshire. The Charge-hand was Dick Stanley. Charles Moore recalls: 'On my arrival at Hawarden there was a large backlog of aircraft that had starting problems. After further liaison with the Officer i/c the MU it was agreed that ATA fitters would take over all adjustments to new aircraft on a daily inspection basis before ferrying them to their destinations.' This is not as patronising as it sounds as there was always a queue of fitters waiting to 'get their spanners going' The ATA favoured schemes of progressive achievement. On the engineering side this manifested itself in the shape of log books with different aircraft types in which an individual

fitter could record his (or her) on-going engineering experience; This in turn gave him a ranking in the pecking order. The same principle applied in the Flying Section, but here giving rise to a new piece of aeronautical jargon — 'Type Hoggers'. Charlie Moore continues: 'As the new system began to sort itself out, we carried out on one day alone 200 movements not including taxi flights. Over 100 aircraft of all types found new homes. One thing that always remained constant was the accident rate. Flying in all conditions, with no radio or navigation aids was the reason for this ….' Statistics for the year ending 1942 show 3,871 Wellington movements by ATA of which 1,356 were new aircraft out of Hawarden and Cranage. Amongst these was Broughton-built R1629, which did much for the war effort in the electronic field by becoming the world's first AEW (Airborne Early Warning) aircraft. It had come off the production line in early March 1941 and was ferried north to outside storage at N° 18 MU Dumfries, from whence into operational service with N° 149 Squadron at Mildenhall (Suffolk). Its career with bomber Command came to a halt on 8 May 1941 after a landing accident. It could not be repaired on unit, but was sent to N° 43 (Repair & Salvage) Group, Maintenance Command. After repair it was sent in June 1941 to the Royal Aircraft Establishment at Farnborough, where it became the flying testbed in the development of ACI and AEW systems.

As D-Day approached Hawarden saw an intensification in the movement of fighter aircraft southwards. A newcomer was the versatile DH Mosquito (all types). The first Mosquito accident enters Hawarden's log on 24 March 1944 when KB116 piloted by Second Officer Grace Stevenson swung on take off collapsing the undercarriage. Despite blotting her copybook Grace went on to become First Officer in the ATA. Being N° 3 FPP based, Grace was one of the women pilots who in the last 18 months of its existence succeeded in breaching that all-male bastion that was Hawarden ferry pool. There are but two further Mosquito entries in the attached accident log, both incurring fatalities. The MAP (Vickers-Armstrong) factory at Hawarden was one of the seven factories that tooled up to meet the mass production of of the Avro Lancaster. Others included AV Roe Manchester, Metro Vickers, Manchester, Austin Aero, Longbridge and Vickers Armstrong, Castle Bromwich. The first four of 235 Flintshire-built Lancasters rolled off the Hawarden assembly line in June 1944 with nine more in July and twelve in August and peaking at twenty a month November 1944–April 1945. Ferrying of these aircraft fell locally to N°s 3 and 14 FPPs, by now often directly to operational units, by-passing MUs and the RAF's own delivery flights. Cheesman illustrates this with the following anecdote:

Sea Cadets prepare to loose moorings on a Catalina whilst
Flight Captain A. E. Chambers turns the props prior to
commencing a long ferry flight.
[Mrs Diana Barnato-Walker via Ken Day]

Wind Down of ATA Pools

Closed	Pool	Opened
1945		
March	Nº 5 (T)FPP Haddenham	15.8.43
June	Nº 9 FPP Aston Down	09.41
	Nº 12 FPP Cosford	07.41 Sub-pool 11.40
	Nº 10 FPP Lossiemouth	10.41
August	Nº 8 FPP Sydenham	03.41
	Nº 15 FPP Hamble	07.41 Sub-pool 11.40
September	Nº 2 FPP Whitchurch	5.11.40
	Nº 14 FPP Ringway	01.41 Sub-pool 11.40
	Nº 16 FPP Kirkbride	07.41 Sub-pool 09.40
October	Nº 4 FPP Prestwick	09.40
	Nº 6 FPP Ratcliffe	11.40
	Nº 7 FPP Sherburn-in-Elmet	11.40
November	Nº 3 FPP Hawarden	11.40 Sub-pool 05.40
1946		
March	Nº 1 FPP White Waltham	11.40 Sub-pool 02.40

Ringway had four Lancasters to deliver to an airfield in Norfolk; and it so happened that the local group Captain was paying a visit to the Watch Office at this station when the Ringway Anson arrived to wait for the expected ferry pilots and fly them back. Right on its tail came a second ATA taxi Anson to park neatly by the first. The Group Captain began to take notice.

No sooner were the Anson propellers still than the first of the Lancasters appeared in the circuit. It was quickly followed by a second, then a third. and in the next few minutes not four but eight had landed and taxied efficiently to their dispersal points. The pilots climbed out and made their way to the Watch Office.

The Group Captain was dumfounded: 'Marvellous organisation! Wonderful! How do you fellows possibly do it? Perfect timing! Think of all the calculation you must have had to make. And no wirless either!

No one troubled to disillusion the Group Captain or station commander. Not one Pool, but two had been involved in the operation, Nº 3 FPP, Hawarden, having contributed the second four Lancasters from Vickers Armstrong. As neither Ringway nor Hawarden knew that the other had deliveries to that particular airfield that day, the whole perfect movement had been by pure chance.

As the tempo of ferrying operations increased 'it was everybody out' (Ken Day's words); it took some effort at Hawarden with its new rest rooms for crew, where there was a growing tendency to linger around the fire and read the paper, a far cry from the days of Walter Handley, when they slummed it in the ATA 'house'. Walter himself was often heard to say to visiting VIPs: 'Look at it here. Things are so bloody awful, that they have got nothing else to do but go out and fly!'. Even 'Operations' people were occasionally forced to leave their office chairs to complete a daily schedule. Not that some chair-bound types needed much persuasion to get back into the air. Charlie More and Ken Day often chuckled recalling a case — on a Christmas Eve some eighteen months earlier, when both helped to strap into a clapped out Hart Special (K4411) of 1935 vintage, a

powerful variant of the pre-war Hawker Hart light day-bomber bi-plane, no less a personage than Senior Commander Philip Wills, ATA Director of Operations at White Waltham who had a penchant for solo flying, taking out any aircraft short of a pilot — the older the better. K4411 had seen operational service with Nº 40 Squadron, Abingdon and later with Nᵒˢ 5 and 10 FTSs, but since August 1942 had been an ATA hack with the Training FPP at White Waltham. but what it was doing in north-east Wales is something of a mystery, and why the Director of Operations no less should have agreed to fly it south is equally problematic considering the choice of more comfortable taxi or communications aircraft at his disposal. Suffice it to say Phil Wills was more than a little 'rusty' on type — he had never flown one before. He gleaned as much information as he could from ground staff and took off without incident, but thirty minutes ito his flight the engine started to cough and then failed. Many a pilot would have abandoned his aircraft but Wills was a peace-time glider pilot of some renown and he skilfully brought K4411 to earth in the hill country at Llandysul, near Montgomery. On landing he found that he had taken off from Hawarden on the reserve fuel tank and had simply run out of fuel whilst his main tank was still full! Owing to the difficult terrain he was unable to take-off again. Later on a guard detail arrived from RAF Cosford and Philip was taken to Cosford where he spent Christmas Day in the Officers' Mess. One thing is almost certain, he was not the flavour of the month with the guard picket.

But Philip Wills's niche in aviation history stems not from finally writing off a prehistoric bi- plane in the wilds of mid-Wales, but for his part at the height of the Battle of Britain in glider radar trials in over the English Channel. In June 1940, following the fall of the Belgian strongpoint Fort Eben Emael to an audacious glider-borne assault as the Germans marched into the Low Countries some consideration was given as to whether the new fangled RDF (Radar) could detect the wooden gliders which might form the spearhead of the expected invasion of England. Such was the urgency, that tests had been carried out and a 'final' report prepared by 17 July. Tests were carried at Worth Matravers AMRE out at a distance of 2–30 miles out to sea off the coast of Dorset and up to 10,000ft. Involved were a number of pre-war gliding experts and their gliders, hastily retrieved from storage, including Philip Wills and his Minimoa. Wills recalls being towed out to sea by a Tiger Moth or one the three Avro 504Ns of the Special Duty Flight. Quite good results were obtained with CH equipment; CHL results were less satisfactory, possibly because of too much aerial activity in the area; It was a nerve-racking experience to be towed to within 20 miles of the enemy coast and then released to glide the 40 or so lonely miles back to base, but not once during the three weeks of the test were they intercepted by enemy aircraft. There was a need for further tests, to modify CHL aerials and to test for gliders very low down over the sea, where there were no cliffs. Hence the move to north Wales, more specifically the RAF stations at Rhuddlan CH, Trewin Sands GCI and Prestatyn and South Stack CHL stations. But, typically for something so sensitive, these Welsh trials warrant no more than three official lines in radar records at the PRO and certainly have not impressed themselves on local folk memory. However, aviation records reveal a glider accident involving Hotspur HH299 on 24 October 1942 in the vicinity of Plas Newydd, Glascoed, Abergele. The crash site is a mile to the SW of AMES N° 65, better known as RAF Rhuddlan. A much bigger glider, a Horsa (the registration of which we have failed to trace), came to grief on 5 June 1943 on the Ruthin side of Clawdd-newydd.

Any history of the ATA in the north-west, must include the work carried out by Class 6 seaplane pilots working into and out of the North Atlantic terminal at Beaumaris, Anglesey. Given the rank of Flight Captains, these men worked out from the three main ATA Ferry Pools, N° 6 Ratcliff, N° 4 Prestwick and N° 8 Belfast. They were abley assisted by co-pilot, flight engineer and one ATC or Sea Cadet (the latter being trained to a high level of seamanship) or, alternatively, an ATA flight engineer and two ATC or Sea Cadets as from July 1943. The log at Saro Beaumaris recalls many well known ATA pilots passing through the terminal: José Carreras from Spain, A. E. Chambers, A. W. Vincent, F. A. W. Mickel, J. L. Glover, W. B. Shaw, E. J. Spiller and E. L. Wilson. A ferry flight could start with the pilot being flown to the nearest airfield to the point of departure, then a taxi to the departure point. Lettice Curtis gives a pilot's opinion of Beaumaris, commenting 'of all the flying boat bases visited, ATA Beaumaris was perhaps the most delightful'. Here there was plenty of room to manoeuvre and plenty of water right up to the Menai Bridge where the aircraft ready for delivery were moored. It was, above all, a good bolt hole if one was caught in bad weather.

The seemingly awkward statistical year ending 14 February 1945 (reflecting the date when the ATA got underway) shows the organisation had reached maturity. During the previous twelve months the 637 pilots who were on actual ferryng had moved 78,851 aircraft of 99 different types, which involved a total of 94,682 flying hours. In addition to the operational work, the taxi fleet of Ansons, Dominies and Fairchilds grew to 218 machines, which logged 40,180 hours of flying time for the same period. A similar set of statistics takes us to standown in November 1945. Making allowance for the gradual closure of ferry pools they are no less remarkable: single engined aircraft 18,150; twin-engined aircraft 9,570; four-engined aircraft 4,311; flying boats 201; total 32,373 on 78 different types. The statistics for the Broughton factory show: Wellingtons delivered 296; Lancaster 235, Lincolns 11 over the nine months. It is remarkable to think that N° 3 FPP over nearly five years must have shifted some 5,780 machines from it next door neighbour. This chapter began with the winding down process and touched on the hurt and vexation felt by the 'forgotten pilots' at the few accolades that came the way of the ATA after hostilities had ceased, and in the lack of any tangible recognition by the RAF itself the greatest beneficiary of ATA services, so one must end by allowing these bare statistics to speak for themselves.

Lettice wallows in nostalgia, recalling her ferry trips in flying boats, relative oases of calm in wartime skies …

The ferrying of these big boats was for both pilot and crew a delightful and fascinating experience and, as can be imagined, there was always keen competition for the job of second pilot. The whole operation was completely unhurried and, to a very large extent, free from the usual irksome route restrictions. Pilots tended to take the longer coastal courses rather than fly direct — the excuse safety, but in reality because of the enormous pleasure derived from flying low over the water sand watching the passing scenery. To fly a Sunderland up the Western Scottish coast and through the Western Isles on a clear, calm day keeping close to the water, approached the ultimate in pleasure flying. Away from cities, balloon barrages and all the other appurtenances of war — for flying boats had little semblance to fighting machines — one was back in an unhurried and timeless age of sea, rocks and sky, able to view it from a new a superior dimension. The places visited had the same timeless quality — it would be interesting to know how many people today could name the connection between such place names as Plymouth, Mountbatten, Felixstowe, Windermere, Lerwick and Sullom Voe!

Some Ferry Mishaps, 1941–5

1941

2.1.41. Curtiss Mohawk: AR658. Flew into HT wires Wroughton. Nº 2 FPP.

1.2.41. Curtiss Mohawk: AR664. Spun in at Ringway. Nº 14 FPP.

5.2.41. Fairey Fulmar: N4074. On ferry from HMS *Kestrel* (RNAS Worthy Down), flies into Minera Mountain, west of Wrexham, in snow storm. S/Lt S. Burden killed.

26.3.41. DH Puss Moth: BK846. Blown over by slip stream of departing Wellington as landing at Hawarden. Nº 1 FPP.

27.4.41. Curtiss Tomahawk: AH892. Forced landing at Wrexham aerodrome under construction. Nº 3 FPP.

12.8.41. Curtiss Tomahawk: AK154. Damages wing after hitting contractor's ditch as landing at Hawarden. Nº 3 FPP.

30.8.41. DH Leopard Moth: AV986 (ex-G-ACRV). Mechanical problem, force landed safely, Rushup Edge Derbyshire; on take off blown into stone wall by wind, undercarriage collapsed. First of four accidents First Officer (later Flight Captain) Bernard Short was to have with ATA. Nº 14 FPP.

7.9.41. Curtiss Tomahawk: AH805. Swung on landing, High Ercall, undercarriage collapsed. Nº 1 FPP.

8.9.41. Bristol Beaufighter IF: X7640. Crashed 3 miles SW Capel Curig on ferry flight Weston, Bristol – RAF Sealand. First Officer V. G. Covett killed. Nº 2 FPP.

10.9.41. DH90 Dragonfly: X9390 (ex-GAEFN). Engine failure on take-off, Cosford en route to Brockton SLG. Swung into trees at sewage works. Nº 7 FPP.

28.9.41. Bristol Beaufighter II: T 3045. Stalled on approach to Atcham, caught fire. Nº 2 FPP.

7.11.41. Handley Page Hampden I: P5396. Stalled and crashed in circuit at Burtonwood, killing First Officer I. J. Parades (Philippines). Nº 3 FPP .

11.11.41. Bell Airacobra: AH598. Engine blew up after take-off, Kirkbride en route for Hawarden. Walter Handley killed. Nº 3 FPP.

24.11.41. Supermarine Spitfire IIA: P7284. Crashed in circuit at Valley, on delivery from Leconfield to Nº 350 Belgian Sqn, then forming. Nº 3 Del.Flt. .

24.11.41. Supermarine Spitfire IIA: P8661. Unable to locate Valley in bad weather. Crashed at Llanfair, killing P/O Philip Vernon. Nº 3 Del.Flt.

7.12.41. Hawker Hurricane: Z5663. On ferry from Brockworth to Nº 48 MU Hawarden; control lost in snowstorm, crashed in Wyre Forest, near Bewdley killing First Officer E. E. Gasser (USA). Nº 2 FPP.

7.12.41. DH Dominie I: X7354. Struck by lightning in snowstorm whilst on taxi duties Lichfield to Hawarden; crashed at Rectory Farm, Hordley, killing P/Os G. K. Eaton and J. E. Moodie. Nº 3 Del. Flt.

7.12.41. Hawker Hurricane: BN130. Force landed in snowstorm on Darland Meadows, Rossett. Nº 3 Del. Flt.

10.12.41. Blackburn Botha: W5103. In-bound to Nº 48 MU from Sherburn-in-Furness; crashed in cloud into Round Hill, Peak District, killing First Officer T. W. Rogers. Nº 7 FPP.

10.12.41. Curtiss Kittyhawk: AK575. Missing on flight Speke – Prestwick. Nº 4 FPP.

1942

13.1.42. Miles Magister: P2468. On ferry flight Whitchurch, Bristol – Kingstown, refuelled Sealand, crashed at Raffels, near Carlisle in mist and fog. Nº 2 FPP.

29.1.42. Hurricane I: V7001. On ferry flight from Rollasons, Hanworth (Surrey) – to Nº 18 MU, Dumfries, via Hawarden In poor visibility ploughed into Bryn Adda Flats, Ysgubor Ucha, Ruabon Mounbtain, killing Second Officer P. J. Collins. Nº 1 FPP.

30.1.42. Curtiss Mohawk: AR671. Engine failure, spun in to ground whilst in circuit RAF Pershore. Nº 3 FPP.

30.1.42. Boulton Paul Defiant I: N3337. Forced landing in foul weather, NE of Tern Hill; undercarriage collapsed; pilot killed. Nº 6 FPP.

6.2.42. Douglas Boston III: W8254 (converted turbinelite), crashed on landing, Ringway. Nº 1 FPP.

7.2.42. Handley Page Hampden I: AT231. Crashed on approach to Nº 33 SLG, Weston Park, killing First Officer E. L. Renicker (USA). Nº 14 FPP.

7.2.42. Lockheed Hudson III: AE487. Iced up, after take-off, crashed ¹/2 mile E of Speke. Nº 3 FPP.

8.2.42. Avro Anson: W1793. On taxi run with Nº 6 FPP; had left Sherburn -in-Elmet but crashed on Buckes Heath, Stain Moor, Cumberland in snowstorm. killing First Officer W. J. Elliott (USA). Nº 6 FPP.

8.2.42. Boulton Paul Defiant I: AA321. Forced landing, Plas Power, Wrexham on ferry from Nº 264 Sqn (West Malling) – RAF Wrexham. Nº 1 FPP.

20.2.42. Supermarine Walrus: W3070. Crashed on delivery, ferry flight Cowes – Donibristle, pilot unhurt (2nd incident involving Bernard Short) Nº 14 FPP.

18.3.42. Handley Page Hampden I: X3130. Missing on ferry flight Kitkbride – Thorney Island; crewed by First Officer T. C. David Bray (Australia) and Second Officer N. A. Berry, of Hawarden Ferry Pool. Nº 3 FPP.

16.4.42. Supermarine Spitfire: BM478. Overshot landing at Burtonwood. Nº 6 FPP.

15.5.42. Supermarine Spitfire: K9961. On ferry from Nº 37MU Burtonwood; crashed at Tern Hill landing in a cross wind. Nº 6 FPP.

26.5.42. Miles Magister I: R1822. Dived into ground at Burgess Farm, High Ercall. Nº 3 Del. Flt.

27.8.42. Hawker Hart Trainer: K6525 Ground looped landing at Hawarden, tipped on nose. (T)FPP.

28.8.42. Bristol Beaufighter IIF: R2470. Difficulties on take-off. Wing hits ground, Burgess Farm, High Ercall. Nº 3 Del.Flt.

8.9.42. Bristol Beaufighter IIF: T3445. On ferry flight from Nº 30 MU Sealand; crashed whilst in circuit, ¹/2 mile E of Shawbury. Nº 3 Del. Flt.

12.9.42. Hawker Hurricane: JS346. On ferry Kirkbride – Abroath. Crashed in bad weather at Eeves Hall, Dumfries, killing pilot HRH Prince Chirosakti (Siam). Nº 16 FPP.

17.9.42. Supermarine Spitfire V: EP983. Took off Hawarden in low cloud, spun in at Saighton, killing pilot First Officer Cyril Walter Morris. Nº 3 FPP.

6.10.42. Bristol Beaufighter VI: V8468. One engine failed, second lost power; hit trees in forced landing near Bridgnorth, Shropshire. Nº 3 FPP.

31.10.42. Supermarine Walrus I: W 3097. On ferry from Donibristle to Sealand, beached at Gronant, (Flintshire), engine problems possibly out of fuel. Nº 8 FPP.

31.10.42. Fairey Swordfish: L9726. Took off Ringway, flew into balloon cable, managed to land safely. Nº 14 FPP (Note: on 26 May 1941. this aircraft credited with damaging *Bismarck's* rudder) .

21.11.42. Hawker Typhoon IB: DN251. Ferry flight Hatfield to

Dumfries crashed into Brown Clee Hills, killing pilot Flight Captain Walter Mason. Nº 5 FPP.

21.12.42. Supermarine Spitfire VC: JG924. Took off Hawarden for Nº 76 MU (Packing Depot), Wroughton. kept very low, clipped trees and tangled with overhead wires and poles, crashed at Mollington, Chester, caught fire killing Second Officer J. H. Stubbs. Nº 3 FPP.

24.12.42. Hawker Hart Special: K4411. Took of from Hawarden on reserve tank, forced to land at Llandysul, Montgomery. Guard picket mounted by RAF Cosford. Pilot, Philip Wills, ATA Director of Operations.

1943

11.1.43. Supermarine Spitfire IX: EN248. On ferry flight from Nº 9 MU Cosford to Nº 47 MU Sealand; landed safely but taxied into soft grass; undercarriage collapsed. Nº 12 FPP.

13.1.43. Fairey Swordfish: HS219. On ferry to Renfrew . Emergency landing at Speke; hit obstruction on runway. S/Lt E. L. Helwell unhurt.

14.1.43. Fairey Swordfish: HS213. On ferry to Renfrew. Crashed near Rootes factory, Speke. S/Lt E. L. Helwell again unhurt.

15.1.43. Miles Master III: W8840. On ferry Sherburn-in-Elmet – Tern Hill; flew into ground in poor visibility at Ashbourne-on-Leek. Nº 7 FPP.

11.2.43. Miles Hawk Trainer: DG666 (ex-GAEAX). ATA communications hack, hit by Percival Proctor LZ675 whilst parked at Hawarden.

13.2.43. Fairey Fulmar I: N1942. On ATA ferry Stockport - Yeovilton collided with Spitfire R7335 on runway at Ringway.

14.2.43. Boulton Paul Defiant I: N1551. Disorientated in cloud, control lost abandoned by pilot, Second Officer R. W. Reisert (USA) over Lindal-in-Furness. Nº 6 FPP.

16.2.43. Avro Anson I: N5154. Forced landing in bad weather at Llanfairtalhaiarn, (Denbighshire) whilst on taxi run. Nº 2 FPP.

2.3.43. Supermarine Spitfire IX: EN205. Crashed making a forced landing at Battingbourn Kingston (Wilts.). Nº 15 FPP.

10.3.43. Supermarine Walrus I: W3100. Tail wheel collapsed on landing Ringway, First Officer L. R. Rawlings (USA) unhurt.

17.3.43. Vought Chesapeake I: AL949. Engine trouble on taxi flight from Lee-on Solent to Nº 770 Sqn, put down at Hawarden, when noticed tail wheel was not locked causing 'waggle'; repaired by ATA mechanics.

2.4.43. Supermarine Walrus I: X9482. Ferry flight from SARO, ground looped on runway Kirkbride, landing in a cross wind; pilot uninjured (3rd incident involving Bernard Short). Nº 14 FPP.

7.4.43. Supermarine Walrus I: W3100. Although picketed down at Ringway, blown over in gale-force winds. Nº 14 FPP.

18.4.43. Bristol Beaufighter VIF: X7887. Ditched off Bradda Head, IoM, on ferry from Ballyhalbert – Nº 29 MU HIgh Ercall; pilot F/O S. Sielinski fatally injured. Nº 3 Del. Flt.

20 5.43. Fairey Fulmar II: DR742. Taxying accident Burtonwood. Firts Officer W. N. Ester (USA) uninjured.

21.5.43. Fairey Barracuda: P9740. Brand new, undercarriage collapsed on take-off, Wroughton; pilot Second Officer Jenie Broad unhurt. Nº 15 FPP.

22.5.43. Miles Master II: W9029. Ferry flight Nº 10 MU Hullavington – Nº 5 (P)AFU Tern Hill; lost propeller over Littleworth (Worcs.) bounced on forced landing, smashed into farm buildings and caught fire, killing trapped pilot, Second Officer Mary Webb Nicholson (USA). Nº 12 FPP.

21.6.43. Vickers Wellington XIV: HF136. Port engine lost power on take-off, Hawarden; veered and crashed on Cop Farm killing pilot First Officer A. Carpenter. Nº 3 FPP.

30.6.43. Fairey Barracuda: P9865. Complete engine failure. Put down safely at RAF Winfield (Berwick) First Officer J. E. G. Johns unhurt.

1.7.43. Supermarine Walrus: X9463. Ground looped at Eastleigh; First Officer Benedetta Will is unhurt. Nº15FPP.

4.7.43. Fairey Swordfish: P4141. Engine failure, put down successfully at Ringway. Nº 15 FPP.

14.7.43. Supermarine Walrus: L2184. On ferry Ringway to Eastleigh; engine failure, landed safely at Eastleigh; pilot First Officer Grace Stevenson (USA). Nº 15 FPP.

27.7.43. Grumman Hellcat I: FN324. On ferry from Nº 8 FPP, Belfast; swung badly while taking off, Speke, collided with hay cart. Pilot S/Lt Barrington FAA .

27.7.43. Fairey Swordfish: LS220. Engine failure; Sgt J.M. Matton (RAF det,) injured in forced landing at East Underton Farm, Bridgnorth. Nº 5 FPP.

29.7.43. Fairey Barracuda: P9655(G).(ASV radar test bed); engine failure on ferry flight; forced landing at Pendeford, Wolverhampton .

29.7.43. Vickers Wellington X: HE819. Crashed Cranage on pre-delivery check flight. F/O Rouff and Vickers test inspector, Mr E. Booth, killed.

19.8.43. Grumman Hellcat: FN355. On ferry from Belfast; engine failure on circuit, belly- landed Millom, P/O J. Robinson (RAF det.) unhurt. Nº 8 FPP.

20.8.43. Fairey Barracuda: BV759. On ferry to Nº 15 MU Wroughton, engine failure, black smoke filled cockpit, control lost, crashed near Rufford bombing range, Mansfield, killing pilot F/Sgt J. C. Milliken (RAF det.). Nº 5 (T)FPP.

8.9.43. Supermarine Spitfire V: AD555. Overshot in flapless landing at South Marston. Nº 15 FPP.

10.9.43. Supermarine Spitfire XI: EN341. Overshot landing South Marston, ploughed through hedge losing undercarriage. Nº 15FPP.

27.9.43. Grumman Wildcat V: JV347. ATA ferry, collided with another aircraft taxying off runway after landing High Ercall.

11.10.43. Hawker Hurricane I: L2026. Engine failure, stalled in forcelanding, crashed and caught fire killing pilot, Second Officer D. J. M. Martin. Nº 16 FPP.

19.10.43. Fairey Barracuda: DT824. On delivery flight from Heaton Chapel, engine failure, force landed successfully at Wheaton Aston aerodrome.

20.10.43. Handley Page Hampden: P2113. On ferry after conversion to torpedo bomber. Fire in port engine. Successful forced landing at Tod Brow, Cumberland. At great risk Flight Captain J. E. Martens turned off fuel cocks and fought fire. Nº 16 FPP.

24.10.43. Grumman Avenger I: FN883. ATA ferry, engine failure, successfully put down at Burscough (Lancs.).

26.10.43. Hawker Hurricane IIC: LE262. Low cloud brought aircraft below safe flying limits, stalled and crashed into hill 10 miles E of St Bees Head, killing pilot First Officer M. Coutanceau (det. RAF). Nº 3 FPP .

3.11.43. Vought Corsair I: JT 253. Engine failure forced S/Lt E. A. Roberts FAA to land on beach at Wallasey; struggle by Nº 48 MU Hawarden to salvage a/c before tide claimed it.

3.10.43. Bristol Beaufighter X: NE203. On ferry flight from Weston-super-Mare to Nº 46 MU Lossiemouth, pilot lost sight of ground, off course, stalled and hit mountainside at World's End, Llangollen killing F/Sgt John Shepherd. Nº 2 FPP.

3.11.43. Fairey Swordfish II: NE862. Engine fire, undercarriage torn off in forced landing at Kiddemore Green (Staffordshire); pilot Third Officer Irene Ferguson survived. Nº 7 FPP.

Issue 3

SPITFIRE & SEAFIRE

IDENTIFICATION TABLE

3 BLADED PROPELLERS. (all with one radiator).	With normal fighter type windscreen.	Spitfire I.	Two fuel contents gauges with starter magneto switch alongside. No jettison tank controls in cockpit.
		Spitfire II.	Cartridge starter with reloading ring on right of dashboard. No jettison tank controls in cockpit.
		Spitfire V.	Guns always. Jettison tank and rear fuselage tank controls in cockpit. Some with clipped wings.
		Seafire I, II.	Deck arrester hook.
	With P.R.U. windscreen i.e. one piece with blisters.	Spitfire IV.	No guns. 66 gallon leading edge tanks.
		Spitfire VII PR.	Guns. Rear fuselage tank controls in cockpit.
		Spitfire XIII.	Guns, cartridge starter, jettison tank controls.
4 BLADED PROPELLERS.	With TWO radiators.	Spitfire VII F.	Pressure cabin with detachable or sliding hood. Retractable tail wheel. Extended wing tips.
		Spitfire VIII.	No pressure cabin. Retractable tail wheel. Extended wing tips.
		Spitfire IX.	No pressure cabin. Non-retractable tail wheel.
		Spitfire XI.	P.R.U. one piece windscreen with blisters. Retractable tail wheel. No guns.
	With ONE radiator.	Spitfire VI.	Pressure cabin with detachable hood. Non-retractable tail wheel. Extended wing tips.
		Spitfire XII.	Griffon engine with humps on engine cowl. Different shaped rudder, and retractable tail wheel. Clipped wings.
		Seafire III.	Deck arrester hook and folding wings.

Engine: Griffon in Spitfire XII. Merlin in all others. Injection carb. on some Mks., indicated by a wobble pump or booster pump switch in cockpit. No mixture lever except on early Mks. Fuel: 100 Octane (87 permitted on Spitfire I).
Supercharger: Some Mks. have 2-speed, 2-stage type, with auto control. Override switch on dash. Keep UP for ferrying. Press button provided to ground test.

SPITFIRE AND SEAFIRE—*Continued.*

Propeller:
3 blade constant speed:—Rotol, or D.H. hydromatic or counterweight.
4 blade constant speed:—Rotol.

Interconnected Throttle and Propeller Control (fitted to some Spitfire IX): The propeller lever has only 2 positions. At "AUTOMATIC," the throttle controls the boost and revs. above 1900 r.p.m. At "MAX. REVS.," automatic device is overridden and higher r.p.m. obtained.

U/C Operation:
Normal: Hydraulic. When raising or lowering U/C (and tail wheel if retractable) pause as soon as lever is out of notch. This allows weight of wheels to be lifted off locking pins. Then move lever to desired position at other end of quadrant, with a steady positive action and without pause. This is a safeguard against selector jamming. Lever will then automatically spring into the other notch (Idle position). (Some Mk. I have hand pump with simple selector lever).
Reserve: None.
Emergency: CO_2 cylinder. Selector must be DOWN. If selector jams midway, apply negative "G" and bang it.
Indicator: Green light locked DOWN. Red light locked UP. No lights IN TRANSIT. On some, stalks protruding above wings show position of each leg. Separate light for tail wheel: Green, locked DOWN.

Flaps:
Normal: Compressed air. 2-positions only.
Reserve: None. Emergency: None.
Indicators: Bell cranks in wings.

Gills:
Manual control with single radiator. Indicator on map box. Automatic control with two radiators. Button for ground testing. Some aircraft have carb. heat control to left of pilot.

Main Tanks:
All aircraft have two main tanks in fuselage; total capacity 85 or 96 gals. A few aircraft have a cock lever for each tank, others, a single cock. Tanks are pressurised on most aircraft. Keep pressurising cock OFF. Some Spitfire V's have an immersed pump in lower tank with switch below rudder trimmer. Keep OFF for ferrying.

Long Range Tanks:
Jettison: 30, 90, or 170 gal. tank under fuselage can be fitted on most aircraft, but should be as empty as possible. Cock lever and jettison hand grip control to right of pilot. Always have cock OFF. No gauge. Always jettison tank before a belly landing. To do so, check cock is OFF, then pull hand grip. Max. permissible speed with jettison tank 220 m.p.h. (191 knots) and only normal flying manoeuvres allowed.
Rear fuselage: Fixed 29-gal. tank on some. Cock lever on right of cockpit. No gauge. Should be as empty as possible. Only normal flying manoeuvres permitted until tank is empty.
66-Gallon leading edge: One in each wing in Spitfire IV and XI. Not normally used for ferrying but may contain 20-gals. each. Cocks on corresponding sides of cockpit. When not marked, ON when fore-and-aft, and OFF athwartships. If required, turn both ON at a safe height, then turn mains OFF. When nearly empty, turn mains ON, then wing tanks OFF. Contents gauges on some aircraft.
14-Gallon leading edge: One in each wing in Spitfire VII F and VIII. Their contents transferred to top main tank by air pressure. Transfer cock below dash, marked "OFF—STAR—PORT." Tanks should be empty and cock OFF. No gauges.
Underslung: Some Spitfire V have a 30-gal. fixed tank under port wing. No gauge. Cock lever near compass. If full, use early in flight to avoid tendency to land one wing low.

(Continued on next card.

Issue 3.

WELLINGTON I.

Engines: Two Pegasus XVIII. 2-speed blowers. Fuel: 100 Octane.
Propellers: D.H. constant speed, counterweight type.
U/C Operation: As Wellington III, except for two-position hydraulic power selector at right of pilot's seat.
Flaps, Gills, Tanks, and Control Locks: As Wellington III.
Starting: Direct electric, 12 or 24-volt. Dopers and starter magneto switches in nacelles.

FLYING PARTICULARS

Take-Off:

Hydraulics:	Blowers:	Boost:	R.P.M.:	Mixture:	Gills:	Trim:	Flaps:
ON.	M.	$+6\frac{3}{4}$.	2600.	Rich.	No. 2.	All Neutral.	UP.

[Safety Speed: 120 m.p.h.

Climb (Max.):

Hydraulics:	Boost:	R.P.M.:	Mixture:	Gills:	A.S.I.:
OFF.	$+2\frac{1}{2}$.	2250.	Rich.	No. 2 (Watch temps.).	130 m.p.h.

A.T.A. Cruise:

Boost:	R.P.M.:	Mixture:	Gills:	A.S.I.:	Consumption:
0.	1900.	Weak.	Closed if possible.	160 m.p.h.	40 gals./eng. hr.

Single Engine:

	Boost:	R.P.M.:	Mixture:	Gills:	Dead Prop.:	Rudder:	Aileron:	A.S.I:
Level:	$+2\frac{1}{2}$.	2250.	Rich.	Closed.	Full Coarse.	Full trim.	5° bank.	95 m.p.h.
Climb:	+5.	Full fine pitch.	Rich.	Closed.	Full Coarse.	Full trim.	5° bank.	95 m.p.h.

Stall: Flaps and U/C UP: 67 m.p.h. Flaps and U/C DOWN: 58 m.p.h.
Glide: Flaps and U/C UP: 120 m.p.h. Flaps and U/C DOWN: 100 m.p.h.

Approach and Land:

Hydraulics:	Flaps:	Effect:	Max. speed for flaps:	Final Approach:
ON.	DOWN.	Powerful nose-up.	120 m.p.h.	80 m.p.h. With Static Vent: 90 m.p.h.

Notes: As Wellington III.

WELLINGTON II.

Engines: Two Merlin X. 2-speed blowers. Fuel: 100 Octane.
Propellers: D.H. constant speed, hydromatic, feathering.
U/C Operation, Flaps, Tanks and Control Locks: As Wellington III.
Gills: Two 3-position radiator shutter controls on floor to right of pilot.
Starting: As Wellington I.

FLYING PARTICULARS

Take-Off:

Blowers:	Boost:	R.P.M.:	Mixture:	Radiator:	Elev.:	Rudder:	Flaps:
M.	+10. (Cut-out UP).	3000.	Rich.	Closed.	Neutral.	5° right.	UP.

[Safety Speed: 135 m.p.h.

Climb (A.T.A.):

Boost:	R.P.M.:	Mixture:	A.S.I.:
$+5\frac{3}{4}$ (Cut-out DOWN).	2600.	Rich.	140 m.p.h.

A.T.A. Cruise:

Boost:	R.P.M.:	Mixture:	Radiator:	A.S.I.:	Consumption:
0.	1900.	Weak.	Closed (85°C.).	170 m.p.h.	35 gals./eng. hr.

Single Engine:

	Boost:	R.P.M.:	Mixture:	Radiator:	Dead Prop.:	Rudder & Aileron:	A.S.I:
Level:	+2.	2600.	Rich.	Closed.	Feathered.	Full trim.	120 m.p.h.
Climb:	+4.	2600.	Rich.	Closed.	Feathered.	Full trim.	110 m.p.h.

Stall: Flaps and U/C UP: 74 m.p.h. Flaps and U/C DOWN: 63 m.p.h.
Glide: Flaps and U/C UP: 120 m.p.h. Flaps and U/C DOWN: 100 m.p.h.

Examples of ATA pilot's notes. Each ATA pilot would have been supplied with notes on every aeroplane type that he/she was likely to fly. The notes were held in a ring-binder and gave sufficient details to enable the pilot to identify the aircraft type and mark. They also gave the flying characteristics and technical specifications of each type. [Ken Day]

15.11.43. Boulton Paul Defiant I: T3927. Engine cut in circuit; belly landed Hawarden. Nº 3 FPP.

22.11.43. Fairey Swordfish II: LS438. Tail-wheel failure on take-off from Cosford, tyre burst on landing at RAF Pershore.

30.11.43. Fairey Barracuda II: LS486. 'Weather-cocked' into wind on landing Ringway; brakes failed, undercarriage collapsed; pilot First Officer T. F. THompson unhurt. Nº 14 FPP.

1.12.43. Supermerine Spitfire VIII: JG546. Contol lost in bad weather. Crashed at Stag Lane, Lowton (Lancs,) Nº 2 FPP.

2.12.43. Bristol Beaufighter X: NE228. Failed to respond to red light: airfield unuseable; failed to gain height, overshot, came to rest on airfield boundary, Sealand. Flight Captain R. F. James unhurt. Nº 3 FPP.

18.12.43. Handley Page Hampden: AD736. Ex-Nº 1402 Met. Flt, (Aldergrove); last flight before breaking up. Port engine failed as landing at Hawarden, 'stabilised yaw', hit building, rolled over and crashed in inverted position, broke up and destroyed by fire killing First Officer J. D. Hurley. Nº 8 FPP.

1944

8.1.44 Westland Whirlwind I: P7097. Swung off runway whilst landing Hawarden, ran into waterlogged ground, undercarriage badly damaged, not repaired. Nº 3 FPP.

23.1.44. Bristol Beaufighter X: NE474. Taxying with three passengers at Hawarden when hit by Mustang AG597 of Nº 41. OTU landing on wrong runway. Explosion and fire killing Mustang pilot F/O E. W. Holford and an ATA passenger. Nº 3 FPP.

24.1.44. Handley Page Halifax II: JP182. On ferry from Nº 45 MU Kinloss to Nº 5. MU Kemble. Hit snow blizzard, became lost, flew into Scott Crag, W of Keswick. Flight Captain B. Short and Senior Flight Engineer A. Bird both killed. Nº 14 FPP .

10.2.44. Supermarine Spitfire IX: MK616. Scheduled ferry flight Nº 9 MU Cosford – Nº 39 MU Colerne. Climbed sharply on take off, went into roll and dived into lake at Tong, Shropshire, killing Second Officer Jane Winstone. Nº 12 FPP.

15.2.44. Curtiss Seamew I: FN460. ATA groundstaff Hawarden reprimanded for damaging tail-wheel of a/c as removing it from hangar, delaying delivery to Nº 15 MU Wroughton.

17.2.44. Bristol Beaufort: AW379. On flight from Cosford to Melton Mowbray.; weather deteriorated, a/c iced up and was abandoned, to crash into Cardigan Bay off Aberdyfi. Pilot Commander F. Francis parachuted onto Darland Meadows, Rossett, north of Wrexham. Nº 6 FPP.

2.3.44 DH MosquitoVI: HP932. First Officer Dora Lang with Flt/Eng Janice Harrington had just delivered a Lockheed Hudson to Cosford; ferry of HP932 back to Lasham (Hampshire), stalled on approach; 20ft above runway reared up and crashed on back, killing both crew members. Nº 15 FPP.

24.3.44. DH Mosquito XX: KB116. Swung on take-off Hawarden, undercarriage collapsed, severe damage. Pilot, Second Officer Grace Stevenson unhurt. Nº 3 FPP.

3.4.44. Avro Anson I: N4875. Went missing on ambulance flight White Waltham–Prestwick. Presumed ditched in Irish Sea. ATA CF.

30.4.44. North American Mustang I: AG612. Complete engine failure on take-off, Ringway; flew straight through boundary hedge and overturned. Nº 14 FPP.

13.5.44. Fairey Swordfish III: NF262. On ferry from Nº 29 MU High Ercall to HMS *Kestrel* (Worthy Down). Engine failure over Wellington, forced landing 4 miles SSW of Shifnal; Second Officer Mollie Rose unhurt.

1.6.44 Vought Corsair II: JS633. Hydraulic failure after take off Hawarden, undercarriage out of action, expended surplus fuel, belly-landed on aerodrome, pilot First Officer J. D. Rochford

(Canada) unhurt. Nº 3 FPP.

9.6.44 Grumman Avenger: JZ560. Takes off Hawarden on ferry flight to Hawkinge, Kent. A/c and pilot First Officer Roy Egginton never seen or heard of again. Nº 3 FPP .

9.6.44 Fairey Swordfish III: NF300. Engine failure, forced landing at Speke. Pilot First Officer Victoria Cholmondeley (Australia) unhurt. Nº 12 FPP.

15.6.44. Fairey Barracuda: DP885. Ferry flight Ringway to Prestwick, lost hydraulic power, stooged round losing fuel, returned to Ringway circuit good belly landing. Flight Captain G. N. Wikner (Australia) and passenger unhurt. Nº 14 FPP.

22.6.44. Supermarine Walrus: K8564. Damaged by ground staff Hawarden as manhandled from hangar; gust of wind blew a/c into soft ground, strain damage to tail unit. Nº 3 FPP .

26.6.44. Vought Corsair II: JT452. On ferry Nº 19 MU St Athan – Nº 29 MU High Ercall, pilot F/Sgt J. de-Little. After landing pilot bcame disorientated and taxied into Hudson IIIA FK743.

23.7.44. Grumman Wildcat VI: JV428. Ground-looped as landing at Hawarden; badly damaged port wing First Officer J. A. MacCallum (S. Africa) unhurt. Nº 8 FPP.

4.8.44 Percival Proctor III: LZ801. VIP ferry flight Heston – Hawarden – Prestwick. Engine failure over Bangor-on-Dee; put down on Shocklach Meadows, fixed undercarriage hit a 'ridge and furrow', tipped on to nose, passenger Katherine Farrer, adjutant Nº 5 FPP, seriously injured; pilot, Flight Captain Margaret Fairweather received fractured skull and lacerations to brain which proved fatal. ATA CF.

13.8.44. Lockheed Hudson I: N7238. Engine caught fire on take-off Littlewick (Berks,); force landed still ablaze; at great personal risk Flight Captain GB Warne (USA) (instructor) rescued conversion pupil then Second Officer Jane Plant (USA) before a/c exploded. ATA (T)FPP.

18.8.44. Airspeed Oxford I: PH235. Crashed at Holmes Chapel on ferry flight; cause not established. Nº 14 FPP.

19.8.44. Sea Hurricane: BW855. On ferry from Sealand to Nº 731 Sqn, East Haven, flew into moorland at Hepple Whitefield, Northumberland, in bad visibility at dusk killing L/Cdr P. N. Medd FAA.

15.9.44. Fairey Barracuda MD859 skidded across the grass whilst taxying at high speed at Hawarden, hit concrete picket post;; pilot Second Officer E. S. Edwards unhurt. Nº 7 FPP.

19.9.44. Fairey Barracuda III: MD898. Engine failure on take-off Hawarden, 'respectable' wheels-up forced landing straight ahead at Park Farm, Broughton. Nº 3 FPP.

27.10.44. Boulton Paul Defiant III: T4019. Destined for Admiralty; on ferry flight Nº 10 MU Hullavington – Donibristle.; planned change of pilot and refuelling Hawarden engine cut on approach to airfield, crashed bursting into flames, killing pilot, First Officer E. E. Vergette.

30.10.44. Avro Anson I: MH230. Forced landing near Ruabon, Wrexham; a/c originally attributed to ATA, but appears to have belonged to Nº 83 Group Communications Sqn, 2 TAF and on a rather mysterious unauthorised flight from airstrip B78 (Eindhoven, Holland) Pilot was F/Lt G. S. Frances, who was on his way to Speke when bad weather intervened. No records of accident or Court of Inquiry exist.

4.11.44. Fairey Swordfish III: NF187. Engine failure at 1,000ft. forced landing ploughing through trees at Summerhill Grange, Kingswinford, (Staffs.). First Officer P. P. Kerrigan survived. Nº 9 FPP.

27.11.44. DH Mosquito VI: NT147. On ferry flight Hawarden – Nº 12 MU Kirkbride; swung on single engine overshoot and crashed to ground killing Third Officer J. F. Wheelock. Nº 3 FPP.

13.12.44. Supermarine Walrus II: X9570. On flight Wig Bay to

Swindon, running out of fuel, with local airfields blotted out by mist and fog landed in sea off Crosby and taxied to moorings off New Brighton. Rescued by ATA team from Hawarden under F/O J. R. Burill, engineer officer from the MU. Nº 3 FPP.

1945

9.1.45. Fairey Swordfish III: NF396. On 4-leg ferry High Ercall – Hawarden – Prestwick – Turnberry. Engine failed at 1,000ft over latter airfield, overshot trying to avoid hangar and MT vehicles and hit embankment, Cadet Pilot (later Third Officer) Patricia Mary Provis survived. Nº 4 FPP.

30.1.45. Grumman Avenger: JZ437. On staged ferry from Belfast; 15mins. after leaving Hawarden engine developed oil leak filling cockpit with black smoke. Returned to airfield and put a/c down safely. pilot First Officer W. Reilly. Nº 8 FPP.

3.2.45. Fairey Barracuda III: PM387, On ferry from Ringway, lost hydraulics; put down safely by First Officer P. Parkes at RAF Pershore. Nº 14 FPP.

4.2.45. Fairey Barracuda III: PM859. Circling a house at Timperley, Cheshire, lost control and crashed into it, killing First Officer R. Williams. Nº 14 FPP.

10.2.45. Supermarine Spitfire VII: MB912. Caught by crosswind and swung on take off Hawarden collided with floodlight; a/c wrecked. Nº 3 FPP. .

10.2.45. Bristol Beaufighter: RD210. On fuel consumption test from Nº 1 Ferry Unit, RAF Peshore; went missing, found completely wrecked on Aran Fawddwy, pilot and navigator dead.

13.2.45. Fairey Swordfish III: NS193. Forced landing at Bridgnorth, Shropshire, whilst on ferry flight after suffering complete engine failure, with smoke pouring from under cowling. Nº 1 FPP.

28.2.45. Fairey Swordfish III: NS133. After landing at Hawarden, burst tyre and swung into soft ground off runway. Third Office Miss K. M. Stanley Smith, shaken but unhurt. Nº 5 (T)FPP.

18.4.45. Chance Vought Corsair II: JS576. Ferry flight from Air Holding Units, Stretton – Woodvale, strong on-shore winds, came in very fast, brakes seized as taxying, First Officer A. Warrington unhurt. Nº 8 FPP.

11.5.45. North American B25 Mitchell II: FK965 (serial re-allocated). On ferry flight from RAF Odiham via Worcester, Severn and Dee valleys to Hawarden. Over Wellington complete instrument failure. After one aborted landing attempt successfully put down in 'daisy cutter', starboard engine burst into flames, having earlier lost white hot exhaust stubs; pilot First Officer Diana Barnato Walker and flight engineer Third Officer John Brown survived. Nº 15 FPP.

12.5.45. Supermarine Seafire XV: SR492. Collected from Nº 43 MU Pengam Moors, Cardiff and flown to Nº 52 MU Rhoose, parts of airfield waterlogged, left runway after landing, sank up to propellers.; pilot Flight Captain the Hon. G. E. Dutton. Nº 2 FPP.

29.5.45. Fairey Barracuda II: MX792. On ferry from Crail (Fife) to Ronaldsway (IoM). Heavy sea mist off Solway Firth, low cloud merged with sea in fading light, stalled into sea; pilot Third Officer Eleanor Keith Jopp, brought to surface in air bubble as a/c sank, picked up by fishing boat. Nº 15 FPP.

8.6.45. Fairey Barracuda II: DR202. On ferry flight from Eastleigh, Southampton; over Bridgnorth engine began to overheat, successfully landed at nearest aerodrome, Halfpenny Green, Wolverhampton. Flight-Captain Philippa Bennett unhurt. Nº 15 FPP. (Pilot had 37 previous ferries on type).

27.7.45. Supermarine Seafire XV: SW810. On ferry from Hawarden to Kirkbride, engine started to fail whilst in circuit, came straight in whilst facing wind, perfect landing; pilot First Officer L. Tompkins. Nº 3 FPP.

15.8.45. Fairey Barracuda II: MX550. On ferry from Ratcliffe to Kirkbride; a/c brought down safely at Church Broughton with falling oil pressure and problems with constant speed unit. Nº 6 FPP.

21.8.45. Blackburn Roc I: L3098. Taxying out over grass area Hawarden for ferry flight to Hatston (Orkneys), wheel dropped into coverless manhole, causing damage to wing section. Nº 3 FPP (N.B. this a/c had lost its tail unit during the bombing raid on Hawarden 14.11.40.

22.8.45. Avro Anson I: NK861. Collided with mobile compressor whilst taxying between hangars 1, 2 and 6. Nº 3 FPP.

3.9.45. Supermarine Seafire XVII: SP196. On ferry Whitchurch (Bristol) to Hawarden, where only runway in use had strong crosss winds; a/c buffeted, slipped from side to side, starboard wing caught runway, swung came to rest in boggy ground; pilot Third Officer Yvonne Eveleigh shaken but uninjured. Nº 2 FPP.

1946

19.3.46. Supermarine Spitfire XIV: NH695. Ferry flight AST Hamble via White Waltham to Nº 29 MU, High Ercall. Weather worsened, a/c ploughed into tree line at Pound Green, NW of Bewdley killing pilot First Officer Rosamund Everard Steenkamp (South Africa). New Nº 1 FP. (Last ATA person killed flying military aircraft).

Further Reading

Action Stations: Military Airfields of ... series, Vols 1–10 (Wellingborough, 1982–1990)

Air Britain (Historians) Ltd, *RAF Serials ...* 18 vols (Tunbridge Wells, 1985–2000)

Air League of the British Empire, *The Story of the Air Training Corps* (London, 1946)

Austen, M., *British Civil Registers 1919–1999* (Tunbridge Wells, 1999)

Barfield, N. *Broughton: From Wellington to Airbus* (Stroud, 2001)

Batt, R., *The Radar Army* (London, 1991)

Bekker, Cajus, *The Luftwaffe War Diaries* (London, 1967)

Berry, A., *et al, Fenn's and Whixall Mosses* (Mold, 1996)

Black, A. & C., *RAF (the Second Year) P(London, 1942)*

Blandford, E. *Target England* (1997)

Bowyer, M. J. *Action Stations Revisited ...* series (in progress, Manchester, 2000–04)

Bragg, M. RDF 1 (Paisley, 2001)

Charlton, L., *Royal Air Force, January 1941–March 1942*

Cleary, A. *Historical RADAR on th Isle of Man* (author, 2004)

Cheesman, E. C. *Brief Glory: the Story of the ATA* (Leicester, 1946)

Chorley, W. R. *Bomber Command Losses* , 8 vols (Hinckley, 1992–2003)

Cordingly, W. R. *From a Cat's Whisker Beginning* (author, 1988)

Cordingly, W. R. *Time to Tell* (author, 1992)

Cordingly, N. *The Era of the Nocturnal Blip* (author, 1994)

Curtis, L. *Forgotten Pilots — A Story of the ATA 1939–45* (Olney, 1982)

Curtis, L. *Lettice Curtis: her Autobiography* (Hinckley, 2004)

Dobinson, C., *Fields of Deception* (London, 2000)

Dobinson, C., *20th century Fortification in England*, 5 Vols/9 parts (York, 1996)

Ferguson, A. P. *A History of RAF Shawbury* (Liverpool, 1977)

Foot, W., *Benches, Fields, Streets and Hills: the anti-invasion landscape of England, 1940* (York, 2005)

Franks, N. *Fighter Command Losses, 1939–41* (Leicester, 1997)

Gough, J. *Watching the Skies: A History of Ground Radar in the Air Defence of the United Kingdom* (London, 1993)

Halley, J. J. *The Squadrons of the RAF & Commonwealth* (Tonbridge, 1988)

Institute of Electrical Engineers, *Radar Development to 1945* (London, 1998)

Jefford, C. G. *RAF Squadrons* (2nd ed., Shrewsbury, 2001)

King, A., *Golden Wings* (London, 1975)

Lake, A., *Flying Units of the RAF* (Shrewsbury, 1999)

Latham, C. & Stobbs, A., *Radar: A Wartime Miracle* (Stroud, 1996)

Latham, C. & Stobbs, A., *Pioneers of RADAR* (Stroud, 1999)

McNeill, R., *RAF Coastal Command Losses of World War 2, Vol. 1, 1939–41* (Hinkley, 2003)

Morgan, E. B. & Shacklady, E., *Spitfire: the History* (Stamford, 1987)

The Origins and Development of Operational research in the RAF (HMSO, 1963)

Orr, W. I. & Cowan, S. D., *Beam Antenna Handbook* (Lake Wood, N.J., 1990)

Osbourne, M., *Defending Britain: Twentieth-Century Military Structures in the Landscape* (Stroud, 2004)

Pearcy, A., *Lend Lease Aircraft in World War II* (Shrewsbury, 1996)

Pratt, D. & Grant, M., *Wings Across the Border*, Vols 1 & 2 (Wrexham, 1998 & 2002)

Price, A., *The Luftwaffe Data Book* (London, 1997)

Ramsey, W. G. (ed.), *The Blitz Then and Now*, 3 vols (London 1987–9)

Ramsey, W. G. (ed.), *The Battle of Britain Then and Now Mk V* (London, 1989)

Ray, J., *The Night Blitz 1940–41* (London, 1996)

Richards, D. *Royal Air Force, 1939–1945, Vol 1, The Fight at Odds* (London, 1953)

Shores, C. & Williams, C., *Aces High* (London, 1994)

Smith, D. *Hawarden: A Welsh Airfield 1939–1979* (author, n.d.)

Sturtivant, R., Hamlin, J. & Halley, J. J., *RAF Flying Training and Support Units* (Tunbridge Wells, 1997)

Swords, S. S., *The Technical History of the Beginnings of Radar* (London, 1986)

Wakefield, K. *The First Pathfinders* (1992)

Wills, H., *Pillboxes: A Study of UK Defences, 1940* (London, 1985)

Wynn, K. G., *Men of the Battle of Britain* (London, 1999)

Zimmerman, D., *Britain's Shield* (Stroud, 2001)